DEATH AND THE
AFTERLIFE
IN THE NEW TESTAMENT

DEATH AND THE
AFTERLIFE
IN THE NEW TESTAMENT

JAIME CLARK-SOLES

t&t clark

NEW YORK • LONDON

T & T Clark International, 80 Maiden Lane, New York, NY 10038

T & T Clark International, The Tower Building, 11 York Road, London SE1 7NX

T & T Clark International is a Continuum imprint.

Cover design: Jennifer Glosser

Except as otherwise specified, the Bible text is from the *New Revised Standard Version Bible,* copyright 1989, by the Division of Christian Education of the National Council of the Churches of Christ in the USA, and is used by permission. KJV refers to the King James Version of the Holy Bible.

William Sloane Coffin. *Credo*. Louisville: Westminster John Knox Press, 2004.

Library of Congress Cataloging-in-Publication Data

Clark-Soles, Jaime, 1967–
    Death and the afterlife in the New Testament / Jaime Clark-Soles.
      p. cm.
    Includes bibliographical references and index.
    ISBN-13: 978-0-567-02902-7 (hardcover)
    ISBN-10: 0-567-02902-6 (hardcover)
    ISBN-13: 978-0-567-02912-6 (pbk.)
    ISBN-10: 0-567-02912-3 (pbk.)
    1. Death – Biblical teaching. 2. Future life – Biblical teaching. 3. Bible. N.T. Criticism, interpretation, etc. I. Title.
BS2545.D45C53 2006
236′.109015 – dc22

2006024402

Printed in the United States of America on Recycled

06   07   08   09   10   10 9 8 7 6 5 4 3 2 1

To Thad, my true partner

CONTENTS

ACKNOWLEDGMENTS

I WOULD LIKE to thank everyone who has helped to bring this book to life. Grants were generously provided by the Louisville Institute, the Catholic Biblical Association, the Wabash Center for Teaching and Learning in Religion, the Perkins School of Theology Scholarly Outreach Program, and the Southern Methodist University Research Council. Susan R. Garrett, Rebekah Miles, Pat Davis, Harold Attridge, Wayne Meeks, William Lawrence, and Marjorie Procter-Smith were all instrumental to my procuring said grants.

Numerous colleagues have contributed in multifarious ways. I have presented related papers at the regional, national, and international Society of Biblical Literature meetings and received useful feedback from each group. The national and international Johannine Literature sections were especially productive arenas, as was the national Hellenistic Moral Philosophy section. Likewise valuable was the Graduate Bible Colloquium at Perkins School of Theology, which includes my biblical studies colleagues Jouette Bassler, Abraham Smith, Mark Chancey, Roy Heller, Richard Nelson, Alejandro Botta, and Serge Frolov. Robert Foster, one of our graduate students, provided especially helpful feedback. Special thanks to Richard Nelson, who gave me more concise language with which to work in my Fourth Gospel chapter. Melissa Dowling in classics has been a stimulating conversation partner, particularly around issues of time and eschatology in the Roman Imperial period. A. Katherine Grieb vetted my Paul chapter and made it better. Warren Carter and A. J. Levine did the same for the Matthew chapter, as did Tom Thatcher and Francisco Lozada for part of the Fourth Gospel chapter. Valerie Karras provided useful discussion and bibliography.

Over the years a host of research assistants have worked tirelessly to move this project along. These include David Watson, Jeremy Bakker, Gena Anderson, and Ann Willet. Pride of place, however, must be reserved for Ila Kraft. If I were a Martin Luther or Fyodor Dostoyevsky, she would be my Kate or Anna. Her attention to detail has augmented my work greatly. But more important, she is a brilliant exegete and concise writer. She is a sheer gift to me.

The team at T&T Clark is first-rate. Hearty thanks is due to Henry Carrigan and S. David Garber, whose editing was impressively thorough, meticulous, erudite, and showed true investment in the success of this book.

I regularly teach a course for seminary students, clergy, and laypeople entitled "Evil, Suffering, and Death in the New Testament," part of which is devoted to the study of how the various NT authors address death and the afterlife. My deepest thanks to each participant who shared their insights, questions, experiences, and enthusiasm for the importance of the topic with me. I have learned far more than I have taught in each instance.

My church, CityChurch of Dallas, is the closest thing to the reign of God I have found to date. They constantly nourish, inspire, love, and challenge me, and, most important, do their best to keep me honest and grounded. With them the platitudinous, the banal, the simple, the silly, the preachy, the evasive, and the inflated do not play well.

Anyone who has attempted a project that takes years knows that one needs superlative friendship along the way. And so, to "the crew" I offer thanks and praise: Teri Walker, Syed Rehman, Mark Chancey, and Tracy Anne Allred.

Finally, to my family I owe the deepest gratitude. To my dear departed father-in-law, who made the contents of this book only too urgent and real to me as he battled cancer for a year and half, dying just before Christmas 2005, I pay homage. To the Soles and Clark families, thank you for your ongoing love and support. To my lifelong partner, Thad, and my two amazing children, Chloe and Caleb, I will never be able to express my love adequately. They are a blessing beyond all telling of it.

INTRODUCTION

Roman beliefs about life after death were extraordinarily varied. No single orthodoxy dominated; polytheism was supplemented by philosophical speculation and by individual sects such as Stoicism, Mithraism, Judaism, and eventually Christianity.

— D. Felton, *Haunted Greece and Rome*, xiii

THE PRECIPITATING QUESTION

I BEGAN THIS PROJECT in order to answer the question "What exactly does the New Testament (NT) say about death and afterlife?" It turns out that it says both more and less than one might hope or expect. By more, I mean that every time the subject of death and what happens after death arises, it is clear that the authors' interests far exceed answering that single question. Their comments emerge from the concerns and experiences of living Christian communities; they relate to a larger theological and pastoral agenda, and the primary focus remains life on earth and the proper living of it.

The texts say less than one may have hoped because no author directly sets out to answer my question. There is no systematic theology in the NT regarding death and afterlife. Certainly resurrection appears throughout. Beyond that, the fascinating aspects of the question are in the details of the texts. Therefore, the appropriate question, as it turns out, is not what does *the NT* say about death and afterlife, but rather what do *the various NT texts* say about it? In other words, the NT texts say a variety of things that cannot be construed as a single view. Others have sought to unify the biblical witness, glossing over the individual pictures presented by the NT authors. I revel in snapshots of the individuals and am less interested in the family photo because the latter invariably obscures or marginalizes certain relatives, leaving the most attractive, assertive, or powerful members of the family at center stage.

Because the texts differ, the structure of the chapters devoted to each must differ. Even so, the reader will see some similarities. Of each author, I inquire after the specific language used with respect to death and life after death; I explore the anthropology, cosmology, eschatology, and where relevant, theology and Christology; finally, I suggest ways that the stated views

1

function in each situation. Always I assume that each author is bright and faithful, having ideas the reader should attend with gravity.

CHAPTER OUTLINE

Chapter 1 sets the investigation against the backdrop of options deployed by thinkers and cultures that contributed to the discussion before the NT authors joined it. This includes ancient Near Eastern, ancient Jewish, Second Temple Jewish, and Greco-Roman materials. I draw upon epitaphs, graves, Roman religions, mystery religions, consolation literature, classical litera-ture, biblical literature, extrabiblical Jewish literature (Philo, Josephus), and Hellenistic philosophy. Particular topics addressed include anthropology; notions of divine judgment; and the origins of heaven, hell, and Satan.

Chapter 2 treats the Pauline literature, using 1 Cor 15 as a primary an-chor, with 2 Cor 5 and Phil 1 playing crucial roles as well. I begin with Paul for a number of reasons. First, Paul's writings comprise no small part of the NT. Second, 1 Cor 15 is often considered to be the classic statement on Christian afterlife. In it Paul speaks not only of resurrection but also of the embodied status it will entail. Third, Paul's eschatology is apocalyptic, and therefore representative of the majority of NT authors. Fourth, Paul's undisputed letters contain no hell language, an apparently strange feature given the usual delight in hell and the accompanying eternal torment that infuses most apocalyptic literature. Though numerous words or phrases for hell appear in the NT — including Hades, Apollyon, Gehenna, "cast into Tartarus," and "outer darkness where there will be weeping and gnashing of teeth" — Paul employs none of them. Paul's comments regarding death and afterlife serve his theological, pastoral, apologetic, and ethical agendas.

Chapter 3 takes up the Gospel of John since it provides points of both comparison and contrast. Unlike Paul's eschatology, the Fourth Evangelist's (FE's) eschatology is realized. Although FE employs dualistic language, a typical component of apocalyptic theology, he does not stress (and may not even entertain) the future, apocalyptic eschatological scenario so fundamen-tal to Paul's theology, preaching, and pastoral exhortation. Paul and FE agree, however, in their omission of hell language. Certainly neither depicts Satan as ruling some godforsaken territory for all of eternity. In this chapter I argue that FE evinces a bestowed, realized immortality.

Chapter 4 is devoted to the Gospel of Matthew. Matthew shares a heav-ily apocalyptic worldview with Paul, but unlike Paul, Matthew has a robust notion of hell. Hell abounds in Matthew in the form of Hades, Gehenna, outer darkness, fire, weeping and gnashing of teeth. Numerous characters play a role in the eschatological scenario, perhaps most notably angels who gather the wicked together and transport them to their eternal fiery destination. Matthew's anthropology imagines humans as either good or evil. The evil will experience the fate just described; the righteous can expect rewards of various sorts. To understand Matthew's view, I attend to Matthew's social setting. I have found Warren Carter's recent work on Matthew and empire most useful and largely compelling and so I allow Carter to set that stage. Clearly, Matthew's community stands in tension with outsiders, both those from the parent tradition as well as the Roman Empire. Justice and righteousness, as characteristics of both God and human beings, are consuming, driving categories for Matthew. Perhaps it is not surprising, then, that Matthew is passionate about hell, for it emphasizes God's justice and righteousness and provides a satisfying theodicy in the face of perceived persecution from outsiders, who apparently flourish despite their unrighteousness. Matthew's depiction of death and afterlife functions to enjoin ethical behavior, encourage faithfulness, and certify God's character as righteous and just.

Like all of our authors, Matthew's material on death and afterlife functions to shape community. In particular, I address the ethical, social, pastoral, liturgical, and theological functions.

Chapter 5 addresses 1 Peter, famous for its supposed depiction of "Jesus' descent into hell" and the subsequent development of the notion of purgatory. The particular texts under consideration, 3:19 and 4:6, have caused ample debate because they are notoriously difficult. The grammatical and syntactical issues leave open any number of interpretive possibilities at any number of places. For instance, it is not clear who the "spirits" are, why they are in prison, where they are in prison (no language of "descent" actually occurs), who preaches to them, or what the purpose of the proclamation is. How does 3:19 relate to the letter as whole, if at all? How does it relate to 4:6 in particular, if at all? And how does any of it relate to the author's own community? After exploring 1 Peter's language related to death and afterlife, I will argue that the beliefs function ethically, pastorally, theologically, and socially.

Finally, in chapter 6 I will summarize my findings and offer concluding comparisons and contrasts among the authors, paying consideration to their social, cultural milieux. I will then indicate implications for future research.

CAVEATS

It is important to state directly what the book will *not* do. First, I do not assume a unified vision among NT authors concerning death and afterlife. Neither do I reject unity a priori.

Second, the chapters on each NT book are devoted solely to the question of death and afterlife. I do not try to write thorough treatments of Paul, the Fourth Gospel, Matthew, and 1 Peter, as interesting as that would certainly be. For instance, there is currently disagreement among Matthean scholars regarding the social situation of the community, the characterization of the author and audience of Matthew, and numerous other aspects of the Gospel. Here I am not interested in writing a monograph about the Gospel of Matthew; rather, I want to attend solely to death and afterlife in the NT, and I employ Matthew only with respect to its contribution to such an investigation. Warren Carter's recent work on Matthew and empire are both provocative and largely compelling, so I have adopted his reconstruction in the chapter devoted to Matthew. I realize that some Matthean scholars contest some of his theses, but I leave that debate in the footnotes since such debates move us away from an investigation of death and afterlife in the NT and into debates within the Matthean guild.

Third, I have chosen only representative books of the NT since it is simply not feasible to canvass every author of the NT in a single book, though it would be a terribly engrossing and worthwhile endeavor. One could imagine devoting a whole study to the Gospels or to following the Pauline trajectory from the undisputed epistles to the Deutero-Pauline material. A number of other texts are tantalizing. Take Heb 2:14–15, for example: "Since, therefore, the children share flesh and blood, he himself likewise shared the same things, so that through death he might destroy the one who has the power of death, that is, the devil, and free those who all their lives were held in slavery by the fear of death." Or Luke 23:43: "He replied, 'Truly I tell you, today you will be with me in Paradise,' " not to mention Revelation. I certainly intend to pursue this line of questioning in a future volume, and I hope others attend to it as well. For the current study, I include materials that (1) add something distinctive to the discussion, (2) highlight some of the variety housed within the NT regarding the topic of death and afterlife, and (3) reveal the ways beliefs function for the community. The authors share many similarities when we consider the category regarding functions.

Fourth, apropos of the above discussion concerning a "snapshot" approach rather than a "red thread" one, I patently do *not* espouse a theory of chronological development within the NT regarding attitudes toward death and afterlife. To do so seems to me to give in to the chronological urge so prevalent among NT scholars, or to phrase it otherwise, to commit a chronological faux pas.

In the end, none of the authors expresses interest in delineating a doctrine of death and afterlife, or constructing a mighty tome on systematic theology for which all posterity would revere them. They focus upon questions of death, and life after death as a springboard for considering contemporary life and the shape it could and should take.

PREVIOUS WORKS

Alan Segal's lengthy and wonderful book, *Life after Death: A History of the Afterlife in Western Religion*,[1] is vast, covering many centuries, countries, and three world religions. He aims to provide a sweeping survey and does it well. Understandably, then, he devotes only brief attention to the NT. In contrast, my book will answer the question "What do the NT texts say about death and afterlife?" by addressing the detailed, complex question rather than painting a broad sweep of the history of ideas. The fact that Segal's book contains no scriptural index indicates that this is simply not his primary focus.

The question "So what did happen on Easter morning?" serves as "the central theme" of N. T. Wright's august 817–page tome, *The Resurrection of the Son of God*.[2] From the outset Wright indicates that the primary purpose of his work is heavily apologetic. On page 6 he lists six aspects of "the dominant paradigm" accepted by "mainline churches" that he intends to challenge, two of which are these: "The early Christians underwent some kind of fantasy or hallucination," and "Jesus' body . . . was not 'raised from the dead' in the sense that the gospel stories, read at face value, seem to require." On the next page he points out that he has six "positive" aims as well, including this one: "To argue that the *only* possible reason why early Christianity began and took the shape it did is that the tomb really was empty and that people really did meet Jesus, alive again, and that, though admitting it involves accepting a challenge at the level of worldview itself, the best historical explanation for all these phenomena is that Jesus was indeed bodily raised from the dead." For my part, I do not have a doctrinal or dogmatic agenda that I will try to prove with my research. I do not intend to prove that Jesus or anyone else was raised from the dead. I want to know what the NT authors thought about death and afterlife. Insofar as Jesus is one part of that question for our authors, I will use some of Wright's research.

R. Bauckham has explored apocalyptic literature, both canonical and extracanonical.[3] While encyclopedic and impressive, *The Fate of the Dead* is limited by its attention to a single genre. Joseph Park has canvassed Jewish

---

1. Alan Segal, *Life after Death: A History of the Afterlife in Western Religion* (New York: Doubleday, 2004).
2. N. T. Wright, *The Resurrection of the Son of God* (Minneapolis: Fortress, 2003), 4.
3. Richard Bauckham, *The Fate of the Dead: Studies on the Jewish and Christian Apocalypses* (NovTSup 93; Leiden: Brill, 1998).

inscriptions primarily to catalog the various conceptions of afterlife alive among Jews in the first century.[4] Park's *Conceptions of the Afterlife in Jewish Inscriptions: With Special Reference to Pauline Literature* is useful background reading, but it actually deals little with the Pauline literature. Longenecker has edited a collection of essays on *Life in the Face of Death*, but it is aimed at lay Christians. As one can detect from its subtitle, *The Resurrection Message of the New Testament* (emphasis added), the book intends to isolate a single, unified thread.[5] In addition, there are histories of heaven and histories of hell that provide information.[6] They tend to cover many centuries and therefore lack the specificity needed for my project. H. C. C. Cavallin has done some preparatory work for 1 Cor 15.[7]

METHOD

All of the NT texts were forged by and written for people who inhabited a Greco-Roman world.[8] To understand fully the texts, then, we must set

---

4. Joseph S. Park, *Conceptions of Afterlife in Jewish Inscriptions: With Special Reference to Pauline Literature* (Tübingen: Mohr Siebeck, 2000).

5. Richard Longenecker, ed., *Life in the Face of Death: The Resurrection Message of the New Testament* (Grand Rapids: Eerdmans, 1998). One might include Pheme Perkins, *Resurrection: New Testament Witness and Contemporary Reflection* (Garden City, NY: Doubleday, 1984) under the category of treatments that take a unitary approach.

6. Alan Bernstein, *The Formation of Hell: Death and Retribution in the Ancient and Early Christian Worlds* (Ithaca, NY: Cornell University Press, 1993); Jeffrey Burton Russell, *A History of Heaven: The Singing Silence* (Princeton: Princeton University Press, 1997); Colleen McDannell and Bernhard Lang, *Heaven: A History* (New Haven: Yale University Press, 2001); J. Edward Wright, *The Early History of Heaven* (New York: Oxford University Press, 2000).

7. Hans Clemens Casesarius Cavallin, *Life after Death: Paul's Argument for the Resurrection of the Dead in I Cor 15*, part 1, *An Enquiry into the Jewish Background* (Lund, Sweden: Gleerup, 1974). Part 2 never appeared. Cavallin expresses his original intentions in the preface (9):

This volume forms the first part of a larger investigation concerning the Pauline argument for the resurrection of the dead in I Cor 15 and its background in Judaism, the Hellenistic culture, the Gospel tradition (above all the controversy with the Sadducees in Mk 12:18–27 parr), the kerygma and didache of the Primitive Church and Paul's first sketch of a resurrection teaching in I Th 4:13–18. For practical reasons this study of the Jewish background is published separately as my doctoral dissertation; yet I want to stress my intention to see this part of my work as a preparation for the study of I Cor 15. So the dialogue with Jewish texts is carried on by questions formulated in a preliminary examination of I Cor 15. This is sometimes developed into an explicit comparison between the Jewish texts. But applying the results of this investigation to the study of Paul will mainly be reserved for the second volume.

8. In chapter 1, on "Backgrounds," I will quickly review the debate in the late 1950s and 1960s instigated by Oscar Cullmann (*Immortality of the Soul or Resurrection of the Dead? The Witness of the New Testament* [London: Epworth, 1958], who made a distinction between the "Jewish" and Christian belief in resurrection of the body and the "Greek" conception of the immortality of the soul. As it turned out, of course, such categories were simpleminded and served only to veil the nuanced complexities of the subject.

them within the context of the options already being deployed by other groups in the Roman Empire. No classicists have studied how the NT texts addressing death and afterlife fit into these contexts. On the contrary, the notable classicist Ramsay MacMullen denies that most Romans had any serious conception of an afterlife, an opinion based on the fact that one could find on tomb inscriptions the acronym for the tripartite exclamation "I was not, I was, I am no more. Who cares?"[9] My own analysis of the evidence contradicts his argument.

I will proceed with this investigation by using the tools of a social historian. Overarching goals that guide the study include the following:

1. *To delineate the various constructs of death and afterlife exhibited within the NT canon.* Casual readers and learned scholars alike assume that the twenty-seven NT books speak univocally about death and afterlife — or at least that one can discern a unifying theme running through them like a red thread. In this book I will show that such an assumption of univocality obscures the rich variety of early Christian ways of constructing the expected future life exemplified by the NT texts. I will delineate precisely the details of the major options.

2. *To account for the similarities and differences discovered.* What factors help us to account for the similarities and differences in certain NT authors' views of death and afterlife? I assume that attention to the interrelated issues of the authors' respective social and geographical locations, chosen genres, anthropological views, and theological beliefs will yield results.

3. *To explore the views of death and afterlife associated with other religions in the Roman Empire in the first century of the Common Era.* The textual and archaeological evidence points to a vibrant religious culture, with temples to multiple gods and goddesses clustered close together in urban centers. In addition to a thriving pantheon and exotic mystery cults, the imperial cult was quite in vogue. It may be that elements of these traditions influenced the treatment of death and afterlife themes in the NT.

4. *To investigate how various schools of contemporary Hellenistic philosophy informed the NT texts on death and afterlife.* One stated goal of the project is to investigate how, if at all, various schools of contemporary Hellenistic philosophy informed NT views on death and afterlife.[10] One may

---

9. Ramsay MacMullen, *Paganism in the Roman Empire* (New Haven: Yale University Press, 1981).

10. As renowned classicist A. A. Long avers: "Hellenistic is a term which refers to Greek, and later, Graeco-Roman civilization in the period beginning with the death of Alexander the Great (323 B.C.) and ending, by convention, with the victory of Octavian over Mark Antony at the battle of Actium in 31 B.C. During these three centuries it is neither Platonism nor the Peripatetic tradition established by Aristotle which occupied the central place in ancient philosophy, but Stoicism, Scepticism and Epicureanism, all of which were post-Aristotelian developments. These are the movements of thought which define the main lines of philosophy

presuppose that the NT authors were influenced by Hellenistic philosophical views related to death and the afterlife because in the first century it was not religion but philosophy that typically addressed questions on the nature of the body, the soul, and the Divine. How did the Stoics, Platonists, Skeptics, Neopythagoreans, Cynics, and Epicureans conceive of death and afterlife? To what extent did erudite philosophical notions trickle down to the daily worldviews of ancient people?

I contend that the NT authors were influenced not only by the categories and contents employed by philosophers, but also by the various functions intended by the philosophers. Those functions include the following categories:

a. *Theological.* To teach people about the existence (or not) and nature of the gods

b. *Pastoral/psychological.* To assuage anxiety

c. *Ethical.* To enjoin proper conduct

d. *Social.* To form and maintain a community characterized by a particular approach to life and death

e. *Political.* To encourage a particular stance toward the state

f. *Apologetic.* To aggrandize the authority of the Founder by depicting him handling his own death in a way commensurate with his teachings

Each NT author who addresses the matter of death and afterlife evinces some combination of these functions.

5. *To articulate what is at stake for each NT author addressed.*

What ideas were circulating before the NT authors composed their material? Let us briefly survey the Ancient Near Eastern (ANE) and Greco-Roman scenes.

in the Hellenistic world, and 'Hellenistic philosophy' is the expression I use in this book to refer to them collectively' " (*Hellenistic Philosophy: Stoics, Epicureans, Sceptics* [Berkeley: University of California Press, 1974], 1).

– ONE –

BACKGROUNDS

Tradition is not repetition, but the transmission of a living reality, which must be renewed and rethought as the community develops.
— Claudia Setzer[1]

The fear of death is common to all peoples at all times. — A. A. Long[2]

T O UNDERSTAND and appraise the biblical texts concerning death and afterlife, we must situate them historically and culturally. To that end this chapter will review evidence from a number of areas. We begin with ancient and Second Temple forms of Judaism and their notions of afterlife and anthropology. We will then briefly discuss the history of notions about heaven and hell to establish the circumambient ideas about each that inhered in our authors when they wrote. Are heaven and hell conceived of as states of being, tangible places, both, or neither? Why did the ancients mention heaven and hell? How does the literary record align with the archaeological record? We will also study what the philosophers have to say about death and afterlife as well as the associated anthropology and ethics. What major concerns elicit or stimulate their thinking and teaching on the subject? What makes them ask about death and afterlife? How do the philosophers influence NT authors, if at all?

DEATH AND AFTERLIFE
IN ANCIENT JUDAISMS

The Old Testament

While there is no robust notion of afterlife in the OT, the idea is not entirely absent. As is commonly understood, the OT considers a person to be a unified subject such that whether in life or death, no part of the person

---

1. Claudia Setzer, *Resurrection of the Body in Early Judaism and Early Christianity: Doctrine, Community, and Self-Definition* (Leiden: Brill, 2004), 17.
2. A. A. Long, *Hellenistic Philosophy: Stoics, Epicureans, Sceptics* (2d ed.; Berkeley: University of California Press, 1986), 50.

enjoys a different ontology from the other parts. In the OT texts that do envision some sort of life after death, wicked and righteous alike endure a shadowy, unenviable, stygian existence in Sheol (the Pit) after a fugacious life. But mostly, the OT is silent on this matter.[3]

Though literary evidence is lacking, the archaeological record assures us of a belief in life after death. The fact that the dead were provided with food and drink, as well as magical items such as jewelry, testifies to this belief. The authors point to terms that appear in the OT, distinguishing "obvious ones" from those that usually do not refer to afterlife but can in specialized contexts. For example, Sheol occurs sixty-five times in the OT, nine of which are in the prose material.[4] The etymology of the word is unclear. *Rephaim* denotes underworld inhabitants.[5] The word "necromancer" (or "medium," *'ôb*, 1 Sam 28:7) indicates a belief in the possibility of communication between the living and the dead.[6] Friedman and Overton find reference to the descent of a high god to the gates of the netherworld, a point relevant to our discussion of the descent of Christ in 1 Pet 3:19 as well as the proclamation concerning the gates of Hades in Matt 16:18. In the end, against the notion of biblical silence, Friedman and Overton contend that "the terms and explicit references to afterlife occur early and late, in poetry and prose, distributed through the course of the Hebrew Bible."[7] Though some might try to explain away one occurrence or another, the authors insist: "When taken with awareness of the historical and archaeological record, they add up to evidence of belief in an afterlife."[8]

Puzzling is the rarity of textual references in light of the abundance of material evidence. The authors recognize that the priestly writers P, E, and D have a stake in centralizing true religion in cultic practices that require a priest, thereby increasing their power and income. *Beliefs function* in forming and maintaining communities. Lay authors, such as J or the prophet First Isaiah (as opposed to prophets like Jeremiah and Ezekiel, who were priests), do not have a vested interest in the cultus. If necromancers and other laypeople could perform efficacious religious functions, it would detract from the power of the priests, so the priests deny or draw attention away from

3. Picking up on the dearth of attention to death and afterlife in the OT, Richard Elliot Friedman and Shawna Dolansky Overton entitle their article "Death and Afterlife: the Biblical Silence," in *Death, Life-after-Death, Resurrection and the World-to-Come in the Judaisms of Antiquity* (vol. 4 of *Judaism in Late Antiquity*; ed. Alan J. Avery-Peck and Jacob Neusner; Leiden: Brill, 1995), 35–57.

4. See ibid., 47, for a list.
5. Ibid., 42.
6. Ibid., 44.
7. Ibid., 45.
8. Ibid., 46.

the underworld and afterlife, making rules against trafficking in such. The authors wisely conclude:

> None of the ideas connected with afterlife beliefs can be traced in a linear historical progression.... On the contrary, conflicting views can prevail simultaneously. Rather than attempting to extract a single, unified notion of the afterlife in ancient Israel that progresses linearly through time, we must instead investigate each reference to mortuary rites, the netherworld, veneration of deceased ancestors, necromancy, and resurrection within its own literary-historical framework, with the understanding that each author, within his or her own political and spatio-temporal context, might have a distinct idea of what happens to humans after they die, what they become, and what the proper relationship should be between the living and the dead.[9]

As the rest of this book will show, this approach pertains as well to each of the NT authors.

For evidence regarding death and afterlife, the Psalms would seem to be a natural place to begin, given their frequent references to death, the grave, and the Pit. John Goldingay, however, argues that the Psalms give no cause for the hope of an afterlife. Just because later Christians used it as such does not mean that hope was the intent of its original authors. Rather, the emphasis in Psalms is on the gift of this life, and the hope is in longevity and progeny.[10]

In her book *Death, Burial, and Afterlife in the Biblical World*, Rachel Hallote provides a lively presentation of the material culture related to biblical views of death and afterlife.[11] Employing both archaeology and biblical material, she declares that burial customs tend to perdure and that one usually cannot tell the difference between Israelite and Canaanite material. Because the dead were believed to have healing powers, they played a powerful role for the living.

There were three types of burial places in ancient Israel. First, there were cemeteries. Tombs were either hewn in rock, made of masonry, or pits in sand. One finds cities of the dead and acrosolia — with shafts leading down to a central burial chamber with offshoots for benches. Second, a person might be buried in the middle of open fields. The dead bodies of "important" people (not women and children) guard the field that one owns while it lies fallow. Third, people were buried under the floors or in the walls of houses.

---

9. Ibid., 56.
10. John Goldingay, "Death and Afterlife in the Psalms," in *Death, Life-after-Death, Resurrection and the World-to-Come* (ed. Avery-Peck and Neusner), 61–85.
11. Rachel S. Hallote, *Death, Burial, and Afterlife in the Biblical World: How the Israelites and Their Neighbors Treated the Dead* (Chicago: Ivan R. Dee, 2001).

This holds true for women, men, and children, but particularly for the very young and old; those who needed special care in life would need special care in death. Infants might be buried in jars. Kings were buried near their cities, while prophets were buried near holy places. Hallote offers an important caveat: "Not everyone is represented in the extant burials because most of society — specifically the lower classes — did not receive the type of burials that survive in the archaeological record."[12]

The ancient Israelites viewed death as "gathering" or "collecting" people to their ancestors — literally placing them in the family tomb with previously deceased relatives. It also may refer to secondary ossuary burial in which, after the body has decomposed, survivors collect the bones and mix them with other family bones. The texts can refer to death as "sleep" (cf. 1 Kgs 2:10; 16:28; 2 Kgs 20:21; 2 Chr 26:23; 28:27), a phenomenon that occurs in the NT as well.[13]

Israelites did not embalm, cremation was rare, and burial markers were not common. Because for the Israelites the family was more important than the individual, it is perhaps not surprising that one finds no coffin or individual grave with a marker. Coffins and ossuaries for individuals arise only in the Second Temple period, probably under the influence of Greeks, Persians, and Romans. What served as burial markers? A pile of stones or a living tree (often oak) because the tree represents life and the body helps the tree grow. Sometimes burial with a marker was done when a person was far from home and could not be buried in a family tomb. Regarding descriptions of tombs and burials, one finds next to nothing in the biblical record. Hallote assumes that this is because everyone already knew the details.

We can characterize the OT attitude toward death mainly as fear: "Once dead you were cut off from God's grace" (cf. Ps 88:4–5).[14] If God does not remember the dead, clearly being dead is not desirable. "This attitude vividly underscores the need for death rites — if God does not take care of the dead, it is up to their family members to do so, placing them in family tombs and tending those tombs in specific ways."[15]

Some Israelites practiced the cult of the dead, worshipping them, sacrificing to their ancestors, asking them to tell the future or heal (normally the prerogative of God), and feeding them (cf. Ps 106:28). Because some saw this behavior as contradicting monotheism, officials had it outlawed, but nevertheless people practiced it, and practiced it exactly as the Canaanites

---

12. Ibid., 31.
13. Ibid., 44. Paul Norman Jackson devotes a monograph to the subject: *An Investigation of* Koimaomai *in the New Testament: The Concept of Eschatological Sleep* (Lewiston, NY: Mellen Biblical Press, 1996). The subject of "soul sleep" has piqued the interest of readers over the years, especially in relation to the ideas of Paul.
14. Hallote, *Death, Burial, and Afterlife*, 52.
15. Ibid., 53.

did. Many kings did not condone it because it threatened the political unity of the state by keeping loyalties focused on family, clan, and tribe.

Hallote argues that across time, burial rituals remain startlingly similar, despite political change. Tomb offerings — such as food, drink, jewelry, and weapons — are exemplary. Either people imagined that the dead needed these things in the next life, or these gifts served as tokens of esteem. Near the Golan Heights unusual Bronze Age above-ground masonry tombs called dolmens have been found.[16] Coffins come into use between 30 and 70 CE. Jesus was not buried in a coffin, but Rabbi Johanan ben Zakkai (first c. [century] CE) was carried out of Jerusalem in one. Ossuaries appear in the Chalcolithic Period, then deliquesce, reappearing in the first century CE. Ossuaries provide evidence for secondary burial, but there is no evidence regarding rituals occurring with the secondary burial.

Whence did Israel derive its burial customs and beliefs? Such a question forces one to turn to Israel's neighbors. "Burial practices are very slow to change."[17] Syria, Mesopotamia, and Egypt all practiced ancestor worship. They wrote down exactly how the beliefs and rituals of death and afterlife were to be practiced. Not so Israel: the Bible is our only source. The written texts from Israel's neighbors provide the missing link about death and burial in Israel. They fill out the picture of death in biblical world. The Bible itself proclaims that its cultural origins are Mesopotamian (Gen 2:10–14); and Abraham is from Ur. To Mesopotamia, then, we turn.

Mesopotamia

All discussions of Mesopotamian views on death and afterlife begin with the Epic of Gilgamesh, in which food, a serpent, and immortality, all themes related to loss of immortality in the Bible (cf. Gen 3), appear.[18] Scholars also make comparisons with the text about Adapa, a man who wishes to be immortal and therefore godlike (cf. Gen 3:4–5), but ultimately cannot.[19] The netherworlds of Mesopotamia approximate those of the OT insofar as both imagine that everyone shares equally in its horrors. In both Mesopotamian

---

16. Ibid., 83.

17. Ibid., 102.

18. All three themes appear in the FG as well. Perhaps the author of FG has the Epic of Gilgamesh (as well as the Genesis creation stories) in mind.

19. Whether or not the Genesis creation stories claim that humans were created to be immortal engenders debate. Richard Nelson (personal correspondence, June 19, 2006) contends that current exegetical opinion tends to assume that Gen 2–3 reflects the loss of a chance at immortality that would have been provided by ongoing access to the tree of life. The Gilgamesh immortality plant is the cross-cultural reference for this. As creatures of dust, humans quite expectedly return to dust (Gen 2:7; 3:19), and being blocked off from Eden and the tree of life means that consequence takes place (3:24). However, premature death (Adam lived 930 years; Gen 5:5) is only one explanation for "in the day that you eat of it you shall die" (2:17). Another is that God backed off from the original threat, or may not have been entirely forthcoming, as the serpent suggested (3:4–5).

texts and the Bible, the netherworld is located beneath the earth, a place of dust. Roads lead there, and gates are at the entrance (cf. Descent of Ishtar 1–13; Gen 37:35; 2 Sam 22:5–6; Job 17:16; Ps 18:5–6; Isa 26:19). Whereas Friedman expresses doubt about discerning the etymology of Sheol, Hallote readily contends that the root of Sheol means hollowness. God's presence is not there (cf. Ps 6:5; 88:4–5; Isa 38:18).

Ereshkigal is the queen of the Mesopotamian underworld. She is not evil. Motu (or Mot) is the underworld deity of the Ugaritic world (Ugarit refers to northern, coastal Canaan, the region known as Phoenicia in the Iron Age). Israelites and Canaanites shared religion. Motu probably appears in the Bible as does Shuwala, a cognate of Sheol, who is the north Syrian goddess of death mentioned in texts from the city of Emar, near the Euphrates. "The goddess of death, Shuwala, has become the place she rules, Sheol" (*šĕ'ôl*; Isa 28:15, 17–19).[20]

Egypt

Death in Egyptian records looks different from death in the biblical and Mesopotamian records. Egyptian religion was quite death-centered, and Egyptians considered the body as essential in the afterlife, as shown by their massive pyramids and the practice of embalming. Egyptians noticed that they were different from Israelites and Canaanites as the story of Sinuhe shows. Sinuhe is an Egyptian who ends up in Canaan. Near the end of his life, he reconnects with Egypt, thereby avoiding a Canaanite burial, described as something an Egyptian would not want to endure.[21] The patriarchs Jacob and Joseph first underwent Egyptian mummification processes and eventually were carried back to Israel for burial (Gen 49:28–50:26).

OT Anthropology: Wolff

Our only source for Israelite anthropology pertinent to life and death is the OT. Greek thought does not heavily influence Hebrew or Jewish thinking until the Hellenistic period. For ancient Israel, *nepeš* seems to combine functions of the Greek *thymos* (intense feeling) and *psychē* (inner self) of the living. *Nepeš* never means the soul. Israelite anthropology, according to Jan Bremmer, was "strictly unitarian and remained so until the first century AD, when the Greek belief in an immortal soul started to gain ground in Palestine and the Diaspora."[22] Not surprisingly, two Hellenized Jews, Josephus and Philo, are the first to demonstrate this transition.

20. Ibid., 113.
21. Hallote, *Death, Burial, and Afterlife*, 116.
22. Jan Bremmer, *The Rise and Fall of the Afterlife* (London: Routledge, 2002), 8.

Hans Wolff's classic work *Anthropology of the Old Testament*, though somewhat dated, still provides a reasonable introduction to OT anthropology.[23] From the beginning, Wolff indicates the variety in the texts: "The fact that every individual document presupposes a particular view of man could be a challenge to a systematic of biblical anthropology."[24] According to Wolff, "Concepts like heart, soul, flesh, and spirit (but also ear and mouth, hand and arm) are not infrequently interchangeable in Hebrew poetry."[25] He gives as an example Ps 6:2–4, where the personal pronoun "I" parallels "my bones" and "my soul," and he calls this feature "stereometry of expression."[26] So, different body parts can represent the person as a whole. In addition to this "stereometric thinking," he posits "synthetic thinking," where the naming of a body part stands in for the function implied. So, when Isaiah declares: "How beautiful upon the mountains are the feet of him who brings good tidings" (52:7), the author is not interested in the physical beauty of the feet but rather, in Wolff's words: "How beautiful it is that the messenger is hurrying over the mountains!"[27]

Nepeš

While many scholars equate *nepeš* with soul, Wolff claims that few instances of the word do so. Many different English words are needed to translate *nepeš* accurately in each of its contexts. In addition to its use as a pronoun, Wolff finds the following meanings for *nepeš*: throat, neck, desire, soul, life, person.

Throat. In treating the meaning as throat, Wolff points to what he calls "the needy man per se." He indicates that thirst, water, and *nepeš* often cluster, a fact that reminds one of the Gospel of John (henceforth FG; as in chs. 4; 7; 19). The throat also participates in taste, which reminds us of the FG and Matthean notions of "tasting death."[28] Wolff points to the tasting *nepeš* as it appears in Num 21:5b: "There is no food and no water, and our *nepeš* feels loathing at this worthless food" (NRSV/au. trans.). Those familiar with FG immediately think of the Bread from Heaven Discourse in chapter 6 and the living water in chapter 4. Wolff also includes the *nepeš*'s function of breathing in this category, thereby linking it to the psychic *pneuma* of Hellenistic philosophy.

Desire. The term *nepeš* also represents "unslaked desire," which causes action somewhat akin perhaps to the Stoic impulse (*hormē*).

---

23. Hans Walter Wolff, *Anthropology of the Old Testament* (trans. Margaret Kohl; Philadelphia: Fortress, 1974).

24. Ibid., 3.

25. Ibid., 7.

26. Ibid., 8.

27. Ibid.

28. The expression occurs in all four Gospels as well as Hebrews.

Life. The word *nepeš* can stand for life itself, as in Prov 8:35–36: "For whoever finds me finds life and obtains favor from the LORD; but those who miss me injure themselves [their *nepeš*]; all who hate me love death." This proverb, certainly known to the Fourth Evangelist, must factor into his thinking on life and death. Blood and *nepeš* go together. The blood is the *nepeš* (cf. Deut 12:23, "life"). The *nepeš* is not an immortal soul: "Rich and abundant though this use of *n.* [*nepeš*] for life is, we must not fail to observe that the *n.* is never given the meaning of an indestructible core of being, in contradistinction to the physical life, and even capable of living when cut off from that life."[29] The departure of the *nepeš* for Sheol is an allusion to the cessation of breathing.

Person. The term *nepeš* can refer to the individual and *nepeš mēt* means a dead person, a corpse (Lev 21:11), probably akin to the Greek *nekros*. Human beings are defined as *nepeš ḥayyâ*, and they become so when God breathes the breath of life into their person (Gen 2:7). Only by this breath does a person become living. Paul will replicate this concept with the word *pneuma*. Yahweh has a *nepeš*.[30]

Bāśār

This word means flesh, body, relationship, weakness. While God has *nepeš*, God has no *bāśār*. Most often, *bāśār* refers to the flesh of sacrificial animals. The NT picks this up by referring to Jesus as the paschal lamb. *Bāśār* also refers to the visible part of the body and, therefore, to the person in one's bodily aspect. In addition, *bāśār* indicates human frailty and weakness (Gen 6:3, 12; Ps 78:38f., Isa 40:6) (much like the NT phrase "the spirit indeed is willing, but the flesh is weak" [Matt 26:41; Mark 14:38]). As Wolff says, "Ethical frailty is added to the frailty of the creature. It is not the Qumran texts, when they talk about 'guilty flesh'... and 'the flesh of unrighteousness,'... that are moving for the first time towards the Pauline recognition that nothing good dwells in my flesh' (Rom 7:5, 18). In complete contrast to this 'flesh' is the 'spirit' (Isa 31:3); but the spirit is also the flesh's hope (Joel 2:28)."[31] One could easily write this last sentence about the FG.

Rûaḥ

This term is distinct from *bāśār* and *nepeš*. In 113 of 389 occurrences it refers to natural power, or wind, and in 136 it is associated with God. The remaining 129 references are related to people, animals, and false gods. So 35 percent of the time *rûaḥ* is associated with God, whereas *nepeš* applies to

---

29. Ibid., 20.
30. Ibid., 25.
31. Ibid., 31.

God only 3 percent of the time and *bāśār* never applies to God. *Rûaḥ* means wind, moving air (not just air), usually as a strong force used as a tool by God.[32] Sometimes it parallels physical breath, *nĕšāmâ*. Sometimes *nepeš* and *rûaḥ* are used synonymously, but the latter emphasizes the wind from Yahweh that enlivens, whereas *nepeš* is related to the process of breathing.[33] *Rûaḥ* can refer to vital powers. Wolff contends that we do better to translate *rûaḥ* as power or authority rather than spirit. Finally, other meanings include spirit(s), feelings, and will. "[*Rûaḥ*] stands twice as often for wind and for the divine vital power as for man's breath, feeling and will. Most of the texts that deal with the r. of God or man show God and man in a dynamic relationship."[34] In some ways one may profitably compare *rûaḥ* with *pneuma* in the NT.

Lēb/lĕbāb

Wolff considers this to be the most important word in a study of OT anthropology. Only 26 of 858 occurrences of *lēb* refer to God's heart. Overwhelmingly it is a word applied to people. *Lēb* refers to the physiological heart. However, ancient Israelites did not connect the heart with the beating of the pulse. Rather, they believed that the heart caused limbs to move. In that respect, for us it corresponds to part of the brain. Israelites did not have exact knowledge about the brain, nerves, or lungs. For them, the *lēb* was not in the head but in the chest. (cf. Jas 5:5; Luke 21:34). *Lēb* also refers to feelings. Its meaning overlaps with *nepeš* when it refers to wish, desire, or longing. *Lēb* primarily means reason. "In by far the greatest number of cases it is intellectual, rational functions that are ascribed to the heart, . . . precisely what we ascribe to the head and, more exactly, to the brain."[35] *Lēb* occurs most frequently in the wisdom literature where the heart is linked to understanding (ear and heart are often connected), insight, consciousness, thinking, knowledge, and memory. God's statutes are to remain on human hearts; people are to remain conscious of them (cf. Paul in 2 Cor 3:2–3). *Lēb* also refers to decisions of the will, conscience, or impulse of the will. It can stand for the person's self. For example, Jesus tells Judas to proceed with what the devil has put it into his heart to do (John 13:2, 27). This approximates 1 Sam 14:7: "His armor-bearer said to him, 'Do all that your mind [*lēb*] inclines to. I am with you; as your mind [*lēb*] is, so is mine.'" Wolff writes: "[*Lēb*] least of all means the emotions; on the contrary, it much more frequently means (and indeed this is its specific characteristic) the organ of knowledge, with which is associated the will, its plans, decisions and

---

32. Ibid., 33.
33. Ibid.
34. Ibid., 39.
35. Ibid., 46.

intentions, the consciousness, and a conscious and sincerely devoted obedience."[36] Finally, *lēb* refers to God's heart. When it does, it always relates to God's relationship with humanity. So in Gen 6:6, God's heart is grieved. Heart refers to God's will and plan over against which humanity is judged. The heart of God is knowable (but see Job 10:13). In sum, *lēb* "includes everything that we ascribe to the head and the brain — power of perception, reason, understanding, insight, consciousness, memory, knowledge, reflection, judgment, sense of direction, discernment. These things circumscribe the real core of meaning of the word [*lēb*]."[37]

Něšāmâ *and* dām

Wolff indicates that breath (*něšāmâ*) and blood (*dām*) are physiological terms. Blood is tied up with blood-guiltiness and sacrifice. Both relate to reverence for life.[38]

POSTMORTEM EXISTENCE
IN THE OT: SHEOL

An OT person who dies descends to Sheol ("Hades" in the Septuagint [LXX]), regardless of one's moral behavior. The notion of God's moral judgment determining one's fate in the afterlife, which will become the norm later, has not yet caught on.

"Sheol" is synonymous with "grave" (cf. Ps 16:10; Gen 37:35); it is subterranean (Ps 63:9) and shadowlike (Isa 14:9); its inhabitants do not think of the living (Job 21:21) or of God (Ps 88). "Good and bad — Sheol received them all (Psalm 89:49 [48])."[39]

In the postexilic period, the good and bad are moved to different compartments in Sheol (*1 Enoch* 22). In the second century BCE, Sheol is supplemented by Gehenna, the fiery valley south of Jerusalem. Gehenna represented the place where children had been sacrificed (Jer 7:32) and eventually the place where sinners would be judged.[40]

In postexilic Judaism, as in Greece, old and new coexist. Josephus (first c. CE) thinks that the Pharisees place the souls of both the just and unjust in the underworld, whereas he, though a Pharisee, assigns the unjust to Hades and the righteous to heaven until the final resurrection. Inscriptions

---

36. Ibid., 55.

37. Wolff, .

38. Wolff goes on to treat inner body parts, but that discussion need not concern us at present.

39. Bremmer, *Rise and Fall of the Afterlife*, 8.

40. Incidentally, the Jewish use of "paradise" arises in the intertestamental period. In the NT it appears only in Luke 23:43; 2 Cor 12:4; and Rev 2:7.

and literature, however, show that the older view, which lacked a robust afterlife for anyone, persisted in the first century.

With respect to the OT (with the possible exception of Dan 12), an apocalyptic moral judgment by God on a designated day of visitation followed by consignment to respective eternities does not yet obtain. If judgment is not primarily aimed at the determination of one's eternal abode, then what function does it serve in the OT texts?

THE FORMATION OF HEAVEN AND HELL

The tale ... will save us if we believe it; ... it will enable us to be dear to ourselves and to the gods both during our sojourn here and when we receive our reward. (Plato, *Republic* 621b–c, regarding his myth of Er)

In tracing the origins of hell and the devil, scholars refer to Canaanite and Persian elements. Hallote is no different. She observes that in Canaanite traditions child sacrifice to Moloch was performed at Tophet in Geh ben Hinnom, the Valley of Hinnom's son. Eventually, the valley becomes Gehenna, and Gehenna replaces Sheol (*šě'ôl*).

The dualism of Persian Zoroastrianism originating from the late sixth century to the fourth century BCE heavily influenced Judaism. In that worldview, the major benevolent god is Ahura Mazda, a god of light. He is opposed by Angra Mainyu, the Lord of Lies, who symbolizes darkness and death. According to Zoroastrian beliefs, the duality will climax in a final cosmic battle between good and evil, in which the soul of human beings will hang in the balance. In the end, evil will be vanquished, the dead will be resurrected, and the kingdom of heaven on earth will begin. The soul is judged posthumously. If the soul is deemed good, it goes to the house of Song. If bad, it will be sent to hell, which is ruled not by Angra Mainyu but by the first man ever to die.[41] Pharisees embraced Zoroastrian ideas of death, afterlife, judgment, angels, and demons; Sadducees did not (cf. Acts 23:8).

Heaven

All of the NT authors in this study use the language of heaven. Christians derive their heavenly designs most directly from the Hellenistic world, which built upon Egyptian and ancient Near Eastern traditions.

Egypt

The Egyptian Old Kingdom (2686–2160 BCE) pyramid texts, Middle Kingdom (2040–1633 BCE) coffin texts, and the New Kingdom (1558–1085

41. Hallote, *Death, Burial, and Afterlife*, 127.

BCE) Book of the Dead reveal a movement from the idea of the Pharaoh alone ascending to dwell with the gods in a celestial place, to democratizing the afterlife so that it includes commoners as well. Egyptian sources do not agree upon the exact location of heaven. Some consider it celestial and others terrestrial, the latter being illustrated by the Fields of Rushes, a mystical place far away but still on earth. While the Egyptians did not invent heaven, they appear to be the first to have democratized it.[42]

Sumer

The Sumerian vision of afterlife registers as far gloomier than the Egyptian vision. Sumer existed from the fourth millennium until 2050 BCE, when the Semitic king Sargon destroyed the Sumerian city of Ur. Sumerian cosmology was tripartite: the high gods inhabited heaven, humans inhabited earth, and dead humans along with the gods associated with death inhabited the netherworld. For the most part Sumerians left the celestial realm to the gods and assumed that humans descended to a netherworld, where an enervated version of earthly life ensued. Punishment was meted out during earthly life. However, there is an occasional hint that the rare person entered a paradise, called Dilmun, located somewhere on earth.[43]

Assyria and Babylonia

The Babylonian creation myth, the *Enuma Elish*, narrates the creation of the world from the slain body of the goddess Tiamat. It has a tripartite cosmology: heaven, earth, and netherworld.[44] As evinced by the Gilgamesh epic, the images of Mesopotamian afterlife closely approximate those of Sumer: a grim, pallid, shadowy existence in a netherworld set up like an ancient Mesopotamian city. The gods reside in a celestial plane that human beings can never attain. Social status and meticulous care by one's surviving family, rather than virtue, determine the quality of one's postmortem existence.

Syria and Palestine

As seen in the Ugaritic materials, the Syro-Palestinian material depicts all humans going to the grave, regardless of social status. No one resides with the gods.

To summarize, with the exception of Egypt, the ancient Near East (ANE) had no concept of a robust afterlife and certainly not one in which the dead

---

42. J. Edward Wright, *The Early History of Heaven* (New York: Oxford University Press, 2000), 25.
43. Ibid., 30.
44. Ibid., 33.

dwell with gods in heaven. "Heaven as a place for humans to join the gods after death was, it seems, an Egyptian invention."[45]

Israelite Traditions

Ancient Israelites envisioned a tripartite universe: heaven (*šāmayîm*), earth (*'ereṣ*), and underworld (Sheol, *šĕôl*). A variety of heavenly models existed, which cannot be systemized. We will simply provide the main features of the most popular options.[46] Wright distinguishes between biblical Israel, a theological entity, and ancient Israel, which includes all peoples of Syria-Palestine in the Late Bronze and Iron Ages as well as all material culture, which includes the Hebrew Bible. Thus, ancient Israel is a broader concept than biblical Israel.

The texts report various physical descriptions of heaven, from depictions of heaven as made of lapis lazuli, as in the Akkadian texts (cf. Ezek 1:26; Exod 24:9–10), to images of heaven made of a substance that restrains the waters of heaven (Gen 1:6–8; cf. *Enuma Elish* 4.135–41).[47]

Angels reside in heaven, as do other gods, a point that chagrins the Deuteronomist and Chronicler, who labor assiduously to eviscerate those other gods and emphasize the regnancy of Yahweh.[48] Wright provides a useful summary:

> The image of heaven in the Hebrew Bible, the foundation document of subsequent Judaism and Christianity, is multifaceted. To be sure, there is the strictly monotheistic depiction that dominates the Bible. On the other hand, however, there is abundant archaeological and textual evidence to show that, for some of the people of ancient Israel, and for their neighbors as well, heaven was populated by myriad gods and goddesses. Judaism and Christianity inherited one of these models; the other was largely suppressed by the biblical editors and nearly lost. This was the heaven of the poly-Yahwists, the people who worshipped Yahweh *and* the other gods. For them Yahweh was just one of the gods or perhaps chief among the gods. The traditional depictions of the biblical image of heaven represent the views of the few parochial and perhaps elitist editors who curated the biblical materials into what became their canonical shape. This was the monotheistic conception of heaven that was inherited by later Judaism and Christianity and that in the course of time would become normative. The depiction offered

---

45. Ibid., 51.
46. For a fuller discussion, see ibid., 52–97.
47. Ibid., 58.
48. Wright states: "Heaven, so it seems, was for most Israelites and Judeans a much more thickly settled region than the strict Yahweh-alone group could have imagined!" (ibid., 72).

here should give life to the voices of those whose views were marginalized, discredited, or otherwise silenced in the course of the Persian and Hellenistic periods, when what was later to become "normative" Judaism began to emerge.

The ancient Israelites, like their Near Eastern neighbors, imagined the cosmos as a tripartite structure: heaven, earth, netherworld. Also like their contemporaries, the Israelites believed that heaven was for the gods, earth for humans, and the netherworld for the mortuary gods and deceased humans. Humans, with the possible exception of Enoch and Elijah, did not ascend to heaven during life or after death. Humans shared the same, inescapable fate—death and the netherworld. The netherworld (Sheol) was not a place for terrible punishments, at least not yet; it was simply a dark, dusty place where one continues in a shadowy form of one's life on earth. Heaven was not the post-mortem destiny of humans. Heaven was for the gods, and humans were not welcome. As Daniel 12:1–3, the latest book of the Hebrew Bible, suggests, however, this idea underwent a dramatic change as the Jews began to interact more intimately with the Persians and Greeks.[49]

Greek Influences on Christian Notions of Heaven

Jeffrey Burton Russell begins his *A History of Heaven: The Singing Silence* by declaring: "The central theme of this book is the fulfillment of the human longing for unity, body, and soul, in ourselves, with one another, and with the cosmos."[50] He considers the period from 200 BCE to Dante's *Divine Comedy* (1321 CE) and the publication of *Benedictus Dei*, a papal decree that established the beatific vision (1336). Russell chooses Dante as the end point because in many ways he is the culmination of what has come before. Russell explores how heaven relates to time, space, and place. How can human language describe or define it? How does a person exist in it? Russell explores the tensions that exist between body and soul, individual and community, abstract versus the physical images, human language versus ineffability of heaven.

For Russell, the limitations of human speech necessitate metaphorical heavenly expressions. Metaphorical ontology is "the use of figures of speech to go beyond science, history, and poetry to indicate the deepest, divine, heavenly reality."[51] Christians take from Greco-Roman culture images of gardens as well as the absence of death, disease, or want. People depict

49. Ibid., 95–97.
50. Jeffrey Burton Russell, *A History of Heaven: The Singing Silence* (Princeton: Princeton University Press, 1997), xiii.
51. Ibid., 8.

heaven in a way relevant to their own context. So desert dwellers imagine water and coolness; those in cold places imagine sunshine.

On the relationship between heaven and time, bodies necessarily require time and space. Singing a hymn of praise demands consecutive time. If we are affected by time and our experience is a subcategory of God's experience, then God must be affected by time as well.[52]

For bodies to exist, there must be space. Some refer to heaven as a space up in the sky, beyond earth, while others speak of heaven as coming down to us on earth. Space metaphors often used include kingdom, garden, city, celestial spheres, a reign, and God's throne. Other metaphors include womb, nut, umbilicus, mandala, book, ladder, bridge, clouds, gates, court.[53] Kingdom language for heaven was popular in the East, city language in the West.[54] The idea of a new or heavenly Jerusalem goes back to Ezekiel (sixth c. BCE). Elysium is a common Greco-Roman heaven and is variously located on earth, in the sphere of the moon, among the stars, or in the Blessed Isles of the West.[55] The ancients differed in terms of the number and arrangement of cosmological spheres. Plato's *Timaeus* has eight, Cicero nine, Plutarch three, and Mithraism seven.

In "Rest in Peace or Roast in Hell: Funerary versus Apocalyptic Portraits of Paradise," McCane argues that funerary images of paradise in late antiquity differ from apocalyptic ones because the former seek to console the visitor to the grave of the recently lost loved one, while the latter seek to inspire those who are about to die.[56] He speaks of *klinē* meals that depict the deceased reclining on a couch, sometimes with a spouse, being fed baskets of food, a female to the left in a chair strumming a stringed instrument, a three-legged table with fish, and a puppy.[57]

The *refrigerium* is a "refreshing" meal eaten at the grave during a ritual commemoration of the dead. In Roman custom, the *cena novendialis* was a feast celebrated graveside nine days after death; the Parentalia, a feast for dead parents, was held each February. The anniversary of the person's death

---

52. The relationship between bodies and time is a lively discussion in the field of metaphysics. See Mark Heller, "Temporal Parts of Four-Dimensional Objects," *Philosophical Studies* 46 (1984): 323–34; idem, *The Ontology of Physical Objects: Four-Dimensional Hunks of Matter* (Cambridge, UK: Cambridge University Press, 1990).

53. Russell, *History of Heaven*, 15.

54. Ibid., 13.

55. Cf. Homer, *Odyssey* 4.561–569; Hesiod, *Works and Days* 167–73; Pindar, *Olympian Odes* 2.61–83.

56. Byron R. McCane, "Rest in Peace or Roast in Hell: Funerary versus Apocalyptic Portraits of Paradise," in *Zeichen aus Text und Stein: Studien auf dem Weg zu einer Archäologie des Neuen Testaments* (ed. Stefan Alkier and Jürgen Zangenberg; Tübingen: Francke, 2003), 488–500.

57. Ibid., 489.

was another occasion for dining at the gravesite. People counted the dead as present and joining in these meals.[58]

In the third to fourth centuries CE we see on sarcophagi and catacomb paintings the *stibadium*, or sigma-meal, in which a group of five to seven people sit around a semicircular table with abundant food and drink. Unlike the *klinē* images in which the deceased figures prominently, in these paintings it is not clear which person represents the deceased.[59]

These funerary portraits perhaps alleviated the pain of loss. As Quintilian says, "I live on, and must find a reason to live on" (*Institutio oratorio* 6.14).[60] The images were "balm for the wound of loss, healing for the psychological experience of grief," and would only have been seen when a loved one was in a catacomb and visiting the grave of the deceased.[61]

In addition to fulfilling these individual functions, such ceremonies also served society and culture. The rite of passage allowed the family members to move on, inherit, and remarry. This was all an upper-class phenomenon.

On the other hand, apocalyptic was typically a response on the part of lower-class and marginalized people to inequities in social structures that threatened to make life meaningless for the righteous who suffered while the wicked flourished. It originated among ordinary religious people. Common to both is the use of images of abundance in the afterlife; thus we can consider all of it as a raging protest against death.[62]

Plato (428–347 BCE). Plato's *Phaedo* ascribes immortality to both *psychē* (the life force in all living things) and *nous* (the mind, existing only in humans), which together constitute the soul. In *Gorgias*, Plato has the dead arrive in a meadow, undergo judgment, and receive reward or punishment on the basis of deeds (thus, ethics), after which they are reincarnated, only to die once again. So there is a cyclical element to his eschatology that does not exist in Christianity. Plato's *Phaedrus* teaches that the soul ascends, and if it is too heavy, it sinks back down and is reincarnated. This process is supposed to lead to eventual purification. *Cicero (106–43 BCE).* Cicero's "Dream of Scipio" (in *De republica* 6) places the land of the just in the Milky Way.

Cicero distinguishes between the body, which perishes at death, and the immortal soul, which is eternal and immaterial. His views are presented in the *Tusculan Disputations.* Stoics, whose philosophy Cicero agreed with in part, believed that souls rise to join the fires of the sky. The earth exists in the center of concentric spheres. As one moves outward, one gets closer and

---

58. See Lucian, *On Funerals*, 9; McCane, "Rest in Peace," 490.
59. McCane, "Rest in Peace," 490.
60. Ibid., 491.
61. Ibid., 492.
62. Ibid., 496.

closer to the empyrean, the place of pure fire where God is and which serves as the soul's true home.[63]

New Testament forms of Christianity share concepts of heaven with both the Jewish parent tradition as well as Greco-Roman ideas. Both early Jewish and Greek notions included the view that all the dead entered a land of shadowy existence (Sheol and Hades). Later, distinctions were made, and the particularly virtuous received special rewards. Even later, the virtuous dead ascended to another place, leaving behind on earth or in Hades those deserving of punishment.[64]

Jewish Materials

Early eschatology had a strong corporate trajectory. The dominant Deuteronomic view finds dead people either entirely dead or living an enfeebled form of life in Sheol. In keeping with this theology, those who do good receive good, and those who do bad receive bad; this judgment takes place during one's earthly life. But after the exile this theology no longer "worked." It became clear that the wicked were often rewarded and the righteous sometimes suffered unjustly (Job). Given God's nature as just, this injustice necessitated some sort of posthumous settling of accounts. We then see the tripartite compartmentalization of Sheol: a fiery Gehenna for the unrighteous, a shadowy, old-fashioned Sheol for the mediocre, and a happy part for the righteous. By the time one gets to the late OT literature, such as parts of Daniel, a more otherworldly eschatology appears. The individual takes center stage, and the corporate aspect of judgment disappears. "The old Deuteronomic view yielded to belief in personal immortality and reward in heaven."[65]

By the first century CE, Pharisees taught resurrection of the body, which the faithful Jew received either at death or at a later time (cf. Acts 23:7–8). "The bodily resurrection was confirmed by the Pharisees at the Council of Jamnia in 90 CE. and has remained orthodox Jewish belief."[66] Resurrection takes place at the Mount of Olives, and all who rise undergo judgment. The faithful attain some sort of heavenly existence, often identified with the temple or courts. Elijah (2 Kgs 2:11–12), Enoch (Gen 5:24; Heb 11:5), and sometimes Moses (Deut 32:5–7; Mark 9:4) are presented as figures who have already attained heavenly existence. Where do the resurrected righteous live? Either in Jerusalem or in paradise. Paradise comes from the Persian *pairi-daēza* (enclosure), which referred to the gardens of the king of Persia. The connection between paradise and the garden of Eden comes only

---

63. Russell, *History of Heaven*, 23.
64. Ibid., 18.
65. Ibid., 29.
66. Ibid., 30.

in third to first centuries BCE, when the LXX could translate both *pardēs* and Eden as *paradeisos*. Paradise becomes the opposite of Gehenna.

The heavenly Jerusalem as a posthumous abode is well established by the second century BCE. Time and space become glorified together so that the Day of the Lord is judgment day, a festival day, the eternal Shabbat. The author of Hebrews adopts this imagery in chapter 4.

As is the case with hell, the intertestamental period saw a sharp rise in heavenly interest, particularly in the apocalyptic literature.[67] In these texts the apocalyptic seer goes through various heavens (the number varies in the different texts, just as it does among Greek authors), receives a vision of how things will eventuate, and returns to earth to share that vision. Two attitudes toward the body obtain: (1) "The future resurrected body is identical with the present body decaying in the grave, so that at the resurrection limbs, organs — the entire body — will be restored."[68] (2) The body will be transformed at the resurrection from an earthly body to a spiritual body that is somehow glorified. We will see that Paul argues for the latter.

First Enoch was compiled from 250–50 BCE.[69] The portion known as the Book of the Watchers (chs. 1–36, ca. 200 BCE) is an important resource for understanding the development of heavenly concepts. It appears to be the earliest evidence of a heavenly ascent and the first to insist that the righteous enjoy otherworldly bliss. Heaven is depicted as a combination of an earthly and a celestial city, where God and the elect dwell. Metaphors include mountains, gates, rivers, trees, the temple, the throne, music, light, and celestial elements. There are many similarities in heavenly images between the Jewish apocalyptic literature and the NT apocalypse known as Revelation.

Ancient Judaism. "Before Zoroastrianism, there was no precedent for a devil in Near Eastern belief, only for underworld rulers."[70] Beelzebub derives from *ba'al zĕbûb*, Lord of the Flies. Likewise, Beelzebul means "Lord of the garbage." Both are meant to derogate the god of the Philistines. Mark 3:22 is the first evidence that connects Beelzebub to the devil. Lucifer, bearer of light, originates in Isa 14:12–15, from a passage about the king of Babylon that later readers took out of context (cf. LXX, Latin Vulgate, KJV). Lucifer will end up in Sheol, which has now become hell. This Isaianic passage is the origin of belief in the devil as a fallen angel.[71]

---

67. See especially Martha Himmelfarb, *Ascent to Heaven in Jewish and Christian Apocalypses* (New York: Oxford University Press, 1993).

68. Russell, *History of Heaven*, 36.

69. For a useful introduction and summary of 1 Enoch, see http://wesley.nnu.edu/biblical_studies/noncanon/summaries/1enoch-notes.htm.

70. Hallote, *Death, Burial, and Afterlife*, 131.

71. See Susan R. Garrett, ch. 3 "Fallen Angels" in *No Ordinary Angel: Jesus and the Angels in the Bible and Today* (New York: Doubleday, forthcoming).

During the Greco-Roman period Judaism borrowed physical character-istics of the devil from classical sources, especially mythological creatures such as Pan and the Dionysiac satyrs. While conceptual ideas and beliefs about hell and the devil developed during this period, the archaeological record indicates no similar development in Jewish burial practices.

Intertestamental Judaism. During the Late Second Temple period, writ-ers produced apocalyptic literature that offered new cosmologies containing specific descriptions of postmortem existence in heaven or hell. In these texts, one goes to heaven as a reward or to hell as a punishment; hence, one's postmortem existence is tied to the moral judgment one undergoes. Satan, called by various names and aided by armies of demons, looms large in this period.

Philo and Josephus. It is not the case that "Jewish" and "Hellenistic" rep-resent two mutually exclusive categories. Nowhere is this better proved than in the works of Philo, who interprets the Jewish tradition largely through the lenses of Hellenistic philosophy. Philo does indeed adhere to a dualism more readily observable in Platonic texts than in the OT.[72] Any categories here are for heuristic purposes and clarity of presentation since Jewish liter-ature and Hellenistic literature show certain similar tendencies, and overlap is inevitable.

Philo (20 BCE–ca. 50 CE). In his article "Eschatology in Philo and Jose-phus,"[73] Grabbe divides the topic into three useful categories: (1) individual eschatology, (2) national eschatology, and (3) cosmic eschatology. In treating Philo's personal eschatology, Grabbe observes that death entails a separation of the soul from the body; the body is a tomb. Philo is a Middle Platonist: he combines Platonism with other ideas, especially Stoicism.[74] Early Stoics had no doctrine of afterlife. Later Stoics held that some souls remained after death until the *ekpyrōsis* (conflagration), the last stage of the universe's re-curring cycle of birth, life, and death. Either way, immortality was not a prominent belief in Stoicism. During Philo's lifetime Platonism and Stoicism were similar in that both had a place for afterlife, though very differently conceived. In Stoicism, the soul was viewed as having eight parts; in Platon-ism, three; in Aristotelianism, five. Philo uses the terms Hades and Tartarus, but not as literal places; rather, they refer to a certain quality of life. Thus Philo can say, "But it is not that mythical place of the impious in Hades. For the true Hades is the life of the bad, a life of damnation and blood-guiltiness,

---

72. For a description of Philo's dualism, see Daniel Boyarin, "Paul and the Genealogy of Gender," in *A Feminist Companion to Paul* (ed. Amy-Jill Levine; London: T&T Clark, 2004), 13–41.

73. Lester Grabbe, "Eschatology in Philo and Josephus," in *Death, Life-after-Death, Resurrection and the World-to-Come* (ed. Avery-Peck and Neusner), 163–85.

74. See John Dillon, *The Middle Platonists: 80 B.C. to A.D. 220* (Ithaca, NY: Cornell University Press, 1977).

the victim of every curse."[75] Such a notion sounds quite existential. On the other hand, Philo can speak of the soul being freed from the body at death to exist in the heavenly sphere. It is somewhat strange that heaven talk would be literal and hell talk existential or metaphorical. Philo has no notion of a cosmic eschatology. There is simply a postmortem judgment of the individual without a general resurrection.

Josephus (37 CE–ca. 100 CE). In treating Josephus, Grabbe indicates that Josephus's personal eschatology envisions a postmortem judgment, where the soul, the essential part of a human being, receives a new life if it is good, but punishment in the netherworld if it is bad. Josephus appears to believe in metempsychosis (the soul at death passing into another body). Regarding the second category, national eschatology, Josephus seems to have had some national eschatological beliefs based on the book of Daniel, and influenced by the fact that he fought in a Jewish war against Rome. National and cosmic eschatology are not prominent in his writings, however, because either (1) he held such beliefs, but kept them to himself so as not to offend Rome; or (2) he no longer held such beliefs. Josephus may have believed in an eschaton and destruction by fire, but he provides little information. Neither does he discuss his belief in the resurrection. Grabbe asks whether this is because belief in the resurrection and the eschaton are not something Greeks and Romans could relate to, or because he did not hold such a belief. Grabbe chooses the former.

Grabbe concludes that both Philo and Josephus believe that the soul is an immortal, incorruptible divine fragment imprisoned in the body. Death is a separation of the soul from this body. Josephus may have believed that all such souls are reborn (into another body). Philo eschews resurrection, as would any good Platonist who hates the physical body. Neither felt extreme compunction toward consistency, and this is especially true of Philo.

Summary. As we will see in the following chapters, "No single view of heaven exists in the New Testament, which left many questions unresolved and open to debate in succeeding centuries."[76] We close with three conclusions regarding heaven:

1. For Hellenistic thinkers, the concept of heaven relates to physics. However, most NT authors do not care about physics. Only Paul hints in this direction.

2. The concept of heaven relates to the question of anthropology and personal identity: *What* am I? *Who* am I? How am I related to God? Greek philosophers and Jewish authors answered these questions differently.

---

75. Philo, *Congr.* 57; Grabbe, "Eschatology," 169.
76. Russell, *History of Heaven*, 40.

3. The concept of heaven relates to ethics: there is reward or punishment based on deeds. The NT authors exhibit particular interest in this feature.

A Brief History of Hell

My baby Acerva was snatched away to live in Hades;...her father asks that the earth may rest lightly on her for ever. (*CIL* 14.1731)

A brief history of hell up to the end of the first century is relevant as we begin to discuss biblical books that have hell as part of their stated theology. Alan Bernstein defines hell as "a divinely sanctioned place of eternal torment for the wicked."[77] As might be expected, various Mediterranean cultures contributed to the NT concept of hell.

Mesopotamia, Babylonia, and Egypt

The Mesopotamian record witnesses to the notion of "neutral death" by the middle of the third millennium BCE. That view, according to which the dead survive en masse in a pallid half-life without either reward or punishment, later informed classical antiquity through Persia.[78] The Babylonian viewpoint is exemplified by the Epic of Gilgamesh, which dates to somewhere around the late third or early second millennium BCE. After witnessing his friend Enkidu's death, Gilgamesh seeks eternal life, but the key to immortality (root of youth) is stolen by a serpent; failing in his quest, Gilgamesh dies. In the Epic, the dead inhabit a great wilderness inaccessible to the living.

Additional evidence is provided by the Babylonian myth of Inanna and Ereshkigal, the Sumerian version of which is dated to the first half of the second millennium BCE and the Akkadian text to the end of the second millennium BCE. Inanna (Ishtar in the Akkadian version), a fertility goddess, descends from the heavens to usurp power from her sister Ereshkigal, ruler of the dead. Inanna is released from the dead so that water might be provided to end drought, continuing the chthonic cycle. Both the Epic of Gilgamesh and the Descent of Inanna assume moral neutrality when it comes to the dead; all of the dead, both good and evil, are in the underworld. Whereas the Epic depicts a wilderness, the Descent's underworld remarkably resembles a Middle Eastern city with gates and palace, and various functionaries (monarchs, judges, guards, et al.).

What is the point of such stories? Bernstein argues that the land of the dead is in the imagination of the living; it is for the sake of the living that such tales are told. The living aimed to distance themselves from death, but

---

77. Alan E. Bernstein, *The Formation of Hell: Death and Retribution in the Ancient and Early Christian Worlds* (Ithaca, NY: Cornell University Press, 1993), 3.
78. Ibid.

the fact that some characters could bridge the gap expresses the doubts and anxieties of the living, who are not entirely successful in sequestering their dead.[79] Such stories speak to the concern for a productive earth so that the living can thrive. "Surely the connection between the grave and the granary must be correctly delineated for a society to function properly."[80] As in the discussion about heaven above, notions of hell in these cultures betray the sociohistorical context of the authors.

Egypt departs from the "neutral death" depictions of Mesopotamia and Babylonia. In the middle of the second millennium BCE, the Egyptian Coffin Texts from the Middle Kingdom testify to their notion of "moral death." "That view, according to which the dead are judged by the standard of known criteria and then rewarded or punished, later informed ancient Greece through its colonies in Sicily and through the influence attributed to the mathematician and mystic Pythagoras."[81] The notion of "mere death," where one simply dies and ceases to exist, was not popular in Egypt. "Mere death excludes the possibility of hell."[82] In the Egyptian texts, the dead live in an underworld called Tuat, which is situated by a river with surrounding fields. In the Pyramid texts we find the pharaoh conflated with the sun-god Amon-Re, so that after death the pharaoh also rises to eternal life in the heavens. The pharaoh must first pronounce himself innocent. Such a concept clearly functioned as political propaganda.

The Coffin texts reflect the democratization of the above system, rewarding the good and punishing the wicked. Here is also the earliest depiction of a scale as tool for assessing a person's moral life. The Book of the Dead was written to help people through the process of judgment. The Egyptian Book of Gates and the Book Am-Tuat consign the wicked to fire and pits (cf. Revelation).

In the Book of Gates we have a zoned underworld, where judgment is based on one's devotion, or lack thereof, to certain gods. Judgments are not eternal, and the use of spells can undermine the attention to moral judgment in the text.[83] "For now it is sufficient to conclude that the morally neutral storehouse of the dead and the subdivided, mapped underworld, zoned (at least potentially) according to ethical principles, were options that formed part of the cultural stock, the conceptual repertory, of the ancient world before the first millennium B.C.E."[84]

---

79. I refer the reader to Mary Douglas, *Purity and Danger: An Analysis of Concepts of Pollution and Taboo* (London: Ark Paperbacks, 1984).
80. Bernstein, *Formation of Hell*, 10.
81. Ibid., 3.
82. Ibid.
83. Ibid., 18.
84. Ibid.

Greece and Rome

Neutral Death. Like the ANE materials, the earliest written Greek mythology sources evidence a notion of neutral death rather than moral death or hell as defined by Bernstein. Emphasis is still on the separation between the dead and the living, rather than separation of the good and the wicked, and all of the dead are located in the same place, living under the same conditions. In the *Odyssey*, the soul survives death, but dead souls reside at great remove from the living. There are two sets of consequences going on in Hades, which is depicted as far away, beyond the edge of the earth, as well as down below. Superhuman characters, like Sisyphus and Tantalus, receive punishment for insubordination to the gods. "In Homer, however, death for all the purely human shades is morally neutral. Distinctions of social status brought over from life, memories and aspirations, vicarious pride or shame at loss of status, characterize the dead, it is true, but these emotions do not affect their basic condition, and as compared to the fact of death, the place itself adds nothing."[85]

Moral Death in Plato (ca. 428–347 BCE) and Socrates (ca. 470–399 BCE). Like the Orphics (below), Plato espouses *sōma sēma* ("the body is a tomb"; *Crat.* 400B–C). Plato has much to say regarding postmortem fate, especially in the *Phaedrus.* He presents a notion of successive incarnations. When a person dies, the soul separates from the body, whereupon it is morally judged and assigned a spot in the place appropriate to that judgment. The underworld is quite complex topographically, involving rivers and holes and seas consisting of hot and cold water and mud. The fundamental center is Tartarus, which serves as a channel to other places. Bernstein lists four potential fates for the dead in Plato: (1) The holy immediately ascend into the ether to dwell with the gods. (2) Those whose moral status is "indeterminate" proceed to the Acherusian Lake and live there until the soul is purified, paying penalties for infractions and receiving rewards for any good actions. (3) Those guilty of "curable" sins are annually washed out of Tartarus through the rivers, seeking forgiveness from those they have offended; if denied, they return to Tartarus for another year; if forgiven, they come out into the lake, and their torment ends. (4) The hopelessly wicked receive eternal punishment by being cast into Tartarus, never to escape. Once again, we see that the point of judgment, reward, and punishment has to do with encouraging behavior that makes for a good orderly society. "These themes... are certainly clear in Plato: the soul is immortal; it is judged for the character it acquires during its life in the body; it can be rewarded or punished after death. The rewards of the blessed and the punishment of the

---

85. Ibid., 33.

incurably wicked endure forever."[86] Plato appears to be "the earliest author to state categorically that the fate of the extremely wicked is eternal punishment."[87]

Moral Death in Virgil (70–19 BCE). In the *Aeneid*, book 6, on the "Descent of Aeneas," Virgil wrote with the encouragement of Augustus to legitimate his rule. His geography of hell includes an entry space, where the dead of a morally neutral type reside (e.g., infants, suicides). They are conscious of being dead and retain their earthly identity. For example, those who died of love still long for the beloved, and the suicides wish they had stayed alive. The road then forks to the right and left: the wicked are sent left to Tartarus, and the virtuous right to the Elysian fields. This resembles Plato's geography insofar as both he and Virgil envision three areas of judgment. In Tartarus superhuman characters such as the Titans are punished, but so are certain categories of humans (fratricides, patricides, adulterers, fraudulent businessmen). No individual humans are named, just the categories. There are three types of souls in Elysium: (1) the perfect, which remain forever in Elysium; (2) the perfectible, those who can complete their purification while remaining in Elysium; and (3) those who need to be reincarnated, to take on additional physical lives to achieve purity.

For all the similarity between Homer and Virgil, Odysseus's journey is a personal one, but Aeneas's is national: his journey is tied to the history of Rome and its rulers. Furthermore, unlike Homer, Virgil's underworld is moral. The prisoners of Tartarus will forever there remain. "Here the punishment of the dead is firmly established."[88]

Moral Death in Plutarch (before 50 CE–after 120 CE). In his *Ethical Works* one finds Plutarch's *On the Delays of the Divine Vengeance*, which investigates whether postmortem punishment is effective and justice is achieved. Plutarch maintains that a delay in divine vengeance allows time for reform. And what about the notion of children punished for the sins of the parents? Plutarch says that when people see how the sins of parents affect their children, they will behave so that their own children are not negatively affected. Plutarch also holds some sort of doctrine of genetic sin, the family nature. This serves a twofold function: the dead are purified for their next life by suffering the knowledge of their progeny's suffering on their account. The progeny are purified in this life by the suffering that stems from their forebears.

In Plutarch, unlike Plato and Virgil, we find the goddess Erinys (Fury) destroying imperfectible souls. Bernstein argues here that Fury does not

---

86. Ibid., 58.
87. Ibid., 61.
88. Ibid., 73.

actually annihilate but rather whisks the souls away to oblivion, "imprison-
ing them in the Nameless and Unseen."[89] The goddess Dike (Justice) takes
the souls that did not receive punishment on earth and does one of three
things with them in order to purge them of their passions: (1) when the soul
lapses, Dike administers more punishment; (2) when the soul lapses due to
ignorance, it is sent to another body; or (3) the soul remains in a state of
unfulfilled passion until the passion extinguishes.

Plutarch deals with two aspects of justice or purification. First, one must
pay for any crimes or misdeeds committed on earth for which the perpetrator
never received punishment. For that, the shade receives physical wounds.[90]
But as indicated above, there is also concern to eradicate the *propensity* for
evil. Plutarch supports postmortem punishment, but not eternal punishment
(with the exception of oblivion, about which we have no details). Punishment and shame factor significantly in Plutarch's thinking. "Through three
techniques — punishment in the afterlife, demotion of the soul into another
body, and denial of reincarnation and enforced frustration until the passion
is spent — Dike can achieve radical purification by uprooting unjust passions, as opposed to 'merely' reversing fortune and inspiring regret as Poine
[Punishment] does."[91]

What we see in Plato, Virgil, and Plutarch is a rather orderly system of
justice and punishment with an eye to encouraging moral behavior in the
living. One almost gathers the sense of an underworld Ellis Island, with ships
of new immigrants regularly arriving and being met by those who have the
power to judge the newcomer. "The moral afterlife in Plato, Virgil, and
Plutarch is dynamic. It judges, divides, processes, rewards, and punishes."[92]

FUNCTIONS OF DIVINE JUDGMENT
IN OT TEXTS

David Kuck argues for a variety of functions related to divine judgment as
evinced by the LXX. The trajectory moves from judgment within history to
eschatological judgment.

First, divine judgment serves as a moral recompense within the life of
an individual or nation. In this vein he makes four points: (1) Some deeds
may carry their own consequences, but the main point is that God controls
recompense; God sees all and judges according to God's justice. (2) The
concept of recompense can explain historical circumstances, but usually it is

89. Ibid., 78.
90. The idea of a shade or soul receiving physical punishment may strike one as
incomprehensible or confusing. Nonetheless, this is the language that Plutarch employs.
91. Bernstein, *Formation of Hell*, 82.
92. Ibid., 83.

used to encourage individual moral responsibility or national responsibility for keeping covenant with God. (3) Recompense is future oriented but remains within history; no definitive act that changes the course of history is imagined. (4) The language is "mostly not drawn from the realm of forensic judgment and lawsuits, but rather from the realm of the economic life: pay, reward, loss, compensation."[93] The Gospel of Matthew employs this economic language extensively.

Second, Kuck addresses what he calls "the announcement of God's decision to recompense God's people." Though closely related to the first point (above), in this case some agent of God announces the wrongdoing and states God's intention to punish it imminently. This feature is typical of prophetic literature and makes heavy use of the language of wrath (*orgē* or *thymos*) and fire as well as "Day of the Lord" language.[94] Here the prophets make four main points: (1) God will punish the nation. (2) The language is heavily forensic. (3) The acts of the whole people against their covenant with God are what require punishment. (4) Punishment will be rendered within the bounds of historical time.[95]

Third, Kuck takes up appeals made to the higher court of God's judgment. Some situations cannot be resolved in human courts for various reasons (e.g., the social status of the victim), so there is an appeal to God for justice. Here Kuck makes six main points: (1) Situations of human conflict precipitate the need for judgment (rather than God-human conflict). (2) The terminology is heavily judicial. (3) Aggression language more than morality language obtains. (4) The emphasis is not on the whole group but on individuals. (5) This court of appeals notion gives hope to those who stand no chance of winning in a human court and provides a social outlet so that violence does not escalate. (6) This type of judgment is envisioned as taking place within history.[96]

Fourth, Kuck attends to Israel vis-à-vis the nations in God's judgment. God opposes those who oppose Israel and Israel's God. Kuck makes three main points: (1) Such a notion bolsters group identity. (2) This idea is useful in situations of defeat. (3) Judgment language here sometimes moves to the cosmic level.[97]

Moving to a later historical period, Kuck discerns three categories. First, he discusses moral recompense for individuals and claims that this concept carries over for paraenetic purposes from the OT through rabbinic Judaism. Moving the judgment to a postmortem period is most evident after 70 CE.

---

93. David W. Kuck, *Judgment and Community Conflict: Paul's Use of Apocalyptic Judgment Language in 1 Corinthians 3:5–4:5* (NovTSup 66; Leiden: Brill, 1992), 43.
94. For primary texts, see ibid., footnotes 29–32. Paul uses such language.
95. Ibid., 45.
96. Ibid., 49.
97. Ibid., 52.

Second, Kuck argues that appeals to the higher court of God's judgment do not really extend beyond the OT. Finally, Kuck points out that the eschatological judgment is addressed to situations of crisis and conflict. Here the idea of God judging Israel's oppressors negatively and faithful Jews positively carries over as a result of Second Temple political crises and defeats. In this section Kuck treats apocalyptic texts (*Jubilees*; 4 Ezra [= 2 Esd 3–14]; *2 Baruch*; et al.).

Kuck then moves into an analysis of judgment language in selected Jewish texts. He treats *1 Enoch* 1–36 and 92–105; *Psalms of Solomon*; Wisdom of Solomon; *Testament of Abraham*; and *2 Enoch*. Also, among the Dead Sea Scrolls he deals with *War Scroll* (1QM); pesharim; *Rule of the Community* (1QS); *Damascus Document* (CD); *Thanksgiving Hymns* (1QH).[98]

Ultimately, Kuck argues that two different functions are at work from the OT to the Tannaitic period (ca. 10 CE–220 CE). First, the individual's place in society and life is defined. There are four corollaries: (1) One should behave morally and thus receive health and success. (2) The faithfulness of individuals will influence the nation and its fate. (3) God is available for individuals who cannot find justice through human systems. (4) God's justice can be postmortem in the later Jewish texts.

Second, a belief in God's judgment can define a group in relation to the larger world or offer encouragement to that group in times of crisis.

Kuck's insights will inform our analysis of the NT texts.

GRECO-ROMAN MATERIAL[99]

Pagan beliefs ranged from the completely nihilistic denial of after-life, through a vague sense of souls' ghostly experience, to a concept of the individual soul's survival and of personal survival in a recognizable form. These individual surviving souls were sometimes subject to purgation which reflected a moral judgment on the virtues and misdeeds of the life just lived.[100]

The Evidence

Epitaphs

Romans predominantly cremated from the fourth century BCE to the end of the first CE and then moved primarily to burial. However, both practices

---

98. Ibid., 68ff, 93.

99. For simple reference issues, the reader may consult the *Oxford Classical Dictionary* (ed. Simon Hornblower and Antony Spawforth; 3d ed., rev.; New York: Oxford University Press, 2003); henceforth, *OCD*.

100. Keith Hopkins, *Death and Renewal* (Cambridge: Cambridge University Press, 1983), 227.

coexisted. The practice of inscribing tombstones became popular only at the end of the first century BCE. Around a hundred thousand epitaphs survive from the western half of the Roman Empire. These epitaphs show that from the first century BCE onward, some Romans envisioned individual postmortem existence.

Graves

Roman graves came in various shapes and sizes. There were grand tombs for the really wealthy and mass graves for the abject poor. Between those two extremes were small graves marked with stone and collective tombs, discussed below. For the most part, the tombs were built with individuals in mind, not families. Relatives of the wealthy built tombs to respect the dead, to impress the living, and to immortalize themselves.[101] In death as in life, the vast majority of the impoverished populace left no trace of their burial; many were dumped in *puticuli*, collective burial pits, mass graves.

Given the problem of the overpopulation of Rome during our period, how to dispose of bodies was of grave concern. One response to the problem lay in the formation of burial clubs. Because the cost of land was so high, Romans turned to burial clubs and collective tombs called columbaria. Though we hear nothing of them in the NT, Christian catacombs came to mirror Roman ones and included the sale of burial spots. By belonging to a burial club, one could be assured of receiving a proper burial, which would be a particular solace to those who, as is typical of urban living, might not have enough nearby blood relatives to rely on for such a purpose. Scholars have compared early Christian communities to burial clubs for a number of reasons. In both, slave and free mingled; they ate occasional meals under the aegis of a patron god; they were social clubs of sorts; the members functioned as fictive kin, fulfilling functions normally satisfied by blood relatives, and so on. Hopkins argues that the primary function of the club was to guarantee a person individuality in a mass society.

Romans tended to the dead, even feeding them. They buried them with items that might make their postmortem life resemble their earthly life. Two major religious festivals, the Parentalia and the Lemuria, were officially devoted to commemorating the dead. During the former, relatives would eat a meal at the graveside, where there were often facilities such as ovens and wells. Pipes linked some tombs with the surface so that food and drink could be provided for the deceased. Improper attention to the dead could result in adverse circumstances for the living. If fear of reprisals by the dead toward the survivors was not enough, there were always wills, through which the wealthy could affect the living even after death. Many willed funds to the

---

101. Ibid., 207.

local community in the form of annual banquets in their name, or educational programs or public memorials that overtly highlighted their generosity and gave them an immortality of sorts.[102]

Roman Religion

"Roman religious beliefs were extraordinarily varied; there was no single dominant orthodoxy; polytheism was supplemented by inventive, philosophical speculation and by individual sects, such as Stoicism, Mithraism, Judaism and Christianity."[103] Unlike the nihilistic Roman attitude expressed so famously by the initials *nf f ns nc* (*non fui, fui, non sum, non curo*; "I was not, I was, I am no more, I don't care"), Christians were optimistic about life after death. "The hope of eternal salvation was likely to appeal to Romans who, as we have seen, honoured their dead, worried about their fate, and were preoccupied by the prospect of their own imminent death."[104]

According to Beard, North, and Price, Roman religion focused primarily upon this life. Though the Roman state encouraged honoring the dead and participating in memorial services such as the Parentalia, "the official state cult did not particularly emphasize the fate of the individual after death, or urge a particular view of the afterlife."[105]

Mystery Religions

Historians of early Christianity typically allude to and make comparisons with ancient mystery cults, which tended to express interest in achieving immortality and involve religious rituals.[106] The most famous cult, the Eleusinian mysteries, centered on the story of Demeter and Persephone and was primarily chthonic. This is also true of the cult of Adonis, Aphrodite's lover. The Dionysian cult may be most famous for the celebration of the Bacchae, a wild, drunken, orgiastic party. The cult of Magna Mater (also called Cybele) tangentially relates to our project insofar as it involves some notion of a dying and rising god. As it turns out, though, the resurrection amounts only to the ability of Attis (Cybele's lover) to grow his hair and nails.

Indubitably, the two most important mystery religions for students of Christianity are Isism and Mithraism. In the former, one finds a dying and

---

102. For a detailed discussion, see ibid., 247–55. For consolation literature as a genre of the NT, see Paul Holloway, *Consolation in Philippians: Philosophical Sources and Rhetorical Strategy* (Cambridge, UK: Cambridge University Press, 2001); and Abraham Smith, *Comfort One Another: Reconstructing the Rhetoric and Audience of 1 Thessalonians* (Louisville: Westminster John Knox, 1995).

103. Hopkins, *Death and Renewal*, 226–67.

104. Ibid., 232.

105. Mary Beard, John North, and Simon Price, *Religions of Rome* (2 vols.; Cambridge, UK: Cambridge University Press, 1998), 1:89.

106. For a fuller introduction to the mysteries, read M. W. Meyer, ed., *The Ancient Mysteries: A Sourcebook* (San Francisco: Harper & Row, 1987).

rising god, Osiris. All students of Isism read Apuleius's delightful novel, *The Golden Ass*, in which the protagonist Lucius converts to the cult of Isis, is reborn, and is promised a blessed life and also a life after death. "There is, however, no word of his being *renatus in aeternum* [reborn for eternity], which is what counts."[107]

Mithraism, restricted to males, enjoyed wide popularity, especially among Roman soldiers. Scholars have made much of its analogues with Christianity and its concern for immortality. Mithras serves as an intermediary between the god of light and human beings. He is most often depicted slaying a bull, and being baptized in the blood of the bull effects certain advantages for initiates. In the end, the evidence is suggestive but does not directly illuminate our subject.[108]

Consolation Letters

The literary record has bequeathed to us a genre known as consolation literature. Seneca's *Letter of Condolence to Marcia* and *Letter of Condolence to Polybius* are significant here. As Hopkins states: "Educated Romans read such literature, however boring we find it."[109] The advice given varies by author. Seneca's letters are peppered with Stoic notions. Plutarch lost a daughter, as did Cicero. In *A Consolation to His Wife*, Plutarch enjoins his wife to control her grief.[110] Typically men were expected to be less emotional than women in the mourning process, and there was concern about excessive female grief.[111] As usual, Lucian satirizes the grieving process (*On Grief*, or *Funerals*), but other evidence takes it more seriously. Such is the case with Cicero's comments on the loss of his daughter, which caused him unbearable grief (*Letters to His Friends* 4; *Letters to Atticus* 12).

The main problem with each type of evidence presented above, of course, is that so much is missing. Also, it is not clear to what degree epitaphs reflect the actual sentiment of the deceased and their families. Epitaphs may simply represent a choice from one of the limited options in a stone mason's repertoire, chosen for appeal or affordability.

---

107. Ramsay MacMullen, *Paganism in the Roman Empire* (New Haven: Yale University Press, 1981).

108. It is instructive to read both Franz Cumont (who published extensively on the mystery religions) and Ramsay MacMullen together on the subject since the former makes much of the evidence while the latter minimizes it.

109. Hopkins, *Death and Renewal*, 218n23.

110. See Sarah Pomeroy, ed., *Plutarch's "Advice to the Bride and Groom," and "A Consolation to His Wife": English Translations, Commentary, Interpretive Essays, and Bibliography* (New York: Oxford University Press, 1999), esp. 59–81, 206–10.

111. The Twelve Tables prohibited women from tearing their cheeks with their nails at funerals. See Gail Holst-Warhaft, *Dangerous Voices: Women's Laments and Greek Literature* (London: Routledge, 1992).

Overview of the Soul

The discussion of the fate of a human being necessarily entails attention to anthropological considerations. Perhaps the most famous aspect of Greek philosophical anthropology is centered on the soul. What one finds overall is some linear development and some parallel development coupled with the waxing and waning of various ideas.

Russell argues that Christian anthropology is confused. For example, NT authors are not as clear as some gnostic authors, who easily divided people into three groups: somatics, who could not be saved; psychics, who might be; and pneumatics, who certainly were.[112] As we will see in later chapters, "no clear distinction between *psychē* and *pneuma* appeared in Hellenistic Jewish thought or among New Testament or other orthodox Christian thinkers."[113] Paul, for example, uses both *pneuma* (spirit) and *psychē* (soul), with *pneuma* being superior to *psychē*, and *sarx* (flesh) inferior to both.[114] Like many Jews, some Christians imagined a person to be a psychosomatic unity. The whole person was to be saved, including the body. Therefore, such believers eschewed any notion of a salvation without the body. The language of "immortality of the soul" is inaccurate insofar as it never appears in the NT. Paul speaks of that which is perishable "putting on" imperishability, but that is an attribute that will inhere only when the Parousia arrives. Later, resurrection of the body and immortality of the soul become confused categories, such that "the idea of the immortality of the soul came eventually to be identified with the Biblical doctrine of the resurrection of the body, a doctrine one of whose original polemical targets was the immortality of the soul."[115]

Homer (ca. 8th c. BCE)

In providing a brief background of Greek concepts of the soul, Jan Bremmer begins with Homer, for whom no one word indicates the seat of a person's psychological attributes; rather, his vocabulary is richly varied.[116] The most important word for emotion is *thymos*, but he also uses *menos* (fury), *noos* (act of the mind), and words for kidney, heart, lungs, liver, and gallbladder. Using the work of Scandinavian anthropologists, Bremmer argues that most

---

112. As usual with survey literature, Russell, *History of Heaven*, overstates the unity of thought in Gnosticism. For an introduction to Gnosticism, see Bentley Layton, *The Gnostic Scriptures: A New Translation with Annotations and Introductions* (ABRL; New York: Doubleday, 1995); or Elaine Pagels, *The Gnostic Gospels* (New York: Random House, 1979). For further study, see The Gnostic Society Library's Web page: http://www.gnosis.org/library.html.

113. Russell, *History of Heaven*, 44.

114. See ibid., 45, for a longer discussion on what Paul might mean by a *sōma pneumatikon*.

115. Jaroslav Pelikan, *The Emergence of the Catholic Tradition (100–600)* (Chicago: University of Chicago Press, 1971), 51.

116. This background is taken from Bremmer, *Rise and Fall of the Afterlife*, 1–10.

primitive peoples have thought that humans have two kinds of soul: (1) a free-soul that is inactive when the body is active, represents the individual personality, and manifests itself in dreams, swoons, or at death; and (2) a number of body-souls that endow the body with life and consciousness, but do not stand for the "part of the person that survives after death."[117] Homer has both *psychē*, a kind of free-soul, and body-souls: *thymos, noos, menos,* and then more physical organs, *phrenes* (lungs/midriff/heart), and *ētor* (heart).

Pythagoras, Orphism, and the Immortal Soul (6th c. BCE)

The Greek philosopher Pythagoras was interested in the immortal soul and reincarnation. In 530 BCE he left Samos and went to southern Italy, where he lived as an aristocrat. He died in Metapontum around 515. Parmenides and Empedocles, also southern Italians, propagated his ideas.

Orphism appears to be connected with Pythagoras and also stems from southern Italy.[118] Orphics were wealthy, as evidenced by the gold leaves, impressive graves in Thurii, and bronze urns. The inscribed gold leaves found in graves are guides to the underworld and passwords into a happy hereafter. A considerable number of women were Orphics. "Orphism, then, was an upper-class movement which paid special attention to the human individual, who was very much concerned with his own survival and salvation."[119] From the fifth century BCE onward, Pindar, Aristophanes, and Plato evince an afterlife with eternal sunlight or beautiful meadows, and the separation of the good, who are blessed in the afterlife, from the bad, who "wallow in the mud of Hades."[120] They teach transmigration or reincarnation of souls, which implies that the soul is quite different from the body. The Homeric idea had to do with the soul of the living; in (the Orphic) Pindar, the human soul is upgraded to divine. Eventually Plato will say *sōma sēma*, "the body is the tomb" of the soul. The task is to divorce oneself from the body. Those who are too attached to the body are doomed to be reincarnated so that they can try again.

Where did Pythagoras get his ideas? Although it is impossible to determine the source, Bremmer offers four explanations, all pointing toward sociohistorical causes. First, he argues that early Greeks did not care about personal survival but rather social survival of the group. Eventually this changes, as grave monuments attest, saying things like, "Look at who lies

117. Ibid., 2.
118. This area of the classics is experiencing numerous new developments due to recent discoveries of the oldest Orphic theogony (Darveni Papyrus), Orphic bone tablets, a steady influx of Gold Leaves (small inscribed gold lamellae found in graves), and new Apulian vases with representations of Orpheus and the afterlife; ibid., 11.
119. Ibid., 18.
120. Ibid., 23.

here," and eschatological ideas such as Elysium (Gk: *ēlysion*) develop. Reincarnation fits this trend toward an emphasis on personal survival in the afterlife.

Second, Bremmer suggests that the development arose from Pythagoras's dismal Metapontum period, when all was going awry for aristocrats like him. Extreme rules (for which the Pythagoreans were known) gave folks a sense of belonging, a place to excel, and a sense of certainty, much like modern sectarian movements.

Third, reincarnation gave people a sense of importance. Bremmer quotes Weber's observation that "the rise of religions of salvation, such as Christianity, were the consequence of a depoliticisation of the *Bildungsschichten.*"[121]

Finally, he suggests that Pythagoras's contribution could not have happened apart from the development of the *psychē* as a person's "self." Plato then takes Pythagoras's views (regarding the immortality of the soul, but not reincarnation) and passes them down to Christianity. "The rise of the soul, then, was the fruit of a combination of political and psychological developments not in India or Egypt, but in Greece itself."[122]

Socrates and Plato (5th c. BCE)

After Homer the meaning of *psychē* expands. With Socrates, *psychē* becomes the center of a person's inner life; according to Socrates, a person's task is to "care for [the] *psychē*." Eventually *psychē* absorbs *thymos*, which probably leads to Plato's notion of the tripartite soul.[123] Preexistence and survival of the soul after death are central Platonic doctrines, as is metempsychosis.

Aristotle (384–322 BCE)

Aristotle posited a separate power in the souls of human beings: reason. Humans have an animal self and a rational self. Aristotle's psychology is a divided self, whereas the Stoics envision a unified self.

Stoicism, Epicureanism, and Skepticism, all post-Aristotelian developments, constitute the main branches of Hellenistic philosophy, the dates of which extend from 323–31 BCE. After that, Platonism and Aristotelianism begin a revival. Epicureanism and Stoicism both assumed that "happiness depends on an understanding of the universe and what it is to be a [human being]."[124] Minor philosophers existed but will not be addressed here. Epicurus was regarded by some as *the* savior of humanity, as one can see in Lucretius. Stoics and Epicureans provided many Hellenistic people "with a

---

121. Ibid., 25.
122. Ibid., 26.
123. The three parts include the rational soul (mind), the spirited soul (volition), and the appetitive soul (desire).
124. Long, *Hellenistic Philosophy*, 6.

set of attitudes that religion and political ideologies might also have supported."[125] This is exactly why it is important to study them alongside
the NT.

Epicureans and Stoics

Epicureans and Stoics as well as some influential physicians continued to
maintain that the *psychē* does not exist independently from its body (see
fuller sections below on Stoicism and Epicureanism).

Christianity

Psychē entered the vocabulary of Greek-speaking Jews and then Christians
by means of LXX. Since the OT does not know of Greek dualism, which
makes body and soul opponents, it would take Christianity some time to develop this notion. For instance, Bremmer argues that Paul rarely uses *psychē*
and never with respect to afterlife. In Paul it tends to mean the "seat of
emotions" (Phil 1:27, au. trans.). Only with the growing influence of philo-
sophically trained Greek theologians like Origen and Clement does Platonic
dualism start to dominate Christianity. Eventually the Greek concept of soul
influences the Germanic world via Latin translations of the Bible and will
thus be responsible for our modern term "soul," from Old English *sāāwol*
and Old High German *sēula*.

The *psychē* (free soul) is what becomes the soul of the dead (as opposed
to body-souls that endow the body with life but do not survive death). The
usage of *psychē* as soul of the dead was taken over by Jews and Christians
(cf. Rev 20:4).

In commenting on the Greek influence upon Christian views of the body,
Russell declares: "Further, the much ignored fact is that neither the New
Testament nor the early Christian writers ever used the term 'immortal soul'
or 'immortal spirit.' The early Christians, like the rabbis, understood that
union with God was union of the whole human, both soul and body. Christian tradition continued to assume this union until, in the third century CE,
Platonic ideas of the soul's great superiority to the body promoted the idea
of the survival of souls apart from bodies."[126] Much of Judaism considered
the body unitary, whereas Platonic notions divided the self.

According to Russell, "The Christian confusion over the relationship
between spirit, soul, and body originated in persistent Greek philosophical inconsistencies about the terms *psychē, pneuma, sōma,* and *sarx.*
These terms resist definition because they frequently shifted in meaning.
...*Pneuma* and *psychē* are interchangeable in some writers and separate

125. Ibid., 12.
126. Russell, *History of Heaven*, 15.

in others, with the resulting permanent confusion in Western languages between 'spirit' and 'soul.' "[127] We will want to attend to this confusion as we
study the NT texts.

Stoicism

The following treatment of Stoicism is longer than those devoted to other
philosophies because Stoicism had more influence on NT authors than did
any other philosophical school. Our main sources for Stoicism include Diogenes Laertius, Cicero (esp. *De finibus*), Chrysippus, and Arius Didymus's
compendium of Stoic ethics in Stobaeus's *Eclogae*. Stoicism enjoys primacy
of place in Hellenistic philosophy in terms of importance and influence.
A. A. Long divides it into three periods: Early (Zeno to Antipater), Middle
(Panaetius and Posidonius), and late Stoicism (Seneca, Marcus Aurelius,
Epictetus). No complete work survives from the first two phases.

Zeno, the founder of Stoicism, was born in Citium around 335 BCE, came
to Athens in 311, and died around 263. He began his Stoic career in 300 by
frequenting the Painted Colonnade (Stoa) at Athens. He actually began as a
Cynic, influenced by the Cynic Crates. From Cynicism, Zeno borrowed the
crucial Stoic principle that the real *physis* (nature; natural condition) of a
person consists in one's rationality, one's *logos*. Socratic notions, such as the
idea that knowledge and goodness go together, also influenced him; a good
person is wise and a bad person is ignorant; from knowledge right action
follows; the greatest evil is a bad condition of soul.[128]

Stoicism clearly borrowed from both earlier and contemporary philosophy. Stoicism was heavily intellectual, displaying a keen interest in ordered
thinking, logic, grammar, and ethics. It thrived in Athens, Rome, and other
Mediterranean cities. Chrysippus was the head of the Stoa from 232–208
BCE and was followed by Posidonius (135–50 BCE), who came from Apa-
maea on the Syrian Orontes. Posidonius departed from earlier Stoicism and
adopted Plato's tripartite soul. Stoics divided philosophy into logic, physics,
and ethics.

Zeno (ca. 335–263 BCE)

We will now review Stoic anthropology. Zeno established Stoicism. *Hormē*,
impulse, is the central concept in the old Stoic analysis of human action. In
addition to *hormē*, language of note includes *phronēsis* (practical wisdom);
psychē, *phantasia* (impressions), *logos*, atoms, virtue, reason, impulse, happiness (*eudaimonia*, happiness, never appears in Bible). A human being is a
special sort of animal, but definitely an animal.

---

127. Ibid., 24.
128. Long, *Hellenistic Philosophy*, 111.

Stoic Philosophy of Nature

Every living creature has its own governing principle (*hēgemonikon*), and in human beings that principle is rational, which implies the ability to use language to articulate thought. *Physis* (nature) and *logos* (reason) are the two primary categories, and they overlap. Nature holds the world together and causes things on earth to grow. God, the rational being par excellence, holds the world together, this best of all possible worlds, and runs things for the benefit of humans (cf. Rom 8:28 NRSV note). God also is referred to as Soul of the world, Mind of the world, Nature, artistic fire, creative reason, the Universe.[129] While *logos* and *physis* both refer to God, they each have different connotations. Nature manifests itself differently in different parts of nature. So plants have *physis* (nature), irrational animals have soul, and human beings have *logos* (reason). Stoic theology is pantheistic and optimistic. One hears of cosmic reason and the divinity of the stars (echoed in 1 Cor 15:41). This notion of a rational, beneficent god is completely opposed to the teaching of the Epicureans, who believe that god is uninvolved and unconcerned with humans. Stoics can speak of fire and *pneuma*, or fiery breath, and maintain that the human soul is an "offshoot of God."[130]

The Structure of Things: Body, Pneuma, Elements

Virtue is a corporeal entity in Stoicism. There are two "principles": one is the active principle, which is Nature or God, and this is related intimately to a second "passive principle," called "matter or 'substance without qualitative determination.' "[131] There is a physical relationship between the two principles, and one immediately thinks of the FE's language of incarnation, of abiding between Jesus, God, and believers (esp. John 15), when one reads the words of the Stoics: "God is mixed with matter, penetrates the whole of matter and shapes it."[132] For something to exist, it must be capable of acting or being acted upon.

"Matter" in Stoicism is not synonymous with corporeality. "It is misleading to describe the Stoics as 'materialists.' Bodies, in the Stoic system, are compounds of 'matter' and 'mind' (God or *logos*). Mind is not something other than body but a necessary constituent of it, the 'reason' in matter. The Stoics are better described as vitalists."[133] For Zeno, fire and breath ("hot breath") are part of soul. Medical writers conceived of *pneuma* as the

---

129. Ibid., 148.
130. Ibid., 150.
131. Ibid., 154.
132. *SVF* 2:310; here and henceforth, *SVF* stands for Hans Friedrich August von Arnim, ed., *Stoicorum veterum fragmenta* (4 vols.; Leipzig: Teubner, 1903–24). Cf. Diogenes Laertius, *Lives of Eminent Philosophers* 7.134, citing Zeno).
133. Long, *Hellenistic Philosophy*, 154.

" 'vital' spirit transmitted via the arteries."[134] For Chrysippus, *pneuma* is the vehicle of the *logos*. "Intelligent *pneuma*" is "something which is both a physical component of the world and an agent capable of rational action."[135] This approximates FG, where *pneuma* is physical (John 1:32–33), the disciples can hear it, it blows where it wills (3:8), but it is responsible for guiding them in all truth (16:13), and so on. *Pneuma* is marked by continuous movement, which leads Long to define it more as "force" or "energy" or "gas."[136]

Fire plays a great role. The traditional four elements — earth, air, fire, water — in Stoicism consist of two pairs; the active pair (fire and air, or *pneuma*) and the passive pair (earth and water). *Pneuma* "holds together" earth and water.

> The universe itself is a sphere, and all its constituents tend to move towards the center, but only earth and water actually possess weight.... The *pneuma*, unlike the passive elements, pervades the whole cosmic sphere and unites the center with the circumference.... This function of *pneuma* in the macrocosm is equally at work in every individual body. Organic and inorganic things alike owe their identity and their properties to the *pneuma*. Its two constituents, fire and air, are blended in different proportions in different things. One arrangement of *pneuma* is the soul of an animal; the structure of a plant is a further arrangement, and the coherence of a stone yet another.... Whatever *pneuma* disposes it also holds together by the "tension" which it establishes between the individual parts. (*SVF* 2:441, 448)[137]

The Stoics, following Aristotle, treated "mixtures" in their writings. Aristotle distinguished between synthesis (combination, where constituent elements retain their individual characteristics) and *mixis* (mixing) or *krasis* (blending, where the components form something homogenous; so bronze results from blending copper and tin). The Stoics called the synthesis "juxtaposition." They specified other forms of mixture as well. "Complete fusion" is much like Aristotelian *mixis*.[138] The concept of complete interpenetration of two bodies is particularly relevant for study of the FG. Alexander of Aphrodisias says: "Certain mixtures occur when bodies are completely extended throughout the substance and properties of one another while

134. Ibid., 155.
135. Ibid.
136. Ibid., 156.
137. Ibid.
138. Ibid., 159.

maintaining their original substance and properties in this mixture. Chrysippus calls this specifically a 'blending' of mixtures" (*SVF* 2:473).[139] As Long says, "But in 'blending,' the components so 'extend' throughout one another that every particle among them shares in all the components of the mixture."[140]

The Stoics defended this theory with examples. "The mixture of wine and water, they argued, is more than a juxtaposition of wine and water droplets. But it is not a complete fusion of these, since if one puts an oiled sponge into such a mixture the two components can be separated (*SVF* 2:472). The idea is clearly that no volume of such a mixture, however small, can be reached in which the constituents fail to exhibit the same properties and relationship to each other."[141] This may be what the author of FG has in mind with respect to Jesus and God being in the believer and the believer in them. A further relevancy comprises this theory of interpenetration as it relates to *pneuma* and matter. Both are corporeal, but *pneuma* is so fine and tenuous that it can simultaneously occupy the same space as matter.

Stoics had four categories: (1) "substance, which corresponds to matter"; (2) but since all matter is permeated by *pneuma*, which gives matter its distinctive shape, there is a second category, "qualified" matter. *Pneuma* is what creates individuality, this man, this dog. "Each of them owes its individuality to *pneuma*, which so qualifies matter that each so-called individual possesses some characteristic shared by nothing else in the universe and which persists as long as it persists."[142] It is extremely important for us to recognize that Stoics distinguish between things that exist and things that subsist. Anything that is incorporeal, such as time, voice, and place, does not exist, but that does not mean that they constitute nothing. They can shape thought, so they subsist. Stoics categorize as a "class" "the something" that includes both substances and incorporeals. (3) "Being in a certain state" is the category used to analyze a person's being somewhere at a given time, acting, having a certain size or color as opposed to a permanent state. (4) "Relative disposition" deserves some attention for our purposes. It is used to define something in its relation to something else and describes how things are dependent upon one another.

Stoics view the entire universe as connected in some way by means of *pneuma*, which inheres in all things; hence, the Stoic notion of "cosmic sympathy," which reminds one of the Apostle Paul's words in Rom 8. Furthermore, for both Paul and the Fourth Evangelist, *pneuma* is the distinctive tie between God and Christians, and God bestows *pneuma* upon

---

139. Ibid.
140. Ibid.
141. Ibid., 159–60.
142. Ibid., 161.

human beings when they become believers. "In Stoicism, to be a good and happy man is to be related in a certain way to Nature or God."[143] Marcus Aurelius says, "We have come into being for co-operation." Jesus' words, "When I am lifted up I will draw *all* people to myself" (John 12:32, emphasis added), echoes this notion of cosmic interdependence. Individualism is not revered among Stoics.

Stoic Causation: Determinism, Human Action, Cosmic Evil

Stoics do not have what many moderns would consider a satisfying theodicy. Because of their strict concern for causation, Stoics inevitably arrive at determinism.[144] Every event has a cause. Furthermore, God, intelligent Nature, in a way that is most beneficial for us, directs the universe. This is the best of all possible worlds. "The world was designed for the benefit of rational beings."[145] This leads to a number of implications. (1) One should be able to figure out the future from the present. This is why many Stoics subscribed to prophecy, divination, and astrology. (2) When bad things happen to any individual, they can comfort themselves with the knowledge that what may be bad for them is good for the universe as a whole. Knowing this to be true, a person can accept whatever comes with equanimity and poise. If we knew all the facts, we would agree that the injury is beneficial, so we must assume that we simply do not have enough knowledge. But we cannot know everything, so we have to trust God. This reminds one of the experience of the disciples in the FG upon the occasion of Jesus' imminent departure, where Jesus tries to explain to his uncomprehending disciples that it is better for everyone if he goes (e.g., John 16). And of course the concept of trust (*pisteuō*) is prominent in the FG (e.g., John 3).

One's highest goal is to align oneself with Nature. Marcus Aurelius prays: "Everything that is in tune with you, O Universe, is in tune with me. Nothing that is timely for you is too early or too late for me" (*Meditations* 4.23). The *logos* is the "indwelling cause of all things," which sounds much like the FG. Although the FG after the prologue never refers to Jesus as *Logos*, the emphasis on his *logoi* continues the theme.[146] The FG differs from Stoicism in that human beings do not have *pneuma* by nature; it is given only to believers. It is a part of the newly constituted person, not the ordinary person. Stoics would argue that when a person makes a choice, one really

143. Ibid., 163.

144. See Abraham J. Malherbe, "Determinism and Free Will in Paul: The Argument of 1 Corinthians 8–9," in *Paul in His Hellenistic Context* (ed. Troels Engberg-Pedersen; Minneapolis: Fortress, 1995), 231–55.

145. Long, *Hellenistic Philosophy*, 168.

146. See Jaime Clark-Soles, *Scripture Cannot Be Broken: The Social Function of the Use of Scripture in the Fourth Gospel* (Boston: Brill, 2003), 294–310.

has no choice; that choice depends on the kind of person one is. The kind of person one is depends upon a combination of heredity and experiences. So, for Stoic and Christian alike, what one needs to do is to become a certain kind of person, which would be virtuous for Stoics, but Christian for John and Paul.

The Soul and Human Nature

A person is a unified but not uniform substance. The soul of a person is a portion of the vital, intelligent, warm breath (*pneuma*) that permeates the entire cosmos, including the body. "Most Stoics supposed that the soul, which is separated from the body at death, survives for a limited time."[147] Only people and animals have souls. For the Stoics, the soul has eight qualities: the five senses, the faculties of speech and reproduction, and the "governing-principle" (*hēgemonikon*). The governing principle is the most influential part of the soul and is located in the heart. From there it sends out the other parts of the soul through the body. It is the seat of consciousness and for us most closely approximates the brain. The soul receives impressions (*phantasia*), and then it can initiate movement known as impulse. This accounts in part for causation of goal-directed action. For Stoics, rationality belongs only to the *hēgemonikon* of the mature person. *Logos* takes either the first seven or fourteen years from birth to develop. Stoics divide people into foolish and wise rather than bad and good. Ignorance, not sin or wickedness, is the foolish person's problem.

Stoic Ethics

"Nature (God, *pneuma*, cause, *logos* or destiny) is a perfect being, and the value of anything else in the world depends upon its relationship to Nature. Accordance with Nature denotes positive value and contrariness to Nature the opposite."[148] The prayer of Cleanthes reminds one of Jesus' prayer in the garden of Gethsemane (Mark 14:32–36 and par.). Cleanthes prays: "Guide me, O Zeus, and thou Destiny, whither I have been appointed by you. For I will follow freely; and if, grown bad, I prove unwilling, I shall follow no less" (Cleanthes, *SVF* 1:527).[149] The starting point for Stoic ethics is the primary impulse of a newborn. Nature dictates that people should advance through five stages since human nature is a progressive, evolving phenomenon. "The goal of the progression is life in accordance with mature human nature, that is, a life governed by rational principles which are in complete harmony with the rationality, goals and processes of universal Nature."[150] Most people

---

147. Long, *Hellenistic Philosophy*, 171n1.
148. Ibid., 179.
149. Ibid., 183.
150. Ibid., 188.

never get to stage five, or even four, but the ultimate goal is still the perfection of one's nature. The FG calls this ultimate goal *zōē* (life). Paul fits well with Stoic notions in that he calls Christians to become *teleioi* (mature/perfect), to leave off spiritual milk, infancy, and childish ways (1 Cor 3:1–2; 14:20). He speaks of a process, of a pressing on toward a goal, keeping one's eye on the prize (Phil 3:12–14). For him, "being saved" denotes a process rather than a punctiliar event. He speaks of being transformed by the renewing of one's mind (*nous*; Rom 12:2) and of acting in accordance with conscience (*syneidēsis*; 2 Cor 1:12).

Stoic virtues can be divided into four categories: practical wisdom, justice, moderation, and courage. Each of these could be divided further. For example, justice can be broken down into piety, kindness, sympathy, and fair dealing.[151] From a Stoic viewpoint, all people develop some concept of values. Nature endows people with the tools to do this and to think analogically. This does not mean, however, that a person will actually attain virtue, or knowledge of what is good. FG shares this position. All people have the ability to know (*ginōskō*), but not all will do so. The external actions of a good person may appear identical to those of a foolish person. The truth lies in the internal motivations, a point not at all lost on the author of Matthew as he attacks the Pharisees (ch. 23). Stoicism might inform a reading of Johannine dualism. This dualism is puzzling insofar as it often is found in apocalyptic texts, of which John is not one. But according to Stoic ethics, which is not grounded in apocalypticism any more than is FG, "a miss is as bad as a mile.... Until a man is good he is bad."[152]

The following, written about Stoic political theory, could have been written about Paul's own vision of God's kingdom:

> I have already referred to Zeno's *Republic* in which the fundamental social and economic institutions of the Greek world are abolished.... In the ideal world the state withers away because each Stoic sage is self-sufficient and his own authority (*SVF* 3:617). But he is united with his fellows by the bond of friendship [cf. Paul and FG on the prominent theme of friendship: *philos, philadelphia, phileō*], for all wise men are friends to each other and it is only between them that friendship in its true sense can exist (*SVF* 3:625). A communal way of life which dispenses with all distinctions based upon sex, birth, nationality, and property — this is the pattern of social behaviour. The theory is utopian and was recognized to be such. But its interest lies in the criticism of

---

151. Ibid., 200.
152. Ibid., 204.

contemporary society which it implies. Stoic political theory is not a blue-print for reform but a paradigm of the world as it might be if men could be united not by artificial ties but by the recognition in each other of common values and common purposes. Money, family, and hereditary status are all seen as divisive factors.[153]

Such rhetoric is reminiscent of Jesus' exhortations to let the dead bury the dead; to "hate father and mother"; to realize that being a son of Abraham counts for nothing in the kingdom, but what counts is being a child of God by faith. Most NT authors express concerns about the problems of money. Paul's famous dictum of Gal 3:28, "There is no longer ... slave or free; ... for all of you are one in Christ Jesus," is similar to much of the Stoic idealism mentioned above.

Epicurus

Epicurus was born on Samos in 341 BCE. Given that the Epicurean inscription of Diogenes of Oenoanda, located in Turkey, was erected around 200 CE, Epicurus was influential for at least five hundred years.[154] For Epicureans, the point of philosophy is to help people attain happiness.[155] Epicurus's philosophy was quite empiricist and particularly Atomistic. In this view, there are atoms and there is the void in which atoms move. The evidence for this is immediate sensation and feeling. "What enters me from things outside is not a motor-car horn if that is what I do genuinely hear, but a cluster of atoms (*eidōla*) thrown off the outer surface of such objects. Provided that these 'effluences' ... enter the sense organ without experiencing any change of structure, the impression they produce on us will be an accurate image of the object."[156] The Atomist theory tries to answer a question: "What principles derived from empirical evidence are necessary and sufficient to account for the physical world as it presents itself to our senses?" The answer is concise: "an infinite number of indivisible bodies moving in infinite space."[157] Aristotle and the Stoics denied the necessity of void to account for motion. In Epicureanism bodies are of two kinds: compound and the units from which compounds are made [i.e., noncompounds, which

153. Ibid., 205.

154. Much work has been done recently with the Herculaneum papyri, which has shed more light on Philodemus, a poet and follower of Epicurus. The Philodemus Project is housed at UCLA and run primarily by Richard Janko, Dirk Obbink, and David Blank. David Armstrong (University of Texas, Austin) has published important materials in this area as well. For an introduction to the project, see http://www.humnet.ucla.edu/humnet/classics/Philodemus/phil.art.html.

155. Long, *Hellenistic Philosophy*, 21.

156. Ibid., 22.

157. Ibid., 31.

are indivisible]. Epicurus does not subscribe to the four elements common in Greek philosophy. Lucretius praises Epicurus for relieving people from the burden of "the weight of religion."[158] Epicurus believed that there are gods, but that they do not meddle with moving celestial bodies and thus with deciding the fates of human beings. He had no respect for popular religion in which people think that by ritual behavior they will pacify or inspire the gods. Epicurus believes that there are infinite other worlds, for if atoms came together in a way to form this world, why should they not do the same again sometime or in a way that varies? Obviously, Epicurus denies the foundations of Platonic and Aristotelian cosmology. No longer does one need Plato's Forms, Demiurge, or World-Soul, or Aristotle's Prime Mover and Heavenly Intelligences.[159]

Theology

Theology and psychology were two areas that mattered a great deal to Epicurus. Epicurus insisted that gods were in no way responsible for natural events. There is no survival of the personality in any form after death. Epicurus thought that by teaching this he could assuage the fear of divine judgment and eternal punishment. Just as the gods will not be involved then, so they are not involved now. This certainly undermines Greek religion as well as Platonism, which insists that the cosmos is under the direction of a divine intelligence.[160] According to Plato, humanity and the universe are possessions of the gods, and the gods act providentially with regard to people. Aristotle also considered the "heavenly bodies as intelligent, divine beings whose movements are voluntary."[161] All movement and life depend on Unmoved Mover, pure Mind, or God, "whose activity of eternal self-contemplation promotes desire and motion in the heavenly bodies, each governed by its own intelligence."[162] While not concerned with the lives of individuals, God is the prime cause of everything, according to Aristotle. Epicurus opposes Aristotle's view of "God." To him, the gods are considered to be sublimely happy and immortal, which they presumably could not be if they were involved in human affairs, according to Epicurus, who defined happiness as "uninterrupted tranquility or freedom from pain." One way he argues this is via theodicy. Looking at the imperfections of this world, it is obvious to him that the world does not stem from the desire or ability of the perfect gods.

---

158. Ibid., 40.
159. Ibid., 20.
160. Ibid., 42.
161. Ibid., 43.
162. Ibid., 43.

The Soul and Mental Processes

In a famous quote, Epicurus declares: "Death is nothing to us; for that which has been dissolved lacks sensation; and that which lacks sensation is no concern to us" (*Principal Doctrines* [*Kuriai doxai*] 2). "The first thing which Epicurus strove to establish in his psychological theory was the complete and permanent loss of consciousness at death."[163] This means that any system of rewards and punishment after death was necessarily nothing more than mythology. Epicurus's audience must have been worried about this permanent unconscious state, or Epicurus would not have spent so much time on it. And Christianity and the mystery cults might not have gained as many adherents.

The fear of death affects people's beliefs about afterlife; hence comes Epicurus's raging against popular religion. On the one hand, people fear eternal damnation. On the other hand, people fear cessation of existence. Epicurus and Lucretius after him address these concerns. They compare death with one's situation before birth: before one was born, one did not exist and did not care that one did not exist; so why should one care that one does not exist after death? He offers this consolation: If there is to be any trouble and pain for a person, one too must exist oneself at that time in order that ill may affect the person. Since death removes this and prevents the existence of one to whom a mass of misfortunes might accrue, we may be assured that there is nothing to be feared in death, and that one who no longer exists cannot be troubled (*Principal Doctrines* 3:861–868).[164]

This certainly is not how Jesus will deal with the fear of death. Both FG (John 14) and Hebrews (ch. 2) validate that the fear of death is paralyzing and strong. "Since, therefore, the children share flesh and blood, he himself likewise shared the same things, so that through death he might destroy the one who has the power of death, that is, the devil, and free those who all their lives were held in slavery by the fear of death" (Heb 2:14–15). In a later chapter we will venture an initial (somewhat speculative) comparison between FG and Epicurus.

Epicurus has a unified view of a person rather than a dualistic or tripartite view. The soul (*psychē*) and body do not exist apart from one another. The soul animates the body but does not survive the body. Aristotle agrees broadly on a body-soul dependence, but he does not view the soul as a physical substance as Epicurus does. For Epicurus, the soul must be corporeal because if it is not, then it is void, and void cannot do anything.[165] The soul consists of atoms that act upon the body and are affected by atoms that make up the body. The soul "resembles most closely breath mixed with heat (Epicurus, *Letter to Herodotus* 63). Lucretius also adds air. The soul is obviously warm and airy because those are the two elements missing from the body when it dies. Since air, breath, and heat are not enough to cause action (and ethics is a primary category for Epicureans), there must be a fourth element, called the unnamed element.[166] None of these elements can be separated or divisible. The unnamed element comprises the distinctive character of the soul.

In Lucretius, there is a spatial distinction drawn between the *animus*, or rational part, and *anima*, the irrational part. The *animus* sits in the chest, and the rest of the soul is distributed throughout the body. The *animus* is the mind, whose function is to allow thought and feeling and to govern the rest of the soul. Putting it into modern terms, Long suggests that the *animus* is the brain, and the *anima* is the nerves. Lucretius uses the terms "mind," "soul," and "intellect" synonymously. The fact that the *animus* is in the chest and that Lucretius speaks of the mind and heart synonymously makes the *psyche* and *kardia* closely related. Long quotes Lucretius: "So you can see that a beginning of movement is engendered by the heart, and it comes forth first from the mind's volition and then is dispatched throughout the whole body and limbs."[167] This is true in the NT as well, especially in the FG. Lucretius's *On the Nature of Things* (*De rerum natura*) attests to his belief that the gods exist (which places him in agreement with the Stoic Cicero), but they are remote and unconcerned (which differs from Cicero).[168]

Sense-perceptions occupy much of Epicurean interests. The ideas are complicated and at times obscure, a problem to which Long responds: "Epicurus and Lucretius leave us in the dark here, and no wonder! For no one has yet succeeded in giving a purely mechanistic explanation of consciousness."[169]

Epicurus wants people to experience pleasure, defined as a life free of trouble. Plato and Aristotle want people to achieve a life of virtue, "excellence of 'soul' which manifests itself in the exercise of those activities appropriate to each faculty of the personality and in moral action."[170]

Skepticism

Sextus Empiricus, a Greek physician who flourished at the end of the second century CE, provides information regarding Skepticism. The founder of Skepticism is Pyrrho of Elis, an older contemporary of Epicurus. Aenesidemus, who operates in the first century BCE, works out Pyrrho's principles.

---

166. Ibid.
167. Ibid., 57.
168. See Beard, North, and Price, *Religions of Rome*, 2:38.
169. Long, *Hellenistic Philosophy*, 54.
170. Ibid., 62.

Earliest Skepticism, then, is really Pyrrhonism. As with the historical Jesus quest, it is difficult to decide which material should be attributed to Pyrrho himself and which to his followers, but surely some goes back to Pyrrho. Pyrrho was born at Elis, northwest of Peloponnese, around 365 BCE. His philosophical goal comprised freedom from disturbance. Timon of Phlius is his most notable follower. Three questions occupied the Skeptics. First is the issue of what things are really like, the answer to which is "unknowable." The second concerns what attitude we should have toward them, and the answer is "suspended judgment," summarized well by the phrase "No more this than that."[171] Finally, Skeptics inquire after what the consequences of such an attitude will be.

According to Long, the question "What are things really like?" "might well be called the basic question of Greek philosophy."[172] The standard title for such an inquiry by Greek philosophers is "On Nature." Pyrrho's answer to the question of the nature of things, what are things really like, is that they are "unknowable" to both senses and reason. Sense perceptions are not necessarily reliable. All one can report on is "what appears," but that is not evidence for "what is."[173] Pyrrho uses "the apparent" for what Epicurus and Stoics call *phantasia* — presentation, impression, image. Skepticism will strike the reader as antithetical to claims made by Paul, Hebrews, and other NT texts that strive in large part to provide a basis for knowledge, confidence, and the possibility of God working in revelatory ways through sense perceptions. See, for instance, Gal 3:1–5 or Heb 11:1.

Pyrrho died in 270 BCE, and the next stage of Skepticism actually occurs in the Academy under Arcesilaus, around 265 BCE, who like Pyrrho denies the possibility of knowledge. "Like the Stoic and Epicurean insistence on the validity of their rational explanations of phenomena, Pyrrho's antithetical skepticism is an alternative answer for men dissatisfied with the traditional values and beliefs of a society in a state of transition."[174] Arcesilaus's goal is not possession of knowledge, but freedom from error; therefore, "suspension of judgment" is his mantra.[175] The third leading figure in Skepticism is Carneades, who is more constructive than Arcesilaus since he introduces probability. He spends much time opposing Chrysippus (the leader of the Stoics) and establishing distinctions between certitude and probability, necessity and contingency, and causal and logical relationships.[176]

---

171. Ibid., 84.
172. Ibid., 81.
173. Ibid., 82.
174. Ibid., 87.
175. Ibid., 92.
176. Ibid., 106.

Later Developments in Hellenistic Philosophy

We should mention a few other figures to round out the background picture of Hellenistic philosophy, which from 150–50 BCE may be characterized as eclectic. Panaetius was a Stoic. Like all Stoics, he taught that the universe is imperishable, but he eschewed the common notion of a cataclysmic fire. "It is often said that he [Panaetius] totally denied any survival of the soul after death, but no Stoic postulated unlimited survival or immortality. Panaetius may have adhered to the orthodox view of survival for a limited duration."[177] For Panaetius, the ideal was to live in accordance with God. The good person is directed by knowledge, and this cannot be reduced to a list of rules. Such a notion sounds familiar to the reader of the FG, a Gospel that is long on knowledge (*gnōsis*) but short on rules (*entolai*).

Posidonius is a Stoic who fights with Chrysippus over the cause of excessive impulses. Unlike Posidonius, Chrysippus does not allow for an irrational aspect of the soul. Though Chrysippus has a monistic concept, Plato's is tripartite; Posidonius adopts the latter since Plato admits an irrational part of the soul. Chrysippus explains bad behavior by external influences; Posidonius sees it as stemming from within the soul. The irrational part must be made to come under the authority of the rational. Cicero speaks of Posidonius's support of divination: "That the dying foresee the future is established by Posidonius with this example: a Rhodian as he was dying named six of his contemporaries and said which of them would die first, second and so on" (*De div.* 64 = F108).[178] Long considers Posidonius one of the most notable personages of the Hellenistic world, whose range of influence included Cicero, Strabo, and Seneca. Antiochus of Ascalon (b. 130 BCE), an eclectic philosopher who was a Stoic and Academic, deserves mention; so does Cicero, who gives us much of our evidence.[179]

Hellenistic Philosophy and the Classical Tradition

"In the Roman world during the first two Christian centuries, Stoicism was the dominant philosophy among educated pagans."[180] The Stoicism of Seneca, Epictetus, and Marcus Aurelius has been the most influential, though "Cleanthes' verses show that the system could provide a basis for genuine religious experience."[181] I would also add the prayer by Marcus Aurelius cited above. The Roman Stoics were monotheistic in practical terms. "God approaches men — no, the relation is closer: he enters men. Without God no mind can be good. In the bodies of men divine seeds have been scattered"

---

177. Ibid., 213n2.
178. Ibid., 221.
179. For a concise presentation of Cicero's importance, see ibid., 229–31.
180. Ibid., 232.
181. Ibid., 234.

(Seneca, *Ep*. 73.16).[182] The Stoa existed until 529 CE, when Justinian closed the four philosophical schools in Athens. Their real influence, though, had expired more than three centuries earlier. Clement of Alexandria (ca. 150–216 CE) is noteworthy for his employment of Stoic doctrine. "He assimilates Stoic *logos* to 'the word of God,' approves of the suppression of emotional impulses, and while teaching salvation as the basis of ethics sees the life of the Christian as 'a collection of rational actions, that is, the invarying practice of the teaching of the Word, which we call faith....' The sinner, like the Stoic 'fool,' is ignorant."[183] These notions make easy a comparison with Matthew and the FG.

The Stoics, the Cynics (especially Dio Chrysostom and Diogenes Laertius), the Epicureans, and less so the Skeptics — all bequeathed their principles to their cultures such that a certain amount of knowledge about each was widespread.

Now that we have viewed the fundamental notions regarding human beings as they are and as they should be, let us now turn to a more detailed discussion of views of eschatology (Dowling) and notions of postmortem judgment (Kuck).

Greco-Roman Eschatology

Dowling argues that a "radical reenvisioning of time in Roman culture" which involved a personification of eternal time, oddly imaged as variously male or female, occurred between the first century BCE and the early second century CE.[184] She begins with Greek antecedents, observing that there is no robust notion of eternal time as a force in either the religious mythology (Chronos has no vital cult) or philosophy (contrast this with the OT, which assumes that God acts in and through time). The first century saw vibrant interest in the calendar. The state calendar, commissioned by Augustus, became linked to the zodiacal calendar such that notions of time in politics and mystical religions combined. Simultaneously, Roman artists display a keen interest in the inexorability of death. Under the emperors Vespasian and Titus, coins bearing personified Aeternitas in female form are minted. The coins, a powerful vehicle for the inculcation of ideology, linked eternal time with world dominion. Images of Aeternitas persist into the third century, which proves, according to Dowling, that it was effective as a propagandistic tool.

Abstract ideas personified as goddesses were common for Romans, but Dowling points out that the moment when an idea becomes personified as

---

182. Ibid., 235.
183. Ibid.
184. Melissa Barden Dowling, "A Time to Regender: The Transformation of Roman Time," *Kronoscope* 3, no. 2 (2003): 169–83.

a goddess marks an important development. Therefore, she wants to know why it occurred particularly during 75–80 CE. She suggests two markers. First, in the East the defeat of Jerusalem and destruction of the temple caused unrest among Jewish and Christian communities. Second, the destruction of Jupiter Optimus Maximus, the center of Roman religion, caused unrest in the West. Dowling suggests that the government needed to assure inhabitants of the empire that peace, prosperity, and security were sure. "It is important to stress, however, that the emergence of a Roman iconography of Aeternitas predates the dissemination of early Christian ideas of eternity, so the influence was not from the Christians to the Romans. But the reverse might be true. Early Christian writers were thinking about Aeternitas in part because many men and women in the Roman world were thinking about eternity, and thinking in a new way."[185] As the imperial calendar took root empire-wide, time became universalized such that people could contemplate time as an abstract idea. All of these factors led to a personification of time.

Time was presented in female form as Aeternitas, but under Hadrian in 121 CE, time became male in the form of *saeculum aureum* (the Golden Age). Later emperors continued to use Aeternitas, and there was fluidity. The images were often accompanied by a globe, a phoenix, and a zodiac. During the reign of Antoninus Pius, the cult of Roma Aeterna was formed. Dowling argues that the fluctuation in gender in images of time coincides with a fluctuation in gender roles in Roman society in the first and second centuries, during which Roman women gained more rights.

Mithraism contributed a new concept of time insofar as it rejected typical Roman cyclical views of time and instead imagined an imminent apocalyptic battle in which eternity would have a starting point. Mithraic time is not only apocalyptic; it also is male.

The Function of Greco-Roman Notions of Postmortem Judgment

Kuck argues that postmortem judgment language was known and used on both the popular and philosophical levels. He identifies the major sources of the beliefs from the classical period and then focuses on the late Hellenistic and Roman uses of the language, since that is the period relevant for Paul. He also shows that the ideas functioned wholly at the level of the individual and were motivated in large part by desire for honor.

Classical Sources

The important classical sources include Homer (who provides the mythology of the underworld), the Eleusinian Mysteries (which emphasize the

---

185. Ibid., 174.

importance of ritual for the attainment of a blessed afterlife), Orpheus and Pythagoras (who popularized discussion of transmigration of souls). The latter, followed by Plato, give us the notion of an immortal soul distinct from the body.

Hellenistic and Roman Period

Kuck introduces both the evidence for vital views of postmortem judgment as well as the functions of such language. He begins by recognizing the "cultured despisers" — including Epicurus, Ovid, the Skeptic Sextus Empiricus, and Lucian — who mocked the popular views. With the exception of Plato, Hellenistic and Roman philosophy had little use for notions of postmortem judgment. But their disdain suggests that many people did, in fact, believe these ideas. We can see this in the mystery religions, in the religious and Platonic philosophies, and in Homeric mythology.[186]

First, poets, drawing on mythology, use the language of postmortem judgment for aesthetic purposes.

Second, such language functions to console and therefore appears in philosophical discussions about death (Epicurus, Cicero, Pseudo-Plato's *Axiochus*), funeral speeches (Aelius Aristides, *Orations* 31 and 32), *epikēdia* (dirges/funeral songs), laments, epitaphs, and consolatory addresses.[187]

Third, the idea of postmortem judgment is used for ritual propaganda. For example, the priests of the mysteries promise rewards for adherents and punishment for nonadherents, and rulers use the concept to control society and keep people law-abiding. Cicero's "Dream of Scipio" (in *De republica* 6) is patriotic insofar as doing good means serving one's country and doing bad equals breaking laws, divine and human.[188] The same function was served by the funerary practices among Roman nobles, whose bodies were placed on public display, replete with insignia and finery that marked them as model citizens. Such displays, according to Hopkins, inspired young men to offer their lives as a sacrifice for the state.

Fourth, warning of postmortem judgment is useful for moral exhortation, as can be seen in Seneca's tragedies and Statius's poetry. Virgil's *Aeneid*, book 6, combines the Homeric underworld judgment and the Platonic metempsychosis tradition. Where Homer only hints at judgment, Virgil

---

186. For a particularly good treatment of Homer, see Christiane Sourvinou-Inwood, *'Reading' Greek Death: To the End of the Classical Period*. Oxford: Clarendon, 1995.

187. These poems honoring the dead, though "theoretically distinct from the dirge (*epikēdeion*), *epitaphios*, or consolation, as being delivered or performed over the corpse and before the funeral, nevertheless are barely distinguishable from these in content, and its common themes (irrevocable fate, cruel destiny, sorrow of survivors, hopes of immortality) are naturally also those of funerary epigrams" ("Epicedium," *OCD*, 531).

188. Kuck, *Judgment and Community Conflict*, 137.

amplifies it into a major theme of Aeneas's journey. Plutarch, especially in his myths, uses postmortem judgment to encourage virtue and discourage vice.

Fifth, the language of postmortem judgment appears in the social satire of Lucian, who does not believe the ideas but capitalizes on the fact that his fellow residents do. In all of these, the basis for judgment is morality.

All of the texts studied by Kuck point to judgment on the basis of the individual's practice of virtue within society.[189] In Plato, the soul's process of purgation mirrors the philosopher's process of attainment of virtue by means of philosophy. In funeral speeches and epigraphy, we see the concern for attaining praise and honor in life and death. There is emphasis on what one deserves, which can be seen by the language of wages (*misthos*).[190] The Greco-Roman models are individualistic and lack the idea of "one common evil fate for the group of the wicked."[191] What about the concept of "conscience," or self-judgment? According to Kuck, wherever one sees a robust view of conscience (as in Seneca), one sees no concern for divine judgment; that is, the conscience acts as a moral compass. On the other hand, wherever there is a focus on divine recompense, the conscience plays no role. This differs greatly from Paul, who incorporates both.

Kuck concludes the following: Greeks and Romans learned of postmortem judgment from the mystery religions, from their own literary heritage (Homer and Hesiod), and their philosophers (Plato), but only the Platonic philosophers used judgment language copiously. Postmortem judgment language served two primary functions: (1) to motivate moral behavior and (2) to console and eulogize by a positive view of the fate of the dead. The language focuses on the individual person.

Greco-Roman materials differ from their Jewish counterparts in that Greco-Roman views did not emerge from situations of group crisis or threat experienced historically. "Greco-Roman conceptions did not generally speak in terms of a divine judgment that would overturn injustice and vindicate a particular group of people."[192] Judgment takes place upon an individual's death, rather than upon an apocalyptic Day of the Lord. There is no real uniformity of ideas since there is no authoritative body to establish such ideas. There is no single divine judge or consistent scenario. In epigraphy, the language functions to eulogize the dead (expressing their piety and deserved reward) and to console the survivors by assuring them that the good earthly reputation enjoyed by the dead would attend and assist them in the underworld.

---

189. Ibid., 141.
190. Numerous NT texts use the language of wages in this way, as we will see in later chapters.
191. Ibid., 144.
192. Ibid., 148.

PAUL:
THE ETHICS OF DEATH
AND AFTERLIFE

The minister, who took his ecumenical and — some felt — slightly impersonal remarks from Saint Paul's sermon on Love from First Corinthians, talked for about half an hour. ("Didn't you feel that was a very inappropriate text?" said Julian, who had a pagan's gloomy view of death coupled with a horror of the non-specific.)"

—Donna Tartt, *The Secret History*[1]

The specific details of the ultimate fates of human beings are anything but clear in Paul's surviving letters.

—Jeffrey A. Trumbower, *Rescue for the Dead*[2]

Resurrection is more than a single, curious belief; it functions as a shorthand for an interlocking web of values, a condensation symbol that helps to construct community.
—Claudia Setzer[3]

T HE APOSTLE PAUL provides the earliest written evidence of a Christian view of death and afterlife and as such deserves to be studied first. Paul's seven undisputed Epistles — 1 Thessalonians, Romans, 1 and 2 Corinthians, Galatians, Philippians, and Philemon — will serve as evidence.

SIX MAIN POINTS

In this chapter I will show the following: (1) Paul insists upon future resurrection of the believer at the Parousia followed by eternal embodied

---

1. Donna Tartt, *The Secret History* (New York: Knopf, 1992), 375.
2. Jeffrey A. Trumbower, *Rescue for the Dead: The Posthumous Salvation of Non-Christians in Early Christianity* (New York: Oxford University Press, 1991), 40.
3. Claudia Setzer, *Resurrection of the Body in Early Judaism and Early Christianity: Doctrine, Community, and Self-Definition* (Leiden: Brill, 2004), 144.

immortality. (2) Paul demonstrates no interest in hell; rather, he focuses on heaven. (3) While Paul *states with certainty* that believers will be raised at the resurrection, he *implies* that others may be as well. (4) The main categories in Paul's anthropology are flesh (*sarx*) and (related) blood (*haima*), spirit (*pneuma*), whole person (*psychē*), body (*sōma*), sin (*hamartia*), death (multiple words), and life (*zōē*). (5) Paul's teaching regarding death and afterlife serves at least four related functions: theological, apologetic, pastoral, and ethical. (6) While Paul has a future and somewhat apocalyptic eschatology, he lacks the typical apocalyptic relish in vindictiveness and shows scant interest in the posthumous fate of unbelievers. Along the way, we will observe the debates about resurrection versus immortality,[4] as well as the "intermediate state" in Paul.

Throughout I will assume that Paul's social context affects his views.[5] Paul's churches are spread far and wide, and for the most part, he does not reside among any of them for very long. This differs from Matthew or John, for example, whose Gospels are identified with single church bodies probably struggling with sectarian schism. Paul is not concerned with breaking away from a parent tradition; rather, he is occupied by drawing boundaries in a Gentile world (for instance, reminding his formerly pagan readers that behavior such as sleeping with prostitutes, suing neighbors, and arrogantly consuming meat sacrificed to idols transgresses acceptable Christian moral boundaries). Always, he must engage the various cultures and terminologies of his audiences.

This chapter will move from the general to the specific. After briefly reviewing Paul's background and chronology, I will provide a general overview of Pauline anthropology (guided by Paul Jewett), after which I will discuss the primary passages of concern moving from the "traditional" loci of Pauline anthropological eschatology, 1 Cor 15 and 1 Thess 4, to the "problematic" passages, 2 Cor 5:1–10 and Phil 1:18b–26.

PAUL'S BACKGROUND AND CHRONOLOGY

Since Paul was a Pharisee, perhaps we should not be surprised to find him arguing for the resurrection of the dead. According to some NT literature (Synoptics, Acts, Paul), as well as Josephus and early rabbinic writings, belief in the resurrection or the afterlife was a distinguishing characteristic

---

4. Those interested in that debate should begin with Oscar Cullmann's famous essay, "Immortality of the Soul or Resurrection of the Dead? The New Testament Witness," *Harvard Divinity School Bulletin* 21 (1955–56): 5–36; repr., *Immortality of the Soul or Resurrection of the Dead? The Witness of the New Testament* (London: Epworth; New York: Macmillan, 1958); online: http://www.geocities.com/pastorkeith/cullmann.html.

5. For a still unparalleled presentation of Paul's social context, see Wayne A. Meeks, *The First Urban Christians* (New Haven: Yale University Press, 1983).

of the Pharisees, as opposed to the Sadducees, who rejected such beliefs.[6] Paul did not derive belief in resurrection from Christianity; he brought the belief with him. "It was not Paul's experience of Christ but his Pharisaism (Phil 3.6) and his Jewish apocalypticism that first bequeathed to him a resurrection language."[7] As a Pharisee Paul likely would have had a concept of disembodied existence between death and resurrection.[8]

Before we study the shape that resurrection takes in Paul's hands, let us remind ourselves of the outline of Paul's career. Pauline chronology is a scholarly morass. Raymond Brown provides one of the best charts for this, sporting a column with "traditional" dating and one for "revisionist" dating.[9] Brown opts for the former; Jewett (among others whom Brown accounts for) falls in the latter camp. Brown's chronology of Paul's letters is simpler than Jewett's. For example, Brown does not posit nearly as many different letters comprising 2 Corinthians as Jewett does (generally 2 Corinthians is thought to contain two to five letters). My argument does not depend on establishing Pauline chronology, but providing an outline will help to situate the reader historically.

34 CE	Paul's conversion in Damascus
37	Escape from Aretas; First Jerusalem Journey
Early 50	1 Thessalonians
Mid 50	2 Thessalonians (if authentic)
51	Second Jerusalem Journey
52–53	Galatians
54–55	Philippians
54–56	1 and 2 Corinthians[10]
55–56	Philemon
Late 56–early 57	Romans
57	Third Jerusalem Journey
59–60	Appearance before Festus; trip to Rome

---

6. Setzer, *Resurrection of the Body*, 21. Josephus J.W. 2; Ant. 18.12–17; Mark 12:18–27 and par; 162–5. Acts 23:6–9; 26:5–8; Lk 18:12.

7. Calvin J. Roetzel, "'As Dying, and Behold We Live': Death and Resurrection in Paul's Theology," *Interpretation* 46 (1992): 5.

8. Josephus, *J.W.* 2.8.14; *Ant.* 18.1.3. We could (and perhaps should) problematize this picture in two ways: First, the nature of Paul's Pharisaism and how it shaped his sense of his own identity is debated (see any standard work on Paul, such as Calvin Roetzel, *Paul: The Man and the Myth* (Columbia: University of South Carolina Press, 1998); or Alan Segal, *Paul the Convert: The Apostolate and Apostasy of Saul the Pharisee* (New Haven: Yale University Press, 1990). Second, the nature of Pharisaism itself is debated (see, e.g., Anthony Saldarini, *Pharisees, Scribes, and Sadducees in Palestinian Society: A Sociological Approach* (Grand Rapids: Eerdmans, 2001); or Martin S. Jaffee, *Early Judaism* (Upper Saddle River, NJ: Prentice Hall, 1997).

9. Raymond E. Brown, *An Introduction to the New Testament* (New York: Doubleday, 1997), 428.

10. Jewett argues that the Corinthian correspondence consists of six letters, which he classifies as A–F. He marks their dates as follows: Letter A, late 54 or very early 55 CE (a few

INTRODUCTION TO
PAULINE ANTHROPOLOGY

Any understanding of Paul's views on death and afterlife must consider Paul's anthropological language. Jewett offers the following useful preliminary theses on Paul's terminology:

1. When analyzed chronologically, Paul's use of anthropological terms is erratic; new connotations emerge, and then fade, giving way to more traditional definitions.

2. Each new connotation is tied to a specific situation in a congregation. When the situation changes, the connotation may change.

3. Paul is sensitive to language used by his opponents, and that language shapes his own.

4. Paul draws anthropological terms from Jewish or early Christian tradition and uses them with varying frequency.

5. Paul is not concerned to establish a consistent anthropological terminology. The later the letter, the more contradictory his usage becomes.

6. The anthropological terms do not constitute the core of Paul's gospel; they are used to defend the core, defined by Jewett as "the eschatological righteousness of God revealed in the Christ event." No single term communicates his conception of humans. Paul's anthropology must be reconstructed from his argument as a whole.[11]

Despite Jewett's cautionary word, I do think it possible to give a general picture of Paul's anthropology as it relates to death and afterlife. We must be satisfied with what we can detect without overstating the case, flagging difficulties along the way.

A few words are in order regarding Jewett's work. First, Jewett argues that Paul's categories are primarily influenced by the situation presented in a given epistle. The context in large part determines the terms. For example, when Paul writes 1 Thessalonians, his earliest letter, the word *sarx* plays no substantial part because *sarx* is unimportant in the Thessalonian context. When he writes Galatians several years later, *sarx* is a central category because the Galatian nomists, who insist on circumcision of the flesh, have made it so. This leads Jewett to a second conviction: one can responsibly

---

months earlier than B); Letter B, spring 55; Letter C, summer 55; Letter D, fall 55; Letter E, spring 56; Letter F, late spring or early summer 56. For details regarding the contents of each, see Robert Jewett, *Paul's Anthropological Terms: A Study of Their Use in Conflict Settings* (Leiden: Brill, 1971), 23–26.

11. Ibid., 9–10.

speak of expansion in Paul's thought. Such expansion becomes apparent across the Corinthian correspondence, as Paul is forced to consider categories previously unimportant to him. Jewett's argument for expansion is nuanced, however. He does not imagine Paul with an anthropological suitcase in hand, empty when he arrives at Thessalonica and surfeited as he makes his way to Rome. Rather, Paul's letters show him packing only categories that are relevant for a particular situation, changing anthropological clothing as he goes. At times he pulls out something from a prior trip, but other clothing may be discarded entirely. For example, Paul uses the term *psychikos/on* in 1 Corinthians when contending against opponents there who likely have contributed the term to the discussion. After he deals with them, the word drops from his epistolary vocabulary. As Jewett states, "Paul did not in general evince any interest in producing a truly consistent anthropology."[12]

Finally, the subtitle of Jewett's book, *A Study of Their Use in Conflict Settings,* anticipates his emphasis on how Paul's anthropological terms are used to combat "heresy."[13] The five forms of heresy detected are the nomists, the libertines, the gnostics, the Divine-Man-Missionaries, and the enthusiasts. Scholarship over the three decades since the book was written have nuanced such discussions about Paul's opponents, but Jewett's investigation is still helpful in generally defining a range of meaning for Paul's anthropological terms.[14]

---

12. Ibid., 447.

13. The first century is probably too early to speak of Christian heresy. Rather, scholars refer to varieties of early Christianity. See Walter Bauer, *Orthodoxy and Heresy in Earliest Christianity* (ed. Robert Kraft and Gerhard Krodel; 2nd ed.; Mifflintown, PA: Sigler, 1996).

14. An egregious lacuna by today's standards lies in the fact that Jewett's book on Paul's view of what constitutes a human being (*Paul's Terms*) contains no reference to the language of male and female, obviously primary categories for Paul. Paul uses *anēr* (male) language 43 times, 38 of them in Rom 7 and 1 Cor 7; 11; 14. Of the 215 NT occurrences of *gynē* (female), 43 occur in undisputed Paul, 40 of these in 1 Cor 7; 11; 14. Fortunately, this lacuna has since been ably filled by numerous scholars, all of whom deepen, nuance, and correct Jewett's work. See, e.g., Antoinette Wire, "Christ and Gender: A Study of Difference and Equality in Galatians 3:28," in *Jesus Christus als die Mitte der Schrift* (ed. Judith Gundry-Volf; Berlin: de Gruyter, 1997), 439–77; Dale Martin, *The Corinthian Body* (New Haven: Yale University Press, 1995), and his article on Gal 3:28: "The Queer History of Galatians 3:28: No Male and Female," in *Sex and the Single Savior: Gender and Sexuality in Biblical Interpretation* (Louisville: Westminster John Knox, 2006), 77–90; Margaret Mary Mitchell, *Paul and the Rhetoric of Reconciliation: An Exegetical Investigation of the Language and Composition of 1 Corinthians* (Tübingen: Mohr, 1991); Elisabeth Schüssler Fiorenza et al., *In Memory of Her: A Feminist Theological Reconstruction of Christian Origins* (New York: Crossroads, 1983); Jouette Bassler, "*Skeuos:* A Modest Proposal for Illuminating Paul's Use of Metaphor in 1 Thessalonians 4:4," in *The Social World of the First Christians* (ed. L. Michael White and O. Larry Yarbrough; Minneapolis: Fortress, 1995), 53–66; and Amy-Jill Levine with Marianne Blickenstaff, eds., *A Feminist Companion to Paul* (London: T&T Clark, 2004). While Paul never directly addresses gender as it relates to death and afterlife, Daniel Boyarin ("Paul and the Genealogy of Gender," in Levine, *Paul*, 13–41) has ably argued that Paul imagines a

Kardia (Heart)

Jewett claims that "if there is an underlying consistency in his doctrine of [the hu]man, it would seem to be most closely correlated with the Judaic term 'heart,' which connotes a view of man as an integral, intentional self who stands in relationship before God." Jewett maintains that *kardia* (heart) is not especially noteworthy in Paul's anthropology.[15] Paul has inherited the term, and it belongs to the earliest layer of his anthropological thought. Hans Wolff delineates the range of meaning for *kardia* in Paul as the center of the emotions, thought, and volition.[16]

Nevertheless, I would not so readily dismiss Paul's *kardia* language since, according to Paul, the heart of each person will be judged (Rom 2:5–11), and upon that basis one will receive either eternal life or wrath and fury. Thus, for Paul the heart determines one's reward in the eschaton.

Psychē

Psychē appears most regularly in what Jewett labels "personal" contexts and much less so in paraenetic, didactic, and epistolary blessing settings. Jewett finds that most uses of *psychē* fall within the following three meanings (all of which derive from the Hebrew Scriptures):

1. the individual's earthly life as publicly observable in behavior;

2. the individual's earthly life which can be lost in death; and

3. the individual person.

Paul does not envision the *psychē* as something that exists after death. Jewett carefully distinguishes Paul's use of *psychē* from that of other Jewish thinkers: "He never uses it in the strict sense of the 'soul,' i.e., the God-related portion of man which survives after death. Furthermore, Paul avoids the interchangeability between *pneuma* and *psychē* which was the mark of the Rabbinic usage, related as it was to the question of the fate of the soul after death."[17] As with *kardia*, Jewett ascribes *psychē* to the earliest layer of Paul's anthropology.[18]

---

nonhierarchical eternity for Christians in genderless spiritual bodies. In the pre-eschaton time period, however, gender is retained, except for occasional ecstatic moments.

15. Jewett, *Paul's Terms*, 447.

16. Hans W. Wolff, *Anthropology of the Old Testament* (trans. Margaret Kohl; Philadelphia: Fortress, 1974); this work does not appear in Jewett's bibliography.

17. Jewett, *Paul's Terms*, 448–49.

18. Jewett, ibid., notices two exceptions. First, in Philippians Paul uses *psychē*, or a compound of it, in exhorting the Philippians to unity (as in 1:27). Later, when Paul adopts the term *en sōma* (in the body) or *sōma christou* (body of Christ), he leaves behind the Philippians' language, an example of "development" in Paul's thought. The second instance is the use of *psychikos* in Letter A to Corinth, as mentioned above (Jewett, *Paul's Terms*, 449).

Osei-Bonsu, on the other hand, argues that although Paul does not use *psyche* in 1 Cor 15, one can assume that Paul believed in the soul as a continuing part of the person. Paul does not make much mention of it because he and the opponents agree that the disembodied soul survives death.[19] Osei-Bonsu argues that the souls of the dead are in heaven, but the bodies sleep in the earth.[20] I disagree with Osei-Bonsu, as will become clear below. Hans Conzelmann claims that Paul does not have a doctrine of the soul.[21]

Nous and Cognates

Nous also seems to belong to the earliest layer of Paul's thinking, and Jewett defines its meaning for Paul as "the constellation of thoughts and assumptions which makes up the consciousness of the person and acts as the agent of rational discernment and communication."[22] Paul does not give the term the weight of "the real me," as Bultmann or some Corinthians might believe. The term is nowhere used with regard to death and afterlife.

Pneuma

Regarding *pneuma tou anthrōpou* (human spirit), the category is complicated. Jewett argues that Paul initially used *pneuma* in a way that did not distinguish between spirit of a human being and Spirit of God: "Standing within the tradition of Hellenistic Christianity which at this particular point closely paralleled the popular Jewish usage, Paul thought of the human spirit simply as the apportioned divine Spirit. This Spirit was thought to so enter human possession that it could be referred to as 'mine.'"[23] However, in dealing with the gnostics of Corinth, who overly identify with God's Spirit, Paul seeks to distinguish the human *pneuma* from the divine (1 Cor 2:11).[24] "This distinction is unparalleled in the Hellenistic world so that one is inclined to believe it was a Pauline creation."[25] For the first time, the human *pneuma* takes on a somewhat negative connotation. Such a usage occurs nowhere outside of Letter B.[26] After dealing with the Corinthian gnostics,

---

19. J. Osei-Bonsu, "The Intermediate State in the New Testament," *Scottish Journal of Theology* 44 (1991): 188–90.
20. Ibid., 190.
21. Hans Conzelmann, *1 Corinthians: A Commentary on the First Epistle to the Corinthians* (ed. G. W. MacRae; trans. J. W. Leitch; Philadelphia: Fortress, 1975), 281.
22. Jewett, *Paul's Terms*, 450.
23. Ibid., 451.
24. Jewett (ibid., 451) recognizes the problem of somewhat conflicting tendencies regarding the human spirit when 1 Cor 5:3–5 is factored into the equation. Paul never addresses the conflict.
25. Ibid., 451.
26. Jewett includes: 1 Cor 1:1–6:11; 1 Cor 7:1–9:23; 1 Cor 10:23–11:1; 1 Cor 12:1–14:40; 1 Cor 16:1–12, p. 24.

Paul reverts to the notion of the divinely apportioned Spirit as the center of the human self.

Jewett flags a problem with the "dichotomous anthropology found most often in traditional Judaic expressions...where man consists of flesh/body and spirit."[27] He claims that, while accepting the practical interchangeability of *sarx* and *sōma* in Jewish anthropology, Paul does not similarly interchange *pneuma* and *psychē*.[28] He also does not use the dichotomy between *sarx/sōma* and *pneuma* to argue for immortality of the soul, as did the rabbis. This popular dichotomy is absent in Paul's technical discussion of *sarx*, *pneuma*, and *sōma*. In reading Paul, one will thus find the popular notions side by side with Paul's more technical meanings.[29]

Sarx

Jewett devotes a substantial portion of his monograph (117 pages) to this word.[30] He determines that the term "flesh" is not a major category in 1 Thessalonians; it becomes so in Galatians, where it is used not only in a personal sense (*sarx* with lowercase *s* as that which can be physically cut) but also *Sarx* in an apocalyptic, cosmic sense as a personified being (*Sarx* with a capital *S*, much like Death and Sin, discussed later in the section on Philippians 1, below). In Gal 4:21–31, "flesh" is associated with "the old aeon, slavery, the Judaizers and the law and contrasted with the 'Spirit' which is associated with the new aeon, freedom and the gospel."[31] "Flesh" can be used neutrally; it becomes negatively personified in the sense that a person puts one's confidence in the flesh rather than in God.

The *sarx* waters grow murky, however, because Paul is not consistent. In Letter A[32] he collapses the distinction between *sarx* and *sōma* (1 Cor 6:15–16; 15:38–39), and in Letter B he himself slips into the very dualism he chastises in the Corinthian gnostics (1 Cor 5:5). In assessing all of these factors, Jewett is led to declare: "This appropriation of gnostic assumptions in Letter B to facilitate the debate with them contrasts strikingly with his avoidance of the technical [*sarx*] category in Letter A and indicates his

---

27. Ibid., 452.
28. Ibid.
29. Ibid.; cf. 1 Cor 5:4; 7:34; 2 Cor 7:1.
30. Jewett treats the history of interpretation from the nineteenth century onward. Of particular concern is the relationship between spirit and flesh. Ludemann argues that Paul's was the "first uniquely Christian anthropology," based on Ludemann's methodology of considering Hellenistic and Jewish options. For Ludemann, soteriology was the strongest influence on Paul's categories (Jewett, *Paul's Terms*, 52–54).
31. Ibid., 453.
32. Which Jewett defines as: 1 Cor 9:24–10:22; 1 Cor 6:12–20; 1 Cor 11:2–34; 1 Cor 15; 1 Cor 16:13–24, p. 24.

lack of interest in maintaining a systematic anthropology," and "the category differs in its definition according to the historical situation in which it is used."[33]

Sōma

In its neutral sense *sōma* simply means the human body. This appears to be its use in 2 Cor 5:10. But Paul uses *sōma* in more technical ways in the Corinthian correspondence. First, the attitudes of the Corinthians toward the body cause Paul great distress. On the one hand, the libertines dismiss the importance of the body so entirely that they have sex with prostitutes, not considering such acts to be in ethical conflict with their religious convictions. On the other hand, certain ascetic married couples make too much of the body and, therefore, do not engage in sexual relations when Paul believes that they should. Jewett defines the human body as "the basis of relationship and unity between persons,"[34] and it is relevant for us because of Paul's discussion of the resurrected body in 1 Cor 15:35–57.

Second, Paul can use the term "body" metaphorically to refer to the church as the body of Christ. Paul sometimes ascribes to a third usage, as in Letter C[35] where he speaks of the body as a prison of the inner man, but he does this for the sake of argument, as a concession to his Corinthian opponents, who believe that the body is a prison (2 Cor 5:6, 8).

Romans is quite different in that here Paul uses *sōma* in the sense of "the basis of unity and relationship" only once (12:5) and never to describe the church as the body of Christ.[36] Rather, the meaning here overlaps with *sarx* insofar as *sarx* can be used to describe the human being in the old presalvation aeon. But salvation is presented in heavily bodily terms, perhaps to combat dualistic notions that degrade the body and lead to libertine behavior. So *sōma* can cross from the old aeon to the new aeon: "unlike the word 'flesh,' *sōma* can be used to depict the whole scope of salvation including the resurrection (Rom 8:11) and redemption (Rom 8:23) of the body and the bodily worship [of God] in the world (Rom 12:1), which is the form of ethical activity the new aeon inaugurates and requires. The agent of this somatic salvation is the 'body of Christ' (Rom 7:4) whose death and resurrection marked the turning of the aeons."[37]

Paul always indicates (1) that sin, not the body, is responsible for death, and (2) that in our earthly embodied existence, the body is subject to death; immortality is not an option for the body as it exists before the second

33. Ibid., 454.
34. Ibid., 456.
35. 2 Cor 2:14–6:13; 2 Cor 7:2–4, p. 25.
36. Ibid., 457.
37. Ibid.

coming of Christ. This body will die and decay, but at Christ's coming believers will experience bodily resurrection. All of this has ethical implications
for Paul.

It is in no way surprising that the part of a human being known as the
body is redeemed and transformed inasmuch as Paul indicates the same for
the mind and heart of the believer. Before a person commits oneself to Christ,
one's mind is reprobate; afterward, it is renewed (Rom 1:28; 12:2). Before
Christ, one's heart is darkened (1:21 KJV); afterward, it is obedient. J. Paul
Sampley writes: "Believers, with their renewed minds, can know, will, and
do the good. For Paul it is the person under the power of sin who is at cross-
purposes, who wills one thing and achieves another, and who does unwilled
things (Rom 7:17–21)."[38]

Syneidēsis, Synoida

The Pauline Epistles use the term "conscience" first to connote knowledge
of one's transgressions, and second to connote the agent that produces such
knowledge. The first is represented by the "weak" in Corinth, who believe
that their consciences cause them to refrain from eating idol meat; and the
second, by the "strong," who argue that knowledge is the remedy by which
the weak might put their consciences in order. Thus, the "strong" in Corinth,
the know-it-alls (cf. 8:1–2), considered conscience to be one's mind, nous,
or the inner self. Paul rejects this and maintains a distinction between conscience as "the autonomous agent which marks one's own transgressions,"
and the nous, or inner self, such that the conscience reigns above the mind
in determining final behavior, even when the conscience is uninformed (cf.
1 Cor 8 and 10).

But Jewett argues that later, in Letter C, Paul uses conscience to indicate
an agent that discerns external matters, especially whether or not the superapostles are worthy of loyalty (2 Cor 4:2; 5:11).[39] In Romans, Paul uses the
words in both senses: as the knowledge of one's transgressions and also as
the agent that produces said knowledge, demonstrating that familiar refrain
from Jewett: "It indicates how little Paul was concerned to work out a truly
systematic anthropology."[40]

Esō/exō Anthrōpos

Paul uses the language of inner and outer human beings in Letter C. The
inner human is associated with the heart and the outer human with the
flesh, which suffers under persecution. The terms were made necessary by

---

38. J. Paul Sampley, *Walking between the Times: Paul's Moral Reasoning* (Minneapolis:
Fortress, 1991), 114.
39. Jewett, *Paul's Terms*, 459.
40. Ibid.

his opponents' concept of the inner person "as the pneumatic core of a person, enabled by its divine nature to receive and comprehend the divine wisdom, but held in bondage by the material body."[41] Hence, Paul must use these terms, but he does so with obscurity. As Oscar Cullmann observes, Rom 8:11 shows that the Holy Spirit is already transforming the Christian's inner person, and the body will similarly be transformed at the resurrection.

We have thus found that Paul has an extremely rich anthropological vocabulary. For the purposes of investigating Paul's view of death and afterlife, *kardia* is important since God's judgment of the motives lodged there affect one's ultimate fate. *Sōma* and *pneuma* constitute the eternal immortal body; *sarx* and *haima* do not. The other anthropological terms are less important.

THE PROMISES AND PUZZLES OF 1 COR 15, PAUL'S "CLASSIC" STATEMENT

Because 1 Cor 15 provides Paul's most extensive treatment of what believers can expect after death, we will allow it to provide the framework for the first part of our inquiry into Paul's views. As 1 Cor 5:9 indicates, the canonical 1 Corinthians is actually at least the second letter Paul has sent to Corinth. In it he responds to a written letter from some of the Corinthians as well as oral reports from Chloe's people (1:11) and Stephanus, Fortunatus, and Achaicus (16:17).[42] The church stands divided over a number of issues, including but not limited to factionalism, spiritual arrogance, fornication, undue abstinence, litigiousness, the consumption of food sacrificed to idols, head coverings, problems at the Lord's Supper, disorderly worship, and misunderstanding over the resurrection.

Some in the congregation seem to have had an overrealized eschatology: they believed that they had already attained the highest level of spiritual maturity possible. Hence, they could claim, "There is no resurrection from the dead." They confused the penultimate with the ultimate.[43] Paul refers to them with the heaviest of irony as *pneumatikoi*, spiritual people (1 Cor 2:15; 3:1). They were so convinced that they had already left the mundane realm of existence that they dispensed with any boundaries on their behavior. Their slogan was, "All things are lawful for me" (1 Cor 6:12), even unto sleeping with prostitutes and disregarding any consequences of their eating

---

41. Jewett, 460.

42. The three men listed in 16:17 may be the *hoi Chloēs* (Chloe's people) mentioned in 1:11. The "church" at Corinth was comprised of a number of house churches, one of which probably met in Chloe's house. For more information, see Meeks, *First Urban Christians*, 75–77.

43. For a different view, see Martin, "The Resurrected Body," in *Corinthian Body*, 104–36, who argues that the problem is not an overrealized eschatology as much as it is an eschatology that dismisses the body.

meat sacrificed to idols. They believed they were fully experiencing the resurrection now and that the future could not improve upon the present. Their slogan might have been, "This is as good as it gets."

Verses 1–11, Setting the Stage via Warrants

Paul's rebuttal, which actually commences at 15:1, is varied and not always concise. While Paul gives much detail in this argument, he really makes only three main points. First, what he preaches is good news (*euangelion*). In the first two verses of his rebuttal (15:1–2), he uses some form of the word three times, so that it stands out as though written in capital letters with red ink.[44] Second, Jesus Christ, who died for our sins, has been raised from the dead (as we will see later, believers also will be raised at the Parousia). Finally, the resurrection of Jesus after his death on the cross comprises the good news by which believers are *being saved* from Sin and, by extension, from Death. Every problem in the Corinthian church could be solved by the Corinthians rightly understanding this last point. In 15:2 Paul characterizes *to euangelion* as that "through which also you are being saved, if you hold firmly to the word that I proclaimed to you" (*di' hou kai sōzesthe, tini logō euēngelisamēn hymin ei katechete*), a phrase that takes the listener back to the thesis statement of the letter laid out in 1:18: "For the message about the cross is foolishness to those who are perishing, but to us who are being saved it is the power of God" (*Ho logos gar ho tou staurou tois men apollymenois mōria estin, tois de sōzomenois hēmin dynamis theou estin*). This saving (*sōzō*) word (*logos*), this good news, serves as an *inclusio* (envelope) for the whole epistle.[45]

Now let us explore the details of the argument. In 1 Cor 15:1–11, to remind them of what they should already know about Jesus' resurrection, Paul provides five different warrants for his argument. First, he appeals to Scripture, which speaks of Christ's death and resurrection: "that Christ died for our sins in accordance with the scriptures, and that he was buried, and that he was raised on the third day in accordance with the scriptures (*graphē*)" (vv. 3–4). Second, Paul appeals to tradition to indicate that what he has taught them is by no means idiosyncratic: "For I handed on to you

---

44. *Euangelion* once; *euangelizomai* twice. Paul uses *euangelizomai* six times and *euaggelion* eight times in 1 Corinthians.

45. One will notice a special emphasis in 1 Corinthians on the cross of Christ: *stauroō*, four times; *stauros*, twice. All six occurrences are in the first two chapters. That is because the "strong," those whom Paul ironically calls "gifted in all speech and knowledge" (1 Cor 1:5, au. trans.) are plagued by arrogance (*physioō*), and Paul needs to direct their gaze upon the humility of Christ on the cross and exhort the Corinthians to imitate that humility as displayed by Paul and Christ. So intent on this is Paul that he says, "I decided to know nothing among you except Jesus Christ, and him *crucified*" (2:2, emphasis added). The kenosis hymn of Phil 2:6–11 profoundly captures this humility.

(*paradidōmi*, from which comes the noun *paradosis*, "tradition") as of first importance what I in turn had received (*paralambanō*)" (15:3). Third, Paul refers to eyewitness accounts: "[the risen Jesus] appeared (*horaō*) to Cephas, then to the twelve. Then he appeared to more than five hundred brothers and sisters at one time, most of whom are still alive, though some have died. Then he appeared to James, then to all the apostles" (vv. 5–7).

Fourth, Paul offers his own testimony, claiming that the eyewitnesses in vv. 5–7 have no advantage over Paul and no more basis for authority. If anything, he surpasses them through sheer diligence born of grace: "Last of all, as to one untimely born, he appeared also to me. For I am the least of the apostles, unfit to be called an apostle, because I persecuted the church of God. But by the grace of God I am what I am, and his grace toward me has not been in vain. On the contrary, I worked harder than any of them — though it was not I, but the grace of God that is with me" (vv. 8–10).

Fifth, Paul makes a final appeal to their own experience, surely a powerful and undeniable basis for argument. He reminds them of what he taught them earlier: "Now I would remind *you*, brothers and sisters, of the good news that I proclaimed to *you*, which *you* in turn received, in which also *you* stand" (v. 1, emphasis added). He also reminds them of the belief that they already have: "so we proclaim and so *you* have come to believe" (v. 11, emphasis added).[46] First Corinthians 15 is the earliest extant Christian evidence of Jesus' resurrection appearances; the Gospels, all of which narrate the appearances more fully, were composed after Paul's Epistles.

Verses 13–19, Christ Has Been Raised: A *Via Negativa* Argument

In the course of his argument, Paul makes a number of assertions, only some of which he bolsters with corresponding rationale. After voicing the argument of those he wishes to correct, namely, that there is no resurrection of the dead, Paul begins by making conditional statements in the form, "If X then Y; but we all know that X is not the case; therefore, we know that Y is not the case." So Paul sets up the condition: "If there is no resurrection of the dead (X), then Christ has not been raised (Y); and if Christ has not been raised (Y), then our proclamation has been in vain and your faith has been in vain (Z)," such that if X is true, then both Y and Z must be true. But Paul obviously believes that there *is* a resurrection of the dead, that Christ

---

46. This hortatory technique is known as paraenesis and is used by most NT authors. It is characterized by the use of memory, maxim, and model. The author "reminds" the hearers of something that they presumably already know. Often a conventional maxim is invoked (e.g., "Bad company ruins good morals"). In Paul's paraenesis, models for imitation often include himself and Jesus.

has been raised, and that his proclamation as well as their faith has *not* been in vain.

Because it is true that Christ has been raised, then it is also true that the Corinthians are no longer "in their sins." Paul envisions human beings "in sin" and Christ's resurrection as transforming this calamitous situation for believers (v. 17). Furthermore, because Christ has been raised it is true that believers a) have not perished (*apollymi*, v. 18) and b) can expect more than "this life" (*tautē zōē*, v. 19). Here *apollymi* has a broader meaning than physical death, for, of course, some believers have already physically died. *Apollymi* has eschatological significance. " 'Eternal life' for Paul means much more than just going to heaven when you die; it means sharing in the life to come, the age of the Spirit that will be consummated when Christ returns to renew the world."[47]

Verses 20–28, Christ Has Been Raised: *Via Positiva*

At verse 20 Paul positively reinforces the very points he has just made so volubly above. Verse 20, which calls Christ the first fruits (*aparchē*), gives important information regarding Paul's view of death and afterlife.[48] According to Paul, to date only Christ has been raised. No one else will be raised until Christ's Parousia, when believers (those who belong to Christ) will be raised.[49]

Verses 23–28 provide a time line:

1. Jesus dies and is resurrected (v. 23).

2. Jesus will come again at the Parousia (v. 23).

3. Those who believe in Jesus Christ will be resurrected and transformed, receiving spiritual bodies.[50] In 1 Thess 4 Paul breaks this down into more detail, specifying that the dead in Christ will rise first, and living

47. A. Katherine Grieb, *The Story of Romans: A Narrative Defense of God's Righteousness* (Louisville: Westminster John Knox, 2002), 66.

48. Paul uses the same firstfruits language elsewhere regarding those who have the Holy Spirit (Rom 8:23), the Jews as God's chosen people (11:16), and individual converts to Christianity (16:5; 1 Cor 16:15).

49. Verse 23 presents a conundrum. Does "all" here mean "all" or does it mean "some, namely, Christians." Scholars disagree about this. Fee argues that "all" means some, "those who are his"; see Gordon Fee, *The First Epistle to the Corinthians* (Grand Rapids: Eerdmans, 1987), 749–50n19. Others find in Paul a trajectory of universal salvation, especially in light of Rom 9–11; see John Gager, *Reinventing Paul* (New York: Oxford University Press, 2000), for example. In ch. 2 of *Elusive Israel*, Cosgrove makes a proposal for extrapolating from Paul a notion of universal salvation, although Cosgrove does not find it explicitly expressed in Paul's letters; see Charles H. Cosgrove, "Hermeneutical Election," in *Elusive Israel: The Puzzle of Election in Romans* (Louisville: Westminster John Knox, 1997), 26–45.

50. Based on v. 22, some might disagree with my contention and assume that Paul contends that nonbelievers will be raised as well. For an argument that corroborates my own, see Fee, *First Corinthians*, 749–50n19, where he claims that "all" refers only to believers (v. 22), "those who are his" (v. 23).

Christians will follow to meet the Lord. All must be done in order (*en tagmati*; 1 Cor 15:23).

4. Jesus will reign for a period during which he will destroy every power and authority that he considers an enemy (*echthros*; vv. 24–25). The last enemy to be destroyed is Death (*thanatos*; v. 26).[51]

5. The end (*to telos*) arrives (v. 24).

6. Jesus will hand over the kingdom to God, and everything will be in subjection to God, including Jesus (vv. 24, 27–28).

In the most stunning statement of all, Paul declares that at this point, it will be possible to say that God is everything to everyone: "so that God may be all in all" (*hina ē ho theos [ta] panta en pasin*; 15:28). What are the ramifications for notions of afterlife herein? Where is Satan? Where is hell? Where are the unbelievers? How can it be that in his most extensive and majestic statement regarding the unfolding of the future, Paul addresses none of these? Paul's theology cannot sustain a notion of afterlife that includes Satan's reign over any territory of eternally tormented souls, because this would impinge unbearably upon God's sovereignty and Christ's victory through the cross. If such a realm existed, then one would have to say that there, in hell, is a place where God is in fact *not* everything to everyone. Something would exist outside of God's purview such that God in fact would *not* be "all in all." Even more egregious would be the notion of a "ruler of the underworld or hell," since that would mean that Jesus has not, in fact, defeated all of the rulers and authorities and powers that he died to destroy. Paul clearly would concede none of this.

The eschatology presented here is consistent with what Paul says elsewhere. In chapter 7 he has already indicated the imminence of the eschaton: "I mean, brothers and sisters, the appointed time [*kairos*] has grown short" (7:29). "For the present form of this world is passing away" (*to schēma tou kosmou toutou*; 7:31). One should also recognize the political overtones of the narrated apocalyptic drama, in which "the intensifying military imagery and processional language liken God's coming triumph to an imperial victory march."[52]

---

51. Death language in Paul includes *analyō* (Phil 1:23); *katalyō* (2 Cor 5:1); *apollymi* (1 Cor 1:18–19); *thanatos* (1 Cor 15:55–56; Rom 7:24: "Wretched man that I am! Who will rescue me from this body of death?"); *apothnēskō* (Phil 1:21); *nekros* (1 Cor 15:29); *olethros* (1 Cor 5:5; 1 Thess 5:3); *koimaomai* (1 Thess 4:15); *syntrimma* (a *hapax legomenon*, Rom 3:16); *diaphtheirō* (2 Cor 4:16, where the outward being rots, but the inner is renewed); *katargeō*, used extensively in the sense of destruction, reduce to nothing, come to an end (cf. Rom 6:6, where the body of sin is crucified with Christ and so destroyed; 1 Cor 2:6, where rulers of this age are doomed to perish; 15:24, where every ruler and every authority and power is destroyed; 15:26, where Death is destroyed).

52. Setzer, *Resurrection of the Body*, 60. For an excellent discussion of 1 Corinthians as anti-imperialist literature, see ibid., 58–70. In fact, numerous other scholars — such as Richard A.

Verses 29–32, Another Appeal to Experience

Paul then appeals once more to the personal experience of the Corinthians, mentioning that their practice of baptizing on behalf of the dead serves to bolster Paul's own argument rather than that of the scoffers mentioned in verse 12. Then, just as he did at the start of the chapter, Paul refers to his own experience (vv. 30–32). In this case, he claims that if he did not believe in the resurrection of the dead, he would be reluctant to die and would, therefore, avoid potentially deadly activities such as evangelizing. But since he knows that the resurrection of dead believers is certain, he freely risks his life for the gospel (cf. Phil 1). His example should convince them of the depth of his belief in resurrection and should inspire their own belief as well.

First Corinthians 15:29 stands alone among NT texts in referring to the practice of baptizing for the dead. Although this verse strikes many modern readers as strange, Paul neither criticizes nor recommends the practice; he seems to accept it without question. There is a body of literature devoted to understanding the idea, but it has led to no widespread consensus. What does Paul mean by baptism for the dead? It likely is an act undertaken by a living person for the benefit of a dead person.[53] In his compelling article Richard DeMaris has argued that the specific Corinthian pagan context influenced the beliefs and practices of the churches there. DeMaris adduces archaeological evidence to show that attitudes toward the dead and burial customs were varied and in flux in first-century Corinth, with both burial and cremation as options. Typically, Greeks buried the dead and Romans cremated them. The Corinthian churches presumably comprised people of various backgrounds. According to the record of material culture, what all shared in common was a strong concern for and interest in the dead. "Put simply, the Corinthian Christians would not have instituted baptism on behalf of the dead if Corinthian religion of the Roman era had not been preoccupied with the realm of the dead."[54]

Horsley (242–52), Helmut Koester (158–66), and Neil Elliott (167–83), all in *Paul and Empire: Religion and Power in Roman Imperial Society* (ed Richard A. Horsley; Harrisburg, PA: Trinity, 1997) — also would argue that 1 Corinthians should be read *primarily* as an anti-imperialist document that aims to establish a counterculture. Already such a move was made in 2 Maccabees, which predates Paul and depicts the religiopolitical aims of Jews against pagan hegemonic powers (the Seleucids, in the case of the Maccabees).

53. For alternative opinions that interpret the verse to mean being baptized for one's own sake, see the discussion in Richard DeMaris, "Christian Religion and Baptism for the Dead (1 Corinthians 15:29): Insights from Archaeology and Anthropology," *JBL* 114 (1995): 661–82, esp. 674.

54. Ibid., 671–72. See also Jeffrey A. Trumbower, *Rescue for the Dead: The Posthumous Salvation of Non-Christians in Early Christianity* (Oxford: Oxford University Press, 2001), 35–39.

To understand the way in which they could conceive of baptism as beneficial to the dead, one should attend to the Greco-Roman belief that death constituted a journey. This is especially prominent in chthonic mythology. Prevalent was the practice of placing a coin in the deceased's mouth to pay Charon his ferry charge for the Stygian journey. Christian baptism would have served especially well as this kind of aid since it clearly marked a transition period. So, if Paul can speak of baptism being a movement from death to life, why not an appropriate ritual for the transition from life to death and, perhaps, to afterlife?[55]

Verses 32–34, Ethical Implications of the Resurrection

Verses 32–34 provide the crux of the matter, not only for chapter 15 and the argument about death and afterlife, but also for 1 Corinthians as a whole: *ethics*. For Paul, the only real reason to speak of death and afterlife is to teach his listeners about how to conduct their lives in the present. Paul never simply wants his audience to believe certain ideas; he always expects certain behavior to follow. In a later chapter we will see that Matthew shares the same conviction. This relationship between belief and behavior is not always recognized, as the following false dichotomy illustrates: "Paul's instructions in 1 Corinthians normally prescribe behavior, not belief, yet the letter ends with Paul's ringing demand for belief in resurrection from the dead."[56]

In fact, chapter 15 is primarily concerned with behavior. If there is no resurrection, then one can simply pursue a hedonistic lifestyle, in which one seeks to maximize pleasure and minimize pain: "If the dead are not raised, 'Let us eat and drink, for tomorrow we die'" (v. 32). This attitude seems to be especially manifest in the Corinthian church, some of whose members indulge in sexual immorality, drunkenness, and gluttony. All things become lawful if one has no expectation of future recompense. But Paul calls his flock to reject such depraved behavior: "Do not be deceived: 'Bad company ruins good morals.' Come to a sober and right mind, and sin no more; for some people have no knowledge of God. I say this to your shame" (vv. 33–34).[57]

---

55. DeMaris, "Corinthian Religion," 676–77, appeals to sociology and anthropology, especially regarding rites of passage, as having three main features: "separation, transition, and incorporation." There is considerable argument as to how 15:29 relates to 15:12. Some argue that the Corinthian practice of vicarious baptism indicates that they do, in fact, believe in life after death. Others contend that they do not believe in life after death and that their practice functions to bridge the breach or disruption caused by death for those still alive. After properly carrying out a ritual to put the dead in their place, the living can proceed smoothly with their own lives. Happily, we do not have to decide the issue here; it is enough to recognize that Paul himself certainly teaches that there is an afterlife for believers.

56. Setzer, *Resurrection of the Body*, 55.

57. See the discussion above regarding *syneidēsis*.

Verses 35–50, Nature of the Resurrection Body

That *bodily* resurrection is a central tenet to which Paul adheres is evident by the fact that it takes up sixteen verses in the chapter. Paul's argument in this section flows as follows:

1. A question is posed: "But someone will ask, 'How are the dead raised? With what kind of body do they come?' " (v. 35).

2. Paul attacks in an ad hominem manner: "Fool!" (v. 36).

3. Paul argues that things have bodies appropriate to their needs (vv. 36–41).

4. Paul loosely describes and compares earthly and heavenly bodies (vv. 42–50).

In this section Paul makes several strong points. First and foremost, God is a creator. Paul thoroughly affirms God's choice to create human beings in bodily form. In Paul's apocalyptic worldview, time is divided into (1) a beginning, when God created the heavens and the earth; (2) a middle, fallen time, in which the cosmos is under the deadly rule of Satan and his cohorts (cf. Rom 8); and (3) a glorious final future, when God will reign supreme and uncontested once again. As is customary in apocalyptic thinking, the end time will be like the beginning (*Endzeit gleicht Urzeit*). So if God chose to create bodies in the beginning, it follows that believers will have bodies in the final age. True, the heavenly body will be different from the earthly body.[58] Paul contrasts the earthly body, which is sown (buried),[59] and the heavenly body, which is raised. The language he uses of the former includes "perishable," "dishonor," "weakness," "physical." In describing the heavenly body, he uses language of "imperishable," "glory,"[60] "power," and "spiritual." But never does Paul indicate antipathy toward bodily existence. Thus, the Platonic or gnostic disdain for the body is untenable for Paul, because imagining the body as a tomb (*sōma sēma*) or some kind of miserable prison entrapping the soul would amount to designating God's creation a

---

58. *Second Baruch* (late first century CE or early second) takes up the issue of a bodily resurrection as well; chs. 49–50 indicate that the living will recognize their resurrected dead, but then a transformation will occur. For a discussion of the similarities to 1 Cor 15, see John J. Collins, "The Afterlife in Apocalyptic Literature," in *Death, Life-after-Death, Resurrection and the World-to-Come* (ed. Alan J. Avery-Peck and Jacob Neusner; vol. 4 of *Judaism in Late Antiquity*; New York: Brill 1995), 130–31.

59. Perhaps Paul uses "sown" imagery to refer to the story of Adam's creation from the dirt of the earth, from which his name derives.

60. See Phil 3:21: "He will transform the body of our humiliation that it may be conformed to the body of his glory, by the power that also enables him to make all things subject to himself"; and 2 Cor 3:18: "And all of us, with unveiled faces, seeing the glory of the Lord as though reflected in a mirror, are being transformed into the same image from one degree of glory to another; for this comes from the Lord, the Spirit."

debacle. It would mean declaring God's choice to create embodied human beings (and stars, animals, and so on) to be misguided at best.[61]

How does gender factor into the discussion of bodies? Unlike Matthew, whose Jesus declares that in the resurrection there will be no marriage because people will be like angels (Matt 22:30), Paul never directly addresses the topic of potentially gendered resurrection bodies. One can, however, assume that Paul and Matthew share a view of genderless afterlife. In his typically luculent and provocative way, Daniel Boyarin argues that Paul's attitudes toward gender are both comprehensible and consistent when one discerns that (1) Paul is working with a notion of the primal androgyne as an ideal, and (2) Paul maintains a hierarchical distinction between spirit and flesh that determines the hierarchy in which male is superior to female in this aeon.[62]

Boyarin argues that Paul "was motivated by a Hellenistic desire for the One, which among other things produced an ideal of a universal human essence, beyond difference and hierarchy."[63] Like Meeks before him, he targets the myth of the androgyne that lies behind Gal 3:28.[64] That myth imagines a creation in which male and female were a unity, as represented in the first creation story in the Hebrew Scriptures: "male and female [God] created them," without hierarchy (Gen 1:27). Boyarin cites Philo as evidence for knowledge of this myth among Jews contemporary with Paul. But Philo distinguishes the first creation story from the second, in which the woman is secondary and derivative from the male, explaining why, in this earthly world, male is superior to female. After an engaging treatment, Boyarin finally concludes that in the Spirit, there is no male and female, but only in baptism and other occasional ecstatic moments can one be in the Spirit prior to the eschaton. However, those who choose to remain unmarried and celibate have, in effect, already become free of gender trappings in this life, and so as celibates already live their lives in the Spirit. The majority of this life is lived in the flesh, where the hierarchy remains necessary for the proper functioning of households. Only at the eschaton will all gender, ethnic, and class distinctions be fully erased.

According to Boyarin, there are in fact, three (not mutually exclusive) options for

a social enactment of the myth of the primal androgyne: some gnostics (and perhaps the Corinthians) seem to have held that having once

61. In *Paul's Terms,* 265, Jewett argues that Paul takes a middle road between the gnostic disdain for the body and the view of 2 Macc 7 that the resurrected body will be identical to the present body.

62. Boyarin, "Genealogy of Gender," 13–41.

63. Ibid., 14.

64. Wayne Meeks, "The Image of the Androgyne: Some Uses of a Symbol in Earliest Christianity," *History of Religions* 13 (1974): 165–208.

attained the spirit humans transcend gender entirely and for ever, whether [in] celibacy or libertinage. Philo, on the other hand, restricts such transcending redemption from gender to celibates and then only to special ritualized moments of ecstasy. Paul's strictures against women with short hair and the speaking out of woman prophets... [11:5–6; 14:33b–36] — if the latter is genuinely Pauline — seem to suggest a third option: for all (not only celibates) there is no male and female, but only momentarily in the ritualized ecstasy of baptism. It is only then, in this life, that people attain the status of life in the spirit, in Christ or in the Lord in which there is no male and female. . . . All three of these possibilities are equally dependent, however, on a notion that gender difference only exists at one ontological level, the outer or physical, the corporeal, but at the level of true existence, the spiritual, there is no gender, that is, no dualism.[65]

Thus, if one applied Boyarin's reasoning to our own topic, the resurrection body would, by implication, be a genderless one.[66]

Second, Paul is not Plato and does not believe that any part of a human being is *inherently* immortal, be it body, soul, or spirit.[67] Why does Paul insist that, in fact, no part of a human being is inherently immortal? Why does he insist that believers attain immortality only when Christ returns and conducts the resurrection? Why does he accentuate the future nature of immortality? To indicate otherwise would be to detract from the efficaciousness of Jesus' work on the cross. If some part of human beings is inherently immortal, why should Christ have bothered being crucified? Did Christ really suffer the cross simply so that human beings could receive a respectable body tacked on to a Platonic soul? Certainly not. Furthermore, if it is the case that the most desirable benefits accrue to one immediately upon death, with a body being tacked on later as a bonus, why should one really care about Christ's Parousia?

---

65. Boyarin, "Genealogy of Gender," 35.

66. If people were created by a good and wise creator with physical bodies, and one extrapolates from this that people will be resurrected with physical bodies, it could also be argued that because a good and wise God saw fit to create people with gendered bodies, then people must be resurrected with gendered bodies. I cannot tell from the quote above if Boyarin agrees with "a notion that gender difference only exists at one ontological level, the outer or physical, the corporeal, but at the level of true existence, the spiritual, there is no gender." He appears to me a bit reluctant to endorse the idea that "true existence" is entirely spiritual.

67. Jewett presents "the most widely accepted definition" of soul (*psychē*) as that which "bears the inner life of man, . . . which will continue to exist after death" (*Paul's Terms*, 334). But in his summary Jewett claims that Paul never uses *psychē* "in the strict sense of the 'soul,' i.e., the God-related portion of man which survives after death." Furthermore, Jewett maintains that in 1 Cor 2:14, *psychikos* (physical), like *sarkinos* (of this world), depicts the mortal realm of a person (ibid., 449).

Paul insists on a doctrine of bodily resurrection because to do otherwise empties both the cross and the Parousia of any real force. Resurrection necessarily requires that a person has first died. Paul believes that, before his resurrection, Jesus was thoroughly dead. Lest there be any mistake, he had been dead for days. Likewise, Paul believes that all people, Christians included, die and remain dead until Christ comes again. At that time, dead believers will be raised. Paul is not at all clear about the fate of unbelievers. One could argue that Paul envisions their annihilation, that they simply remain dead forever. Conversely, after canvassing other writings, particularly Rom 9–11, one could argue that Paul expects universal salvation. One can assume with reasonable certainty that, unlike Matthew, Daniel, or most intertestamental apocalyptic literature, Paul does not appear to believe that after the resurrection following the coming of Christ, some will be rewarded with heaven while others will be consigned to a fiery hell. In fact, Paul never uses any language for hell. He has no Hades, no Gehenna, no outer darkness, no weeping or gnashing of teeth, no Apollyon, no Tartarus. By contrast, he certainly refers easily to heaven and even speaks of "Paradise" (2 Cor 12:4). Why is this? Why the bias toward heaven?

Perhaps two explanations are in order. First, remember Paul's conviction that in the end, God will be "all in all." This certainly will be the case if unbelievers simply do not rise. They cease to exist and therefore have no consciousness, no knowledge that they do not exist, no suffering. This is far different from spending an eternity in a fiery hell, à la Matthew. Second, remember our conviction that most statements on the part of NT authors regarding death and afterlife are aimed at getting people to conduct their earthly lives in a particular way. Paul takes a different tack from Matthew. Paul appears to believe that he has been called to preach *good* news, not bad. He seems to think that if he preaches the good news, God will find a way to make it irresistible. Thus, Paul's preaching is unbalanced, constantly emphasizing the good news and the benefits that emerge from accepting it, and trusting that the good news will be compelling.

Matthew, on the other hand, hedges his bets. To be sure, Matthew preaches good news, but for those who fail to find the gospel of grace irresistible, life-giving, and completely transformative (as in Paul's story about his own call to Christian faith), Matthew's threats and terrifying prospects are intended to make one reconsider. The prospective Matthean Christian might think: "I would rather believe and find out I was wrong than not believe and find out I was wrong." Matthew appears to be less certain than Paul about the gospel's irresistibility and has a Plan B prepared in case Plan A fails.

Verses 51–58, Assured Victory in the Future

In this passage one of Paul's main goals is to emphasize the future aspect of his eschatology, perhaps in response to some Corinthians' overrealized eschatology. Notice then the number of times in the chapter that Paul uses the future tense to indicate that final victory is yet to come, although in the very near future, as we learned in chapter 7. Currently, believers are dead, but they *will be* made alive (*zōopoiēthēsontai*) at the Parousia (15:22–23; cf. 2 Cor 4:14). Likewise, at 15:28 we learn that the son *will become* subject (*hypotagēsetai*). Only at this future date will the glorious, ecstatic declamation of Paul come to pass: "When this perishable body puts on imperishability, and this mortal body puts on immortality, then the saying that is written *will be* fulfilled: 'Death has been swallowed up in victory.' 'Where, O death, is your victory? Where, O death, is your sting?' " (15:54–55). Now this would seem to be a brilliant, sweeping, exhilarating rhetorical note on which to end. But Paul simply cannot resist — he must push his rhetoric into the service of ethical application. Waxing a bit pedantic, he explains that, in fact, "The sting of death is sin, and the power of sin is the law" (15:56). Then, as though catching himself being too preachy, he moves back to exhilaration: "But thanks be to God, who gives us the victory through our Lord Jesus Christ" (v. 57). Paul concludes with ethics: "Therefore, my beloved, be steadfast, immovable, always excelling in the work of the Lord, because you know that in the Lord your labor is not in vain" (v. 58).

For Paul, death is related to sin (Rom 5:12, 6:16). Where there is sin, there is death; where there is death, there is sin. To say that death has already been vanquished would be foolish, since a quick glance within and around manifests that sin is alive and well. "The wages of sin is death" (Rom 6:23; cf. 1 Cor 3:8, 14). Wage or reward (*misthos*) language appears regularly in Matthew as well. For the Corinthians to argue for a realized eschatology would imply that there is no longer sin, and to be sure, they seem to believe that "all things are lawful" (1 Cor 6:12). Correcting them on all counts, Paul shows that sin, salvation, death, judgment, and resurrection are inseparably related topics, and all Christian ethics are dependent upon a correct understanding of them. Paul makes this point exactly when he chastises the know-it-alls among the Corinthians (here his use of "knowledge" is ironic, not literal): "So by your knowledge those weak believers for whom Christ died are destroyed. But when you thus sin against members of your family, and wound their conscience when it is weak, you sin against Christ" (*apollytai gar ho asthenōn en tē sē gnōsei, ho adelphos di' hon Christos apethanen. Houtōs de hamartanontes eis tous adelphous kai typtontes autōn tēn syneidēsin asthenousan eis Christon hamartanete*; 1 Cor 8:11–12).

Though Paul does not explicitly refer to the eschatological judgment in 1 Cor 15, one can assume it belongs there. Paul has already made reference to judgment in 1 Cor 3:13, referring to it there simply as "the Day" (*hē hēmera*). It is alluded to in our chapter by the presence of the trumpets ("at the last trumpet. For the trumpet shall sound"; *en tē eschatē salpingi: salpisei gar*; 15:52), a feature of judgment that Paul has inherited from apocalyptic thinkers before him.[68] In a passage strikingly similar to ours Paul writes:

> For since we believe that Jesus died and rose again, even so, through Jesus, God will bring with him those who have died. For this we declare to you by the word of the Lord, that we who are alive, who are left until the coming of the Lord, will by no means precede those who have died. For the Lord himself, with a cry of command, with the archangel's call and with the sound of God's trumpet, will descend from heaven, and the dead in Christ will rise first. Then we who are alive, who are left, will be caught up in the clouds together with them to meet the Lord in the air; and so we will be with the Lord forever. (1 Thess 4:14–17)[69]

In Paul there is both a corporate and an individual aspect to judgment day (1 Cor 3:13; 4:5; 2 Cor 5:10; Rom 2:16). No one faces judgment until all face it, at the Parousia (1 Cor 15:51–52). Finally, however, it must be individually faced, and believers will not escape judgment. As in Matthew, where believers will judge the twelve tribes of Israel (19:28), Paul maintains that believers will judge angels (1 Cor 6:3). "Whereas a writer like Luke views repentance of sins as a condition for becoming a believer (cf. 3:3; 5:32), to Paul repentance functions at the juncture of a believer's misbehavior, remorse, and desire for reinstatement within the community of believers."[70] What is the basis of judgment for Paul? Ethics, most obviously displayed by marching in step with the Spirit, excelling in the work of the Lord: "In Paul's thought world, surviving the end-time judgment depends on the works the believer has to offer.... For Paul, not even faith is the key to eternal access to God's presence such that one's having it would merit

---

68. The trumpet is standard fare in apocalyptic within the NT. It appears in Matthew's apocalyptic discourse (Matt 24:31) as well as numerous times in Revelation.

69. There is no mention of soul or spirit in the passage, though at 1 Thess 5:23 Paul speaks of body, soul, and spirit as being "kept complete" until the coming of Christ. This implies that those parts will participate in the eschaton (Jewett, *Paul's Terms*, 251). Jewett argues that 1 Thess 5:23 probably picks up the triad from "enthusiastic libertinists" in Thessalonica who "opposed 'body and soul' to 'spirit' in typical Gnostic fashion, believing that redemption consisted of gaining transcendence in the spirit" (ibid., 347). Employing a more "traditional Judaic definition," "Paul insists in this benediction that God works to sanctify the whole man" (see also ibid., 3, 175ff., 183–84, 250–51). Jewett may be overextending his argument here.

70. Sampley, *Walking between the Times*, 69.

inheritance of God's kingdom."[71] One is repaid (*apodidōmi*) according to one's works (Rom 2:6, drawing on Ps 61:12 LXX and Prov 24:12).

David Kuck's work on 1 Cor 3:5–4:5 is instructive here. First Corinthians 3:8 and 14 are the only places where Paul uses *misthos* (reward) in an eschatological sense, but he certainly refers to God's future judgment here.[72] Verses 3:8b and 4:5 emphasize that each individual will be judged on the results of one's labor. This judgment will take place on the "day" (cf. Rom 13:12; 1 Thess 5:4).[73] That day will bring salvation or condemnation, according to Kuck. Closely related is language of Parousia, or coming (1 Cor 4:5; 1 Thess 2:19; 3:13).

First Corinthians 3:13c depicts the day of judgment, with Christ arriving in a fiery theophany (cf. Dan 7:9–10; Isa 66:15). In verse 13d the function of the fire is to test the work of each (Pss 12:6; 66:10; Mal 3:2b–4).[74] A third use of fire appears in verse 15c, where Paul portrays some as barely escaping fiery destruction. Because fire in Jewish and Christian imagery is usually a tool with which God punishes or a tool for purification,[75] some have argued that the fire in verse 13d refers either to eternal hell or to purgatory. Kuck argues against both interpretations, first because Paul never depicts a two-stage judgment scene, and second because the fire here is not said to purify or to burn the person, but rather to reveal the quality of the person's work. Those whose labor is made of durable material will be more

---

71. Ibid., 70. Not all will agree with Sampley. For a discussion of works and grace, see Anthony Thiselton, *The First Epistle to the Corinthians: A Commentary on the Greek Text* (Grand Rapids: Eerdmans, 2000), 1303–4, on 15:57; on the same passage, cf. also Fee, *First Corinthians*, 807. This seems to correlate well with Richard Hays, *The Faith of Jesus Christ: An Investigation of the Narrative Substructure of Galatians 3:1–4:11* (Grand Rapids: Eerdmans, 2002), 109. Hays finds an often-unspoken narrative underlying Paul. So, when Paul says that we are judged by our works, the entire underlying narrative is assumed and implied. Speaking of Gal 4, he writes: "The absence of an explicit reference to Christ's crucifixion and death . . . is of no particular importance, because any allusion to a part of the story presupposes the story as a whole." I would apply this to the places in Paul where he speaks of judgment based on works. Without God's gracious act in Christ Jesus, which motivates and empowers us to perform good works, we would not be found righteous in the judgment. The entire narrative is implied.

72. David W. Kuck, *Judgment and Community Conflict: Paul's Use of Apocalyptic Judgment Language in 1 Corinthians 3:5–4:5* (NovTSup 66; Leiden: Brill, 1992), 167.

73. Paul uses the fuller expression "day of the Lord" or "of Christ" at 1 Cor 1:8; 5:5; 2 Cor 1:14; Phil 1:6, 10; 2:16; 1 Thess 5:2; and 2 Thess 2:2 (if authentic). In Rom 2:5 he says "day of wrath" and at 2:16 "day of judgment" (paraphrased). For other NT references to judgment day, see ibid., 179n146.

74. Raymond Collins emphasizes that the work of each is the work of building up the community/"temple" (as opposed to building up one's own stack of "good works" for one's own personal reward in the coming eschaton); members do have varieties of gifts. In Judaism the Spirit of God dwells in the temple (this may be to counter the *pneumatikoi*). Raymond F. Collins, *First Corinthians* (SP 7; Collegeville, MN: Liturgical Press, 1999), 150ff, 151.

75. R. Collins, *First Corinthians*, 153: "The Spirit is the eschatological power of God, a power tradition frequently associates with fire (cf. the Q saying found in Luke 3:16 = Matt 3:11). With the motif of the Spirit of God, Paul maintains the eschatological perspective introduced by the motifs of the day and the fire" (in 1 Cor 3:13).

richly rewarded than those whose missionary work is burned up. Perhaps the best image is that of receiving tickets for each durable work and then redeeming them at the prize counter — the more tickets, the bigger and better the reward. Those whose work is burned up will have fewer tickets and, therefore, a less impressive reward. "Whatever difficulties this passage may create for systematic theologians, it is quite certain that Paul here promises final salvation even to those laborers who present work of poor quality at the final judgment."[76] However, those who actually destroy the church, God's temple, should not expect salvation. Thus Paul serves them a strong warning regarding factionalism, using eschatological destruction as a deterrent.

Who are the actors in Paul's eschatological scenario? God (Rom 14:10) and Christ (2 Cor 5:10) judge. Rom 2:16 indicates that God judges through Christ. Kuck indicates that Paul does not often speak of Christ as the future judge (2 Cor 5:10 and possibly Rom 14:4 and 1 Thess 4:6). Even in 1 Cor 4:5, it is Christ's job to reveal the person's thoughts, while God judges. Kuck argues that this fits the whole train of thought in 3:5–4:5, that God judges and Christ plays an intermediate role (3:5c, 23; 4:1, 4c) as supervisor.[77] Yet 1 Cor 6:2–3 shows Christians helping to judge the world and even the angels in the eschaton, Christians being superior to everyone and everything. First Corinthians 6:9–10 manifests serious differences between Christians ("holy ones," vv. 1, 11, au. trans.) and non-Christians ("unrighteous outsiders," vv. 1, 9, au. trans.).

For Paul, a central feature of judgment day will be the disclosure of one's motives and thoughts. There is no way to know what someone's motives are until that day. Paul sees the *heart* as the seat of knowledge, emotion, and volition.[78] It can also harbor ignorance and evil (Rom 1:21 KJV, 24; 2:5). Paul contrasts external appearances with internal realities of the heart (2 Cor 12; 1 Thess 2:17). Each Christian will be judged individually (2 Cor 5:10; Rom 14:12).[79]

First Corinthians 4:5 distinguishes between Christ's revealing and God's judging; Rom 2:16 combines them. Both passages indicate that only God knows each heart, so Christians should not attempt to judge each other (the same does not hold true for judging non-Christians).[80] First Corinthians 3 has only the judgment of Christians in view. They will receive *epainos*, "praise/commendation" (Rom 2:29; 1 Cor 4:5).[81]

---

76. Kuck, *Judgment and Community Conflict*, 183.
77. Ibid., 201.
78. See Jewett, *Paul's Terms*, 447–48.
79. Romans 8:13 is similar to 2 Cor 5:10 insofar as it speaks of the deeds of the body.
80. See Kuck, *Judgment and Community Conflict*, 208.
81. Elsewhere Paul speaks of boast (*kauchaomai*) in the sense of reward (e.g., crown in Phil 4:1 and 1 Thess 2:19, prize in 1 Cor 9:24 and Phil 3:14).

First Corinthians 15 has more to do with anthropology than chronology. Paul here teaches the Corinthians to value the body, thereby continuing his argument from chapter 6. It is not so much about chronology, realized versus future eschatology. Paul never explicitly connects judgment and resurrection, nor does he ever mention a resurrection of unbelievers.[82]

Those who do good are rewarded with glory, honor, peace (*doxa de kai timē kai eirēnē*; Rom 2:10), and with prizes (Phil 3:14; 1 Cor 9:24). What counts as doing good? While Paul readily provides virtue lists (as well as vice lists), what counts as "the good" may vary for different believers. It is important to act in line with one's conscience and not to impose that decision on anyone else. For example, whether or not one should eat idol meat depends upon one's own convictions. If it causes affliction of one's conscience, one should refrain. However, at all times one must consider how one's choices affect the faith of others in the body of Christ, the church. Whenever possible, one should not cause scandal to another's faith (1 Cor 10:32).[83] Sampley makes a nice move in comparing the endings of three statements regarding circumcision and uncircumcision. Neither are important, but only faith expressing itself through love (*agapē*; Gal 5:6), being a new creation (Gal 6:15), and keeping God's commandments (1 Cor 7:19).[84]

Will others be judged? According to Romans, the answer is yes:

By your hard and impenitent heart you are storing up wrath for yourself on the day of wrath, when God's righteous judgment will be revealed. For he will repay according to each one's deeds: to those who by patiently doing good seek for glory and honor and immortality, he will give eternal life; while for those who are self-seeking and who obey not the truth but wickedness, there will be wrath and fury. There will be anguish and distress for everyone who does evil, the Jew first and also the Greek, but glory and honor and peace for everyone who does good, the Jew first and also the Greek. For God shows no partiality. (Rom 2:5–11)

What constitutes "doing evil" for Paul? One can look to the vice lists for concrete examples, but Sampley calls *porneia* "Paul's all-inclusive vice."[85]

---

82. Kuck, *Judgment and Community Conflict*, 257.
83. With respect to following one's conscience, see also Rom 14:5: "Some judge one day to be better than another, while others judge all days to be alike. Let all be fully convinced in their own minds"; and 14:22–23: "The faith that you have, have as your own conviction before God. Blessed are those who have no reason to condemn themselves because of what they approve. But those who have doubts are condemned if they eat, because they do not act from faith; for whatever does not proceed from faith is sin."
84. Sampley, *Walking between the Times*, 78.
85. Ibid., 76. Cf. Rom 13:13; 1 Cor 5:10–11; 6:9–10; 2 Cor 12:20; Gal 5:19–21.

By what resources does one know and achieve the good?[86] First, believers
have the Spirit of God that God gives them to help discern the will of God.[87]
Second, believers can imitate Paul as he imitates Christ (1 Cor 11:1). He
writes: "Keep on doing the things that you have learned and received and
heard and seen in me, and the God of peace will be with you" (Phil 4:9;
cf. 3:17; 1 Thess 1:6; 2:9–12; 1 Cor 4:16) Third, Christians can imitate
Christ as Paul so eloquently presents in the kenosis hymn (Phil 2:6–11). Paul
also exhibits saintly examples ranging from individuals (Timothy, Phil 2:22;
Euodia and Syntyche, Phil 4:3) to a household (of Stephanas, 1 Cor 16:15) to
entire churches (e.g., the Macedonian churches as they exemplify generosity:
2 Cor 8:1–2). Finally, one can use the Scriptures that were "written for our
instruction" (Rom 15:4).[88]

Summary and Conclusion:
Where We Are after 1 Cor 15?

What are the main points to be gleaned regarding death and afterlife in Paul
based on our analysis thus far?

1. Some believers have died and remain in the grave. Some are alive and
    can expect to be taken up when Jesus returns.

2. One should behave because at the judgment God will judge people on
    their works.

3. Paul provides no clear argument about the fate of unbelievers, but in
    1 Cor 1:18 he directly contrasts unbelievers with those who are being
    saved, referring to them as in the process of being destroyed. He later
    makes the distinction again that the believers have died but are not
    destroyed (2 Cor 4:9).

4. At the resurrection, believers will receive bodies, but these bodies will
    be immortal, incorruptible, and probably genderless.[89]

---

86. Here I follow Sampley's discussion, ibid., 87–100.
87. Regarding how this might relate to conscience, see Jewett, who emphasizes the *autonomy* of the conscience: "Paul never explains the autonomy of the conscience in terms of its relation to God or the Holy Spirit. It is a purely human function, equally at work and equal in inviolability whether it be within Gentile or Jew, believer or unbeliever" (*Paul's Terms*, 460).
88. See Richard Hays, *Echoes of Scripture in the Letters of Paul* (New Haven: Yale University Press, 1989); idem, "Paul: The *Koinōnia* of His Sufferings," in *The Moral Vision of the New Testament: Community, Cross, New Creation; A Contemporary Introduction to New Testament Ethics* (San Francisco: HarperSanFrancisco, 1996), 16–59. I am, however, inclined to agree with Louis J. Martyn, whose comments serve to nuance the place of Scripture in Paul's ministry; see "The Galatians' Role in the Spirit's War of Liberation," in *Galatians: A New Translation* (AB 33A; New York: Doubleday, 1997), 524–40.
89. Dale Martin argues that 1 Cor 15 depicts different ideologies of the body that are tied to different views on cosmology and physiology (*Corinthian Body*, 104–36). He argues against those who see the debate between Paul and the Corinthians as the difference between a realized

But we need more information to fill out the picture and we need to pursue further questions.

ON 2 COR 5:1–10 AND PHIL 1:18B–26

After reading 1 Cor 15, the picture seems fairly clear and is corroborated by 1 Thess 4. But passages such as 2 Cor 5:1–10 and Phil 1:18b–26 complicate matters. If believers are resurrected at the Parousia and not a moment before (1 Cor 4:5; 15:23, 52; 1 Thess 4:13–18), then we wonder how Paul can declare: "My desire is to depart and be with Christ, for that is far better" (Phil 1:23). If Death is the enemy, we wonder how can he say, "Dying is gain" (Phil 1:21). And what exactly is going on in 2 Cor 5? Is Paul expressing fear that after he dies, he might be bodiless during the time period between his death and the Parousia, in a so-called intermediate state? Is he finding his own teaching in 1 Cor 15 to be deficient when faced with his own death? Or has he simply changed his mind or developed his thinking in the brief time span between 1 and 2 Corinthians such that he envisions individuals receiving their new bodies immediately upon their deaths?

Generally speaking, those who have specifically taken up the topic of the "intermediate state" or "soul sleep" write from a biblical theology perspective and tend to make claims about "the" NT perspective on the topic. Representative of this perspective is J. Osei-Bonsu, whose article "The Intermediate State in the New Testament" epitomizes his unpublished dissertation on the subject:[90]

> The notion of a post-mortem disembodied existence of the soul fol-
> lowed by resurrection on the last day has been part of traditional
> Christian theology for centuries. Though some modern theologians
> are unhappy with this doctrine and have tried to re-interpret it or

---

and future eschatology. The Corinthians probably had a future eschatology, but they rejected the *bodily* part of it. Martin warns against defining Paul's anthropological terms too sharply (ibid., 15). Both Martin and J. Edward Wright, *The Early History of Heaven* (New York: Oxford University Press, 2000), 194, agree that Paul's insistence on bodily resurrection does not contradict his notion that flesh and blood will not inherit the kingdom. Flesh and blood is simply shorthand for living outside the ethics of the Holy Spirit. Following Martin, Setzer (*Resurrection of the Body*, 56–70) argues that Paul's use of anthropological terms mirrors the social situation among the Corinthian Christians and makes an anti-imperialist statement. On the other hand, Wayne Meeks explicitly states that he finds no basis in Paul for viewing Roman imperialism as the cause of the evil state of the present age (*First Urban Christians,* 189). Martin (*Corinthian Body*) assumes that the *pneumatikoi* (spiritual ones) are the wealthy who probably were influenced by Hellenistic philosophy, which had a tendency to disdain the body and elevate the spirit. Siding with the weak who express anxiety over body boundaries (such as eating meat sacrificed to idols, having sex, and so on), Paul draws attention to the value and importance of the body as part of God's present and future drama. Taking it to the level of empire, Paul highlights Jesus as crucified in the flesh by Rome.

90. Osei-Bonsu, "Intermediate State," 169–94.

reject it altogether, it cannot be denied that traditional Christian theology has always taught this.... In recent times the traditional view
has been attacked by several scholars some of whom claim that it is
unbiblical....[91] It is the aim of this article to show that the New Testament supports the view of the intermediate state of the soul followed
by resurrection at which body and soul are reunited.[92]

Osei-Bonsu takes up the passages treated by Cullmann: Luke 16:19–31;
23:43; 2 Cor 5:1–10; Phil 1:23; Rev 6:9–11; to them he adds Matt 10:28
(par. Luke 12:4–5); Acts 2:26–31; 1 Cor 15:35–54; and 1 Thess 4:13–18.
In each case, he argues that the NT text supports, or at least does not argue
against, the intermediate state of the soul as described in his thesis statement.
Here we will take up only the Pauline texts, treating the others in successive
relevant chapters.

Second Corinthians 5

There are two main approaches to 2 Cor 5. The first and perhaps most
common (M. Harris, Boyarin, Jan Lambrecht)[93] is to view 5:1–10 as an
isolated unit on the subject of "Paul's (changing?) view of the afterlife."[94]
This approach contends that Paul's magniloquent exposition in 1 Cor 15 has
been vitiated by his close brush with death in Asia Minor (1:8–9), thrusting
him into a state of anxiety regarding the fate of his body between his death
and the Parousia. In this interpretation, the earthly, tentlike house is the
physical body destroyed at death, and the building from God is the immortal
body bestowed by God, either at death or at the Parousia, depending upon
the scholar. Those who argue for bestowal at the Parousia find Paul here
expressing discomfort at the bodiless (being "naked") state that he will have
to endure if he dies before the Parousia.

The second and far less common approach argues that the sensible unit
runs from 4:16–5:5, which finds Paul concerned not with the resurrection
body or intermediate state of the soul, but rather with defending his apostleship against the critique of the superapostles and with calling the Corinthians
back to correct belief and behavior. In other words, Paul is concerned with
the present, with the difficulty believers experience as they live between the
times, a subject that consumes Paul in all of his letters. I will lay out the major

---

91. Here he has in mind R. E. Bailey, "Life after Death: A New Testament Study in the
Relation of Body and Soul" (Ph.D. diss., University of Edinburgh, 1962); Murray J. Harris,
Raised Immortal: Resurrection and Immortality in the New Testament (Grand Rapids: Eerdmans, 1985); Karel Hanhart, *The Intermediate State in the New Testament* (Groningen: printed
by V. R. B. Kleine, 1966).

92. Osei-Bonsu, "Intermediate State," 169–71.

93. Jan Lambrecht, *Second Corinthians* (SP 8; Collegeville, MN: Liturgical Press, 1999),
80–90.

94. Roetzel, 14.

details of each argument in turn.[95] From beginning to end, 2 Cor 5:1–10 is beset with exegetical difficulties ranging from the syntactical, grammatical, and philological to the conceptual and theological, and no argument smoothly accounts for all of the data without remainder.

Argument 1

The initial verses of 2 Cor 5 sound much like 1 Cor 15 and Rom 8 in that Paul sympathizes with the fact that, although earthly life is difficult, nevertheless a heavenly body awaits believers: "For we know that if the earthly tent we live in is destroyed, we have a building from God, a house not made with hands, eternal in the heavens. For in this tent we groan, longing to be clothed with our heavenly dwelling" (5:1–2). And much like 1 Cor 15, where God's resurrection of Christ serves as a guarantee, here the Holy Spirit serves that role: "He who has prepared us for this very thing is God, who has given us the Spirit as a guarantee" (2 Cor 5:5; cf. 1:22). Echoing Phil 1:21 ("Living is Christ and dying is gain") is 2 Cor 5:8–9: "Yes, we do have confidence, and we would rather be away from the body and at home with the Lord. So whether we are at home or away, we make it our aim to please him." As in 1 Corinthians, all of this body talk has ethics as the focal point: "For all of us must appear before the judgment seat of Christ, so that each may receive recompense for what has been done in the body, whether good or evil" (2 Cor 5:10).

The first issue concerns the meaning of "a heavenly dwelling" and "building from God." Paul uses *oikia, oikodomē,* and *oikētērion* in this passage.[96] This language has been variously interpreted: (1) the church as the body of Christ, (2) the church as the heavenly temple, and most commonly, (3) the resurrection body of the individual believer.[97]

Second, the debate over the timing of the receipt of the resurrection body centers on the proper translation of *echomen* (we [believers] have/possess): should it be rendered present or future? Osei-Bonsu argues for a future meaning, at the time of the Parousia, after the body has long decayed: "*echomen* has a future reference because the possession of the 'building

95. Within each of the two main approaches, one finds many differences on detailed points. The interested reader should consult the major commentaries.

96. For a discussion of the nuances of meaning among the three words, if any, see Victor Paul Furnish, *2 Corinthians* (AB 32A;. Garden City, NY: Doubleday, 1984), 264–65.

97. Those who support the view of the church as heavenly temple include F. F. Bruce, *1 and 2 Corinthians* (Grand Rapids: Eerdmans, 1980); R. H. Gundry, *Sōma in Biblical Theology: With Emphasis on Pauline Anthropology* (Grand Rapids: Academie Books, 1987), 223–44; M. J. Harris, "Paul's View of Death," in *New Dimensions in New Testament Study* (Grand Rapids: Zondervan, 1974), 317–28. Those who argue for the church as the body of Christ include J. A. T. Robinson, *The Body: A Study in Pauline Theology* (London: SCM, 1952), 75–79; and E. Earle Ellis, "II Cor V 1–10 in Pauline Eschatology," *NTS* 6 (1960): 211–24, esp. 217–19. See also Furnish, *2 Corinthians*.

from God' comes only after the dissolution of the tent."[98] Others opt for the present, arguing that it indicates "the possession of the spiritual body at the time that the tent-dwelling is dismantled, i.e., at the moment of death," even before the body has decayed.[99] In 1 Cor, Paul is quite insistent that believers will receive their spiritual bodies only at the time of the Parousia and not a moment before.[100] Arguing that Paul has in mind immediate reception of the body at death means holding that he has completely reversed the position he held with great conviction just one year earlier. He does not, however, indicate to the Corinthians that he has changed his mind. Oscar Cullmann states confidently: "Because resurrection of the body is a new act of creation which embraces everything, it is not an event which begins with each individual death, but only at the End."[101]

The third issue is the concern about nakedness (*gymnos*). One is reminded immediately of the parable of the wedding garment in Matthew, where the one who should have been properly clothed for the occasion was found wanting in dress and banished to outer darkness (Matt 22:1–14). Is Paul indicating some knowledge of such an idea? We know that Paul often uses clothing language metaphorically: putting on Christ (*endyō*, in Rom 13:14; Gal 3:27), "armor of light" (Rom 13:12), "the breastplate of faith and love" (1 Thess 5:8), putting on imperishability and immortality (1 Cor 15:53–54). What is the power of the metaphor in 2 Cor 5:2–4? Osei-Bonsu maintains that Paul is personally discomfited by the notion of bodiless existence between death and the Parousia. Paul uses *endyō* (clothe) in 1 Cor 15:53–54. Why does he switch to *ependyomai* (put on [in addition]) in 2 Cor 5:2, 4? Osei-Bonsu argues (along with Barrett) that Paul has in mind here those who are living when Christ returns, who will then receive, as it were, another body to wear on top of the body they already have ("superclothing," as Lambrecht calls it).[102] This is in contrast to the dead Christians, who are naked (*gymnos*), bodiless, stripped (*ekdyō*; 5:3). Paul appears to prefer to be alive when Jesus returns.[103] Paul's longing to be clothed reiterates his esteem for bodily resurrection already argued in 1 Cor 15 against those in Corinth who had a derogatory or dismissive attitude toward the body. If Paul assumed that one receives the spiritual body at the moment of death,

---

98. Osei-Bonsu, "Intermediate State," 178. In my opinion Osei-Bonsu heavily overexegetes on a frequent basis. I present his case, however, in an effort to demonstrate various ways that people construe the evidence.

99. Ibid., 179.

100. See F. Blass and A. Debrunner, *A Greek Grammar of the New Testament and Other Early Christian Literature* (trans. and rev. by Robert W. Funk; Chicago: University of Chicago Press, 1961), 168: "In confident assertions regarding the future, a vivid, realistic present may be used for the future."

101. Cullmann, *Immortality or Resurrection?* 38.

102. Lambrecht, *Second Corinthians*, 83.

103. Osei-Bonsu, "Intermediate State," 180–81.

then, so the argument goes, he would not have expressed concern about the naked intermediate period.

But if Paul is concerned about being dead with its attendant nakedness, then why does he speak so highly of dying in 2 Cor 5:8, where he indicates that, in some way, the dead are closer to Christ than the living? He appears to express the same conviction in Phil 1:21–23: "For to me, living is Christ and dying is gain. If I am to live in the flesh, that means fruitful labor for me; and I do not know which I prefer. I am hard pressed between the two: my desire is to depart and be with Christ, for that is far better."

There are two puzzles in Osei-Bonsu's argument. First, nowhere else does Paul express concern about a bodiless existence after death and before the Parousia. From 1 Thess 4, his first letter, through 1 Cor 15, and Phil 1, to Rom 8, his final letter, Paul emphasizes the victory over death won by Christ such that nothing can separate the Christian from the love of God in Christ.[104] "Whether we live or whether we die, we are the Lord's" (Rom 14:8).

Second, to Osei-Bonsu, Paul appears to believe that he will be in the presence of the Lord immediately after death. If so, it appears that it would be in bodiless form. But I would argue that this is a problem since it would seem to contradict 1 Cor 15, where the emphasis is on *bodiliness* and waiting for *future* rewards. If Osei-Bonsu is correct, it would appear that Paul adopts the very Platonic dualism that he so vociferously contests elsewhere. This problem can be solved if we agree with Daniel Boyarin that Paul is dualistic but not in a Platonic way that disparages the body. That is, body and soul can be and are separated at death, but this is a negative state of affairs due to sin and will finally be put right at the resurrection, where the two are reunited.[105]

Roetzel claims that Paul, arguing against the opponents who deny any real distance between heaven and earth, divine and human existence, seeks to emphasize the distance, to draw attention to the painful reality of death. A balm is provided in the form of the Holy Spirit such that death's sting is deadened but its power to inflict itself on people remains until the eschaton. The fact that Paul is in polemical mode is further implied by 2 Cor 5:9–10, which warns of God's judgment. Paul believes he will pass muster. Do the Corinthians believe the opponents, imagining them victorious on judgment day? Or does Paul detect some trepidation that might make them reconsider his message?

---

104. In fact, Paul specifically lists "nakedness" as one of the things that will not separate us from the love of God in Christ Jesus (Rom 8:35).

105. Cf. Osei-Bonsu, "Intermediate State," 185.

One might take 2 Cor 5:10 to indicate that everyone will be raised and some will be sent to heaven and some to hell. But looking more closely, such a reading cannot stand. Paul says all "of us," by which he means Christians. Paul does not explicitly claim, as does Matthew, that everyone will be raised. If he does have universal resurrection in mind, he certainly does not depict anyone going to hell.

Problems with Argument 1

If 2 Cor 5:1–10 finds Paul holding forth on a doctrine of the intermediate state or a doctrine regarding the resurrection body and the timing of its receipt, then the following problems arise. First, it would appear that Paul is revising his grand position in 1 Cor 15, written only recently. If such is the case, then why does he not indicate this to the Corinthians? Why does he not use the same terms (physical body, spiritual body, resurrection, transformation, Christ's return, etc.) in 2 Cor 5 to suggest that it is a corrective to 1 Cor 15? Second, Argument 1 depends upon a psychological assessment of Paul as having become suddenly nervous about death, which does not seem consistent with a man who constantly speaks of facing mortal danger with confidence (cf. 1 Cor 15:30–31 and hardship lists: 1 Cor 4:11–13; 2 Cor 6:4–10; 11:22–27). According to Paul, his experience in Asia has given him more confidence, not less (2 Cor 1:9–10).

Argument 2

The second interpretive path (Furnish, Roetzel, Jewett) argues that the unit comprises 2 Cor 4:16–5:5 (or some close variation), having as its primary goal a simultaneous defense of Paul's ministry and a refutation of Paul's opponents, the "super-apostles" (11:5; 12:11), who have slunk in with a Panglossian gospel and turned the Corinthians away from the logic of the cross (*ho logos tou staurou*; 1 Cor 1:18) toward self-centered power and boasting. "Paul's rivals in Corinth promised what everyone desires — an immediate rescue from the one great absolute — death. By contrast, Paul's gospel spoke only of a future resurrection, coupled with a call to suffer with Christ in the present."[106]

Furnish argues that the earthly, tentlike house is synonymous with outer person (4:16b), mortal flesh (4:11), and body (4:10) subject to decay and death. By inner person, Paul signifies the "new creation" of 5:17, "the one whose life, no matter how miserable and adverse the conditions of its mortal existence, has been transformed by the resurrection life of Jesus through which God's own incomparable power is present and manifest (4:7, 10–12)."[107] Inner person and mind are used synonymously. By destruction, Paul

106. Roetzel, 18.
107. Furnish, *2 Corinthians,* 289.

means death.[108] The "building from God, a house not made with hands, eternal in the heavens" has been interpreted in three ways. First, it has been seen as the resurrection body provided for the believer either at the individual's death, at the resurrection, or at the final transformation into a spiritual body. Second, some have seen here a reference to the church such that it means believers are incorporated into Christ's body. Furnish opts for a third explanation previously proposed by Lang: the building from God comes from the apocalyptic milieu and connects to the temple of the new Jerusalem to which all of the righteous are destined to go. In this approach, Paul reiterates his earlier point that those who endure will receive abundant reward as well as the point that believers are to focus on what is unseen and eternal and not on temporary suffering. The purpose would be a hortatory call to persevere and stay the course. Furnish argues that Phil 3:12–21 makes the same argument, reminding believers that their true home is heaven.[109]

In treating 2 Cor 4:16–5:5, Furnish points out a close parallel between 4:17 and Rom 8:17: suffering precedes glory, faith relies on what is not seen (2 Cor 4:18; Rom 8:24–25), and God's provision of the Holy Spirit serves as a guarantee (2 Cor 5:5; Rom 8:23). Furnish distinguishes the groaning (*stenazō*, 2 Cor 5:2, 4), which points to the knowledge of a reality on the cusp of coming to realization, from the dualistic Hellenistic notion found, for example, in Epictetus, which exhorts people to overcome groaning by vanquishing the power of external circumstances.[110]

Furnish argues against the usual anthropological interpretation that sees "clothing oneself over (*ependyō*) with our heavenly dwelling" language (v. 2) to be a reference to a spiritual body, opting rather for a more broadly eschatological meaning that refers to a believer's mortal existence (and more to the point, to Paul's own mortal sufferings) between the two ages. Such an existence always has a moral connection for Paul. Taking this broader approach then allows Furnish to posit that Paul's choice to use two different words for clothing oneself is intentional; that is, *endyō* and *ependyō* are not synonymous. The *endyō* language refers primarily to a baptismal context, which is tied to moral transformation. Furnish concludes: "Therefore, given the context of the present passage (2 Cor 4:16–5:5), it would appear that the longing *to clothe ourselves over with our dwelling which comes from heaven* (v. 2 = v. 4, that '*mortality may be engulfed by life*') is the longing for the fulfillment of that salvation inaugurated at baptism."[111]

---

108. Others argue that the destruction refers to the Parousia, when the current body is destroyed and transformed. See ibid., 293.
109. Ibid., 294–95.
110. Ibid., 296.
111. Ibid., 297.

Paul interrupts his presentation with the comment about being naked in
5:3. The verse is problematic from a text-critical, grammatical, and therefore
interpretive point of view. There are two text-critical issues here. First, one
must decide whether to read *eiper* or *ei ge*. Whoever chooses the latter must
decide how to interpret the *kai* immediately following. Furnish considers the
kai to be separate and to link with what follows, rendering the phrase "pre-
supposing, of course."[112] Second, one must decide whether *ekdyō* (take off)
or *endyō* (clothe) is the original reading. *Endyō* is certainly better attested
externally (P[46], B C D[2] et al), but the *Textual Commentary* team chooses
to place *ekdyō* in the text, though with a D rating, arguing that *endyō*
makes little sense since it simply amounts to a tautology: "when we have
been clothed, we will not be naked."[113] Furnish argues instead for *endyō*
and points out, as we will see below, that the idea "having once clothed
ourselves we shall not be found naked" is not necessarily tautological.[114]

According to Furnish, some compare Paul's use of the word naked (*gymnos*) here with that in 1 Cor 15:37–38, the naked kernel, and argue that Paul
has been influenced by a Hellenistic dualism that speaks of the soul being
naked after sloughing off the body. This dualism has led Paul into fear about
a bodiless state between death and the Parousia.[115] Other interpreters say
that Paul uses naked in the sense of moral shame when standing in the presence of God on judgment day.[116] Furnish, however, argues differently. He
has established that the language of putting on clothing refers to baptism so
that *endyō* refers to the transformation begun at the believer's baptism (cf.
Gal 3:27) and *ependyō* refers to the longing for the fulfillment of the guarantee begun by receiving the Spirit during baptism. Hence, Furnish maintains:
"In this context nakedness would most naturally refer not to the 'nakedness
of the soul' at death (which is not the subject here), but to alienation from
Christ, to having in some way denied one's baptism."[117] Paul's comment,
which interrupts his discussion of the sighing, has a polemical edge. That
is, Paul speaks as though there may be some in Corinth who are not to be
reckoned among the clothed who have received the Spirit as a guarantee and
live and walk by said Spirit. Indeed, he may have the superapostles (or false
apostles) in mind and be warning the Corinthians to turn away from them.

The passage thus serves to highlight Paul's apostleship, to speak to the
reality of apostolic hardships, to emphasize the hope that belongs to all who,

112. Ibid., 267.
113. Bruce M. Metzger, *A Textual Commentary on the Greek New Testament* (2nd ed.; New
York: United Bible Societies, 1994).
114. Furnish, *2 Corinthians*, 268.
115. Ibid.
116. Ellis, "II Cor V 1–10," 219–21; Mathias Rissi, *Studien zum zweiten Korintherbrief:
Der alte Bund—Der Predigt—Der Tod* (ATANT; Zurich: Zwingli, 1969), 92.
117. Furnish, *2 Corinthians*, 268.

like Paul, have been baptized and received the Spirit and continue to walk by that Spirit in faith, not by sight. Meanwhile, they await the full completion of salvation, for which the Spirit has been given as a down payment. The fulfillment of all of this will arrive with the Parousia. This message is familiar, and Paul often repeats it in various times and places throughout his Epistles. Furnish's interpretation has the advantage of taking into account both precise exegetical considerations including text-critical, grammatical, philological, and literary observations (so he sees 4:16–5:5 as a defined unit, rather than 5:1–10 standing alone), as well as taking into account the Paul who emerges when the whole corpus is consulted. He is able to show, therefore, that far from exhibiting a strange, vastly out-of-character, unique moment of deep uncertainty that is diametrically opposed to the counsel Paul gives his congregants elsewhere, this passage is in keeping not only with Paul's theology as a whole, but also with his rhetorical style. The opponents against whom he argues can be found in the text itself without appeal to Jewish or Christian Gnosticism. Perhaps Furnish is correct when he states, "Here as elsewhere in this part of the letter the apologetic and polemical motifs have errant views of apostleship in view, not false notions about life after death."[118]

Second Corinthians 5:6–10

How, then, does Furnish relate vv. 6–10 to what precedes? Paul's language of being at home (*endēmein*) and away from home (*ekdēmein*) appears nowhere else in the NT or LXX, and he uses the language in different ways in this passage. Hence, Furnish argues that Paul has adopted the language of his opponents in order to correct them. If so, then the opponents would hold that being at home in the body is equivalent to being at home in the Lord, a position that we know led the Corinthians into immoral uses of their bodies. Moving them out of their realized eschatology into a more future-oriented eschatology, Paul insists that believers are still, in Sampley's title phrase, "walking between the times." Paul makes his point by taking an opposite position: while we are at home in the body, we are *away from* the Lord. This is similar to the statement he makes in v. 1, which also speaks to the in-between, longing state in which current believers find themselves.

Furnish senses that Paul is uncomfortable with his statement in verse 6b such that he interrupts the confidence language (which resumes in v. 8) to make the statement about faith and sight (v. 7). Against the common view, Furnish argues that Paul is not saying that faith is a stopgap provision until one attains sight in the eschaton, but rather that Paul is referring to two modes of living in the present: by faith (Paul and the believers) or by

---

118. Ibid., 300.

appearances (the superapostles and their followers). Rather than resuming the sentence begun in verse 6, Paul changes his tack. He does want to argue against those with a realized eschatology, but he does not want to imply that living in the body means alienation from life in Christ. Therefore, he moves away from the language of *location* and turns to language of *direction.* "The issue is not one's present place of residence but what one gives as one's 'home address,' what place claims one's loyalty, where one longs to go. The alternatives presented in v. 8b are *body/Lord,* and these correspond to the alternatives of 4:18, *things . . . seen/things . . . not seen,* and of 5:7, *appearance/faith.*"[119]

As usual, Paul closes the section with ethics. Simultaneously, Paul defends his own apostleship (he aims to please the Lord, not himself or any other human being) and exhorts the Corinthians to do the same. A difficulty in verses 9–10 has to do with Paul changing the way he uses the language of at home and away from home. In verse 6b he uses the language to correct his opponents, to create distance as it were between them and the Lord. In verse 8 he reconceives the language to avoid the implication that the distance is so great as to induce hopelessness. In verse 9 he abandons the troublesome language altogether. Because Paul does not supply any clarifying descriptors for the participles in verse 9, commentators have suggested some of their own, such as "in the body" or "with the Lord," to somehow align it with verse 6b. In doing so, however, Furnish argues that commentators are not sensitive to Paul's movement in the passage and actually make verse 9 then contradict verse 6b. "It seems likely that Paul intends to leave the object of the participles unclarified, precisely in order to be done with the imagery entirely. The effect of his formulation here, whether we are at home or away from home, is to relativize the matter of 'residency' so thoroughly as to dismiss it as an irrelevant issue. For him, what is alone important is whether one's service as an apostle (or as any ordinary believer) is finally adjudged acceptable to the Lord."[120]

Verse 10 indicates that a day of judgment will reveal the facts. There are difficulties in this verse, syntactical and otherwise. Particularly, the body language requires some interpretation. One might argue that Paul is reminding the Corinthians about the importance of morality, the proper use of one's body, an issue he has stressed in 1 Corinthians. Or perhaps he is concerned that his comments in verses 6 and 8, improperly understood, could lead the Corinthians to disregard the importance of the body. At any rate, Paul makes

---

119. Ibid., 302–3. Furnish warns against appealing to Phil 1:23 and 1 Thess 4:17, the contexts of which are quite different and in which being alive and being with Christ are exclusive; Phil 3:13, with its image of the life of discipleship as a race, comprises a better comparison to 2 Cor 5:6–10.

120. Ibid., 304.

it clear that their present behavior in the body matters. He is not interested in depicting a detailed scenario of reward and punishment. As usual, any comments he makes about the eschaton are merely for the sake of present conduct.

Summary of 2 Cor 5

In sum, as Furnish, Roetzel, and Jewett argue, Paul's argumentation in this passage is heavily determined by the nature of the opposition he is facing in Corinth. In defending his gospel, Paul makes these primary points:

1. Valid eschatology is future-oriented; overrealized eschatology is not tenable.
2. A bright future awaits believers.
3. The path to that future leads through the valley of the shadow of death.
4. Dead believers are somehow closer to Christ than are the living.
5. Understanding the nature of the resurrected spiritual body has ethical implications (5:15) and, therefore, eschatological implications related to judgment.
6. The Corinthians should return to Paul's teaching since he is a valid apostle, and they should eschew the teaching of the superapostles.

Philippians 1:18b–26

This passage contains a number of puzzles. First, whereas in 1 Cor 15 and elsewhere death is described as an enemy whose days are numbered, here death appears to be a friend since it means residence with Christ. Second, 1 Cor 15 emphasizes that believers are not resurrected until the Parousia, when they will attain immortality; but Phil 1 implies that immediately upon death the believer finds oneself "with Christ." What does this phrase mean? If it means that the "essential" part of a person, the soul, does not die, then Paul is in the realm of immortality, a position he argues against in 1 Cor 15. Let us work through the passage and take up important issues in turn.

The Philippian Community

Paul has founded the Philippian community around 50 CE. Paul writes the letter from prison to thank and praise the Philippians for their solicitousness toward him. Depending on which imprisonment theory one follows, Philippians was written either in the midfifties or early sixties.[121] The letter is irenic in tone and has been variously considered a letter of consolation, a

---

121. For the various arguments, see Bonnie Thurston and Judith M. Ryan, *Philippians and Philemon* (ed. Daniel J. Harrington; Collegeville, MN: Liturgical Press, 2005), 28–30. As mentioned earlier, Jewett, *Chronology*, espouses a 54–55 CE date for Philippians.

letter of friendship, or a family letter.[122] Certainly Paul's relationship with the Philippians differs greatly from his relationship with the Corinthian community.

The Passage

Is death a friend or an enemy for Paul? To judge only by 1 Corinthians, one would unequivocally have to call death an enemy since Paul expressly declares such at 15:26. Paul does not, as do many moderns, consider death "natural"; it is only a temporary phenomenon, and it coincides completely with the present rule of Satan on earth. God is in the business of life and salvation; Satan is in the business of death and sin. But what about Phil 1:18b–26, where Paul seems to contemplate his own death with elation, wistfully longing to depart this world?

> Yes, and I will continue to rejoice for I know that through your prayers and the help of the Spirit of Jesus Christ this will turn out for my deliverance. It is my eager expectation and hope that I will not be put to shame in any way, but that by my speaking with all boldness, Christ will be exalted now as always in my body, whether by life or by death. For to me, living is Christ and dying is gain. If I am to live in the flesh, that means fruitful labor for me; and I do not know which I prefer. I am hard pressed between the two: my desire is to depart and be with Christ, for that is far better; but to remain in the flesh is more necessary for you. Since I am convinced of this, I know that I will remain and continue with all of you for your progress and joy in faith, so that I may share abundantly in your boasting in Christ Jesus when I come to you again.

Here death has no sting. Deliverance (v. 19) may imply release from prison, vindication in the Roman trial, or "God's final approval of his life's work at his death."[123] By body (v. 20), Thurston takes Paul to mean the whole self that endures, rather than *sarx*, which is ephemeral. *Sarx* rather than *sōma* appears at verses 22 and 24. But in contrast to Thurston, Fee declares: "This hoped-for glorification of Christ will take place 'in my body,'

---

122. According to Thurston, *Philippians*, 34–38, Philippians is a consolation letter. In 1:12–21, Paul is trying to turn their minds away from the negative and toward the positive. Paul A. Holloway, "Notes and Observations *Bona Cogitare*: An Epicurean Consolation in Phil 4:8–9," *Harvard Theological Review* 91 (1998): 89–96, argues thus, calling the technique *avocatio-revocatio*. He also considers 1 Thessalonians as consolatory.

123. Thurston, *Philippians*, 62.

by which Paul intends his 'physical presence,' *not* his 'whole person' " (emphasis added).[124] Fee claims that Paul's use of body as "physical presence" makes the most sense since Paul is literally speaking of his body, which is in real physical danger.

The idea that "living is Christ and dying is gain" (v. 21) usually prompts commentators to cite Gal 2:20; Rom 6:3–11; and 2 Cor 5:2–8 as parallels of sorts. In Phil 1:23 Paul assumes that to die is to be with Christ. The notion of being "with Christ" is an interpretive morass without consensus. It would appear that Paul views death as a means of becoming closer to Christ. Thurston goes so far as to say: "The idea is like that encountered in Sufi poetry and Islamic mysticism, that death is the friend that takes one to God."[125] She finds the same sentiment in 2 Cor 5:1–10; life in the flesh creates a distance that death somehow bridges. Likewise, in Rom 8 Paul seems to eviscerate death by proclaiming that it cannot separate the believer from the love of God in Christ. For his part, Fee admits: "But what Paul understands by this is not so clear, and is therefore a clause around which considerable, but ultimately irresolvable, theological ferment has boiled.... At issue is the question of consciousness, for which in Paul we have no direct evidence one way or the other."[126] Fee surmises that Paul expected to be with Christ in full consciousness. He tries to solve the apparent contradiction or "tension," as he calls it, between this notion in Philippians (which he finds paralleled by 2 Cor 5) and the belief in future bodily resurrection by distinguishing between spatial and temporal elements in Paul's eschatology. A Christian is always with Christ, and this remains true, even in death. But death does not escort one into timeless existence. In a move reminiscent of the apostle himself at the end of the tortuous Rom 9–11 (see esp. 11:25) as well as at 1 Cor 15:51, Fee finally appeals to "mystery" and pastoral theology:

> Ultimately this matter lies in the area of mystery. At issue is the interplay between "time" and "eternity" involved in the implied period of "time" between death and resurrection. From our human perspective, earthbound and therefore time bound as it is, we cannot imagine "timeless" existence; whereas from the perspective of eternity/infinity these may very well be collapsed into a single "moment," as it were.

In any case, Paul understood death as a means into the Lord's immediate presence, which for him and countless thousands after him

---

124. Gordon D. Fee, *Paul's Letter to the Philippians* (Grand Rapids: Eerdmans, 1995), 137. Jewett (*Paul's Terms*, 253) argues that *sōma* here means the actual physical body "as the place where the suffering of the apostle is most plainly visible."

125. Thurston, *Philippians*, 64.

126. Fee, *Philippians* (Eerdmans), 148–49.

has been a comforting and encouraging prospect. Very likely he also expected such "gain" to include consciousness, and for most believers, that too has been a matter of encouragement — although in this case such a conclusion goes beyond the certain evidence we possess from Paul himself.[127]

I think that there are two main potential responses to the contradiction between Phil 1 and 1 Cor 15. First, Paul's message is determined by its particular context. In 1 Cor 15, he depicts the apocalyptic scenario, reminding the troubled and troubling Corinthians of this primary feature of his message: there will be a future judgment, at which time believers, including the Corinthians, will be held accountable for their behavior. Therefore, the Corinthians should quickly shape up their ethical act so as to receive the rich rewards that await believers in the eschaton. The genre is exhortation. On the other hand, when Paul writes the Philippians, he writes to console them and to show that ultimately death does not injure the Christian, Paul included. His own particular death is in mind rather than the day of judgment scenario of 1 Cor 15.

The second response is to differentiate Paul's language of death. Perhaps the best way to think about it is in terms of Death (with a capital *D*) and death (with a lowercase *d*). The lower case denotes individual deaths and sins. Paul speaks both of Sin and sin, Death and death. Death (capital *D*) is a personified being who acts in the cosmic apocalyptic drama. Personified Death may manifest itself through concrete political rulers; for example, those who killed Jesus and those who will kill Paul himself. Personified Death is the enemy. This comes from Paul's apocalyptic worldview. As long as the present evil age endures, any death, even a "good" death whereby suffering is brought to an end, must still be considered only "the lesser of two evils." Because Death is so fundamentally anti-God, it cannot be good in any absolute sense. This is why, Paul would argue, people experience a deflated numbness, a gaping hole after a loved one dies; because people are created by God, they are hardwired to "rage against the dying of the light."[128]

In the same way Paul personifies Sin, a close relative of Death.[129] Sin can dominate people, it has power to act of its own accord, and it is intentional and volitional. Thus Paul says in Romans: "Do not let [S]in exercise dominion in your mortal bodies, to make you obey their passions" (6:12). "Sin

---

127. Ibid., 149.
128. Dylan Thomas, "Do Not Go Gentle into That Good Night."
129. "Both Sin and Death are personified by Paul and perform as actors on the stage of man's history," writes Joseph A. Fitzmyer, "Pauline Anthropology," in *The Jerome Biblical Commentary* (ed. R. E. Brown, J. A. Fitzmyer, and R. E. Murphy; vol. 2; Englewood Cliffs: Prentice-Hall, 1968), 818. J. Louis Martyn's work on Paul's apocalyptic elements is unparalleled; see, for instance, his "Galatians' Role," esp. 524–40.

exercised dominion in death" (5:21). "Sin, seizing an opportunity in the commandment, produced in me all kinds of covetousness" (7:8). "It is no longer I that do it, but [S]in that dwells within me" (7:17).[130]

God is fundamentally a creator, a God of life. Because of this, anything that is antilife is opposed to God. This is why, according to Paul, Christians have the best of all possible worlds. On the one hand, they have every right to grieve over the death of a loved one; it is only mete since in their deepest being and understanding of God, they feel and know that Death is not God's will; Death is an enemy, not a friend. "So, grieve and grieve hard, fully, and loudly," Paul would say. But because it is certain that Death's days are numbered, that Jesus Christ has defeated Death and we are simply watching the final act play itself out, Christians cannot grieve as those who have no hope would grieve (1 Thess 4:13). Grieve, but do not despair. Grieve, but recognize and even proclaim the temporary nature of such pain. Such is the advice from Paul.

Further encouragement comes from Paul's conviction that death can actually bring one closer to Christ. Paul even claims that it is abundantly and exceedingly far better to die and be with Christ (*syn Christō einai*; Phil 1:23). Under the 1 Cor 15 model, I spoke of death as "the lesser of two evils"; Phil 1:23, however, depicts dying as the better of two goods: "I am hard pressed between the two: my desire is to depart and be with Christ, for that is far better" (*synechomai de ek tōn dyo, tēn epithymian echōn eis to analysai kai syn Christō einai, pollō [gar] mallon kreisson*). If this means being with Christ immediately following death, then it is the only place in Paul that does not refer to this reunion as taking place in the eschaton (cf. 1 Thess 4:13–14, 17; 5:10; Rom 6:8; 2 Cor 4:14; 13:4). Given Paul's insistence that the resurrection body is bestowed only at the resurrection and given Paul's anthropological dualism, it is reasonable to assume that Paul implies a disembodied intermediate state, followed by the reunion of the body and soul at the Parousia.[131]

Again, Boyarin's article is instructive. He begins by comparing Paul to Philo: Paul "is mobilized by as thoroughgoing a dualism as that of Philo."[132] Unlike Philo, though, Paul never denigrates the body. Taking up 2 Cor 5:1–4, Boyarin points out Paul's distinction between the earthly body and the heavenly body: "The image of the human being that Paul maintains is of a soul dwelling in or clothed by a body, and, however valuable the garment, it

---

130. For an excellent presentation on Sin and Death, see Grieb, *Story of Romans*, 64–79.

131. I use the word "implies" advisedly here because the claim I am making is controversial. Different denominations (not to mention scholars) take different stances toward such claims; in addition, some are preoccupied with the details of it while others barely acknowledge the subject.

132. Boyarin, "Genealogy of Gender," 17.

is less essential than that which it clothes. It is 'the earthly tent that we live in'; it is not *we*. The body, while necessary and positively valued by Paul, is, as in Philo, not the human being but only his or her house or garment."[133] Thus, to "depart" is to die, and to be "with Christ" is to be absent from the body.

The Philippians passage elicits at least two questions similar to those provoked by 2 Cor 5. First, there is the theological and anthropological question regarding whether one is conscious between death and resurrection. Some would insist that Paul must imagine the dead believers to be asleep, in a state of unconsciousness (soul sleep). Such an argument takes seriously Paul's conviction of the "not yet" aspect of Christian life; death still stings, and Christians do not receive the prize until the resurrection (Cullmann, Jackson).[134] Proponents of this view would argue that if the believer immediately moves consciously into the presence of Christ upon death, then immortality has been achieved before the Parousia; this does not cohere with 1 Cor 15. Others would argue that believers go through stages: upon death each is ushered into the presence of Christ in a conscious state (Fee, et al.), but this state is still within time, and the "not yet" aspect is maintained since no one receives a body or achieves immortality and eternality until the Parousia.[135]

Paul has certain pastoral concerns, theological convictions, and messages to convey with each statement. Rather than trying to make them all completely consistent, we must ask about the reason for each statement given the social context of each letter.

BELIEVERS IN HEAVEN

Paul does not answer the question about whether non-Christians of various sorts are going to hell. In Paul's theology no one goes to hell. Those who believe in Christ receive bodily resurrection and eternal life in intimate relationship with Christ. Where will this relationship with Christ take place?

---

133. Ibid., 18. He also argues that Phil 1:19–26 is analogous to 2 Cor 5 with respect to Pauline anthropology.

134. Jackson, *An Investigation*, is guided by a conservative evangelical agenda that seeks a "proper thanatology," and which insists from the outset that there can be no inconsistency in Paul: "One must be careful not to accept any idea which would suggest the apostle Paul was later correcting an earlier mistaken eschatological view" (3n6). He states his agenda strongly: "It is my desire that this work will serve to help the lay person, the pastor, and the teacher reevaluate current thanatological beliefs and, if need be, realign those beliefs with New Testament teaching" (preface, v.). So one finds a coercive element to his argument as well as the notion that the entire NT teaches the same thing. In addition, "The purpose of this work is to establish the reality of an 'interim' period."

135. Gordon D. Fee, *Philippians* (IVPNTC; Downers Grove, IL: InterVarsity, 1999), 72. I think that Fee moves far beyond what Paul has written here.

Paul envisions multilayered heavens, as indicated by 2 Cor 12, and he believes in "Paradise," although the word occurs only once in the Pauline corpus (2 Cor 12:4). In fact, it appears only three times in the NT (cf. Luke 23:43; Rev 2:7) so it is unlikely to have played a significant role in visions of the afterlife among NT Christians. Furthermore, of the 273 occurrences of *ouranos* (heaven) in the NT, only eleven are found in the undisputed Pauline letters.[136]

THE FATE OF UNBELIEVERS

Do the Pauline letters suggest a resurrection of the unrighteous followed by their annihilation, or does he envision no resurrection for nonbelievers? It is impossible to say. Because Paul never directly addresses the ultimate fate of non-Christians, any argument must be made from silence abetted by a few stray verses. It would appear that the main options are as follows:

Possibility 1: Annihilation

At the resurrection only believers arise; unbelievers simply do not rise. While Paul consigns no one to hell, he does seem to imagine extinction or "annihilation" or "destruction" for unbelievers (Rom 9:22), that is, a ceasing of existence rather than some state of perpetual punishment of which the wicked are conscious.[137] This idea is present also in a roughly contemporaneous document, the *Psalms of Solomon* (end of the first century BCE). Like Paul, this author expects a time of judgment based on works with concomitant raising up of the righteous and continued existence in the presence of God: "The destruction of the sinner is forever, and he will not be remembered when (God) looks after the righteous. This is the share of sinners forever, but those who fear the Lord shall rise up to eternal life, and their life shall be in the Lord's light, and it shall never end" (3:11–12; *OTP* 2:655).

Possibility 2: Universal Salvation — All Rise and All Are Saved

As mentioned earlier, Paul may have universal salvation in mind. This would render comprehensible his language about God finally being "all in all" (1 Cor 15:28). In addition, various passages from Romans would be explained:

---

136. Of the six disputed letters, *ouranos* appears four times in Ephesians, five times in Colossians, and once in 2 Thessalonians.

137. According to BDAG, *apōleia* (Rom 9:22) can mean "hell" as well as destruction. One can see this, e.g., in A. Oepke, "*apōleia*," *TDNT* 1:396–97, who says of this word: "What is meant here is not a simple extinction of existence, but an everlasting state of torment and death." This does not cohere with Paul's thought. This is presumably why translators do not capitalize the word in Paul.

There is no distinction since all have sinned and fall short of the glory of God; they are now justified by his grace as a gift, through the redemption that is in Christ Jesus, whom God put forward as a sacrifice of atonement by his blood, effective through faith. (Rom 3:22b–25a)

Just as one man's trespass led to condemnation for all, so one man's act of righteousness leads to justification and life for all. (Rom 5:18)

God has imprisoned all in disobedience so that he may be merciful to all. (Rom 11:32)

Other passages to be considered are Rom 8:38–39; 1 Cor 13:4–8; Phil 2:10–11.

Possibility 3: It Remains a Mystery

If the reader will momentarily entertain an argument (somewhat from silence), I suggest that our wisest move is to follow Paul's own lead from Paul's language of mystery (*mystērion*) found in 1 Cor 15:51. Finite human logic (as opposed to the logic of the cross) takes one only so far, and not impressively far at that. Paul again finally concedes to mystery in Rom 11:25, after an energetic quest to establish indubitably what God will do with the non-Christians closest to his own heart: his Jewish compatriots. His final move? Humility paired with doxology:

O the depth of the riches and wisdom and knowledge of God! How unsearchable are his judgments and how inscrutable his ways! "For who has known the mind of the Lord? Or who has been his counselor?" "Or who has given a gift to him, to receive a gift in return?" For from him and through him and to him are all things. To him be the glory forever. Amen. (Rom 11:33–36)

It may be that Paul envisions a universal resurrection, and we do not know what happens to the non-Christians. In Acts, Paul envisions resurrection for the righteous and unrighteous (24:14–15). One might argue that since Paul speaks of himself as a Pharisee in Phil 3:5 (cf. Luke in Acts 23:6), and since the Pharisees imagined a resurrection for all, therefore it is likely that Paul did as well. But Paul certainly modifies his beliefs in numerous other ways that contradict his earlier Pharisaism, so why not here? In the undisputed letters, however, Paul never expressly speaks of unbelievers being resurrected, so the data would argue against his belief in such a general resurrection.

CONCLUSION

What Paul Says

Regarding death and afterlife, Paul teaches that, with the exception of those who are alive when Christ returns, Christians should expect to die. Neither the dead nor the living Christian has an advantage since death cannot separate the Christian from the love of God in Christ. "To live is Christ, and to die is gain" (Phil 1:21 KJV). To die is to be with Christ, and to live is to be with Christ. Whether in the thought of Paul the dead Christian is *conscious* in any way has been ground for much debate. Those who argue for what is commonly called "soul sleep" maintain that the Christian is not conscious. The benefit of such an argument is that it takes death seriously. If the Christian immediately after death is transferred to a conscious life with Christ, then the Parousia is robbed of its significance, and the doctrine of immortality has vanquished that of resurrection. Others (e.g., Fee) claim that the Christian is in conscious union with Christ immediately upon death, and that part of the problem may lie in the concept of time and eternity with which exegetes interpret Paul. Still others (e.g., Furnish) maintain that Paul never addresses the so-called intermediate state.

With regard to the body and a bodily state, in 1 Cor 15 Paul clearly argues for a future bodily resurrection to occur at the Parousia. First Jesus returns, then dead Christians arise and, joined by living Christians, they meet Christ in the air (1 Thess 4:16–17). Then comes the end, in which everything that is anti-God (powers, rulers, Death) will be destroyed (1 Cor 15:24–26), and God's created order will be renewed (Rom 8). Since God saw fit to create bodies in the beginning, so will God create or re-create those bodies in the new beginning.

Some take 2 Cor 5:1–10 to mean that Christians are in a postmortem, conscious, bodiless state, a state the apostle hopes to avoid. As this argument goes, naked (*gymnos*, v. 3) means without a body, and Paul's anxiety over being naked or bodiless implies that he will be conscious after death (why would he be worried unless he thought that he would be conscious of the nakedness?). Others argue that, in the interim between writing 1 and 2 Corinthians, Paul has had an opportunity to contemplate more fully his own death and has changed his mind, deciding that Christians will receive bodies immediately upon their individual deaths.

In the end, it is not possible to ascertain whether Paul considered the Christian to be conscious or unconscious, embodied or disembodied during the time between death and the Parousia. I think the evidence leans most heavily toward a notion of unconscious pneumatic disembodied existence with Christ in the interim.[138] At the Parousia the Christians receive new, eternal bodies. Because Paul expected the Parousia imminently, the question "What happens when a person dies?" was most likely not primary among the subjects he wished to address.

Paul is even less interested in the question "What happens to non-Christians when they die?" He never mentions hell or any other "place" where non-Christians will suffer forever. He may envision them merely ceasing to exist at death, which would amount to "destruction." Some would argue that Paul has in mind a universal salvation whereby eventually everyone will be saved and granted eternal life (Trumbower). In doing so they draw particularly upon the "all [*pas*]" language of Rom 11:32: "God has imprisoned all in disobedience so that he may be merciful to all."[139] I suggest that it remains a mystery in the Pauline sense. God knows; we, on the other hand, "see through a glass, darkly" (1 Cor 13:12 KJV). Because Paul was writing to and for Christians, he never treats the subject of the fate of non-Christians directly.

Why Paul Says It

In the end, it may be just as interesting to ask not only what Paul says but why he says it. In her provocative study, Claudia Setzer names numerous ways that beliefs in resurrection function, and many of her insights apply to the present investigation.[140] First, Setzer argues that, as a symbol, resurrection condenses a worldview. It is shorthand for a set of attendant beliefs. As indicated above, Paul simultaneously uses bodily resurrection to undermine power plays in the church and in the world:

> The work of Horsley, Elliott, Martin, and Wright helps us understand Paul's use of resurrection, his claim that it is not the immortal *pneuma* that is the site of God's power, but the fragile *sōma*.... These scholars have demonstrated how Paul co-opts the imperial and military language and substitutes an entirely different set of symbols: not the emperor, but the crucified criminal; not the strong, but the weak; not worldly wisdom, but foolishness; not the citizen assembly of the *polis*, but the *ekklēsia* of believers; not the immortal *pneuma*, but the earthy

---

138. Recall Dale Martin's argument (*Corinthian Body*, 17–23) that the *pneuma* endures, though not the *sōma* or *psychē*.

139. See Trumbower, *Rescue for the Dead*, 40–41. The debate over universal salvation would be conducted vigorously in later centuries, with Origen, Gregory of Nyssa, and Hosea Ballou (nineteenth century, Universalist Church) arguing in favor of it, and most others rejecting it. See Trumbower, ibid., ch. 6, "Posthumous Progress and Universal Salvation," 109–25. Another engaging treatment, "Dare We Hope for the Salvation of All? Origen, St. Gregory of Nyssa, and St. Isaac the Syrian," is in Kallistos Ware, *The Inner Kingdom* (Crestwood, NY: St. Vladimir's Seminary Press, 2000), 193–215.

140. Much of the following comes from Setzer, *Resurrection of the Body*, 65–75.

sōma. Paul's apocalyptic language paints a broad picture into which his hearers can plug the particulars of Rome: the emperor, the local aristocracy, and the system of patronage as well as the program of an emerging alternative community.[141]

Second, resurrection is an imprecise and abstract symbol and thus contains room for variety. Paul does have limits; one may not need to subscribe to a precise notion of the spiritual body, but one does need to subscribe to some kind of bodily resurrection.[142] Because of this fact, we can say that belief in resurrection draws boundaries. In 1 Cor 15 Paul insists that Christians believe in a bodily resurrection.

Belief in resurrection constructs community, and implicit in such defining beliefs is countercultural behavior, such as participating in worship, not sleeping with prostitutes, not suing, and so on. Paul fashions his view of resurrection in part from the tool kit of Jewish culture. Belief in resurrection confers legitimacy on those who preach it ("I handed on to you..."; 1 Cor 11:23; 15:3). If resurrection is not true, then Paul is washed up, and he and the Corinthians alike are to be pitied. However, since resurrection is true, Paul is proved to have authority and to authentically represent God and God's gospel.

Resurrection solves a number of problems, one of which is theodicy. Resurrection allows its adherents to live in the world, full of evil as it is, and to persevere in the knowledge that God is about to set all things right by fully inaugurating God's good kingdom.[143] As in the case of Josephus, Tertullian, and others, a single author may evince more than one view. The question becomes, what is the payoff of each view for the author? For Paul, those accrued benefits fall into four overlapping categories: theological, apologetic, pastoral, and ethical.

Theological Reasons

1. As the Creator, God is glorified by the notion of bodily resurrection. Because the good God chose to create bodies, then bodies must be good. Given Paul's apocalyptic views, he imagines that the end will be like the beginning. The creation stories pervade his writings from discussions concerning gender and sexuality (1 Cor 11:8–9), to the

---

141. Ibid., 67.

142. The reader must be aware that "physical" and "bodily" are not synonyms. Though I do not necessarily agree with all or most of their arguments (favoring Schneiders much more than Chilton), this important distinction appears in both Sandra Schneiders, "The Resurrection (of the Body) in the FG: A Key to Johannine Spirituality," in *Life in Abundance: Studies in Tribute to Raymond E. Brown, S.S.* (ed. John R. Donahue; Collegeville, MN: Liturgical Press, 2005), 168–98; and Bruce Chilton, "Resurrection in the Gospels," in *Death, Life-after-Death, Resurrection, and the World-to-Come* (ed. Avery-Peck and Neusner), 215–39.

143. Setzer, *Resurrection of the Body*, 66–70.

reason for sin (15:22; 2 Cor 5), to the power of the Holy Spirit to precipitate "a new creation" (*kainē ktisis*; Gal 4:6; 5:25; 6:15), to the fallen nature of the world (Rom 8), and so on.[144]

2. God alone, not Rome, is sovereign even to the degree that God can destroy not only political powers, but also Death itself. Despite appearances to the contrary, God is currently involved in history; God has not abandoned God's people. God is just and will, ultimately, put all things in order, enacting a thoroughgoing justice.

3. In citing Scripture as part of his argument, Paul assumes and thus teaches that Scripture is authoritative in some way for believers.

4. Platonizing or Gnosticizing notions that denigrate the body are eschewed by those who believe in the resurrection of the body.

Apologetic Reasons

Paul's apostolic authority rests upon the truth of the resurrection (1 Cor 15:12–19).

Pastoral Reasons

1. Paul's doctrine of resurrection followed by immortality takes seriously the power of death and the believers' anguish and fear concerning it, both for themselves and for those who have already died (1 Thess 4). He teaches that proportionate grief is appropriate.

2. Assurance of future immortality provides hope (*elpis*), a key characteristic of Paul's good-news message. In a world dominated by the Roman Empire, under which the apostle himself was probably martyred, resurrection served as a social coping strategy. Setzer makes the following comments about the Pharisees' teaching on resurrection that, *mutatis mutandis*, also apply to Paul the Pharisee:

> Resurrection carried with it a set of affirmations about God's power, ultimate justice, vindication of the righteous and punishment of the wicked. Yet it could seem innocent to an outsider, and as Josephus shows, it could be packaged to sound like the Greco-Roman idea of the immortality of the soul. For the people who looked to the Pharisees as their patrons or representatives it would be a shorthand that reassured them of the continuing power of the God of Israel and Scripture's story, as well as their own eventual vindication. For the local Roman bureaucrat or

144. Regarding the Genesis creation accounts in Paul's writings, see Boyarin, "Genealogy of Gender," and N. T. Wright, *The Resurrection of the Son of God* (Minneapolis: Fortress, 2003), 334.

his deputies, it would be an innocuous belief, perhaps not recognizably different from Greco-Roman ideas of immortality. For the Pharisees and their successors it serves as a useful tool in the symbolic construction of community in a period of social change.[145]

3. Comforting is Paul's message that for believers, intimate connection with Jesus begins immediately and cannot be disrupted, even by death. Paul can be confusing, however, because he really has a notion of *degrees* of separation or intimacy with the Lord. So, while it is true that nothing can fully separate believers from Christ, Paul has in mind being "with Christ" and "even more with Christ," or "close to Christ" and "closer to Christ." Hence, while all believers are with Christ no matter what their circumstances, those who have died are closer than those who have not. In his famous essay, Cullmann declares: "1 Corinthians 15 has been sacrificed for the *Phaedo*" (8), by which he means that Paul's teaching about resurrection has been eclipsed by modern adoption of immortality, a position that Cullmann finds to be opposed to Paul.[146] As it turns out, pitting the terms "resurrection" and "immortality" against one another as binary opposites may be less helpful than arguing along a spectrum, with the goal being proximity to Christ.

Ethical Reasons

Because resurrected believers will be judged according to their deeds on the Day of the Lord, they should behave ethically in this world.

---

145. Setzer, *Resurrection of the Body*, 36.
146. Cullmann, *Immortality or Resurrection?*

– T H R E E –

DEATH AND AFTERLIFE
IN THE FOURTH GOSPEL

T HIS CHAPTER will be laid out somewhat differently from the others.
First, I will discuss death and afterlife in the Fourth Gospel (FG) by
means of a conversation with an earlier Johannine scholar, John A. T. Robinson.[1] Second, I will argue that the Fourth Evangelist (FE) may have been in
conversation with Epicurean ideas concerning death and afterlife. Though
the latter is somewhat speculative, it will exemplify how one might explore
the influence of Hellenistic philosophy on NT authors.[2] Finally, I will glean
the possible functions of the death and afterlife material for the community
of the FG.[3]

◆ ◆ ◆

PART 1:
A CONVERSATION WITH
JOHN A. T. ROBINSON

In 1962 John A. T. Robinson republished an essay of 1957 as "The New
Look on the Fourth Gospel," listing five presuppositions of the (then) "current critical orthodoxy on the Fourth Gospel."[4] Under presupposition 4 —

---

1. An earlier version of portions of this chapter appears as Jaime Clark-Soles, " 'I Will
Raise [Whom?] Up on the Last Day': Anthropology as a Feature of Johannine Eschatology," in
New Currents through John: A Global Perspective (ed. Francisco Lozada Jr. and Thomas W.
Thatcher; Atlanta: Society of Biblical Literature, 2006), 29–53. Used by permission of the
Society of Biblical Literature.
2. I am currently shaping a monograph tentatively entitled *John and the Popular Philosophers* that develops further the idea that the FE converses with various forms of Hellenistic
philosophy.
3. For a full presentation of my views on the community of the FG, see Jaime Clark-Soles,
Scripture Cannot Be Broken: The Social Function of the Use of Scripture in the Fourth Gospel
(Boston: Brill Academic Publishers, 2003).
4. John A. T. Robinson, "The New Look at the Fourth Gospel," in *Papers Presented to
the International Congress on "The Four Gospels in 1957" Held at Christ Church, Oxford,
1957* (ed. K. Aland et al.; Studia evangelica 1; Texte und Untersuchungen zur Geschichte der
altchristlichen Literatur 73; Berlin: Akademie Verlag, 1959): 338–50; repr. as "The New Look

that the FG represents only the latest stage of theological development in first-century Christianity — Robinson addresses eschatology. In his estimation, "critical orthodoxy" assumes that John has finally achieved a realized eschatology; "critical orthodoxy" further asserts that the final form of FG sloughs off the "crude adventism" of an earlier apocalyptic eschatology. In contrast, Robinson argues that neither Jesus nor the primitive church held an apocalyptic eschatology; rather, apocalyptic eschatology, which distinctly emphasizes a future, second advent of Christ, developed only gradually: "The Synoptists witness to a progressive apocalypticization of the message of Jesus."[5]

Robinson thus argues against "critical orthodoxy" in claiming that FG actually reflects an earlier, nonapocalyptic phase quite in line with Jesus himself. This would mean, then, that the reference to Christ's return found in John 21 is *not* the remains of an early, first-stratum apocalyptic eschatology that the author has failed to bury entirely. Rather, according to Robinson, FG has no future, apocalyptic eschatology in its first stratum of theological thinking (a layer already fully formed but not committed to writing by Paul's time). Instead, Robinson argues, the strains of apocalyptic found in FG crept in only after "the Johannine tradition" (which lies behind and is quite distinct from the text known as FG) originally located in "the relative isolation of its Palestinian milieu" came into contact with "the more cosmopolitan world of Asia Minor."[6] That contact, he argues, resulted in the accretion of apocalyptic elements not originally present, thus causing the Johannine tradition finally to participate in the growing trend toward the "apocalyptic *faux pas*."[7] The final stage of the Johannine literature, Robinson contends, is represented by the thoroughgoing apocalypticism of Revelation. In this essay, I will argue for "a still more excellent way" to approach the subject of Johannine eschatology.

Robinson's discussion of Johannine eschatology centers exclusively on a diachronic methodology, trying to understand John's eschatology by positing very early layers of theological rumination, followed by the bulk of the written Gospel, followed by an "epilogue" (John 21). To compel readers to accept his idea that the FE is in conversation with a growing tendency toward a doctrine of the Parousia (Christ's second coming), Robinson would need to argue the case in much finer detail: In conversation with whom, specifically? Where? At one level, Robinson answers the question when he refers to "the more cosmopolitan world of Asia Minor," but this answer

---

on the Fourth Gospel," *Twelve New Testament Studies* (London, SCM Press, 1962), 94–106 (cited below).

5. Robinson, "New Look" (1962), 103.
6. Ibid.
7. Ibid.

is too vague to be meaningful. Why would Robinson imagine apocalyptic thought as more prominent in Asia Minor than in Palestine, especially given his heavy reliance on the Dead Sea Scrolls? Robinson would further need to reflect upon whose best interest is served by a doctrine of the Parousia.

Writing in the 50s, Paul already had a notion of the Parousia (cf. 1 Cor 15; 1 Thess 4). If FG's initial theology was already developed by the time of Paul, as Robinson maintains, then why should one *not* assume that John also had a doctrine of the Parousia at the earliest stage? Robinson argues that "the Johannine tradition" followed a wholly independent trajectory ("Indeed, he *is* his own tradition"[8]) that bypassed Paul and leads directly back to Jesus. But the presence of apocalyptic elements in FG could just as easily support the conclusion that John and Paul come from a similar trajectory, one that was apocalyptic at an early stage. If Robinson adjudicates the matter by assuming that the southern Palestinian trajectory must be different from the Pauline trajectory, this would be problematic on at least two quite different counts. First, as indicated above, the Dead Sea Scrolls community in southern Palestine is extremely apocalyptic, so the notion of southern Palestine as isolated from apocalyptic thought does not stand. Second, the notion of southern Palestine as "isolated" is easily contested by reference to the works of Josephus, if not by Paul's own letters, which attest to social exchange between the Palestinian churches and those outside of Palestine.

Finally, that Robinson looks to Revelation as part of his diachronic picture of the development of Johannine thought is now peculiar, for what has Revelation to do with FG? Though his article is certainly helpful, insightful, and multifariously informative, much of Robinson's eschatological argument is too hypothetical.

In what follows I will avoid the language so prominent in Robinson's article and common to many diachronic analyses, such as "remarkably primitive" versus "extraordinarily mature," or "essential maturity" versus "formal maturity." Furthermore, rather than continue endless debate about source-critical issues or which eschatology the historical Jesus likely held, I will explore the ways in which understanding FG's *anthropology* might illuminate the study of its eschatology. By "anthropology," I refer to a question that occupied the minds of philosophers and theologians alike in antiquity just as it does today: What is a human being? As feminist, gender, and postcolonial studies have taught us, not everyone signifies the same thing when using the language of personhood. In what follows I will provide some preliminary soundings regarding the composition of human beings according to FG, but only with a view to informing the discussion of their fate. The

---

8. Ibid., 98.

thesis of this disquisition is that the FG maintains a *bestowed, realized immortality* for believers rather than a doctrine of future resurrection. I will return to this claim at the conclusion of this chapter.

THE COMPOSITION OF HUMAN BEINGS

The Fourth evangelist does not present her or his anthropology under the categories of logic, ethics, and physics, the traditional triumvirate among Hellenistic philosophers. Rather, one must piece together the FE's view of the person by attending to the language present in, and perhaps even the language absent from, the text of FG. A large section of Robert Jewett's *Paul's Anthropological Terms* is devoted to an analysis of individual anthropological terms: *sarx* (flesh), *pneuma tou anthrōpou* (human spirit), *sōma* (body), *kardia* (heart), *psychē* (soul), *nous* (mind), *exō / esō anthrōpos* (outer/inner person), and *syneidēsis* (conscience/consciousness).

I will take a similar approach here, guided by several precautions in my analysis of the relevant Johannine anthropological terms. First, I warn against what Jewett calls "the lexical method," which abstracts words from their literary and historical contexts.[9] Instead, one must take into account the literary context of the sentence, the paragraph, and the document as a whole; relate the terms to the historical situation (including the author's battle against opponents, which may dictate some of the terms chosen); and relate the terms to the linguistic horizon of the first century. Second, one must engage in the comparative task. What might we learn from the Hebrew Bible, consolation literature, medical texts, and Hellenistic religion and philosophy? Third, one must account not simply for the strict meaning of a term but also for any discernible fluctuations in meaning.[10] Following these guidelines, I will analyze FG's anthropological vocabulary, looking particularly for clues to the FE's eschatological outlook.

The Johannine Terms

Four times the Johannine Jesus repeats his promise to raise up the believer "on the last day" (*en tē eschatē hēmera*), all in chapter 6 (vv. 39, 40, 44, 54). Jesus refers again to this "last day" at 12:48, where he indicates that his word *will* judge (*krinei*) the nonbeliever. What is the nature of the believer, such that on this "last day" one will be raised? When does the author envision the occurrence of this "last day"? Is the believer to continue some sort of existence after dying? To answer such questions, one must understand what

---

9. Robert Jewett, *Paul's Anthropological Terms: A Study of Their Use in Conflict Settings* (Leiden: Brill, 1971), 6–8.
10. Ibid., 6–7.

the author means by such terms as *sarx* ("flesh"; and closely related, *haima*, "blood"), *pneuma* (spirit), *anthrōpos* (person, human being), *sōma* (body), *psychē* (soul), *kardia* (heart), *noeō* (perceive, comprehend), and *koilia* (belly, womb).[11]

For the sake of brevity, let me state directly a number of conclusions, moving quickly over the least important to more significant features. (1) The terms *gynē* (woman, female) and *anēr* (man, male) do not factor into a discussion of anthropology in a way that affects the FE's eschatology. (2) *Koilia* and *noeō* occur only infrequently in FG. (3) *Nous* (mind) does not appear at all in FG, which is surprising given (a) its customary role in anthropological discussions as evidenced not only by other biblical authors but also by Hellenistic philosophers, and (b) the FE's general interest in knowledge (*ginōskō; gnōsis*). (4) The FE never applies *kardia* to Jesus, only to his disciples, and the term always maintains the OT range of meaning for "heart" (*lēb*), the seat of emotions, understanding, and volition.[12] (5) *Psychē, sarx* (to which *haima* relates closely), *sōma, pneuma,* and *anthrōpos* are key features of the FE's anthropology. (6) Four of the FE's key anthropological terms — *psychē, sarx, haima,* and *anthrōpos* — are used of both Jesus and others, whereas *pneuma* and *sōma* are used *only* in reference to Jesus. Thus, the FE's anthropology categorizes Jesus as both similar to and different from human beings; he is both divine and human, God enfleshed. (7) Aspects of these terms/categories overlap with one another.

Although one can imagine various fruitful ways to present the discussion — for example, by discussing the terms in the order of their appearance in the text — I will analyze FG's anthropological terms in descending order of usage frequency.

In a total of six ways, the FE variously uses *anthrōpos*

1. as the generic word for an individual person or for humanity in general, before value judgments are attached and categories of believers and unbelievers obtain. In John 16:21, the FE speaks of a woman giving birth to an *anthrōpos,* not to a soul, mind, or spirit. The Samaritan woman testifies about Jesus to *anthrōpoi* (4:28), and Nicodemus wants to know how an *anthrōpos* can reenter the womb (3:27). I initially assumed that passages such as 2:10 and 5:7 fall under this category as well, but now I am not so sure. In 2:10 the steward observes that an *anthrōpos* serves the good wine first. True enough, but as the reader

---

11. "Flesh, in John's anthropology, is not a part of the human but the human being as natural and mortal," writes Sandra M. Schneiders, "The Resurrection (of the Body) in the FG: A Key to Johannine Spirituality," in *Life in Abundance: Studies of John's Gospel in Tribute to Raymond E. Brown, S.S.* (ed. John R. Donahue; Collegeville, MN: Liturgical Press, 2005).

12. Hans W. Wolff, *Anthropology of the Old Testament* (trans. Margaret Kohl; Philadelphia: Fortress, 1974), 40–58.

comes to learn in the unfolding narrative, Jesus, who provides abundant wine for the wedding feast, is much more than *anthrōpos*. This may be an example of Johannine irony. If the steward had known who Jesus was, he might have asked Jesus for living wine, or wine that does not perish. At 5:7 the lame man at Bethesda has no *anthrōpos* to help him attain healing. True enough, but Jesus, who is much more than an *anthrōpos*, is available to heal him. Again, I think this is an example of *Doppeldeutung* (double meaning).

2. negatively of human beings. For instance, its usage overlaps that of *sarx* (treated below) in a sinister sense when we learn at John 2:25 that Jesus did not need anyone to testify concerning human beings because he knew what was in the human being, presumably qua human being. The FE may have Gen 6:5–6 and 8:21 in mind. At John 17:6 *anthrōpos* approximates the more neutral meaning of *sarx* when Jesus designates his followers as the "*anthrōpoi* whom you [the Father] gave to me out of the world" (au. trans.).

3. for a specific individual: "There was a *person* whose name was John" (1:6, au. trans.); Jesus met "a *person* blind from birth" (9:1, au. trans.). The term *anēr* is never used to refer to a specific male individual; only *anthrōpos* is used in such contexts. By contrast, the word *anthrōpos* is never used of a specific female individual. When women are referred to at all, as in chapter 4, gender is indicated: *gynē* (woman). Presumably this bespeaks the common cultural assumption that male is the default of "person," while female, as the "other" or unusual part of the equation, requires some secondary or specific identification. Thus in chapter 4 the storyteller displays some discomfort with the Samaritan woman's otherness, or flags some sense of it. Why tell us she is a woman of Samaria rather than an *anthrōpos* of Samaria? If the author had used *anthrōpos* of this character, first-century readers would probably have pictured a male. Though I do think the author maintains patriarchal assumptions (cf. 6:10), I do not think that these assumptions factor into the FE's eschatology. Neither the Samaritan woman nor Mary Magdalene (ch. 20) must "become male" (cf. *Gos. Thom.* 114) to receive the rewards the FE's Jesus has to offer. In other words, although the terms *gynē* and *anēr* do reveal important anthropological assumptions on the part of the author, they do not significantly affect the *eschatological* picture. The FG is not the *Gospel of Thomas*.

4. to refer to Jesus in his role as "Son of Man" (*huios tou anthrōpou*). In John 3:13 Jesus refers to the Son of Man simultaneously as the one who will be lifted up and the one who has already (perfect tense) ascended, thereby collapsing present and future in a way that reflects

the author's postnarrative perspective. In addition to collapsing time, the FE artfully uses titles to collapse the role and reward of Jesus into the role and reward of those who believe in him. Jesus repeatedly calls himself "Son of Man" (1:51; 3:13, 14; 5:27; 6:27, 53, 62; 8:28; 9:35; 12:23, 34; 13:31), the last occurrence of the phrase coming just as he enters his passion. Because Jesus, who is equal to God and *is* God, is also the Son of Man, believers become children, not of flesh and blood, but of God (1:13). Jesus is brought down, but on his way back up believers latch on and become elevated as well.

5. incorrectly by opponents to label Jesus. There is a vast difference between *huios tou anthrōpou* and *anthrōpos,* a point the author makes through the use of irony. Jesus' incorrigible opponents designate him as *anthrōpos,* but when they do, the FE indicates that the characters lack understanding of Jesus' true identity. This is true of Caiaphas (11:50), those who question the blind man (9:16, 24), the woman who questions Peter by the gate (18:17), and, famously, Pilate (19:5). This lack of understanding is writ especially large in chapter 5 and at 10:33, where Jesus' opponents accuse him of making himself God when he is only an *anthrōpos.* At 8:40 Jesus calls himself an *anthrōpos,* but only because he is taking up his opponents' line of argument. Surely they should agree that there have been *anthrōpoi* sent by God, but Jesus is not even treated as well as one of those, let alone as one who is united with God (10:33–36).

6. by potential followers who have not yet arrived at a revelation of Jesus' full identity. When these characters apply the word to Jesus, the FE always makes it clear, through irony, that such a designation implies "not enough." Thus the Samaritan woman mistakes Jesus for an *anthrōpos* in 4:29, as does the man born blind in chapter 9. Although both begin in ignorance, each eventually calls Jesus by more appropriate titles ("prophet" and "Christ," 4:19, 29; "prophet" and "Lord," 9:17, 38).

Pneuma ("spirit") occurs twenty-four times in FG. It can refer to

1. the Holy Spirit.

2. the category that is the opposite of "flesh," as in the Nicodemus story (John 3) and the bread-of-life discourse, where the spirit makes alive but the flesh is useless (6:63).

3. the *nature* and *identity* of God: "God is spirit" (4:24).

4. the *manner* in which God is to be worshipped: "in spirit and in truth" (4:23, with dative of manner).

John 7:39 addresses the distinctiveness of the Holy Spirit: "Now he [Jesus] said this about the Spirit, which believers in him were to receive; for as yet there was no Spirit, because Jesus was not yet glorified." Here we learn that, while Jesus is conducting his earthly ministry, no one except Jesus enjoys the gift of the Spirit. This is quite unlike the Gospel of Luke, then, where little of import occurs without the aid of the Spirit, who has been active in the lives of the characters even before Jesus arrives. In John, the inspiriting of the believers takes place only after Jesus has died and risen, when from the cross Jesus bestows the Spirit (19:30) and when he breathes on his disciples and says, "Receive the Holy Spirit" (20:22). The Holy Spirit is available, therefore, only to believers. Jesus calls the Spirit "another Advocate," implying that Jesus is the first Advocate (14:16); in many ways the Spirit serves the same role as Jesus and is intimately related to both God and Jesus.

The word *pneuma* is not used in reference to a part of human composition until John 11:33, where we learn that Jesus is disturbed in spirit and troubled (*tarassō*; cf. 13:21). Here, *pneuma* appears to approximate *kardia,* though the FE refuses to use *kardia* when speaking of Jesus' agitation, preferring *pneuma* and *psychē* instead. The FE describes Jesus' death by saying that Jesus "handed over his spirit" (19:30, au. trans.), presumably to the God who inspirited Jesus at his baptism. It remains an oddity, however, that Jesus finally gives up his *pneuma* when earlier he has said that he will "lay down" his *psychē* for his sheep (10:15, 17–18). Mary Coloe provides a partial solution to this problem when she insists that Jesus does not "give up" his spirit but rather "bestows" the Spirit from the cross:

> After Jesus' word of completion *tetelestai* ["It is finished"; 19:30], he performs his final sovereign act as he bows his head and hands down (*paredōken*) upon the nascent Christian community the promised gift of the Spirit (v. 30). The phrase *paredōken to pneuma* is frequently seen through a Synoptic interpretative model — Jesus gives up his spirit (i.e., his life). This is not what the Johannine texts says. The term *paradidōmi* is not a euphemism for death; it refers to the handing on or bequest of something to a successor.... At this moment Jesus' words to Nicodemus are realized as a disciple experiences being "born from above" (3:3, 5).[13]

What makes *pneuma* such an interesting category for an anthropological discussion is the way the FE has taken one of the most common features of ancient anthropology and made it a specifically Christian category. Hellenistic philosophers, particularly Stoics, hold forth at length about *pneuma* as

---

13. Mary L. Coloe, *God Dwells with Us: Temple Symbolism in the Fourth Gospel* (Collegeville, MN: Liturgical Press, 2001), 189.

a feature of a person. For Zeno, fire and breath ("hot breath") are part of soul. Medical writers conceived of *pneuma* as the "vital" spirit transmitted via the arteries. For Chrysippus, *pneuma* is the vehicle of the logos. "Intelligent pneuma" is "something which is both a physical component of the world and an agent capable of rational action."[14] This approximates FG's usage: *Pneuma* is physical, the disciples can feel it, it blows where it wills (3:8), and it is also responsible for guiding the disciples in all truth (16:13), and so on.

For the Stoics, *pneuma* serves a connective function: It "holds together" earth and water. "The universe itself is a sphere, and all its constituents tend to move towards the center; but only earth and water actually possess weight.... The *pneuma,* unlike the passive elements, pervades the whole cosmic sphere and unites the center with the circumference.... This function of *pneuma* in the macrocosm is equally at work in every individual body. Organic and inorganic things alike owe their identity and their properties to the *pneuma.*"[15] The FE follows suit by arguing that *pneuma* is a connective entity. In FG, however, *pneuma* does not connect the human being with the cosmos; rather, the *pneuma* connects certain human beings (believers) with the *Creator* of the cosmos. *Pneuma* is now defined as the Holy *Pneuma,* whose role is definable (teaching truth, guiding, reminding, and so forth).

The authors of the Hebrew Bible use "spirit" (*rûaḥ*) in reference to God and human beings.[16] With respect to God, the term signifies God's vital power; with respect to humanity; it signifies breath, feelings, and will. In his *Anthropology of the Old Testament,* Wolff entitles the chapter on spirit "*Rûaḥ* — Man as He Is Empowered" and states in the first paragraph, "*Rûaḥ* must from the very beginning properly be called a theoanthropological term."[17] He concludes the chapter by claiming, "Most of the texts that deal with the r[*ûaḥ*] of God or man show God and man in a dynamic relationship."[18] Although the latter statement, mutatis mutandis, could be made of FG insofar as *pneuma* serves as a critical link between God and humanity, there is a crucial difference: OT anthropology, like that of the Stoics, imagines *pneuma* as constitutive of all persons, whereas FG takes great pains to argue otherwise.

To summarize, Jesus is the only character in the narrative of FG who is said to have *pneuma* before the resurrection appearances. *Pneuma* descends on him early in the narrative, and he hands over *pneuma* at the end. Clearly,

---

14. A. A. Long, *Hellenistic Philosophy: Stoics, Epicureans, Sceptics* (2nd ed.; Berkeley: University of California Press, 1986), 155.

15. Ibid., 156.

16. Wolff, *Anthropology,* 32–39.

17. Ibid., 32.

18. Ibid., 39.

pneuma is not a natural, normal part of a person's constitution. It is a gift bestowed by God and available only to those who believe in Jesus. The bestowal of the gift on believers takes place by the end of the narrative (John 20:22), so *pneuma* is yet another gift promised to the believing reader and realized in the readers' present. There is no indication that any fullness is lacking here and now for the believing readers, a feature in harmony with the FE's realized eschatology. Because believers have received the spirit who is connected with truth, they can worship God appropriately in spirit and in truth. There is no hint of an enigmatic Pauline "mirror" (1 Cor 13:12). Light, truth, and clear vision have been granted in fullness with the bestowal of *pneuma* effected by Jesus' death and resurrection.

The FE uses the word *sarx,* often translated "flesh," thirteen times. On first glance, one might assume that *sarx* is a highly esteemed thing, since Jesus, the "word," has become *sarx* (John 1:14). More than half of the occurrences of this term appear in chapter 6, the bread discourse, where for the most part it is Jesus' *sarx* that is addressed. By eating Jesus' *sarx* one receives life (6:33, 51). He gives his *sarx* as bread for the sake of the life of the world, the world for whom God sent God's son. Anyone who does *not* eat his flesh (*sarx*) and drink his blood (*haima*) has no life (*zōē*; 6:53–54). In this discourse, a comparison of *sarx* with the quail provided by God in the wilderness is probably implied (Exod 16:13; Num 11:31–32). This is especially indicated by the otherwise inexplicable use of *trōgō* for "eat" (6:54, 56, 57, 58; 13:18), instead of *esthiō,* the usual word. *Trōgō* implies chomping, crunching, or gnawing, as the Israelites gnawed the quails' flesh off the bones. Just as Jesus, the "bread of life," is superior to the manna given in the wilderness, so Jesus' *sarx* is superior to the *sarx* of the quail.

Negatively, at John 1:13 the FE links *sarx* with "blood" and "the will of man" in specific contrast to God. One who is "born of flesh" is different from one who is "born of spirit" (3:6). Jesus' opponents "judge according to the flesh," which obviously casts *sarx* in a negative light (8:15, au. trans.). In 6:63 *sarx* is useless, while *pneuma* gives life, an exception to the discussion of *sarx* in the bread discourse. The category *sarx* need not be negative in and of itself; it is negative only when compared with Jesus. Before Jesus, bread was bread, water was water, and flesh was flesh — certainly nothing to testify about. After Jesus, all of these categories become options for human beings: if one chooses plain bread, water, and flesh over Jesus as bread, water, and flesh, one will miss out on life.

This reminds us of Jewett's notion of "fluctuation in meaning."[19] Jesus transforms *sarx,* a negative phenomenon apart from participation in him, into something good and life-giving. *Sarx* alone ends in death, just as bread

---

19. Jewett, *Paul's Terms,* 6–7.

alone, the kind that Moses gives (6:49), ends in death; and as water alone, the kind that Jacob's well gives (4:13), ends in death. Jesus transforms the mundane into the spiritual by his participation in the mundane. Just as the water from Jacob's well is not necessarily negative in and of itself, the *sarx* just *is*, before Jesus transforms it by participating in it. This is the force of 17:2, where Jesus, the word made flesh, announces that he has authority over *all* flesh. Because of Jesus' participation in *sarx*, those who believe in Jesus no longer live according to *sarx* alone. They align their *sarx* with *pneuma* so that spirit, God, and life are associated with the believer.

All human beings, including Jesus, have *sarx* and *haima* (blood). When referring to Jesus, these words have a positive connotation; when referring to other human beings, they represent the human being apart from Jesus. Because of and through Jesus, *sarx* and *haima* can become *redeemed* categories if one chooses to abide in Jesus. The FE seeks to pull the reader out of the mundane into the sublime. The possibility of the sublime is fully present by the end of the narrative, when Jesus returns.

Psychē (soul, life) appears ten times in FG. Four of these occurrences refer directly to Jesus' *psychē*. Jesus lays down his *psychē* for the sheep (John 10:11, 15, 17), and Jesus' *psychē* is troubled (12:27). Twice *psychē* refers to what Peter wants to lay down for Jesus (13:37–38). Three times this term occurs in general statements about would-be disciples: Jesus says that those who love their *psychē* will lose it; those who hate it in this world will guard it for eternal life (12:25). Finally, *psychē* is what one lays down for one's friends (15:13). Jesus certainly models each of these elements.

In every instance save one (12:25), *psychē* can be taken to refer to something like the post-Homeric expanded *psychē*, which combines aspects of the free-soul and body-soul.[20] It represents the individual personality (Jesus and Peter declare it to be their own), the seat of emotions (Jesus' soul is troubled), and that which "endows the body with life and consciousness, but does not stand for the part of the person that survives after death."[21] One could argue, however, that the FE has been influenced primarily by the Septuagint (LXX), which renders the Hebrew *nepeš* as *psychē*, thus making any discussion of the pagan literature superfluous at this point. For purposes of the present study, we should recognize two important features of the FE's use of *psychē*. First, the FE imbues the term with a new meaning unparalleled in either the Hebrew Bible or pagan literature. The FE's *psychē* is far more robust than the OT *nepeš*, which does not endure for eternity; it is also unitary, unlike the meaning of the term in Platonic-based philosophies. Second, in FG *psychē* has no meaning of its own; it draws meaning from its

---

20. See Jan Bremmer, *The Rise and Fall of the Afterlife* (London: Routledge, 2002), 1–10.
21. Ibid., 2.

relationship to *other* Johannine anthropological terms. To those terms we now turn.

The word *kardia* (heart) appears only seven times in FG, most often in the Farewell Discourse (John 14–17). It occurs in only two other verses: twice in the Isaiah quote at 12:40, which, following customary OT anthropology indicates that the heart is the seat of understanding; and in 13:2, where the *kardia* is susceptible to the wiles of the devil. Chapter 14 opens and closes with virtually identical language: Jesus exhorts his disciples to let their hearts be untroubled (*tarassō*; 14:1 and 27). The heart is a seat of the emotions. Both the disciples' grief over losing Jesus and their subsequent joy when they see him again will be located in the heart. Yet it is Jesus' *psychē*, not his *kardia*, that is troubled (*tarassō*) in 12:27. Never do we hear a word about Jesus' own heart, and the FE uses the word less than any other Gospel writer.

The FE uses *sōma* (body) only six times, four of which appear in John 19:31–40, the deposition of Jesus' body. *Sōma* first appears in 2:21, where the narrator explains that in speaking of the temple, Jesus means "the temple of his body" and alludes to his resurrection (cf. 2:20, 22). The last occurrence finds Mary Magdalene telling the angels she wonders where others have laid Jesus' body (20:12–13). So, in FG the word *sōma* relates *only* to the body of Jesus, particularly with regard to his death. We hear nothing about anyone else's body — not Lazarus's, not the centurion's slave's, not Peter's, not the Beloved Disciple's. *Sōma* occurs near the beginning of the Gospel and near the end, but not in between. I find highly debatable, then, Sandra Schneider's contention that "bodiliness is the linchpin of resurrection faith."[22]

Twice FE uses the word *koilia* (belly/womb), a term also employed by Matthew, Mark, Luke, Paul, and the author of Revelation. In Matthew, Mark, and Revelation, *koilia* refers only to the stomach. In Luke it always refers to a woman's womb; in Paul it can refer to stomach or womb. Consistent with these usages, John 3:4 finds Nicodemus wondering how to reenter his mother's womb. The use of the word in 7:38, however, is quite enigmatic, and much attention has been devoted to deciphering its meaning. The NRSV translation, "Out of the believer's *heart* shall flow rivers of living water," implies that the word *koilia*, which appears in this text, is synonymous with *kardia* — but this cannot be accurate since the FE uses the word *kardia* elsewhere in a more distinctive fashion. It is not even clear whether the rivers of living water are to come out of the believer's heart (most likely) or Jesus' heart. The experienced reader of the FG will immediately think of the water that flowed from Jesus' side on the cross (19:34); viewed against this backdrop, 7:38 seems to suggest that those who believe in Jesus will have the

---

22. Schneiders, "Resurrection," 168.

same experience, as is often the case in the FG (14:12). Clearly, the language is metaphorical and is tied to other "abundant water" themes in FG. At most, it is an anthropological category relevant only to believers, not human beings in general.

For a text so concerned with knowledge, the lack of noetic (*noeō*) language in FG is striking. The FG does not include the famous dictum found in the Synoptics, "You shall love the Lord your God with all your heart, and with all your soul, and with all your mind, and with all your strength," and "your neighbor as yourself" (Mark 12:30–33 and pars.). *Noeō* language appears only once in FG, in the Isaiah quote at 12:40. Noetic language is inconsequential for Johannine anthropology.

Summary

What key ideas should be gleaned from the foregoing discussion of Johannine anthropological terms? First, an *anthrōpos,* or human being, consists of *flesh and blood,* a *psychē,* and a *heart.* The *psychē* bears the primary anthropological weight, since this is the feature of a person that is capable of eternal life, the primary eschatological reward in FG. The FE connects the *psychē* with *zōē* (12:25), thus avoiding any strict dichotomies between earthly/heavenly, this life/next life. This connection supports the FE's eschatological project, which seeks to blur, if not entirely erase, the distinction between the present and the future, both for the believer and the unbeliever. *Psychē* and *zōē* each belong to what a Pauline scholar might call *both* realms, the present and the future, the earthly and the heavenly; for the FE, it is all *one* realm, already available in fullness for the believer and already fully unavailable for the unbeliever. Second, the FG uses anthropological language carefully both to unite Jesus with other human beings and to distinguish him from them. Like other human beings, Jesus has flesh, blood, and a *psychē.* But a distinction is created when the author avoids using heart language for Jesus. Thus, the disciples' *hearts* are the seat of their trouble (*tarassō*), but Jesus experiences trouble in his *psychē.* Third, *pneuma* is a rich feature of Johannine anthropology. Given Jesus' privileged access to spirit throughout the narrative, *pneuma* serves both to distinguish Jesus from other humans and finally to unite Jesus with believers by his inspiriting them at his death and resurrection, which are presented as a single, unified moment in FG.[23] Fourth, Johannine anthropology is distinctive: though one can cite points of contact with OT ideas, Hellenistic philosophy, other NT concepts, and even emergent gnostic ideas, FG nevertheless coincides exactly with none

23. As Mary Coloe states, "There are not two bestowals of the spirit [in FG]. I would rather speak of two moments within the one Hour, one moment where the focus is on the believer's relationship to Jesus, and a second moment where the focus is on the believer's relationship to the world, as the agent of Jesus in the world" (*God Dwells with Us,* 97).

of them.[24] Perhaps we will not be surprised, then, to learn that this distinctive anthropology contributes to a distinctive eschatology, particularly with respect to the ultimate fate of human beings. The FE is neither Paul nor Plato.

THE FATE OF HUMAN BEINGS

Now that we have some idea concerning what the FE does and does not think about the *nature* of human beings, we are prepared to ask about the *fate* that this author envisions for them. We have already seen that, unlike some Hellenistic philosophers, the FE does not present any part of a person as inherently immortal. What can FE mean, then, in stating that believers will never die, since such a statement seems to imply immortality? To answer this question, we will explore the author's comments relating to life and death; this inquiry will, in turn, help us answer the question of how a human being can *become* immortal (by being inspirited). In the process, we will need to discern *which* human beings become immortal. Further, for those who participate in immortality, when does this quality of life begin? Is it available in the present (i.e., realized eschatology) or only in some near or distant future (e.g., at one's own death or at the Parousia)? If not all human beings become immortal, what happens to those who do not? In this section, I will marshal the evidence necessary to hypothesize soundly that, although all human beings experience physical death, beyond that one's fate depends upon whether or not one believes in Jesus. The author of FG claims a bestowed, realized immortality for believers, an eternal life that begins now. Unbelievers can expect eternal death, which also begins now.

Death and Life Language

The FE uses a number of terms in reference to death: *thanatos* (death), *apollymi* (to destroy), *apōleia* (destruction), *nekros* (dead), *apokteinō* (to kill), *koimaomai* (to sleep), *koimēsis* (sleeping), and *thyō* (to slaughter in sacrifice). The last three terms — *koimaomai, koimēsis,* and *thyō* — each occur only once or twice in the FG. By far, *apothnēskō* is the term used most often in reference to death in FG: twenty-eight of the 111 total occurrences of *apothnēskō* in the NT appear in the FG. This word appears in eight of John's twenty-one chapters, with the majority of occurrences in chapters 8 (six times) and 11 (nine times).

In the Johannine view, all human beings start in death and are given the opportunity to transfer to life. This would be similar to a student starting

---

24. For a full and interesting argument about the relationship between Johannine and gnostic anthropology, see Jeffrey A. Trumbower, *Born from Above: The Anthropology of the Gospel of John* (Tübingen: Mohr, 1992).

with a zero and working to earn an A over the course of the semester, rather than starting with an A and trying not to lose it. Thus, the Johannine Jesus says, "Very truly, I tell you, anyone who hears my word and believes him who sent me has eternal life, and does not come into judgment, but has transferred from death to life" (5:24, au. trans. of "transferred"). The perfect tense of the verb "has transferred" (*metabebēken*) indicates that the action has been fully completed, yet with continuing effects in the present.

Death appears to have a double meaning in FG, signifying both physical death, which no one escapes, and Holy-Spiritual death, which only believers escape. By "Holy-Spiritual death" I mean lacking receipt of the Holy Spirit, a death that the author describes in 8:24 as death-in-sin. I avoid saying "spiritual death" so as to prevent the reader from thinking of a physical/spiritual dichotomy. *Pneuma* is not naturally part of any human being; it is bestowed by Jesus on the basis of belief. This differs vastly from Platonic, Stoic, or gnostic ideas, all of which contend that *pneuma* is constitutive of all human beings.

There is no Greek word that directly renders the English word "afterlife," and even if there were, the FE would never use it. He takes great pains to show no discontinuity between present life and future life. Life before death and life after death are all simply the same life. In FG, such ideas are expressed through the language of "birth" (*gennaō*), "life" (*psychē, zōē, zōopoieō, zaō*), and "resurrection" (*egeirō, anistēmi, anastasis*). Like death, life also has a dual meaning in FG: everyone has physical life (*psychē*), but not everyone has Holy-Spiritual life (*zōē*): the kind of life that is characterized by receipt of the Holy Spirit. Although FG occasionally mentions the former, its emphasis is on the latter. Any person who believes in Jesus will not experience Holy-Spiritual death, and this is the only death that matters.

At John 6:50, Jesus says, "This is the bread that comes down from heaven, so that one may eat of it and not die." On the other hand, those who do not believe that Jesus is who he says he is *will* experience Holy-Spiritual death: "I told you that you would die in your sins, for you will die in your sins unless you believe that I am" (8:24). That there are two layers of meaning is evidenced by the ironic exchange at John 8:51–52, where it is clear that Jesus is speaking "from above," with an eye to the present revelation embodied in himself, while his opponents are speaking "from below," with their eyes set on the past. Jesus says, "Very truly, I tell you, whoever keeps my word will *never see death*" (8:51; emphasis added). They answer, "Now we know that you have a demon. Abraham died [*apethanen*], and so did the prophets; yet you say, 'Whoever keeps my word will *never taste death*.' Are you greater than our father Abraham, who died? The prophets also died. Who do you claim to be?" (8:52–53; emphasis added). Clearly, Jesus' opponents have no understanding of Holy-Spiritual death or life.

Jesus' enemies are not the only ones who do not understand the double meanings of "life" and "death"; neither do his disciples. When Lazarus dies, Jesus says, "This illness does not lead to death" (*ouk estin pros thanaton*; 11:4). Yet it does; Lazarus is dead, dead, dead, rotting away (11:39). Jesus is speaking a higher truth, a heavenly concept beyond their comprehension. When Jesus says, "Our friend Lazarus has fallen asleep, but I am going there to awaken him" (11:11), the disciples take Jesus' *koimaomai* (sleep) language literally. Jesus uses "sleep" language to indicate that death is not ultimate. For the duller reader, the narrator explicitly says, "Jesus, however, had been speaking about his death, but they thought that he was referring merely to sleep. Then Jesus told them plainly, 'Lazarus is dead' " (11:11–14).

Martha appears to be ahead of the disciples in her understanding of life and death when at 11:24 she quotes from Jesus' own words (in 6:40) on the subject: "I know that he [Lazarus] will rise again in the resurrection on the last day." But rather than affirming Martha's regurgitation of his own words, which sound quite traditional by Pauline or Synoptic standards, Jesus *corrects* her understanding: "I am the resurrection and the life. Those who believe in me, even though they die, will live, and everyone who lives and believes in me will never die" (11:25–26). It is not that believers do not die, as the opponents in 8:52 had assumed; it is that physical death has been rendered inconsequential by Jesus' self-revelation. The concessive "even though" shows that he is coming down to her level, acknowledging rather than denying actual death, but trying to move her toward the only real point: eternal life is found in the person of Jesus.

Jesus' Paradigmatic Death

The FG indicates that the experiences of the disciples will mirror some of Jesus' experiences. The world hates him; the world will hate them. The world does not keep Jesus' word; it will not keep theirs. Physical death should be no big deal for Jesus' disciples because, for FG's Jesus, physical death is not a crisis: "For this reason the Father loves me, because I lay down my life [*psychē*] in order to take it up again. No one takes it from me, but I lay it down of my own accord. I have power to lay it down, and I have power to take it up again. I have received this command from my Father" (John 10:17–18). Jesus' death is a sacrifice that glorifies God (11:50; 21:19); that sacrifice is thrown into ironic relief by the comment that the thief seeks to steal and sacrifice (*thyō*) and destroy (10:10). Death holds no surprises for Jesus; the narrator often reminds us that Jesus knows what kind of death he is to die (12:33; 18:32; 21:19). His death is, in fact, an exaltation:[25] no

25. John uses *hypsoō* and *doxa* language to make this point; for the former, see John 3:14; 8:28; 12:32, 34; for *doxazō*, see 7:39; 12:23; 13:31.

suffering servant of Mark's Gospel here; no *kenōsis* hymn (Phil 2:6–11); no "Cursed is everyone who hangs on a tree" (Gal 3:13). Instead, Jesus says, "Very truly, I tell you, unless a grain of wheat falls into the earth and dies, it remains just a single grain; but if it dies, it bears much fruit. Those who love their life [*psychē*] lose it, and those who hate their *life in this world* [*psychē*] will keep it for *eternal life* [*zōē*]. Whoever serves me must follow me, and where I am, there will my servant be also" (12:24–26; emphasis added).

Clearly the author is trying to reeducate believers who might consider death to be a terrifying prospect by having Jesus use consolatory rhetoric: "I have said these things to you to keep you from stumbling. They will put you out of the synagogues. Indeed, an hour is coming when those who kill you will think that by doing so they are offering worship to God" (16:1–2). "But because I have said these things to you, sorrow has filled your hearts" (16:6). "I have said this to you, so that in me you may have peace" (16:33). Why do they need consolation? Jesus' death, their struggle with his absence, and their own persecution have left them fearful. This fear manifests itself in the language of being "alone." Jesus says, "You will leave me *alone* [*kame monon aphēte*]" (16:32), but "I will not leave you *orphaned* [*ouk aphēsō hymas orphanous*]" (14:18, emphasis added). For the believer, death does not involve being orphaned or forsaken; it has no power to sting, and it need not be considered an "enemy," as Paul puts it in 1 Cor 15:26.

The Distinctiveness of Jesus' Death

Although the author provides Jesus as a model of encouragement, it is important to realize that FE distinguishes Jesus' death from that of the disciples. Only Jesus' death is presented in sacrificial cult language, and only the resurrected *sōma* of Jesus is addressed. The FE insists that Jesus' death is a sacrifice that glorifies God (11:50; 21:19). It is widely recognized that FG's passion chronology differs from that of the Synoptics in its emphasis on Jesus as the paschal lamb. There is an ironic comment at John 10:10 that is missed by almost every English translation (NRSV, NIV, KJV, NASB). In the statement *ho kleptēs ouk erchetai ei mē hina klepsē kai thysē kai apolesē* ("the thief comes only that he might thieve and sacrifice and destroy," au. trans.), translators typically render *thyē* as "kill." Surely "sacrifice" is closer to the author's meaning, given Jesus' comment in 16:2: "They will put you out of the synagogues. Indeed, an hour is coming when those who kill [*apokteinō*] you will think that by doing so they are offering worship to God." If at 10:10 the author had simply meant "kill" instead of "sacrifice" in some cultic sense, he would not have added *thyē* to *apollymi*.[26]

---

26. An argument could be made against the Jesus-as-paschal-lamb proposition on the basis of the details of the OT texts. Nevertheless, the author of the FG takes Jesus' death to be

Chapter 21, which I take to be an appendix to FG, brings Jesus back to deal with the physical deaths of Peter and the Beloved Disciple (cf. 13:23; 20:2; 21:20). As is widely argued, John 21 serves, in part, to rehabilitate Peter. I am among those who think that this chapter reflects some level of conflict between the Johannine community, whose hero is the Beloved Disciple, and the "Petrine church down the street," whose hero is Peter. Peter's death is described as glorifying God (21:19), (language elsewhere reserved for Jesus' death) and the BD is not expected to die at all. The fact that the appendix must deal with the rumor that the Beloved Disciple would not die (21:23) indicates that some in the Johannine community misunderstood Jesus' realized eschatology and expected no physical death. This appendix, then, was a necessary corrective.

The Fate of Nonbelievers

Given the fact that the FE is generally thought to represent a perse-cuted group of Jews who have been excised from their parent tradition, one might expect the sort of vehement and vindictive invective against nonbelievers that one finds in Matthew, where "hell" — in the form of Gehenna, Hades, outer darkness, and unquenchable fire — abounds. The terms "Gehenna" (*geenna*), "Hades" (*hadēs*), "the outer darkness" (*to skotos to exōteron*), "consign to Tartarus" (*tartaroō*), "Abaddon" (*Abaddōn*), "abyss" (*abyssos*), and "Apollyon" (*Apollyōn*), all perfectly good words used elsewhere in the NT, never appear in FG. All the Synoptics use "Gehenna"; Matthew and Luke also have "Hades." The Synoptics all refer to "the unquenchable fire," which Mark pairs with hell (*hē geenna, to pyr to asbeston*; 9:43). In FG, fire (*pyr*) appears only once, without the word "unquenchable," and then in the context of a parable (15:6). The FG has no Son of Man coming on the clouds, no wars and rumors of war, no trumpets sounding where believers are changed in the twinkling of an eye, and no rider on a white horse.

Although there is no hell in the FG, there is judgment. Let me high-light two verses in FG that specifically contrast the fates of believers and nonbelievers. John 3:36 contrasts seeing eternal life with having the wrath of God remain upon one; and 5:29 contrasts doing good, which leads to resurrection of life, with doing bad, which leads to resurrection of judg-ment. The believer sees eternal life; the nonbeliever has the wrath of God remaining (*menō*) upon oneself. This *menō* language is not accidental; it is special Johannine vocabulary, and the FE plays on the word here. In the FG, the ultimate reward granted to the believer is to have the Father and Jesus

---

sacrificial, and that is what is important here. The author of 1 John 2:2 understands the FG to mean that Christ served as "the atoning sacrifice."

abide, remain, dwell (*menō*) with that believer (as in 14:23: *eleusometha kai monēn par' autō poiēsometha*). This is nothing less than eternal life. The nonbeliever, by contrast, has only the *wrath* of God; God's self does not abide (*menō*) with the nonbeliever.

What about Satan? Does Satan still hold sway in this world? In John's view, no. "*Now* is the judgment of this world; *now* the ruler of this world will be driven out" (12:31; emphasis added). "The ruler of this world has been judged [*ho archōn tou kosmou toutou kekritai*]" (16:11, au trans.). There is no indication that Satan is a cosmic force opposing God. He is not the strong man whose house Jesus has begun to plunder (cf. Mark 3:27); he is a puny character. Satan does not rule over hell or anything else, although believers do need protection from him (John 17:15).

There is no sense in the FG that the judgment is ongoing. Matthew can speak of eternal fire (*to pyr to aiōnion*; as in 25:41) and eternal punishment (*kolasin aiōnion*; 25:46). In FG, however, the phrase "eternal" is never paired with judgment or death but is often paired with "life."[27]

The Fate of Believers

Believers inherit eternal life, which starts now. To indicate eternal life, the FE uses *zōē* (often in conjunction with "eternal," *aiōnios* or *eis ton aiōna*) as well as *zōopoieō* and *zōe*. Sandra Schneiders astutely observes that "eternal life" in the FG signifies not "indefinite temporal extension of natural life but...a qualitatively different kind of life."[28] God, Jesus, and the Spirit all enliven (*zōopoieō*) the believer (5:21; 6:63). God and Jesus are said to raise up (*egeirō*) believers (God — 5:21; Jesus — 12:1, 9, 17). That Jesus makes alive, with an emphasis on the present, is evidenced by the use of "living/live" (*zaō*). Jesus' conversation with the Samaritan woman about living water pits past against present (Jacob versus Jesus; John 4). *Zaō* also appears in the living bread discourse, where past is again pitted against present (Moses versus Jesus; John 6), as well as in the story of Jesus revitalizing the official's son (4:46–54). In the FG there is no judgment day for believers in the traditional sense of the Synoptics, Paul, and Revelation. Judgment has already happened, one's fate has been decided, and there is no second chance. In typical Johannine fashion, John does use traditional language but empties it of its traditional significance and infuses it with new meaning.

---

27. One could also treat the FE's attitude toward "the world" (*kosmos*) under the heading of "unbelievers." For discussion and bibliography, see N. H. Cassem, "Grammatical and Contextual Inventory of the Use of *Kosmos* in the Johannine Corpus with Some Implications for a Johannine Cosmic Theology," *NTS* 19 (1972–73): 81–91. Likewise, one might also include the FG's "Judeans" (*hoi Ioudaioi*) in this category.

28. Schneiders, "Resurrection," 5.

The FG uses the word *anistēmi* in three contexts in reference to resurrection, always in the future tense. The term appears thus in the bread discourse (John 6:39, 40, 44, 54), the Lazarus discourse (11:23, 24), and in reference to Jesus' own resurrection (20:9). As recognized above, Martha assumes that Jesus' declaration, "I will raise them up on *the last day*" (6:40, emphasis added), refers to a notion of future resurrection, but Jesus corrects her (11:25–26). The "last day" has already come in the package of Jesus' incarnation, death, and resurrection. Thus, Jesus says, "Very truly, I tell you, the hour is coming, *and is now here* [*kai nyn estin*], when the dead will hear the voice of the Son of God, and those who hear will live" (5:25, emphasis added). At 5:28, Jesus declares that "the hour is coming when all who are in the tombs [*mnēmeion*] will hear his voice." The next time the word *mnēmeion* appears, it is in the story of Lazarus, who hears Jesus' voice and comes out of his tomb into the resurrection of life. He has been raised from the dead. In narrative time this resurrection is incomplete because Lazarus, unlike the postresurrection reader, does not yet have access to the Holy Spirit, since Jesus has not yet been glorified.

Unlike Paul (see 1 Cor 15), the FE contends that one can have everything that matters here and now. As it is now, so it will be then; as it will be then, so it can be now. After all, what more can be given than Jesus and God making their dwelling place with you? To say that there is some reward to which one does not presently have access is to say that the revelation of Jesus is somehow lacking. There is no language in the FG about the Holy Spirit as a down payment for future glory (2 Cor 1:22), or about Jesus as firstfruits (1 Cor 15:23). Jesus defines eternal life: "This is eternal life, that they may know you, the only true God, and Jesus Christ whom you have sent" (John 17:3). With Jesus, you have all you need; without him, you have nothing.

We have already seen that the Lazarus story takes the meaning of "resurrection" out of the future and puts it more firmly into the present. The final uses of tomb language in the FG refer to Jesus' burial and resurrection. Clearly, Jesus' resurrection is accomplished in the present as well. All that matters is finished by the end of the story. Keck understands the FG's notion of "resurrection on the last day" in the Pauline sense, a reading that leaves him perplexed: "It is not explained [by John] why resurrection is necessary, but we may assume that the same consideration is at work here as in Paul: 'what God created, the body, God will redeem.' "[29] Keck fails to recognize that the FG has taken the tradition's language of future resurrection and *corrected* it so that the future is completed not at a second coming but rather

---

29. Leander Keck, "Death and Afterlife in the New Testament," in *Death and Afterlife: Perspectives of World Religions* (ed. Hiroshi Obayashi; New York: Greenwood, 1992), 93.

at Jesus' resurrection. Put differently, for the FE, Jesus' appearance after the resurrection and his bestowal of the Holy Spirit constitute the second coming (John 20:19–23). The Coptic Nag Hammadi codices remind one that an author can use traditional language but infuse it with untraditional meanings. Even a cursory scan of these texts reveals that they use traditional language for death and the afterlife: "underworld" (*amnte* or *emnte*); "pit" (*khieit*); "day of judgment" (*mphoou n^{e}tkrisis*); and perhaps particularly interesting for our present purposes, "house" (*hi*). The latter term appears, for example, at *Trimorphic Protennoia* 40.19–32, in which we find a wisdom character, First Thought, dwelling with the believer. The FE is neither the first nor the last theologian to breathe new life into old terms.

Heaven

To denote "heaven," the FE uses the words *ouranos, epouranios, anōthen,* and *anō*. Three points deserve mention. First, "heaven" language in the FG designates the realm of God the Father: it serves as a metonym for God. Such language is used to emphasize source and agency. Heaven is God's command center. Second, most modern understandings of the FE's view of heaven seem to rely on the opening verses of John 14: "In my Father's house there are many dwelling places [*monai*, from *menō*]. If it were not so, would I have told you that I go to prepare a place for you? And if I go and prepare a place for you, I will come again and will take you to myself, so that where I am, there you may be also" (14:2–3). People often interpret this to mean one of two things: (1) at the general resurrection, believers will go to heaven, and nonbelievers will not; or (2) at the time of an individual's death, Jesus will take one up to a heavenly mansion in the sky.[30] I contend that the FE has neither in mind. Although John uses *ouranos* eighteen times, the term never appears in chapter 14. The FE's failure to use *ouranos* in chapter 14 is a clue suggesting that the "many dwelling places" do not have anything to do with heaven. Mary Coloe analyzes John 14 in detail and argues quite compellingly that the image (*paroimia*) about the father's house (*oikia*) that has many dwelling places (*monai*) "introduces the theme of the abiding of the *divine presence*" and "draws upon and transforms Israel's Temple traditions."[31] After careful exegesis, with particular attention to the language of John 14 as it relates to the rest of the book as well as to the Hebrew Scriptures, Coloe concludes that "the action therefore is not the *believers* coming to dwell in God's heavenly abode, but the *Father,* the *Paraclete* and *Jesus* coming to dwell with the believers. It is a 'descending' movement from the divine realm to the human, not an 'ascending' movement from the human to the

---

30. Ibid.: "In other words, Jesus promises to come to the believers in the hour of death and to take them to where he is — with God in heaven."
31. Coloe, *God Dwells with Us,* 159.

divine."[32] In short, John 14 is about a familial relationship, not a castle in the sky (cf. 8:35, "The slave does not have a permanent place in the household; the son has a place there forever").

Third, I want to draw attention to what John does *not* say about "heaven." He indicates no belief in layered heavens, as one finds in Stoic philosophy, the Apostle Paul, and Gnosticism. He never uses the language of paradise (*paradeisos*) as do Paul, Luke, and Revelation. He certainly never uses language such as "believers go to heaven when they die."

Summary

It may be useful here to review the most salient points in our discussion about the fate of human beings. The FG has a rich vocabulary for death, but its primary concern rests with Holy-Spiritual death. Everyone experiences physical death, including Jesus and the Beloved Disciple, but believers do not experience Holy-Spiritual death. Correlatively, believers gain Holy-Spiritual life (also called "eternal" life), the highest reward possible. Unbelievers do not. For believers, *pneuma* is added to *psychē*. Believers can face death with the same confidence that Jesus exhibits, for death has no power to interrupt Jesus' and God's dwelling with the believer (John 14:23): the qualitatively abundant life that is available now extends forever. Heaven is not envisioned as a place where believers go posthumously; rather, it serves metonymically to signify God's agency. Likewise, the FE never imagines an afterlife in which Satan, a fallen angel, rules over a hellish territory to which unbelievers are carried by angels (cf. Matt 13:41–42). With the revelation of Jesus Christ, Satan becomes ultimately impotent. All people receive judgment, with its concomitant fate in this life, a fate that continues into the future.

CONCLUSION

I began this chapter by looking at Robinson's approach to eschatology in the FG, a heavily diachronic approach. I then decided to take up the issue of eschatology differently, using a more synchronic approach. In Robinson's discussion, to "solve" the puzzle of Johannine eschatology means to determine whether or not there was ever a pure (or at least purer) form of Christianity (of which he finds hints in the earliest layers of FG and refers to as "the Johannine tradition"), located in a particular geographical spot (an isolated Palestine), that was later adulterated by the apocalyptic faux pas (due to contact with Asia Minor). Without wholly eschewing the benefits of diachronic investigation (indeed, I have used some diachronic tools in this investigation), I treat the topic more synchronically and assume that one

---

32. Ibid., 163.

has not "solved" Johannine eschatology until one has presented a hypothesis about the possible *significance* of the FG's eschatology rather than its *derivation.* The primary question becomes, What does the author *mean* in making particular statements throughout the text? rather than, How did the author end up with such ideas? Because my goals are different from those of Robinson, one should expect what we consider important conclusions to be different as well.

To offer a hypothesis regarding the FE's eschatology, I inquired after FG's view of "the ultimate fate of human beings," a point of interest for OT writers, NT writers, and Hellenistic philosophers alike. Such a question cannot be responsibly pursued until one has discerned the author's view of what actually constitutes a human being. Is it a bipartite model (body and soul)? Tripartite? Monistic? And which "parts," if any, are assumed to last beyond the grave? If they do persist, is that because they are inherently invincible or immortal (Plato), or is such a characteristic bestowed upon a person (FG)? If bestowed, when? Is that which persists enervated (OT *nepeš*) or robust (Plato's "immortal soul"; the FG's pneumatic *psychē*)? Do people or parts of people "go" somewhere in the future (e.g., to heaven or hell) after death (as in Paul or Matthew or Peter), or do rewards and punishments accrue and occur in life before death (FG)? Having explored these questions, I now state the most important conclusions regarding the FG's anthropological eschatology and their implications with respect to Robinson's essay.

Earlier I claimed that FG evinces a notion of *bestowed realized immortality* for the believer. I am now in the position to elaborate. In the FE's view, immortality is bestowed, not innate. It is realized, not future. Functionally, death has been rendered inconsequential for the believer — and only for the believer. Death is not the Last Great Enemy. But we must distinguish this notion of immortality from both Platonism and Paulinism. On the one hand, unlike Platonism or Gnosticism, no person or part of a person is inherently immortal in the FG; rather, immortality characterizes only the *psychē* of the believer, whom God gifts with Holy-Spiritual (i.e., pneumatic) *zōē*, a "life" that starts now and continues uninterrupted forever. On the other hand, unlike Paul's bestowed futuristic immortality, which *follows* resurrection, the FE claims that the believer never dies and has *already* passed from death to life. Where Paul insists that the quality of future life is far different from the present (cf. Rom 8), for the FE the future is simply more of the same (abundant life). There is no interest in the Parousia (the term never occurs in FG), no blowing of the shofar, no new heaven and new earth, no spiritual body.[33] Speaking of the FG, Robert Kysar has claimed that "in few other

---

33. Contra Mary Coloe (ibid., 177), who appears to see John as a hesitant maverick: "Just as the Spirit is a proleptic gift of the eschaton, so also the worshiping, remembering community

pieces of Christian literature is the tension between the present and future dimensions of salvation more evident."[34] I disagree. John is one of the few NT documents to exclude the language of "hope" (*elpis/elpizō*). Paul says, "Hope that is seen is not hope. For who hopes for what is seen? But if we hope for what we do not see, we wait for it with patience" (Rom 8:24–25). None of this would make sense to a Johannine Christian, who has *seen* Jesus and therefore has seen the Father and hence has no need for hope because of having the ultimate *now*. Strange, then, that Robinson would nominate the FG as "essentially the Gospel for those who have not seen, because they were not there to see." Robinson himself misses the FE's meaning because, much like Jesus' opponents, he is preoccupied by earthly things, such as the "perfectly clear" notion that the FG is written "for a non-Palestinian situation."

In the FG, resurrection adds nothing to the believer that one does not already enjoy. The FG is not Paul, nor is it the Synoptics. For Robinson, such a statement would require a diachronic explanation with an aim to placing proximate value judgments on the various texts. We would have to decide whether John's distinctiveness lies in his correcting the tradition as represented by Paul or in his ignorance of such a tradition. Robinson is hoping for the latter, so that John's trajectory might be both "mature" and "remarkably primitive" at the same time.[35] The drive to prove that John is primitive coheres with Robinson's conviction that "primitive" means "closer to the historical Jesus" and therefore better. Robinson's enthusiasm for the promises of diachronic approaches appears also in his attitude toward the Dead Sea Scrolls: "*For the first time they present us with a body of thought which in date and place (southern Palestine in the first century BC–AD), as well as in fundamental, and not merely verbal, theological affinity, may really represent an actual background, and not merely a possible environment, for the distinctive categories of the Gospel.*"[36] With respect to anthropological and eschatological categories, however, the Dead Sea Scrolls actually indicate as much dissimilarity as affinity with the FG. The Dead Sea Scrolls community

is a proleptic experience of the eschatological House of God. Stibbe's conclusion is along similar lines: 'The realized eschatology in the rest of John 14 suggests that this house is not so much an eternal home in heaven as a post-resurrection, empirical reality for the true disciples.' I add a qualifying note to Stibbe in presenting the role of the Paraclete as mediating this 'empirical reality' and also in claiming that it is not so fully realized that there is no sense of a further Parousia." The only textual evidence that Coloe cites for a future eschatology are the passages in John 5 and 6 discussed, which I have already argued do not actually point to a future eschatology. The only truly difficult piece of evidence is Jesus in John 21:22 saying, "until I come," but Coloe's monograph does not address this verse because she (like me) considers ch. 21 to be an appendix with certain tendencies that move against the rest of the Gospel.

34. Robert Kysar, *John, the Maverick Gospel* (rev. ed.; Louisville: Westminster John Knox, 1993), 99.
35. Robinson, "New Look," 102.
36. Ibid., 99, emphasis original.

evinces a thoroughly apocalyptic eschatology and certainly does not grant women the place of witness and value that FG does.

Post-Robinson synchronic approaches have reminded us that meaning is not determined by diachrony; diachrony may or may not contribute to meaning, but meaning certainly does not depend on a diachronic approach. Today it seems odd to operate with models of trajectories and growth, primitive and mature — heavily judgmental language that forces biblical texts to compete with one another on the basis of age and development. Robinson's goal is to find his favorite theology at the earliest possible stage of Christianity so that he can validate it as the best theology. Consider this comment, which he makes when critiquing an opposing reconstruction:

> This reconstruction I believe to be correct at one point, namely, that the path into apocalyptic was a *faux pas*. It was not, I am persuaded, the original eschatology of Jesus, which was much more in the line of the prophets than of the apocalyptists, nor was it that of the most primitive Church. The Synoptists witness to a progressive apocalypticization of the message of Jesus, ... as the Gospel of Matthew most forcibly illustrates.[37]

Let me draw attention to a few of the striking elements in this statement. First, notice the force with which Robinson expresses his own theological convictions. It is not enough for him to notice that John does one thing and Matthew another; what Matthew does is unequivocally wrong. Second, his ideal goal is to get back to the original eschatology of Jesus, to reach behind the text. It is not enough to discern the FE's eschatology; rather, one must dig through the sediment that is FG to get to the real treasure. Third, who are these mutually exclusive "prophets" and "apocalyptists," and where do Daniel and the intertestamental literature fit into such categories? Fourth, scholars no longer axiomatically assume that there was such a thing as "the" (rather than "a") "*most* primitive," capital-C "Church." Perhaps, contra Robinson, we might opt for a more synchronic approach, informed rather than dominated by concerns external to the text itself. Perhaps we could treat the text as a moment in time and space, a snapshot of one author or community as distinct from, but not better or worse than, another NT author or community. If we did this, we could spend our time uncovering, experiencing, and perhaps even creating meaning from the text, rather than performing an autopsy. After doing so, one just might find that these words were written not that one might understand the original eschatology of Jesus and/or the primitive church, and not that one might see that the FG was correct and Matthew a failure, but "that you might come to believe that

---

37. Ibid., 103.

Jesus is the Christ, the Son of God, and that by believing you might have life in his name" (John 20:31, au. trans.).

♦ ♦ ♦

PART 2:
"THAT TO PHILOSOPHIZE IS TO LEARN TO DIE"

— Michel de Montaigne,
sixteenth-century philosopher

As stated in the introduction, one goal of this project on death and afterlife is to investigate how, if at all, various schools of contemporary Hellenistic philosophy informed NT views on death and afterlife. Here I will argue that the author of the Fourth Gospel (FG) is in dialogue with Epicurean treatments of death. Making such an argument entails a certain amount of repetition: ideas presented in the introduction, chapter 1 on "Backgrounds," and the previous chapter on the FG will resurface, but I hope that the results from the new mixture will come across as fresh despite some redundancy.

In his book *Lucretius on Death and Anxiety*, Charles Segal writes: "Dying, therefore, is inseparable from the conduct of life; dying well is part of living well. For the poets and moralists of antiquity, therefore, death is the recurrent, indeed the inevitable, subject of ethical thought."[38] If Segal is correct, then we might envision the Fourth Evangelist (FE) as seeking to establish an alternative to the philosophical schools of Stoicism and Epicureanism, which were so influential during his day. The FE agrees with the philosophers on at least two fundamental points: (1) Death, or perhaps more important, the fear of death, threatens to obstruct the good life. (2) Knowledge (or belief) is the solution to the problem. With the proper knowledge, one can expend one's days on earth in a way that is characterized by fullness and peace.

THE PROBLEM OF DEATH

Epicurus may be famous for his dictum found in *Principal Doctrines* (*Kuriai doxai*) 2: "Death is nothing to us; for that which has been dissolved lacks sensation; and that which lacks sensation is nothing to us."[39] Nevertheless, he momentarily reveals a pastoral capacity in his *Epistle to Menoeceus*, when he declares death to be the most terrifying of evils (*phrikōdestaton tōn*

---

38. Charles Segal, *Lucretius on Death and Anxiety: Poetry and Philosophy in "De rerum natura"* (Princeton: Princeton University Press, 1990).

39. *Ho thanatos ouden pros hēmas; to gar dialythen anaisthētei, to d' anaisthētoun ouden pros hēmas.*

kakōn; quoted by Diogenes Laertius, *History of Philosophy* 10.125). Epicurus and his disciples aim to free human beings from the anxiety that attends death and help them to achieve instead the untroubled state (*ataraxia*), pleasure (*hēdonē*), and tranquil resting places (*sedes quietae*; Lucretius, *On the Nature of Things* [*De rerum natura*] 3.18–24) befitting the gods. Such freedom comes through knowledge, especially as it is expressed in Epicurus's Atomistic theory.[40]

The author of Hebrews understands the nature of the problem as well: "Since, therefore, the children share flesh and blood, he himself likewise shared the same things, so that through death he might destroy the one who has the power of death, that is, the devil, and free those who all their lives were held in slavery by the fear of death [*phobō thanatou dia pantos tou zēn enochoi hēsan douleias*]" (2:14–15). Paul and the FE would agree.

Let us put to rest once and for all, then, the asseveration of the notable classicist Ramsay MacMullen, who claims that most Romans had no serious conception of an afterlife, an opinion based on the fact that one could find on tomb inscriptions the acronym for the tripartite exclamation: "I was not, I was, I am no more, I don't care."[41] On the contrary, it is clear from reading consolatory texts, epigraphy, plays, Homer's *Odyssey*, Virgil's *Aeneid*, philosophical literature, magical papyri, blessing-and-curse tablets, and the NT that the fear of death threatened to enslave the ancients no less than it does moderns.

---

40. Numerous Atomistic theories were maintained by ancient philosophers. For a brief synopsis of each, see Robert B. B. Wardy, "Atomism," in *The Oxford Classical Dictionary* [OCD] (ed. Simon Hornblower and Antony Spawforth; 3d ed., rev.; New York: Oxford University Press, 2003), 208–10.

Epicurus's Atomist theory tries to answer the question "What principles derived from empirical evidence are necessary and sufficient to account for the physical world as it presents itself to our senses?" The answer is concise: "an infinite number of indivisible bodies moving in infinite space" (Long, *Hellenistic Philosophy*, 31). In Epicureanism, bodies are of two kinds: compound and the units from which compounds are made (i.e., noncompounds, which are indivisible). Epicurus does not subscribe to the four elements common in Greek philosophy. Epicurus believes that there are other worlds, infinite worlds, for if atoms came together in a way to form this world, why should they not do the same again sometime or in a way that varies? Obviously, Epicurus denies the foundations of Platonic and Aristotelian cosmology. No longer does one need Plato's Forms, Demiurge, or World-Soul, or Aristotle's Prime Mover and Heavenly Intelligences (ibid., 20).

Epicurus adopted but modified Democritus's views. Epicurus is a materialist. Atoms of matter are permanent elements and are indivisible. The world came into being through the random collision of atoms and will someday break back down into those atoms. Gods exist, also made of atoms. "Both creation, as in Plato's *Timaeus*, and the eternity of the cosmic order, as in Aristotle's world picture, are rejected: natural movements of atoms are enough to explain the origin and growth of everything in the world.... Epicurus was a thoroughgoing physicalist in his philosophy of mind. The soul is composed of atoms, all extremely small but distinguished by shape in four kinds: fire, air, and breath (but all somehow different from their ordinary namesakes), and a fourth, unnamed kind. At death the component atoms are dispersed" (David John Furley, "Epicurus," OCD, 533).

41. On inscriptions as *nf f ns nc*, to stand for *non fui, fui, non sum, non curo*.

THE PROBLEM OF DEATH IN THE FOURTH GOSPEL

Death constitutes a serious problem for a group that characterizes itself as a community of eternal life. The FE copiously employs various forms of "live/living" (*zaō*) language. In addition to this specific language, the narrative itself evinces these concerns. I have in mind especially the Lazarus incident (11:1–45), which treats the problem of the death of believers (also called those whom Jesus loves); and the Farewell Discourse (chs. 14–17), which treats the problem of Jesus' own death. Reading the Lazarus pericope alongside Lucretius's *On the Nature of Things* is educational. In many ways, the FE approximates Lucretius, a follower of Epicurus, much more closely than Epicurus himself insofar as both FE and Lucretius each deal with philosophical issues in poetic rather than prosaic terms. Epicurus rather pedantically insists that his Atomistic theory should lead to immediate relief of anxiety if not to sheer glee that one will have the opportunity to donate one's atoms for the benefit of future people. Lucretius is far more willing to explore the dark side of death and, more important, the fear of death. He also ventures occasionally into the realm of the personal, individual nature of death, especially in books 3 and 6. Commenting on the end of book 6 and Lucretius's claim that "they fight bloodily for the wrong kind of corpora (6.1286)," Segal says, "Lucretius, however, does not merely castigate their error. He enters into it sympathetically, dramatically; and he thereby makes us his readers feel, in our own skin, what it is to fall prey to uncontrollable anxiety when death's touch is upon us, when we too 'are given over to death and disease' and see ourselves 'entangled' in the nets of a disease that condemns us to certain death."[42] The same could easily have been penned to describe the Lazarus incident in the FG.

THE FOURTH GOSPEL AND EPICUREANISM

At least four aspects of the possible dialogue between FG and Epicureanism deserve attention: (1) freedom from disturbance, (2) posthumous existence, (3) posthumous punishment, and (4) the importance of a community of friends.

Freedom from Disturbance: Peace (*eirēnē*) and Joy (*chara*)

The first sign that the FE may be in dialogue with Epicureanism comes in his frequent use of the verb "trouble" (*tarassō*), which he employs seven times, more than any other NT author. Given that being untroubled (*ataraxia*) is a

---

42. Segal, *Lucretius on Death*, 41.

fundamental principle of Epicureanism (appearing also in opposite form as *tarachos* and *tarachē*), I doubt that this is accidental. Perhaps not surprisingly, the uses congregate in the Lazarus passage and the Farewell Discourse. In 11:33, we read: "When Jesus saw her weeping [*klaiousan*], and the Jews who came with her also weeping [*klaiontas*], he was greatly disturbed in spirit and deeply moved [*enebrimēsato tō pneumati kai etaraxen heauton*]." Two verses later, Jesus himself weeps (*edakrusen*). Jesus is here depicted as anti-Epicurean. He is disturbed and he weeps. One chapter later John has him say: "Now my soul is troubled [*nun hē psychē mou tetaraktai*]" (12:27). And one chapter after that we learn that "Jesus was troubled in spirit [*Iēsous etarachthē tō pneumati*]" (13:21) when contemplating his own death, or "hour."

By depicting the leader of the movement as plagued by disturbance of spirit, John takes much more seriously the troubling nature of death and its concomitant anxiety than does Epicurus, rejecting the notion that this anxiety should be belittled in any way. As we will see, John's path to being untroubled (*ataraxia*), or to peace (*eirēnē*), as he will designate it, leads *through* being troubled (*tarachos*), not around it.

Like Epicurus, however, John does ultimately want to alleviate disturbance. Thus 14:1 and 14:27 evince an *inclusio* that is dependent upon the language of being troubled (*tarassō*): "Do not let your hearts be troubled. Believe in God, believe also in me [*mē tarassesthō hymōn hē kardia; pisteuete eis ton theon kai eis eme pisteuete*]" (14:1). "*Peace* I leave with you; my *peace* I give to you. I do not give to you as the world gives. Do not let your hearts be troubled, and do not let them be afraid [*eirēnēn aphiēmi hymin, eirēnēn tēn emēn didōmi hymin; ou kathōs ho kosmos didōsin egō didōmi hymin. mē tarassesthō hymōn hē kardia mēde deiliatō*]" (John 14:27, emphasis added).[43] Chapter 14, then, appears to be in direct dialogue with Epicureanism. Like the Epicureans, John argues that his followers can be free from disturbance, from fear, thereby achieving an untroubled state (*ataraxia*). John's "peace" (*eirēnē*) is the counterpart to Epicurean "calm" (*ataraxia*).

The goal of Epicurean philosophy is to achieve tranquil resting places (*sedes quietae*), befitting the gods. Epicurus's gods dwell remote from earth. Because the gods do not meddle with the celestial bodies, believed to control human fates, the gods therefore are not involved in deciding the fates of human beings. Certainly there is no notion that humans will join the gods posthumously, since Epicureans do not hold to any survival of the personality in any form after death. Epicurus maintains these beliefs and thinks that by teaching them he can assuage the fear of divine judgment and eternal punishment. Just as the gods do not involve themselves in deciding human

---

43. *Deiliaō* is a hapax legomenon in place of the usual *phobeō*.

fate in this life, so they will not be involved in our judgment or punishment.[44] Theology and psychology are two areas that matter much to Epicurus. He has no respect for popular religion in which people imagine that they will pacify or inspire the gods by ritual behavior. For his part, Lucretius praises Epicurus for relieving people from the burden of "the weight of religion."[45]

I would argue that FE directly addresses Epicurean theology in a number of ways in chapter 14. Jesus tells the disciples that the way out of disturbance (*tarassō*) is belief in him and in God (14:1). He assures them that God has a house in which there are many dwelling places (*monai*). Jesus is going to prepare this place (*topos*). How does Jesus prepare the place? By going to the Father through the cross and resurrection. This is why it is good for him to go, to die: "If you loved me, you would rejoice [*echarēte*] that I am going to the Father" (14:28).

Why should death bring joy? The wonderful benefits that result from Jesus' departure, his death, include peace (*eirēnē*), eternal life (*zōē*), the birth of the church as he bestows the Spirit from the cross (19:30), the receipt of the Paraclete (19:30; 20:22), and the complete unity of the believer with God and Jesus.[46] Jesus' way to the Father prepares a place for them so that they will dwell intimately with God (cf. 1:12; 11:52). This is the effect of 14:23: "Those who love me will keep my word, and my Father will love them, and we will come to them and make our home with them [*ean tis agapa me ton logon mou tērēsei, kai ho patēr mou agapēsei auton kai pros auton eleusometha kai monēn par' autō poiēsometha*]." I must emphasize that this constitutes the ultimate Johannine answer to the problem of death: God and Jesus making their dwelling place among the believers *here and now*, in this life and then projected into an eternal future. Absolutely contrary to the typical interpretation that imagines individual Christians being whisked

---

44. This would certainly have undermined Greek religion as well as Platonism, which insists that the cosmos is under the direction of a divine intelligence (Long, *Hellenistic Philosophy*, 42). According to Plato, humanity and the universe are possessions of the gods, and the gods act providentially over people. Aristotle also considered the "heavenly bodies as intelligent, divine beings whose movements are voluntary" (ibid., 43). For Aristotle, all movement and life depend on the Unmoved Mover, pure Mind or God, "whose activity of eternal self-contemplation promotes desire and motion in the heavenly bodies, each governed by its own intelligence" (ibid., 43). While not concerned with the lives of individuals, God is the prime cause of everything. For Epicurus, the gods are considered to be sublimely happy and immortal, which they patently could not be if they were involved in human affairs since, according to Epicurus, happiness is defined as "uninterrupted tranquility or freedom from pain." Hence, with respect to theodicy, Epicurus surveys the imperfections of this world and surmises that the world does not derive from the desire or ability of the gods.

45. Ibid., 40.

46. John uses the word *heis* (one) forty times. Add the occurrence of *menō* (remain, dwell) and the use of the dative of location meaning "in" and the evidence of the emphasis on unity becomes staggering.

away upon their deaths to some mansion in the sky,[47] John indicates that the peace and tranquillity that Epicurus imagines to be the possession of remote gods, dwelling in remote places of quietude, is actually available to all human beings who know (*ginōskō*) and believe (*pisteuō*) in the revelation of Jesus.

John's view diametrically opposes Epicurus's view in holding that God is not remote and disinterested but is fully and intimately related. In chapter 17 John declares believers to be one (*heis*) with Jesus and God, who also are one. Out of this unity, which is available immediately, peace (*eirēnē*) and joy (*chara*) become available. The FE approximates Epicurus in his fundamental concern to assuage thanatological anxiety so that one's present life may be characterized by pleasure (*hēdonē*) in Epicurus's scheme or joy (*chara*) in FE's message. For the FE, peace, joy, and freedom come through knowledge and belief. In chapter 14 alone, the word *ginōskō* (know) appears eight times (57 in all), *oida* (know) three times (84 in all), and (*pisteuō*) seven times (98 in all). Certainly the Epicurean system, cast in terms of knowledge, could be characterized just as easily by language of belief.

Belief is functionally equivalent to *knowledge* in the FG. Just as the belief is focused on God and Jesus and the Paraclete, so too is the knowing: "If you know me, you will know my Father also. From now on you do know him and have seen him [*ei egnōkate me, kai ton patera mou gnōsesthe. kai ap' arti ginōskete auton kai heōrakate auton*]" (14:7; cf. 14:9, 17, 20, 31). Knowledge leads to truth and peace in John, certainly elements an Epicurean could admire.

Eternal Life versus Recycled Life

But John goes farther than Epicurus regarding the rewards of knowledge. In opposition to the Epicureans, John offers eternal life rather than dissolution of soul and body into atoms that will be reused. Both acknowledge death as a problem for their followers ("the greatest of evils," to quote Epicurus), largely because it is not understood rightly. Both ultimately declare that death is of no consequence for their followers. Epicurus says: "Death is nothing to us; for that which has been dissolved lacks sensation; and that which lacks sensation is no concern to us" (*Principal Doctrines* 2). And the FE's Jesus says: "I am the resurrection and the life. Those who believe in me, even though they die, will live, and everyone who lives and believes in me will never die [*egō eimi hē anastasis kai hē zōē; ho pisteuōn eis eme kan apothanē zēsetai, kai pas ho zōn kai pisteuōn eis eme ou mē apothanē eis ton aiōna*]" (11:25–26). But the solution differs. Where Epicurus urges his readers to happily relinquish the atoms that comprise them as individuals to make way

---

47. Keck perpetuates this misunderstanding in "Death and Afterlife," 83–96. For alternative views, see Coloe, *God Dwells with Us,* and Clark-Soles, " 'I Will Raise [Whom?] Up on the Last Day.' "

for other lives, to give others their turn, John opposes any notion of planned obsolescence with regard to individual persons. In the FE's view, God and Christ both participated in creation to such a degree that the following can be declared: "All things came into being through him, and without him not one thing came into being [*panta di' autou egeneto, kai chōris autou egeneto oude hen*]" (1:3). God, far from being remote and disinterested, is depicted as willing things (*thelēma*, 11 times; *thelei*, 23 times) related to this cosmos and desiring that certain things happen and certain other things do not (cf., e.g., 4:34; 5:30; 6:38–40; also 3:16).

Disregard of Posthumous Punishment

Evidence that the FE stands among philosophers more comfortably than among apocalyptic forms of Judaism so common elsewhere in the NT arises from the fact that the FE excludes any language of hell. The words "Gehenna" (*geenna*), "Hades" (*hadēs*), "the outer darkness" (*to skotos to eksōteron*), "consign to Tartarus" (*tartaroō*), "Abaddon" (*Abaddōn*), "abyss" (*abyssos*), "Apollyon" (*Apollyōn*), all used elsewhere in the NT, never appear in the FG. Epicurus himself argued vociferously against any notion of posthumous judgment, thus implying that such notions were influential among the populace. Both Epicurus (and Lucretius after him) and the FE sought to draw the attention of their students away from fear or motivation grounded in the Greek myths of Hades and to focus it instead on living the present well. "The first thing which Epicurus strove to establish in his psychological theory was the complete and permanent loss of consciousness at death."[48] This means that any system of rewards and punishment after death was necessarily nothing more than mythology.

> Cerberus and the Furies, in truth, and the lack of light, Tartarus belching dread fire from its jaws — these surely neither exist anywhere, nor can exist. But in life there is great fear of punishment for great deeds of evil, and there is penalty for crimes: prison, the terrible casting from the Rock, whips, executioners, stocks, pitch, hot plates, torches; and even if these are missing, yet the mind, conscious of its deeds and fearful, applies goads to itself and burns itself with lashes, and meantime sees neither what end there can be of misfortunes, nor what limit there is for punishments, and fears lest these same become more severe in death. In a word, the life of fools becomes a hell [Acheron] on earth. (Lucretius, *On the Nature of Things* 3.1010–1023)

Fear of punishment for crimes committed in this life, rather than the Acheron (river in Hades) of myth, is the real hell (3.1013–1023). Epicurus's and

---

48. Long, *Hellenistic Philosophy*, 49.

Lucretius's audiences must have been worried about this or both men would not have devoted so much time to it. Perhaps Christianity and the mystery cults drew followers by addressing the fear in some way as well. I maintain that, like Epicurus, the FE contends against notions or doctrines of hell, and like Lucretius, the FE is fully aware of the fact that the mind, conscience, or knowledge of one's evil deeds and the concomitant misery that inheres in the present as a result is more powerful and meaningful a judgment than any mythological underworld. Is this not, after all, the effect of John 3:17–21, which lays stress on judgment taking place on this earth in this life, at the very moment that good or evil deeds are perpetrated?

> Indeed, God did not send the Son into the world to condemn the world, but in order that the world might be saved through him. Those who believe in him are not condemned; but those who do not believe are condemned already, because they have not believed in the name of the only Son of God. And this is the judgment, that the light has come into the world, and people loved darkness rather than light because their deeds were evil. For all who do evil hate the light and do not come to the light, so that their deeds may not be exposed. But those who do what is true come to the light, so that it may be clearly seen that their deeds have been done in God. (John 3:17–21)[49]

The fear of death affects people's beliefs about afterlife; hence, Epicurus's raging against popular religion. On the one hand, people fear eternal damnation. On the other hand, people fear cessation of existence. Epicurus and Lucretius after him address these concerns. They compare death with one's situation before birth: before one was born, one did not exist and did not care that one did not exist, so why should one care about death? Lucretius offers this consolation:

> If there is to be any trouble and pain for a man, he too must exist himself at that time in order that ill may affect him. Since death removes this and prevents the existence of him to whom a mass of misfortunes might accrue, we may be assured that there is nothing to be feared in death, and that he who no longer exists cannot be troubled. (*On the Nature of Things* 3.861–868)[50]

---

49. *Ou gar apesteilen ho theos ton huion eis ton kosmon hina krinē ton kosmon, all' hina sōthē ho kosmos di' autou. Ho pisteuōn eis auton ou krinetai; ho de mē pisteuōn? ēdē kekritai, hoti mē pepisteuken eis to onoma tou monogenous huiou tou theou. autē de estin hē krisis hoti to phōs elēlythen eis ton kosmon kai ēgapēsan hoi anthrōpoi mallon to skotos hē to phōs; ēn gar autōn ponēra ta erga. pas gar ho phaula prassōn misei to phōs kai ouk erchetai pros to phōs, hina mē elenchthē ta erga autou; ho de poiōn tēn alētheian erchetai pros to phōs, hina phanerōthē autou ta erga hoti en theō estin eirgasmena* (John 3:17–21).

50. Long, *Hellenistic Philosophy*, 50.

A Brief Word on Epicurean Anthropology

Epicurus has a unified view of the person rather than a dualistic or tripartite view. The soul (*psychē*) and body do not exist apart from one another. The soul animates the body but does not survive the body. For Epicurus, the soul must be corporeal because if it is not, then it is void, and void cannot do anything.[51] The soul consists of atoms, which act upon the body and are affected by atoms that make up the body. The soul "resembles most closely breath mixed with heat" (Epicurus, *Letter to Herodotus* 63). Lucretius also adds air. The soul is obviously warm and airy because those are the two elements missing from the body when it dies.[52] Since air, breath, and heat are not enough to cause action (and ethics is a primary category for Epicureans), there must be a fourth element, called the unnamed element.[53] None of these elements can be separated or divisible. The unnamed element comprises the distinctive character of the soul.

Lucretius draws a spatial distinction between the *animus,* or rational part, and *anima,* the irrational part. The *animus* sits in the chest, and the rest of the soul is distributed throughout the body. The *animus* is the mind, whose function is to allow thought and feeling and to govern the rest of the soul. Putting it into modern terms, Long suggests that the *animus* is the brain and the *anima* the nerves. Lucretius uses "mind," "soul," and "intellect" synonymously. The fact that the animus is in the chest and that Lucretius speaks of the mind and heart synonymously makes the *psychē* and *kardia* closely related. Lucretius writes: "So you can see that a beginning of movement is engendered by the heart, and it comes forth first from the mind's volition and then is dispatched throughout the whole body and limbs" (*On the Nature of Things* 2.251–293).[54] As our exploration of *kardia* in the NT authors, the heart is a center of emotion and volition. This chapter of the FG under consideration, with its identified *inclusio* at 14:1 and 27, finds the heart (*kardia*) as the source of being troubled (*tarassō*).[55]

A Community of Like-Minded Friends

A. A. Long writes this plaudit on Epicurus:

> There is an elegant simplicity to Epicurus' ethics, a refreshing absence of cant, and also much humanity. He was born into a society which, like most societies, rated wealth, status, physical attributes and political power among the greatest human goods. It was also a slave-based

---

51. Ibid., 51.
52. I think that John's pneumatology also is determined in part by what Epicurus and Lucretius taught about *pneuma.*
53. Ibid.
54. Ibid., 57.
55. Regarding *kardia* language, see the paragraph on *kardia* in the previous chapter, above.

society which reckoned men as superior to women and Greeks as superior to all other peoples. The good for [the hu]man which Epicurus prescribes ignores or rejects these values and distinctions. Freedom from pain and tranquility of mind are things which any sane [hu]man values and Epicurus dedicated his life to showing that they are in our power and how we may attain them [consider Johannine realized eschatology]. His ethics is undeniably centered upon the interests of the individual, and some have, with justification, praised the nobility of Epicurus more highly than his moral code. Yet we must see it in its social and historical context. No Greek thinker was more sensitive to anxieties bred by folly, superstition, prejudice, and specious idealism. At a time of political instability and private disillusionment Epicurus saw that people like atoms are individuals and many of them wander in the void. He thought he could offer them directions signposted by evidence and reason to a way of being, a way of living, a way of relating to others, other individuals. Negative, self-centered, unstimulating we may regard it; we cannot say priggish or self-indulgent, and in antiquity many found liberation and enlightenment in Epicureanism.[56]

Though we may find objectionable such features as FG's sectarianism and vitriolic treatment of "the Jews," his community, too, was clearly a source of enlightenment and liberation for some. To that end, notice the extensive use of language related to light (*phōs/phōtizō*) and sight (*theōreō, horaō, blepō*) as well as liberation (*eleutheros/eleutheroō*). In John 8:32 Jesus proclaims: "You will know the truth, and the truth will make you free [*gnōsesthe tēn alētheian, kai hē alētheia eleutherōsei hymas*]."

Viewing the community of the Beloved Disciple as similar to (or maybe even, for some, an alternative to) Epicurean communities may also help to explain two noteworthy features of this Gospel: (1) the closed nature of the community, in which friendship language (*philos/phileō*) figures prominently; and (2) the lack of overtly stated ethical prescriptions such as those found in Matthew's Sermon on the Mount.[57] The Epicureans were sometimes criticized for their lack of attention to justice. Since the ideal of Epicurean moral philosophy entails the avoidance of disturbance, avoidance of intense emotional commitments, and avoidance of participation in the social system, which leads to competition and the possibility of stress associated with failure, it is difficult to see how concern for others outside of the group fit into Epicurean philosophy.[58] The Epicurean circle was known

---

56. Long, *Hellenistic Philosophy,* 72–73.

57. See Wayne A. Meeks, "The Ethics of the Fourth Evangelist," in *Exploring the Gospel of John* (ed. Alan Culpepper and Clifton Black; Louisville: Westminster John Knox, 1996), 317–26.

58. David John Furley, "Epicurus," *OCD,* 534.

to live together in a secluded, quietistic fashion, in a place known as The Garden. The ideal of friendship characterized the Epicureans. Epicurus writes in *Principal Doctrines* 27: "Of all the things which wisdom secures for the attainment of happiness throughout the whole of life, by far the greatest is the possession of friendship."[59]

The FE's Jesus, with his single commandment, "Love one another," stands in stark contrast to Matthew's Jesus, who goes much further: "You have heard that it was said, 'You shall love your neighbor and hate your enemy.' But I say to you, love your enemies" (Matt 5:43–44). Furthermore, this Gospel, unlike the others, has the hero declare in language that one can imagine the Master Epicurus himself employing: "No one has greater love than this, to lay down one's life for one's friends. You are my friends if you do what I command you. I do not call you servants any longer, because the servant does not know what the master is doing; but I have called you friends, because I have made known to you everything that I have heard from my Father" (John 15:13–15).[60] Again, notice that of the six times friendship language is used, three occurrences appear within the context of the Farewell Discourse on the verge of Jesus' death, and one in the Lazarus pericope, in which Jesus says, "Our friend Lazarus has fallen asleep, but I am going there to awaken him" (11:11).

For the community of eternal life, part of the solution to the problem of death lies in the peace and joy that results from being a part of an intimate community. Again, in the FG this language is prominent in the Farewell Discourse, in which Jesus speaks only to the disciples, the insiders. Just as the ultimate solution to death lies in God and Jesus making their dwelling place among the believers from the day of belief into eternity, so also participation in the community assuages anxiety related to death. Just as the Epicureans gathered to be reminded that death was inconsequential since everyone would dissolve into atoms and suffer no eternal consequences, so too the community of eternal life gathered to be reminded by the Paraclete of the Master's teachings. The crucial difference? John's community recited these words: "Very truly, I tell you, anyone who hears my word and believes him who sent me has eternal life, and does not come under judgment, but has passed from death to life [*amēn amēn legō hymin hoti ho ton logon mou akouōn kai pisteuōn tō pempsanti me echei zōēn aiōnion kai eis krisin ouk erchetai, alla metabebēken ek tou thanatou eis tēn zōēn*]" (5:24).

---

59. *Hon hē sophia paraskeuazetai eis tēn tou holou biou makariotēta polu megiston estin hē tēs philias ktēsis.*

60. *Meizona tautēs agapēn oudeis echei, hina tis tēn psychēn autou thē hyper tōn philōn autou. hymeis philoi mou este ean poiēte ha egō entellomai hymin. ouketi legō hymas doulous, hoti ho doulos ouk oiden ti poiei autou ho kurios; hymas de eirēka philous, hoti panta ha ēkousa para tou patros mou egnōrisa hymin* (John 15:13–15).

The FE's community could certainly be accused of an ethical quietism similar to that in the Epicurean community. Jesus specifically calls the disciples out of the world and establishes a love/hate relationship between the community and the world. "If you belonged to the world, the world would love you as its own. Because you do not belong to the world, but I have chosen you out of the world — therefore the world hates you" (John 15:19).

If Epicurus's community of friendship was ideally characterized by happiness and freedom from pain, so too in the FG the language of joy clusters with the language of friendship (*philos/phileō*) and concentrates in the Farewell Discourse. Ideally the community is a place where sorrow or pain (*lypē*; cf. 16:6), though real, can be turned into joy. Thus in John 16:20 Jesus: "Very truly, I tell you, you will weep and mourn, but the world will rejoice; you will have pain, but your pain will turn into joy [*amēn amēn legō hymin hoti klausete kai thrēnēsete hymeis, ho de kosmos charēsetai; hymeis lypēthēsesthe, all' hē lypē hymōn eis charan genēsetai*]." And in John 16:22: "So you have pain now; but I will see you again, and your hearts will rejoice, and no one will take your joy from you [*kai hymeis oun nyn men lypēn echete; palin de opsomai hymas, kai charēsetai hymōn hē kardia, Kai tēn charan hymōn oudeis airei aph' hymōn*]."[61]

The community is an antidote to pain. John's community also appears to have been a community of equals, where hierarchy based on gender or economic status did not prevail.[62] As reported by Long (above), the same is true of the Epicurean community.[63]

CONCLUSION

Content

Similarities. In conclusion, I maintain that the FE's treatment of death *coincides* with Epicureanism in the following ways:

1. Both share a concern for death as the ultimate problem for humanity.

2. Both the FE and Lucretius transform some form of their Master's sayings into symbolic, poetic statements.

3. Both emphasize a realized eschatology that demythologizes contemporary religious models. They eschew future-oriented religions that cause

---

61. For other passages relevant to Johannine believers' receipt of joy, see 3:29; 15:11; 16:21–24; 17:13.
62. See Sandra M. Schneiders, *Written That You May Believe: Encountering Jesus in the Fourth Gospel* (New York: Crossroad, 2003), esp. ch. 6, "Women in the Fourth Gospel" (93–114), and ch. 8, "Inclusive Discipleship (John 4:1–42)" (126–48).
63. As David Furley points out, slaves and women resided in The Garden and are counted among Epicurus's devoted followers ("Epicurus," *OCD*, 533).

adherents to squander the joy or pleasure available in the present by focusing too intently on the future.

4. Both promote sectarian friendships that necessitate some separation from the world.

5. Both evince an interest in providing for their disciples peace and freedom from disturbance, which can be attained by following a certain set of beliefs.

6. Both depict the Master approaching death nobly and in accordance with his teachings.

7. Neither countenance a posthumous judgment day resulting in eternal torment for certain people.

Differences. The FE's treatment of death *differs* from Epicureanism in certain ways:

1. In the FG, the freedom from disturbance or anxiety about death comes from the knowledge that the disciple will live forever rather than from the knowledge that consciousness will cease, as in Epicureanism.

2. The FE argues against the planned obsolescence envisioned by Epicurus and celebrates the individual. The FE indicates that God and Christ not only created the world, but they also dwell in the individual believer. This Gospel is known for the encounters between Jesus, considered God, and certain individuals: The Samaritan woman, Nicodemus, Lazarus, Mary of Bethany, the Beloved Disciple, and Mary Magdalene.[64] Whereas the gods of Epicurus and Lucretius are remote and untouched by the vicissitudes of earthly life, the FE revels in the complete intimacy and unity shared by the believer and the Creator of the universe via the Holy Spirit (*pneuma*). In this way, he parallels in part or even borrows from the Stoics. But that is another essay for another day.

3. John acknowledges the reality and strength of pain (*lypē*) but relativizes it. It is not to be avoided (unlike the Synoptic Jesus, FE's Jesus does not ask that the cup may pass from him), but it certainly should

---

64. Thanks to Ila Kraft, who in personal correspondence points out the following: As I mentioned on "Backgrounds" (ch. 1, above), Epicurus was convinced that creation took place by a random joining of atoms. On the contrary, the "Word" of the FE is intimately involved: "All things came into being through him, and without him not one thing came into being" (1:3). This might explain the "motive," if God can be said to have motives, of God to overcome death. Epicurus's gods would have had no such motivation. One might say of FG that the relationship of God with believers is one of friendship. See especially J. Massyngberde Ford, *Redeemer, Friend and Mother: Salvation in Antiquity and in the Gospel of John*. Philadelphia: Fortress, 1997.

not be cause for fear or despair (unlike Matthew and Mark, where Jesus cries out, "My God, my God, why have you forsaken me?").

4. Finally, Lucretius ends with eternal death (*On the Nature of Things* 3.1091); John ends on eternal life.

Function

Regarding function, the Epicureans and the FG share commonalities:

Theological: to teach people about the existence (or not) and nature of the gods. Although they disagree radically about the nature and nearness of the gods, the teachings about death and afterlife for both the Epicureans and the FE serve a theological function. For the Epicureans, just as humans share no intimacy with the gods now, neither should they expect any interaction with the gods after death. For the FE, the case is exactly opposite: just as disciples currently enjoy complete intimacy with God and Christ, so they can expect to do so eternally. For FE, the category "theological" should be greatly expanded because under it fall anthropology (What is a person?), cosmology (What is the nature of the world or the universe?), eschatology (What is the destiny or fate of persons?), theology proper (Who is God?), Christology (Who is Jesus as the Christ? What is the significance of his death and resurrection, if any?),[65] pneumatology (Who or what is the Holy Spirit?). Finally, how do God, humans, Christ, and the Spirit relate to one another in time and space?

Pastoral/psychological: to assuage anxiety. Both Epicurean writers and FE teach about death and afterlife in a way that is intended to relieve anxiety among their disciples concerning death.

Ethical: to enjoin proper conduct. Both the Epicureans and the community of the FG stand out among their peer groups for lack of attention to issues of social justice.[66]

Social: to form and maintain a community characterized by a particular approach to life and death. The stances toward death starkly defined both the Epicurean and Johannine communities and provided part of the social glue that held the community together. The teachings helped to form and maintain sectarian boundaries and provide in-group language for the disciples.[67]

---

65. A provocative exchange of ideas is available in John Donahue, ed., *Life in Abundance*. Craig Koester's essay, "The Death of Jesus and the Human Condition: Exploring the Theology of John's Gospel," (141–57) is responded to by Gail O'Day (158–67); and Sandra M. Schneider's "The Resurrection (of the Body) in the Fourth Gospel: A Key to Johannine Spirituality" (168–98) is responded to by Donald Senior (199–203).

66. Long, *Hellenistic Philosophy,* 69–71. Also, for the FG, see Meeks, "The Ethics of the Fourth Evangelist," 317–26.

67. Elsewhere I have presented my views on the Johannine community: Clark-Soles, *Scripture Cannot Be Broken.*

Political: to encourage a particular stance toward the state. Given their views toward death and emphasis on quiet (*hēsychia*), the Epicureans discouraged political involvement. Lucretius's *On the Nature of Things*, book 6, certifies that he would be unlikely to wave a flag of patriotism, especially if it involved war. This political function does not figure prominently in the FE's teachings regarding death and afterlife. One could extrapolate by interpreting Jesus' death and especially his claim that his kingdom is not from this world and that any power Pilate has is from above, but FE does not overtly address the topic.

Apologetic: to aggrandize the authority of the founder by depicting him handling death in a way commensurate with his teachings. Both Lucretius and the FE present their leaders as dying in accordance with their own teachings on death and afterlife, thereby lending authority to those teachings.

In sum, the content and functions evinced in a study of Epicurean and Johannine philosophizing on death and afterlife suggest that the FE was in conversation and, perhaps, competition with the school of Epicurus, the Garden. It leaves one wondering whether or not the FE has this in mind when he has Mary meet Jesus post-Resurrection and pre-ascension and mistake him for The Gardener. Not *A* Gardener, but *The* Gardener (*ho kēpouros*, a hapax legomenon in the NT; 20:15). As it turns out, John's Jesus is far greater than that: he is nothing less than "the way, and the truth, and the life [*hē hodos kai hē alētheia kai hē zōē*]" (14:6).

DEATH AND AFTERLIFE IN MATTHEW

> *The dismal Situation waste and wilde,*
> *A Dungeon horrible, no all sides round*
> *As one great Furnace flam'd, yet from those flames*
> *No light, but rather darkness visible*
>
> —John Milton, *Paradise Lost*

> *So that's what Hell is. I'd never have believed it.... Do you remember, brimstone, the stake, the grid-iron?... What a joke! No need of a gridiron. Hell, it's other people.* —Jean-Paul Sartre, *No Exit*

> *Hell is oneself. Hell is alone, and the other figures in it merely projections. There is nothing to escape from and nothing to escape to. One is always alone... the final desolation of solitude in the phantasmal world of imagination, shuffling memories, and desires.*
>
> —T. S. Eliot, *The Cocktail Party*

> *The ribs and terrors in the whale,*
> *   Arched over me a dismal gloom,*
> *While all God's sun-lit waves rolled by,*
> *   And lift me to a deeper doom.*
>
> *I saw the opening maw of hell,*
> *   With endless pains and sorrows there;*
> *Which none but they that feel can tell—*
> *   Oh, I was plunging to despair.*
>
> —Herman Melville, "The Ribs and Terrors"

INTRODUCTION

IN MATTHEW, one finds the scribe who brings out something old and something new (13:52).[1] What is old is God's expectation of righteousness and God's concomitant judgment, all of which appear in the OT. What is new is hell. For those who need a robust notion of hell for their theology to work, Matthew provides abundantly. Unlike John and Paul, who nowhere use the language of hell, Matthew relishes it. We read of Hades, Gehenna, eternal fire, outer darkness, where there is weeping and gnashing of teeth. Does Matthew have a different notion of death and afterlife than either Paul or the Fourth Evangelist (FE)? If so, how might one account for the differences?

In some ways, Matthew's notion of death and afterlife is simpler than that of Paul or the FE. If one does good, one receives good, identified alternately as heaven, reward, or life. If one does bad, one receives bad, identified as Hades, Gehenna, outer darkness. The Deuteronomistic theologian had not imagined hell; nevertheless, Matthew's theology is partly Deuteronomistic.[2] There is nothing in Matthew's anthropology that we cannot find in the OT. The metaphysical speculation of Paul (1 Cor 15; 2 Cor 5) and John (ch. 3, Nicodemus) finds no home in this Gospel. John and Paul speculate about the nature of human beings; Matthew does not. Where Paul sees a sincere conflict between spirit and flesh (Gal 4:21–31), Matthew sees only hypocrisy. Where John sees a difference between those from above and those from below, those born of the flesh and those born of the spirit (John 3:3, 6), Matthew in typical OT style sees those who are good and those who are bad, those who are righteous and those who are wicked.

Matthew expresses less interest in what one believes than in what one does. This differs greatly from John and Paul, who each in his own way attend heavily to belief. Testifying publicly that Jesus is the Messiah is a key soteriological category for John (see 15:27 and the story of the man born blind in John 9). Matthew is suspicious of public piety, evidenced in his Jesus quote: "Not everyone who says to me, 'Lord, Lord,' will enter the kingdom of heaven, but only the one who *does* the will of my Father in heaven" (7:21, emphasis added). In Matthew, then, rewards and punishments are based on whether or not one does the will of Jesus' Father in heaven. As God's agent,

---

1. In using "Matthew" to refer to the author, I adopt all of the normal caveats. We do not know who actually wrote the Gospel, though we can reasonably surmise that the author was a Jewish-Christian writing for a community in tension with the rest of the Jewish community. As Donald Senior writes: "When using the term *Matthew* in connection with the evangelist and his perspective, the commentary is not referring to the apostle Matthew as such but to the anonymous author of the Gospel whose identity is no longer known to us except through the pages of his text" (Donald Senior, *Matthew* [ANTC; Nashville: Abingdon, 1998], 22).

2. Warren Carter points out that the Deuteronomist would have thought of punishment in terms of concrete historical events (*Matthew and the Margins: A Sociopolitical and Religious Reading* [Maryknoll, NY: Orbis, 2000], 41).

Jesus definitively reveals God's presence and will. As in Mark, Matthew depicts Jesus undergoing tests of understanding; his success establishes him as an agent of God and therefore deserving of persons' commitment to him (e.g. 8:13; 9:28; 18:6; 21:25, 32; 24:23, 26; 27:42). Furthermore, Matthew works assiduously in the opening chapters to establish Jesus' identity and commissioning as the basis for the rest of the Gospel (1:1–4:16).

There are three resurrections in Matthew. First, there is the mini-resurrection of the bodies of the saints when Jesus dies (27:50–54). Second, Jesus is resurrected (28:1–10). Both Jesus and those saints make resurrection appearances, the saints in "the holy city" (27:53), Jesus in Jerusalem (28:9–10) and Galilee (28:16–20).[3] Third, when Jesus returns as the Son of Man, the judgment earlier envisioned in Dan 7–12 will occur (16:27). Unlike John, Paul, and Peter, where only believers are assured of resurrection, everyone will be resurrected in Matthew. The righteous gain heaven and the unrighteous gain hell. This means that one must pay some attention to Matthew's cosmology and eschatology that adds hell to Deuteronomistic theology. Matthew gives no indication that individual persons, whether as a whole or in part, will be transported to heaven or hell at death. Every person's due will come on judgment day, which lies entirely in the future.

Matthew's view of the world is dichotomous.[4] People are either good or evil, good seed or weeds, producers of good fruits or bad. People can kill the body but not the soul. Matthew's anthropology, cosmology, and eschatology are directed at achieving ethical behavior by people obeying the commandments and attaining righteousness through that behavior. Scholars define righteousness variously, some emphasizing God's action and others human action. Carter incorporates both:

---

3. James Tissot's illustrated Gospels contain a black-and-white image of his arresting watercolor depicting these resurrected saints visiting the Holy City. James Tissot, *The Life of Our Saviour Jesus Christ: Three Hundred and Sixty-Five Compositions from the Four Gospels* (trans. Mrs. A. Bell [N. d'Anvers]; New York: McClure-Tissot, 1899).

4. Syreeni argues that Matthew polarizes heaven and earth. God lives in heaven and humans live on earth. Jesus acts as a mediator since he has been given the authority to do so (Matt 28:18). Jesus grants this authority to Peter (16:19) and also the church (18:18). The mediation then comes from above through Christ and from below through Peter and the church. Syreeni then problematizes the schematic by attending to the Lord's Prayer: "Yet it is instructive to ask which of the two types of mediation is closer to Matthew's theological basis. Is the evangelist a whole-hearted spokesman for an institutionalized system of mediation which would effectively overcome the separateness of the human world from God's reality? Or does he, despite his assertion that there are means of mediation in both directions, leave his community in considerable uncertainty in practical life when it should avail itself of these means?" (4). Syreeni sees Matthew working with idealized images of how things "should be," as in the Lord's Prayer. He also detects Matthew's ambivalent mediation techniques at work in his treatment of Israel and the church, as well as the law and Jesus' teachings. See Kari Syreeni, "Between Heaven and Earth: On the Structure of Matthew's Symbolic Universe," *JSNT* 40 (1990): 3–13.

[Righteousness] denotes God's will or saving reign enacted in human actions.... Righteousness or justice (3:15; 5:6) means reconciling and faithful relationships (5:21–26, 27–32), integrity of one's word (5:33–37), nonviolent resistance to evil (5:33–37), love and prayer even for one's enemy (5:43–48), mercy in giving alms (6:2–4), prayer (6:5–15; 7:6–11), fasting (6:16–18), an anxiety-free existence [while] trusting God (6:19–34), refraining from judging others (7:1–5). It creates a distinctive way of life not shared by the wider society and for which disciples are persecuted (5:10).[5]

Through his death, Jesus practices what he preaches in 16:24–26 regarding forsaking one's life as well as serving others (20:26–27). How does Jesus' death serve others? Jesus' own death and resurrection are part of the legal system of righteousness, a ransom (Matt 20:28; Mark 10:45).[6] His death is not posed as an act of grace. Matthew never even uses the word *charis*, one of Paul's favorite words. For Matthew, Jesus' death is certainly not an efficacious replacement of the temple cult, as in John; instead, it is the fulfillment of it.[7] Neither does Jesus die for his friends so that the Paraclete might be given, thus enabling the disciples to do greater works than Jesus himself had done (John 14:12).

In this chapter, then, we learn the following: (1) Matthew's views on death and the afterlife can be explained as a combination of Deuteronomistic theology and apocalyptic notions (angels, earthquakes, Son of Man), especially as found in the intertestamental writings. (2) Matthew's views are both similar to and distinct from Paul and John. (3) Matthew assumes a bodily resurrection but not an explicit theology concerning it. (4) The primary actors in Matthew's eschatology are the righteous, the wicked, God, the Son of Man, angels, demons, and Satan (also called "the devil," "the evil one," and "Beelzebul"). (5) Matthew's anthropology shows no real dialogue with Hellenistic philosophy. Paul must both combat opponents within the church and reshape Hellenistic anthropological categories that his Gentile readers would probably assume. John works to correct a competing Christian eschatology

5. Carter, *Margins*, 13. Cf. Senior, *Matthew*, 55: "The term 'righteousness' (*dikaiosynē*) is another key Matthean concept (Przybylski 1980). 'Righteousness' or 'justice' is a divine attribute, signifying God's fidelity and right relationship to Israel. It also characterizes proper human response to God, implying faithfulness, obedience, and ethical integrity." Cf. Benno Przybylski, *Righteousness in Matthew and His World of Thought* (Cambridge, UK: Cambridge University Press, 1980).

6. For a fuller discussion on the ransom language, see Carter, *Margins*, 405–7. The idea of "ransom" and therefore the force of the preposition "for" is that of substitutionary death. Given Carter's own interests, it is not surprising that he interprets the act as freeing "others who live in the sinful world of imperial control" (406).

7. See the Temple Cleansing (John 2:13–22) and the exchange with the Samaritan woman (John 4:1–42). For a full exposition of the replacement theme, see Mary L. Coloe, *God Dwells with Us: Temple Symbolism in the Fourth Gospel* (Collegeville, MN: Liturgical Press, 2001).

that looks much like Matthew's own. Unlike Paul and John, Matthew does not appear to be arguing against another view of death and afterlife. Unlike John, who uses tradition to *correct* tradition, Matthew prides himself on *transmitting* tradition. (6) The *telos* of Matthew's eschatological scenario is: (a) to inspire clearly delineated ethical behavior; (b) to offer encouragement to a group that perceived itself as persecuted; and (c) to justify inclusion of Gentiles in the church.[8]

MATTHEW'S COMMUNITY

Beliefs, doctrines, and texts function for those who lend them authority. Whether consciously or unconsciously, the author of Matthew had an agenda when he composed the Gospel. Those who heard the text listened for some reason just as Matthew wrote for some reason. How might those two facts converge? I have argued on the basis of the Qumran, Fourth Gospel (FG), and Branch Davidian communities that Scripture functions to help sectarian groups form and perdure:

Table 1:
Categories of Potential Scriptural Functions within Sects[9]

A. Breaking Away: Creating and Degrading "Them"
B. Formation of Sect
   1. Etiology: Celebrate the origins of the community; ground the community in the hoary past
   2. Show sect's founder to have special insight regarding Scripture
   3. Define and elevate "us"
C. Creating a Distinct Way of Life
   1. Ethical behavior
   2. Ritual practice
   3. Language and rhetoric
   4. Use of sacred texts
      a. The sectarian community as Scripture's *telos*
      b. Scripture is authoritative and validates sect's views

---

8. Carter depicts death and resurrection in Matthew in terms of conflict with the imperial elite — Rome and Jerusalem allied (20:18–19) — because Jesus challenges their imperial social structure. So the unrighteous oppose God's faithful agent, but Jesus' resurrection reveals the limits of imperial power: it does not have the last word. Rome can neither keep Jesus dead nor prevent his return, and this fact amounts to the eschatological end of Rome's system (24:27–31). Carter, *Margins,* 399–400, 476–79.

9. Jaime Clark-Soles, *Scripture Cannot Be Broken: The Social Function of the Use of Scripture in the Fourth Gospel* (Boston: Brill, 2003), 24.

　　5. Roles of authoritative leaders: Leader is righteous, chosen, or otherwise admirable; leader is unjustly persecuted; leader is privy to special insight; leader warrants fidelity and belief — salvation depends on one's stance vis-à-vis him
　　6. Definition of the future
D. Opposition to and from the Parent Tradition
　　1. Named opponents
　　2. Those who break Scripture
E. Opposition from within the Sect: Dealing with Defection
　　1. Reward sticking with the sect
　　2. Castigate potential and actual deserters
F. Opposition to and from Without
G. Judgment against Opponents
H. Growing the Sect
　　1. Proselytizing
　　2. The next generation

In using "sectarian" language, I rely upon William Bainbridge's approach to sects and cults. As I have indicated elsewhere:

Bainbridge recognizes some basic tendencies which inhere in groups one might call sectarian. First, sects tend to arise from a schism between an established parent tradition and the smaller group. Second, sects tend to represent "an intense form of a standard religious tradition."[10] Bainbridge is quick to note that while these tendencies appear, they do not always inhere together. Rather than attempting to define the essential characteristics of a "sect," Bainbridge operates with a model that estimates "degrees of tension" between a group and its environment. Those considered "sectarian" are on the high tension end of the continuum.... Whether or not a group will maintain its original level of tension, increase it, or decrease it depends on a number of factors. Bainbridge suggests the following as those which decrease tension:

　　1. Birth of a new generation of members, who must be raised in the religion rather than converted to it.

　　2. Improvement in the economic level of members due to the ascetic values or other features of the sect.

　　3. Sociocultural assimilation of the ethnic group to which members belong.

---

10. William Sims Bainbridge, *The Sociology of Religious Movements* (New York: Routledge, 1997), 24.

4. Increase in the number of members, bringing the sect out of minority status.

5. Development of a stable leadership structure that builds a bureaucracy and emphasizes the needs of the bureaucratic leaders.

6. Random processes, including regression toward the mean, that tend to reduce the deviance of individuals or groups.

As parallels, Bainbridge offers the following as factors that maintain or increase tension:

1. A high level of recruitment of new members, which emphasizes their needs rather than those of members born into the group.

2. Failure of members to rise in the surrounding socioeconomic system, perhaps due to widespread economic depression and social chaos.

3. Rejection of members by powerful groups in society because they belong to a suppressed ethnic group.

4. Failure of a conversionist group to grow causes members to stress specific compensators in lieu of worldly evidence of success.

5. A sequence of charismatic leaders stages numerous revivals that pump up the tension.

6. Holy Scriptures or other well-established traditions that anchor the group near a particular level of tension.[11]

Matthew's group may be loosely defined as sectarian, and I would argue that Matthew's views on death and afterlife both derive from and shape the social context of Matthew's community. Certainly Matthew's ideas of death and afterlife promote the formation of group identity, of a "righteous us" (bound for angel-like existence) and a "wicked them" (bound for hell). Likewise, they help to create a distinct way of life.

Expanding on "Creating a Distinct Way of Life" (C above), Matthew uses death and afterlife categories to enjoin ethical behavior (the parable of the Sheep and the Goats, ch. 25; C2). During the eucharistic meal Matthew has Jesus indicate that the disciples can expect to be with him again (26:29; C2). Language and rhetoric of judgment and resurrection abound in Matthew (C3). Matthew refers to Scripture, especially Daniel and Ezekiel, to press his eschatological views (C4). This evangelist has Jesus himself announce the principles of death and afterlife, thereby validating their authoritativeness

---

11. Clark-Soles, *Scripture Cannot Be Broken*, 22.

(C5). Finally, Matthew uses death and afterlife language to outline the future of the community (C6).

In addition to shaping the faithful, however, Matthew must simultaneously attend to other issues. So, for those who may be on the periphery of the group, or for those whose knees are growing weak, Matthew's language of death and afterlife, with its potential rewards for adherents and certain destruction for apostates, might convince them to stay. In addition, he must address the tension with the Jewish parent tradition, and he does so with verve (see, for example, ch. 23). Finally, the community must also situate itself within a larger reality. John describes that larger reality with the term "world" (*kosmos*); Matthew expresses special concern for the community vis-à-vis Rome.

Drawing more heavily upon narrative categories than sociological ones, Carter has made a similar argument. He finds Matthew's community on the margins of a world that has the synagogue and the Roman Empire at its center. Matthew aims to subvert the center and provide his readers with an alternative world. He considers it a "counternarrative," a "work of resistance."[12] Matthew's small community probably lived in Syrian Antioch sometime around 80 CE. It represented a cross-section of the city's population and experienced and perhaps created tension with both the parent tradition and the empire. It was "familiar with Jewish scriptures, traditions and piety which, interpreted by Jesus, shape[d] their identity and lifestyle."[13] Although Matthew specifically treats the mission to the Gentiles favorably (see the magi [ch. 2] and the Great Commission [28:16–20]), Matthew's community was probably predominantly Jewish.

Carter identifies three particular points of conflict between Matthew and the parent tradition: Matthew contends (1) that Jesus forgives sins (indicated already in 1:21 by his prescribed name, Jesus, which means "Yahweh saves"); (2) that Jesus manifests God's presence in a unique way (indicated already in ch. 1 by his prescribed name, Emmanuel, which means "God with us"); (3) that Jesus can interpret and decree God's will, as indicated by the antitheses in the Sermon on the Mount (i.e., "You have heard that it was said..., but I say... ").[14] The conflict would have cost Matthew's community dearly in terms of social relationships, political power, and economic well-being, all of which may affect physical well-being (see the exhortation to avoid worrying in 6:25–34).

Perhaps Carter's greater contribution lies in his analysis of Matthew's relationship with Rome. He sketches a picture of life in an imperial city where

---

12. Carter, *Margins*, 1.
13. Ibid., 9.
14. Ibid., 34–35.

only five to ten percent of the population enjoyed pukka lives; the rest eked out a living in decidedly squalid conditions, strapped at every turn by a Pax Romana built on the backs of the masses.[15] If Jews in Antioch were an oppressed minority in the dominant culture, how much more so Christians? Drawing upon evidence provided by ancient buildings and coinage as well as literary remains, Carter indicates that Rome took every opportunity to impress upon its inhabitants that its power was divinely ordained, ubiquitous, draconian, eternal, and inevitable. Matthew, however, insists upon the temporary and moribund nature of Rome's power.[16] Just as Satan's end has begun, so Rome, as an agent of Satan (4:8), will fall. Ironically, Matthew uses the language of empire to predict and precipitate its defeat. He speaks of God as a king, of Jesus' coming (*parousia,* a word typically associated with the arrival of the emperor or other notable), of Jesus as bringing the kingdom of heaven, and of God destroying with raging fire, much as Titus and Vespasian had so recently destroyed the Jewish temple in 70 CE.

This section on Matthew's community has drawn attention to the fact that beliefs, ideas, and texts function powerfully in community formation and maintenance. Now it is time to focus narrowly upon what, after all, Matthew wishes to convey to his community with his treatment of death and afterlife.

MATTHEW'S COSMOLOGY

How does Matthew envision the universe? We saw in chapter 2 that Paul believes in a layered universe, part of which can be labeled "paradise." Matthew uses language that references heaven, earth, and various forms of hell. He does not indicate whether he envisions the multileveled or compartmentalized heaven of Paul in 1 Cor 12; nor does he include paradise (*paradeisos*) in his cosmological topography. I will examine his concept of heaven more fully below.

Matthew quotes Isa 9:1–2, drawing on a cosmology that ascribes a physical location to the dark realm of death: "The people who sat in darkness have seen a great light, and for those who sat in the region and shadow of death [*en chōra kai skia thanatou*] light has dawned" (Matt 4:16).[17] A similar cosmology may be found in Job: "If I look for Sheol as my house, if I spread my couch in darkness, if I say to the Pit [*šaḥat*], 'You are my

---

15. Ibid., 18.

16. See Warren Carter, "Are There Imperial Texts in the Class? Intertextual Eagles and Matthean Eschatology as 'Lights Out' Time for Imperial Rome (Matthew 24:27–31)," *JBL* 122 (2003): 467–87.

17. For a sociopolitical interpretation of darkness as a feature of Jewish life under Roman imperial rule, see Carter, *Margins,* 115–16.

father..." (17:13–14); or "Let me alone, that I may find a little comfort before I go, never to return, to the land of gloom and deep darkness, the land of gloom and chaos, where light is like darkness" (10:20–22). In imagery unusual for Matthew, he has blurred the line between the living and the dead inasmuch as he uses language of the Pit, to which one goes after death, and applies it to both the living and the dead. To be sure, those sitting in the realm of death include the living among whom Jesus teaches, but also, in the course of Jesus' ministry as portrayed by Matthew, people who are literally dead (*nekros*) arise. These include those dead individuals whom Jesus resuscitates and who can expect to die again, as well as those long-dead saints who arise and hie to the Holy City at the time of Jesus' death and resurrection.

MATTHEAN ANTHROPOLOGY

For Matthew, human beings are either evil or good, unrighteous or righteous (5:45). So, the slaves of the king gather "all whom they found, both good and bad" (22:10). Matthew has no category for "somewhere in between." Matthew uses *agathos* (good) language sixteen times, as opposed to Mark and John, who use it only four and three times respectively. Paul uses *agathos* as well, but almost always in Romans (21 of 30 times) and almost never to designate a person "good" (only Rom 5:7). In Romans he uses *agathos* most often of conduct or as an abstract noun, "the good." Fully one-third of all NT occurrences of *poneros* (evil) appear in this single Gospel. Matthew uses it twenty-six times, while Mark and John use it only twice and thrice respectively. At times Matthew characterizes *everyone* as evil and sinful (7:11). When he does so, he may have Gen 6:5 in mind: "The Lord saw that the wickedness of humankind was great in the earth, and that every inclination of the thoughts of their hearts was only evil continually"; or 8:21: "And when the Lord smelled the pleasing odor, the Lord said in his heart, 'I will never again curse the ground because of humankind, for the inclination of the human heart is evil from youth'" (cf. Matt 15:19). At other times Matthew distinguishes between those who are sinners, evil, children of the devil, and those who are righteous, good, and children of the kingdom. This is no more or less contradictory than the OT presentation of the Israelites as both "evil from youth" (Gen 8:21) and "chosen" (Deut 7:6; 14:2; Ps 135:4; Isa 41:8).

Apparently the maturing process is likely to lead away from goodness, since one must become like a child to gain entrance to heaven: "Truly I tell you, unless you change [*strepho*] and become like children, you will never enter the kingdom of heaven" (Matt 18:3). Here Jesus is addressing the disciples, who presumably have been listening to him throughout his preceding ministry! Where John prefers to speak of "believers," Matthew prefers "doers." It is easy to determine who the doers are because they produce good fruits, obey the commandments, and by implication avoid hypocrisy and ostentatious piety. "The good person brings good things out of a good treasure, and the evil person brings evil things out of an evil treasure" (12:35).[18] The evil person is the plant that the "Father has not planted" (15:13) and therefore produces "bad fruit" (7:17). It is that simple.[19]

Matthew summarizes his view of the human person and one's fate, complete with an orderly sequence of events and discrete roles for each character:

> He answered, "The one who sows the good seed is the Son of Man; the field is the world, and the good seed are the children of the kingdom; the weeds are the children of the evil one, and the enemy who sowed them is the devil; the harvest is the end of the age, and the reapers are angels. Just as the weeds are collected and burned up with fire, so will it be at the end of the age. The Son of Man will send his angels, and they will collect out of his kingdom all causes of sin and all evildoers, and they will throw them into the furnace of fire, where there will be weeping and gnashing of teeth. Then the righteous will shine like the sun in the kingdom of their Father. Let anyone with ears listen!" (13:37–43)

COMPARING ANTHROPOLOGICAL LANGUAGES

How does Matthew's anthropological language compare with that of Paul and John?

Kardia

As in the OT, the heart (*kardia*) is seen as the location of volition, character (11:29), and emotion. It is the seat of purity (5:8), evil (9:4), and lust (5:28). Matthew's quotation of Isa 6:9–10 illustrates his belief that the heart is the center of understanding: "For this people's heart has grown dull, and their ears are hard of hearing, and they have shut their eyes; so that they might not look with their eyes, and listen with their ears, and understand with

---

18. Carter, *Margins*, 276, shows the link between treasure and heart: "Treasure denotes fundamental commitments (see 6:19–21) which are evidenced in speech and actions." Cf. Senior, *Matthew*, 142–43.

19. Or is it? Inevitably, the perennially difficult questions here arise concerning predestination, grace, and free will. Commentators mull over it and offer various explanations: Senior (*Matthew*, 150–51) determines that predestination is part of the "foreseen plan of God." For Carter's view, see *Margins*, 283–85.

their heart and turn — and I would heal them" (13:15). Matthew is keen to align the external with the internal. Since what is in the heart determines how a person acts, he wants the heart to understand what God commands: "What comes out of the mouth proceeds from the heart, and this is what defiles. For out of the heart come evil intentions, murder, adultery, fornication, theft, false witness, slander. These are what defile a person, but to eat with unwashed hands does not defile" (15:18–20). In 18:35 he wants his readers not just to forgive, but to forgive from the heart. Again, that Matthew borrows his anthropology from the OT is clear when he cites Deut 6:5 (LXX [Septuagint]): "You shall love the Lord your God with all your heart, and with all your soul, and with all your mind" (Matt 22:37; cf. Mark 12:30; Luke 10:27). Like the FE, Matthew never speaks of Jesus' own heart.

Psychē

Psychē *as Physical Life*

The word *psychē* appears sixteen times in Matthew. It can occasionally represent the animating principle, and as such it signifies physical life rather than soul. Herod seeks the young Jesus' *psychē*. Jesus gives up his *psychē* (physical life) as a ransom for many (20:28). One certainly would not declare that he gives up his soul.

Psychē *as Soul*

There appears to be a second, less biological meaning as well. In using *psychē* Matthew blurs the line between mundane physical life and a higher spiritual life. At 10:28 we learn that a human being can kill the body (*sōma*) of another human being, but only God is able to destroy both body and *psychē*. If read only on a literal level, this would, of course, contradict 2:20, where Herod distinctly seeks Jesus' *psychē*. In 6:25 *psychē* may be distinct from *sōma*. Alternatively, this may be an instance of Hebrew parallelism (cf. 21:5). Then there is the paradox concerning those who find their life (*psychē*) and yet lose it, and those who lose their life for the sake of Jesus and yet find it (10:39). One might be physically put to death for Jesus' sake, but in the process one gains some kind of better *psychē*. Perhaps a more accurate translation would draw upon both the life and soul connotations represented by *psychē*: By clinging to physical life, one will lose one's soul, but by willingly forsaking one's physical life for Jesus, one will find one's very soul. The NRSV translators use both definitions of *psychē* elsewhere ("life" at 2:20; 6:25; "soul" at 10:28), so why not here? Jesus makes the same claim again at 16:25–26.

At 11:29 we learn that souls find rest in Jesus (cf. Heb 4). Matthew directly quotes Isa 42:1, thereby indicating that God has a soul (12:18). But in 3:17, which only alludes to the same text in Isaiah, Matthew has removed the language about God's soul; here it is God, rather than God's *psychē*, that is well-pleased. Jesus' *psychē* is of a spiritual sort that can be grieved to death (26:38).[20]

Sarx

Talk of the flesh (*sarx*) occurs less frequently in Matthew than in John or Paul. Matthew once distinguishes the flesh from the spirit, presenting them as opponents (26:41), something that both Paul and John often do. Also, he can use the term "flesh" in place of human being (24:22) or "flesh and blood" to refer to that which marks human beings as merely human, rather than divine (16:17). Additionally, when two people marry, they become one flesh (19:5–6). We never hear of Jesus' flesh, and certainly nothing about eating it, as in the FG.

Pneuma

Many of Matthew's "spirit" (*pneuma*) references are to the Holy Spirit or to demonic beings that possess people (8:16; 10:1). Anthropologically speaking, there are only two relevant passages. The first (5:3) indicates that one's spirit is similar to one's heart as the seat of humility. The other (26:41), already referenced above, is the saying about the spirit being willing and the flesh weak, a phrase adopted from Mark. Matthew mentions Jesus' own spirit only once, and like the references to his *sōma* and *psychē*, "his spirit" is what he gives up (27:50). In terms of Matthew's anthropology, then, *pneuma* is not as significant a category as it is for John and Paul.

In Matthew, the Holy Spirit participates in Mary's pregnancy (1:18, 20) and in Jesus' baptism and temptation (3:11, 16; 4:1), and provides the persecuted followers with words to speak (10:20), just as for OT characters (22:43). By the Spirit's agency demons are exorcised (12:28), and in the Spirit's name people are baptized (28:19). It is far more serious to blaspheme the Holy Spirit than the Son of Man (12:32). Unlike both John and Paul, Matthew never explains how one accesses the Spirit.

---

20. Carter, *Margins*, 240: *psychē* (in 10:28) means (1) the whole self and (2) life in relation to God. "But here it also contrasts with body to refer to the disembodied soul which survives bodily death, but, subject to God's power, is reunited with the body in resurrection." Senior (*Matthew*, 251) points out that the belief in the resurrection in Matthew is based not on the immortality of the human soul, but rather on the power of God to defeat death. W. D. Davies and Dale C. Allison (*A Critical and Exegetical Commentary on the Gospel according to Saint Matthew* [3 vols.; Edinburgh: T&T Clark, 1988], 2:206) on 10:28: "*Psychē*, the disembodied soul, can survive bodily death and later be reunited with a resurrected body. The conception, whether due to the influence of Hellenism or whether a faithful continuation of OT thought, is 'dualistic.'"

Sōma

Half of the fourteen occurrences of Matthew's body (*sōma*) language appear in the Sermon on the Mount, where Jesus is concerned with ethics. So, if one's eye is causing one to sin, one should pluck it out, since it is better to enter heaven with a partial body than to enter hell with a whole one (5:29). Matthew is clearly not concerned here with the nature of the resurrection body. Rather, he is speaking metaphorically and hyperbolically, to emphasize an ethical point. Therefore, it is difficult to determine certainly whether or not Matthew imagines resurrected believers as taking their earthly bodies with them to heaven or to hell. But based on the other evidence around his use of the language, including frequent apocalyptic categories, it is reasonable to assume that Matthew does indeed have a literal notion in mind. Matthew is clear that one should not be anxious about clothing that one dons for the sake of the body (6:25).

Three other chapters of Matthew (10, 26, and 27) use *sōma* language. At 10:28 Matthew exhorts the reader not to fear those who can kill only the body; rather, one should fear only the one who is able to destroy both body and soul. Presumably this statement serves simultaneously to warn and console. The consolation lies in the fact that even if their persecutors manage to kill them, their ultimate fate is under God's control. Yet being in God's hands should cause them some concern: though the power of their persecutors is puny, the power of God is not, and God is certainly able to destroy not only the body, but also the soul. This passage may indicate that Matthew imagines the body participating in the resurrection. It is an ambiguous verse, however. If the body is destroyed at the end of one's earthly life, with what does the person enter heaven or hell (cf. 5:29–30)? Perhaps that is pushing the question too far for Matthew.

In chapters 26 and 27, Matthew turns to the significance of Jesus' own body. The references to his body always are in the context of his crucifixion and death. At 26:12 we learn that the anointing has to do with preparing Jesus' body for burial. Jesus' body as well as his physical life (*psychē*) will be given up in the crucifixion. At the Last Supper (26:26), Jesus refers to the sacrifice of his body (*sōma*): like the sacrifice of his *psychē,* his body is given for the sake of his disciples. The last specific use of *sōma* comes in 27:58–59, when Joseph requests the dead body of Jesus. Nevertheless, Jesus' body is the issue a few verses later with the speculation that his disciples may steal Jesus' body from the tomb. The final allusion to *sōma* appears in 28:11–15, where the readers are told about the venal behavior of Jesus' enemies and the rumors with respect to the theft of Jesus' body. Matthew clearly places extreme import upon the part Jesus' body plays in the resurrection. In keeping with Matthew's assumptions about the body, resurrection requires that Jesus' physical body no longer be in the tomb. His resurrection is further proved by his appearing to various followers after he was raised (28:9–10, 16–20).

Relevant for our study is the odd piece about the bodies of the saints rising from the graves upon Jesus' death:

> Then Jesus cried again with a loud voice and breathed his last. At that moment the curtain of the temple was torn in two, from top to bottom. The earth shook, and the rocks were split. The tombs also were opened, and many bodies of the saints who had fallen asleep were raised. After his resurrection they came out of the tombs and entered the holy city and appeared to many. Now when the centurion and those with him, who were keeping watch over Jesus, saw the earthquake and what took place, they were terrified and said, "Truly this man was God's Son!" (27:50–54)

Notably, instead of indicating that the saints were raised, Matthew specifies that their bodies (*sōmata*) were raised. Apocalyptic categories are on display once again here.[21] Most commentators relate this event to Ezek 37 and assume that the saints are figures from the OT. Neither Paul nor John speaks of this "special resurrection."

Conclusion on Anthropological Terms

Matthew evinces an OT anthropology as defined by Wolff (see ch. 1, above).[22] The most meaningful categories for Matthew's view of humanity are good, evil, *kardia,* and *psychē.* He shows some interest in *sōma* (body) since for this Gospel what happens to people on judgment day is based upon how they have behaved with their bodies. By implication from the story of the dead saints being raised, it appears that Matthew envisions a bodily resurrection at least for saints. *Sarx* (flesh) and *pneuma* (spirit) are not significant anthropological categories for Matthew.

LANGUAGE OF DEATH AND DESTRUCTION

Given that Matthew's community lived a precarious urban existence as a minority group on the margins of synagogue and empire, it is no wonder that Matthew's death and destruction language is richly varied and voluminous. Matthew's language about death includes *apothnēskō, anaireō, apokteinō,*

---

21. Senior, *Matthew,* 334, locates the background in Dan 12; Ezek 37; and intertestamental Jewish apocalyptic.
22. Hans W. Wolff, *Anthropology of the Old Testament* (trans. Margaret Kohl; Philadelphia: Fortress, 1974).

apollymi, thanatos (as well as *thanatoō* and *geusomai thanatou*), *nekros,*
teleutaō (and the phrase *teleutaō thanatos*), *taphos,* and *mnēmeion.*

Apothnēskō simply means "to die, to cease biological life."

Anaireō means "to kill." The word occurs in Matthew only at 2:16,
where Herod tries to kill Jesus. Exodus 2:15 (LXX) uses this same word
when narrating that Pharaoh sought to kill Moses, which only serves to
emphasize Herod as a type of Pharaoh, a theme that recurs throughout
Matthew's infancy narrative.

Apokteinō also means "to kill." In Matthew the killing is directed primarily at Jesus and his followers. The named killers include Herod and the
Pharisees. In 16:21, Matthew emphasizes that Jesus will *be killed,* instead of
simply saying that Jesus will die. The same is indicated in 17:23, where the
verbs for kill and raise are passive. This is quite different from John 10:18,
where Jesus ascribes to himself the power to lay down his life (*psychē*) and
take it up again. In Matthew, as it will happen to Jesus, so will it happen to
his followers (24:9). In 21:35, Jesus identifies the chief priests and the Pharisees as his killers, and the accusation is not lost on them (21:45; see also
22:6; ch. 23). The speech of chapter 23 perhaps reaches its rhetorical pinnacle with Jesus' lament over Jerusalem, the killer of prophets (23:37). What
Jesus has repeatedly and forcefully predicted begins to unfold in 26:3–4:
"Then the chief priests and the elders of the people gathered in the palace
of the high priest, who was called Caiaphas, and they conspired to arrest
Jesus by stealth and kill him."

Thus, eleven of the thirteen occurrences of *apokteinō* refer to leaders
killing Jesus and others of God's servants, including the disciples. Whether
or not this reflects the actual experience of Matthew's own community, presumably it speaks to the group's perceived setting as dangerous because one
chooses to be associated with Jesus.

The only other usage of *apokteinō* occurs at 10:28, where *apokteinō* and
apollymi, both meaning "kill," are contrasted with one another. The verse
serves as both warning and encouragement for the readers of the Gospel;
they should not worry because people can only kill (*apokteinō*) one's body,
but cannot kill (*apokteinō*) one's soul. On the other hand, they should maintain righteousness at all costs, including the death of their bodies, because if
they do not live aright, God can destroy (*apollymi,* see below) not only their
bodies but also their souls (10:28). As with Job (1:12), so in Matthew, even
Satan is not given the power to destroy. For the most part, though, God is
in the business of life, not death (22:31–32): "As for the resurrection of the
dead, have you not read what was said to you by God, 'I am the God of
Abraham, the God of Isaac, and the God of Jacob'? He is God not of the
dead, but of the living" (cf. 18:14). Certainly Matthew's audience, as inher-
itors of the Jewish Scriptures, would be familiar with this tension between

God as giver and sustainer of life and the dark side of God as Destroyer. For moderns, it is one of the enduring problems of the nature of God in the biblical witness. Where many modern interpreters ignore or otherwise account for the "problem," Matthew assumes it to be an incontrovertible, consoling, and even refreshing fact of God's nature. God, the Destroyer, will finally destroy all the enemies of Matthew's community, be they Jerusalem leaders, the imperial power of Rome, or Christian hypocrites and apostates.

Apollymi first means "to destroy," "to perish," and "to lose." It is Matthew's favorite word for destruction; he uses it nineteen times. Its meaning overlaps with other words that mean kill — not only does Herod want to kill (*anaireō*) Jesus (2:16); he also wants to destroy (*apollymi*) him (2:13). The same is true of the Pharisees, chief priests, and elders (12:14; 27:20).

Second, *apollymi* has a broader meaning as well: The disciples do not want to "perish" (8:25). They are to go to the "lost" sheep of the house of Israel (10:6; 15:24). God wants none of the "little ones" to be lost (18:14). All of these uses of *apollymi* imply being outside of God's fold rather than undergoing mere physical death. People can kill (*apokteinō*) the disciples, but God can utterly destroy them (*apollymi*; 10:28).[23] Consider 21:41: the extremely harsh behavior of the owner of the vineyard, who will "wickedly destroy the wicked" (*kakous kakōs apolesei*), symbolizes God's vehement rage. Likewise, in his wrath (*orgizō*) the snubbed king will destroy (*apollymi*) and burn (*empimprēmi*) metaphorical Jerusalem (22:7), an eschatological prediction of God's judgment on Jerusalem's unrighteous. According to Matthew, it is God's prerogative to destroy people forever by excluding them from God's fold.[24] This Matthean sense is conveyed accurately by Christians who customarily pray for those who are "lost" and will thereby be consigned to a postmortem eternal hell, experienced with some level of consciousness. Jesus speaks of the mission to the "lost" sheep of the house of Israel, using a perfect participle (*apolōlota*), which has the effect of putting the matter in very strong terms (10:6; 15:24).[25]

The theological meaning of "lose" (*apollymi*) looms large in Jesus' enigmatic declaration that the one who loses his life for Jesus will find it, and the one who finds it will lose it (16:25). One must lose one's life to find

23. Matthew simultaneously maintains conceptions of hell as both a place of ongoing burning and torment as well as a place of destruction.
24. Not all commentators agree on this. Carter (*Margins*, 240–41) says that physical death (presumably by killing: *apokteinō*) is better than total destruction (*apollymi*). Does Carter envision hell as annihilation (in the Pauline sense described in ch. 2, above) rather than eternal torment? Senior (*Matthew*, 121) takes *apollymi* to mean "eternal judgment." Davies and Allison (*Matthew*, 2:207) answer that the aorist of *apollymi* "is usually translated 'destroy,' and there are some Jewish texts in which the wicked are annihilated. ... It would appear, however, that the author of Matthew shared the prevalent view that the wicked would suffer for ever."
25. The perfect tense indicates action completed in the past, with continuing effect into the present.

it (10:39); this gives the term eschatological meaning, and this presumably is the same meaning Matthew intends when he has the disciples ask Jesus to save them because they are "perishing" (8:25). By using this word, the disciples clearly signify more than drowning. Those still in doubt can refer to 16:25, where the statement about gaining the whole world but losing one's life is immediately followed by heavily apocalyptic language about the arrival of the Son of Man and God's repaying everyone's deeds. Jesus' followers should expect to be killed for their service to him (24:9).

I have indicated above that Matthew uses *apokteinō* language to depict Jesus' prediction that the chief priests and the Pharisees will kill him, and soon afterward to portray that the prediction has been fulfilled. The same thing happens with the *apollymi* language where Matthew intentionally parallels Jesus' prediction in 12:14 that the leaders will kill him with its fulfillment in 27:20, which finds the chief priests and elders steering the people toward destroying Jesus. One might protest that in 12:14 the Pharisees are the leaders, but in 27:20 the leaders are the chief priests and elders. Matthew routinely uses these words synonymously. Is it accidental that the last use of both *apokteinō* and *apollymi* is to show fulfillment of an earlier prophecy of Jesus? While Jesus appears to be a victim of the leaders (as well as *pas ho laos* [all the people], 27:25), Matthew clearly indicates that appearances are deceiving; Jesus is far more in control than his persecutors, a message probably not lost on Matthew's own community.

Thanatos means "death," *thanatoō* means "to put to death," and *geusomai thanatou* means "to taste death." Matthew uses both *thanatos* and *thanatoō* language. In 10:21 he refers to the divisions that will cause family members to seek to put one another to death, and he uses these cognate terms during the passion to refer to the same opponents mentioned above, who seek to put him to death (26:38, 59, 66; 27:1).

The phrase *geusomai thanatou* (16:28) is a colorful phrase for dying: "Truly I tell you, there are some standing here who will not taste death before they see the Son of Man coming in his kingdom." In this case, Matthew has borrowed the logion from Mark 9:1, deleting the word "God" in accord with his reluctance to use God's name, and clarifying that it is the Son of Man who will be responsible for making manifest the power spoken of in Mark. The saying also appears in Luke 9:27. That the phrase was available as an idiom is shown by its additional appearance in both John 8:52 and Heb 2:9.[26] Though Matthew has Jesus declare that hearers themselves will not taste death, Hebrews insists that Jesus himself, by his suffering, tastes

---

26. Also, in the context of the end of the world, 2 Esd 6:26 says, "And they shall see those who were taken up, who from their birth have not *tasted death*" (emphasis added).

death for everyone (2:9).[27] Pertinent to our purposes and discussed further below, the phrase occurs in an eschatological setting: Jesus predicts that the Son of Man will return before some of his auditors die: "There are some standing here who will not taste death before they see the Son of Man coming in his kingdom" (Matt 16:28). This indicates that Matthew envisioned the eschaton arriving imminently. Assuming that Matthew was written around 80 CE, some fifty years after Jesus made the statement, some of Jesus' auditors would be quite aged. If Matthew did not expect the end to arrive quickly, he likely would have omitted the tradition altogether to protect Jesus from such a blunder; therefore, we can assume that Matthew did actually expect the end to come soon.[28]

As with both *apokteinō* and *apollymi* (discussed above), the "whole Sanhedrin" (26:59, au. trans.) and "all the chief priests and elders" (27:1) and the "scribes" (20:18) seek to put Jesus to death (*thanatoō/thanatos*). Again, just as with *apokteinō* and *apollymi,* the last occurrences of both *thanatoō* and *thanatos* in Matthew find Jesus' opponents fulfilling his prediction about them (27:1; 26:66). Is this a coincidence? Matthew heaps up the killing and destroying language when speaking of Jesus' opponents, giving one the distinct impression that these people are thoroughly evil and irredeemable. Matthew's reader feels not the slightest sympathy for them: they never appear to have the slightest bit of humanity in them.

Nekros means "dead." First, there are dead people other than Jesus. At 8:22, Jesus rather starkly commands, "Let the dead bury their own dead," thus defying the notion that one should attend to one's dead family members, and thereby drawing a rather sharp line between the dead and the living. He makes the same point at 22:32, where he declares God to be God of the living, not the dead. Again, he indirectly draws the line at 23:27, when he eviscerates the Pharisees by calling them "whitewashed tombs, . . . full of the bones of the dead and of all kinds of filth." Matthew thus implies that he considers the bones of the dead to be unclean.

In imitation of Jesus' ministry, his disciples are commanded to "raise the dead" (10:8). Jesus' raising of the *nekroi* serves as a sign of his identity, in his attempt to convince John the Baptist that Jesus is "the one who is to come" (11:3, 5). While it strikes the modern skeptic as unlikely or at least odd, we can safely assume, by reading the OT (1 Kgs 17:17–24) as well as contemporary pagan literature (2 Kgs 4:25–37; e.g., Philostratus, *Life of Apollonius of Tyana* 4.45), that for Matthew's audience the ability to raise dead people was a prerequisite for anyone who would deeply impress

---

27. See Bruce Chilton, " 'Not to Taste Death': A Jewish, Christian and Gnostic Usage," *StudBib* 2 (1978): 29–36.

28. It is commonly accepted that Matthew's redaction demonstrates a commitment to presenting both Jesus and the disciples in the best possible light.

potential disciples. At 14:2 Herod assumes that Jesus is John the Baptist redivivus, and Matthew offers no apologetic comment to the reader, thereby indicating that the author expects the audience to understand and perhaps accept the possibility of such things.

Second, there is Jesus as *nekros.* Matthew also speaks of Jesus being "raised from the dead" three times, using two different expressions, *ek nekrōn egerthē* (17:9) and *ēgerthē apo tōn nekrōn* (27:64; 28:7).[29] The first expression is found on the lips of Jesus as he commands his disciples to silence regarding the transfiguration until he has been raised. The second expression comes from the mouth of the chief priests and the Pharisees gathered before Pilate, who say, "Sir, we remember what that impostor said while he was still alive, 'After three days I will rise again.' Therefore command the tomb to be made secure until the third day; otherwise his disciples may go and steal him away, and tell the people, 'He has been raised from the dead [*ēgerthē apo tōn nekrōn*],' and the last deception would be worse than the first" (27:63–64). Once again, the last occurrence of the word fulfills Jesus' prediction and is spoken by an angel: "Then go quickly and tell his disciples, 'He has been raised from the dead [*ēgerthē apo tōn nekrōn*]'" (28:7).

Teleutaō means "to die," and *teleutaō thanatos* means "surely to die." Of the eleven NT appearances of the rather unusual verb *teleutaō,* Matthew uses it the most (2:19; 9:18; 15:4; 22:25). Outside of the Gospels and Acts, it occurs only at Heb 11:22. *Teleutaō* has a rather neutral feel to it. However, the phrase *teleutaō thanatos* (surely die) is stronger. Matthew took this expression from Mark, who took it from the OT (Exod 21:16 LXX).

Tomb language appears as *taphos* and *mnēmeion*. Matthew uses both *taphos* and *mnēmeion* for tombs, and at one point he uses both in a single verse (23:29). *Mnēmeion* is the more typical word, occurring forty times in the NT, seven in Matthew, and only sixteen times in the LXX. Matthew uses it to describe the dwelling place of the demoniac of Gadara (8:28). The righteous lie in a *mnēmeion,* which the Pharisees decorate (23:29); the saints emerge from them (27:52–53). Jesus is laid in one that clearly is cavelike since a stone is rolled to open and close it (27:60, 66; 28:2).

Taphos is a rather unusual word in the NT, but it occurs sixty-five times in the LXX. Six of the seven NT occurrences appear in Matthew. Paul uses it once (Rom 3:13), but there he quotes from the OT. It would appear, then, that Matthew is heavily influenced by the LXX in his choice of grave language, while the other NT authors are not. Matthew calls the Pharisees "whitewashed tombs" (23:27) and claims that the Pharisees build the tombs of the prophets (23:29). Strangely, the word is also used of Jesus' tomb

---

29. The passive here is a divine passive, to indicate that God is responsible for the raising.

(27:61, 64, 66), indicating that *taphos* and *mnēmeion* are synonymous for Matthew.

Perhaps it is easier to understand Matthew's view of death if we compare him with John. For John, death is a state; for Matthew it is an event, and a fairly destructive and violent one at that.

ESCHATOLOGICAL SCENARIO

Matthew's view of the eschaton deserves detailed treatment. To impose order on such a process, this section generally follows a chronological outline. I am aware, however, that it is impossible to keep each aspect entirely separate from the others. I will address the overlap of the future eschaton with the present, the arrival of judgment day, resurrection, gathering, the basis for judgment, sentencing, and the fate of the good and the bad.

Eschatologically, there is overlap between the present and the future since the eschaton begins with Jesus' asseveration: "Repent, for the kingdom of heaven has come near" (Matt 4:17). Resurrections, signs of the eschaton, occur during Jesus' lifetime. Not only does Jesus tell John the Baptist that the dead are being raised (11:5); also, unique to Matthew, certain saints rise at Jesus' death rather than at his resurrection. Matthew appears to be somewhat concerned about this notion, adding at the beginning of 27:53 that they did not actually appear until *after* Jesus' resurrection. Where they were in between is not clear.[30] Along with the saints, Abraham, Isaac, and Jacob seem to be already resurrected (22:32).[31] While in Matthew one can enter the kingdom now, one can only enter hell in the future, on judgment day. Matthew always speaks of people being "raised from the dead" (14:2; 17:9; 28:7); he has no holding tank, purgatory, or intermediate place or state. When people die, they remain dead until they are raised.

At 8:29 we find demons shouting: "What have you to do with us, Son of God? Have you come here to torment us *before the time*?" (emphasis added), which indicates that the time of judgment has not yet arrived. At 12:32 we find judgment taking place across two related but somehow distinct periods: "Whoever speaks a word against the Son of Man will be forgiven, but whoever speaks against the Holy Spirit will not be forgiven, *either in this age or in the age to come*" (emphasis added). At 24:3 we learn that Jesus' coming (*parousia*) will constitute an end: "When he was sitting on the Mount of Olives, the disciples came to him privately, saying, 'Tell

---

30. See Senior, *Matthew,* 333–35.

31. Alternatively, Davies and Allison (*Matthew,* 3:231) say of v. 32: "The argument seemingly implies not resurrection but continued existence and therefore an interim state. The two things were, however, not mutually exclusive; indeed, many no doubt thought the one to imply the other."

us, when will this be, and what will be the sign of *your coming* and of *the end of the age?*' " (emphasis added). Matthew assumes that global preaching is a prerequisite for "the end": "This good news of the kingdom will be proclaimed throughout the world, as a testimony to all the nations; and then the end will come" (24:14). Perhaps Matthew uses this as the "carrot" to inspire his timid community to get out there and preach the gospel. In a passage that stresses the future, Jesus says, "I tell you, I will never again drink of this fruit of the vine until that day when I drink it new with you in my Father's kingdom" (26:29). But just a few verses later, Jesus blurs the time frame: "From now on you will see the Son of Man seated at the right hand of Power and coming on the clouds of heaven" (26:64). All of this then makes strange the famous final line of Matthew's Gospel (28:20): "Remember, I am with you always, to the end of the age." What could it mean? Is Jesus not with them after the end of the age? We can make sense of this if we argue that here Jesus means he is with them until judgment day, after which they will not need him because they will be fully in the kingdom themselves.[32]

Judgment Day

Before resurrection can occur, the "day of judgment" (*hēmera kriseōs*) must arrive. On the Day of Judgment, all will be raised, gathered, and separated into their appropriate categories: the righteous will receive reward, while the rest (the wicked) will receive punishment. Matthew contains four of the seven NT occurrences of this phrase.[33] What do we learn about this day? Any town that rejects Jesus' disciples will fare even worse than Sodom and Gomorrah (10:15).[34] On the day of judgment, "you will have to give an account for every careless word you utter; for by your words you will be justified, and by your words you will be condemned" (12:36–37). This special concern echoes the Sermon on the Mount, which declares that anyone who calls a brother a fool is liable to hell fire (5:22).

Apart from the specific expression "day of judgment," Matthew uses justice (*krisis*) language eight more times and in various ways (12:18, 20; 23:23). It appears as shorthand for the day of judgment, combined with

---

32. As Davies and Allison (ibid., 3:687) observe, there is no ascension scene in Matthew. Carter (*Margins*, 553–54) suggests an assumption/imitation of imperial apotheosis traditions. See also Wendy Cotter, C.S.J., "Greco-Roman Apotheosis Traditions and the Resurrection Appearances in Matthew," in *The Gospel of Matthew in Current Study* (ed. David Aune; Grand Rapids: Eerdmans, 2001), 127–53.

33. Matt 10:15; 11:22, 24; 12:36; elsewhere at 2 Pet 2:9; 3:7; 1 John 4:17.

34. The same fate is declared specifically for Capernaum (11:24). One would have thought that Sodom and Gomorrah had already experienced thorough judgment, but apparently the final nail has not yet been pounded into that coffin. Tyre and Sidon, Chorazin and Bethsaida are grouped with the above problematic towns (11:21–22).

notions of hell. Thus, when he says, "at the judgment [*en tē krisei*]," he specifies a particular point of judgment that makes *krisis* synonymous with the day of judgment (12:41–42). At 23:33 we hear of "the judgment of Gehenna" (au. trans.). Everyone undergoes judgment at Jesus' second coming (the "end of the age"); Jesus' followers will not escape. This differs from John but is in keeping with Paul.

Matthew is the only canonical Gospel to use the term *parousia* to refer to Jesus' future appearance on the day of judgment. The disciples are the first in the narrative to utter it: "When he was sitting on the Mount of Olives, the disciples came to him privately, saying, 'Tell us, when will this be, and what will be the sign of your coming (*parousia*) and of the end of the age?' " (24:3). Jesus provides a threefold, almost formulaic, response in 24:27, 37, 39. In each of the three verses, he speaks not of "my" coming but of "the coming of the Son of Man" (*hē parousia tou huiou tou anthrōpou*), and he compares it with some other phenomena such as lightning or the days of Noah. The *parousia* will mark the "day of judgment" [*hēmera kriseōs*], which will come suddenly and will catch people unaware: "For as in those days before the flood they were eating and drinking, marrying and giving in marriage, until the day Noah entered the ark, and they knew nothing until the flood came and swept them all away, so too will be the coming of the Son of Man."

Raising and Gathering

The first step in the judgment process involves raising and gathering all those to be judged. One quarter of all NT uses of *egeirō* (raise up) appear in Matthew. He uses it twice as often as any other Gospel writer. How significant is this language for Matthew?[35] The first time the word appears, we find it applied to Joseph, who "is raised up" (passive form of *egeirō*) from an extraordinary dream involving an angel who speaks to him in the imperative concerning what to do about Jesus (1:24). The last occurrences come from the mouth of an angel who announces to the women that Jesus has been raised (passive form of *egeirō*) and speaks to them in the imperative concerning what to do about Jesus (28:6–7). In the first two chapters an angel and Joseph interact, with use of the verb *egeirō* several times. This means either that this word does not always refer to resurrection from the dead or to the eschaton, or it means that the raising up of Joseph from the dream has eschatological/soteriological overtones. The latter seems less likely.

---

35. Matthew rarely uses *anistēmi* (raise); however, Luke in Luke-Acts uses it extensively, in 62 of 108 NT occurrences.

However, the eschatological use of *egeirō* language appears in multiple other passages. For instance, at 3:9 John the Baptist proclaims that his Jewish audience should not think that they are included in God's kingdom merely because Abraham is their father. He predicts that God can raise up children for Abraham from stones. The stones, as it turns out, are the Gentiles who will be resurrected into Abraham's family, children by their participation in the church built on the rock, meaning Peter's church (16:18).[36] In the story of the paralytic (9:2–8), *egeirō* (getting-up) language blends into language of salvation and resurrection. The paralytic is raised from his bed (v. 6) and he himself is *raised* (*egertheis*, v. 7). The same is true in the following story, involving the sleeping girl (9:18–26). One's memory flashes back to Joseph, who was raised from sleep, and it flashes forward to Jesus in the tomb, who will be raised from death. Only a few verses after he has raised the sleeping girl, Jesus commands his disciples to do exactly as he has done: "Cure the sick, raise the dead [*nekrous egeirete*], cleanse the lepers, cast out demons" (10:8). In the next chapter, John the Baptist is to be told that, inter alia, "the dead are raised [*nekroi egeirontai*]," a sign that Jesus is the "one who is to come (11:4–5)." Given Jesus' description of his own ministry in 11:5, along with the announcement that he has come "to the lost sheep of the house of Israel" (15:24), we must see theological and eschatological language in his question about raising up the single sheep (12:11). He is clearly not simply speaking of saving a four-legged animal here. He is speaking of the salvation and resurrection of those lost people whom God pursues.

The passage about the people of Nineveh in 12:41–42 is striking in its use of resurrection language. At 12:42 Jesus rather oddly declares that

A the queen of the South will rise up [*egeirō*] at the judgment

B with this generation and condemn it [*katakrinō*],[37]

C because she came from the ends of the earth to listen to the wisdom of Solomon,

D and see, something greater than Solomon is here!

---

36. Senior (*Matthew*, 284) suggests that Matthew might envision separate judgments for Jews and Gentiles, citing 23:38–39 as a reference to Jews who do not accept Jesus.

37. It is not clear whether Matthew imagines the queen actually pronouncing judgment or whether she only participates in the sentencing once the judgment has been made. The theological implications of the former trouble some readers because it would imply that someone other than God, and a mere mortal at that, renders the final judgment. But the argument falters given that the disciples are also said to judge (*krinō*, 19:28) Hence, one cannot fully protect God's territory here, but one could lower the status of the queen and the Ninevites vis-à-vis the disciples by insisting that Matthew distinguished between *katakrinoō* (condemn) used in the queen of the South and the Ninevites passage, and *krinō* (judge) used of the disciples.

Here we learn that this queen of the South receives resurrection at the judgment along with everyone else, and then she will be in a position to judge this generation. Just one verse earlier (12:41), Matthew makes a parallel statement about the Ninevites but uses *anistēmi* instead of *egeirō*, which is unusual for him.[38]

A' The people of Nineveh will rise up [*anistēmi*] at the judgment

B' with this generation and condemn it,[39]

C' because they repented at the proclamation of Jonah,

D' and see, something greater than Jonah is here!

This kind of presentation is in keeping with Matthew's tendency to provide both positive and negative models of faith from the Scriptures.

Matthew 14:2 finds Herod worrying that Jesus is John the Baptist resurrected. This illustrates the belief, common at the time, that someone could come back from the dead before judgment day as well as the notion that if someone does come back from the dead, that person has special powers.[40]

Jesus' Resurrection

Perhaps not surprisingly, many of the occurrences of *egeirō* refer to Jesus' own resurrection from the dead. He predicts it (16:21; 17:9, 23; 20:19; 26:32), the chief priests and Pharisees worry about it (27:63–64), and the angel both announces its completion (28:6) and commissions the women to proclaim it (28:7). Unlike John's Mary Magdalene (John 20:11–18), Matthew's women have no trouble recognizing Jesus. They grab his feet, signaling that Matthew considers the risen Jesus to be fleshly (28:9). Matthew's Jesus does not move through locked doors, as he does in John's Gospel. In the NT, Matthew alone uses the word *egersis* (resurrection), and it appears in his comment clarifying that the saints did not appear in the "holy place" until "after his resurrection [*meta tēn egersin autou*]" (27:53).

Matthew uses *anastasis* (resurrection) only four times, all in the debate about the wife of the seven brothers (22:23–32). There both Jesus and the Sadducees can speak of "the" resurrection, which Jesus expands to "the resurrection of the dead" (22:31). Though the Sadducees do not ascribe to this doctrine, their argument with Jesus attests to its prevalence. Their understanding of the resurrection is similar to that generally described in

---

38. Matthew only uses the word four times, one of which is an OT quotation (22:24), two of which involve someone standing up (9:9; 26:62), and here.

39. Like the queen of the South (= of Sheba; 1 Kgs 10:1–10), the Ninevites may be limited to sentencing rather than judging.

40. Perhaps this explains why the raised saints were able to appear in the holy city (27:51–53). Consult Debbie Felton's rich and entertaining volume, *Haunted Greece and Rome: Ghost Stories from Classical Antiquity* (Austin: University of Texas Press, 1999).

the apocalyptic intertestamental literature. Luke uses the same language in his parallel passage (20:35), and he carries the Sadducean argument over into Acts, with Peter and John replacing Jesus: "While Peter and John were speaking to the people, the priests, the captain of the temple, and the Sadducees came to them, much annoyed because they were teaching the people and proclaiming that in Jesus there is the resurrection of the dead" (Acts 4:1–2). Luke depicts Paul teaching about "the resurrection of the dead" (17:32); as with Jesus, Peter, and John, he ends up defending the doctrine in the presence of Sadducees (23:6) as well as before Felix (24:21). At Acts 26:23 Luke's Paul speaks of the Messiah as "being the first to rise from the dead," but Matthew's Jesus does not appear to be the first (see 27:52–53). Paul also uses the phrase "the resurrection of the dead" (1 Cor 15:42). The author of Hebrews declares that wives received their dead by resurrection (11:35), thereby apparently contradicting what Jesus himself says about postmortem relationships in Matt 22:30. Hebrews 6:2, which speaks of "resurrection of the dead, and eternal judgment," sounds much more like Matthew. First Peter speaks of Jesus being resurrected from the dead (1:3). Luke uses the phrase most often.

Matthew has clearly inherited the notion of resurrection, and he reflects contemporary debate in his first-century Jewish context, wherein the Sadducees eschew "the" resurrection. By calling it "the" resurrection, Matthew demonstrates that it is a known phenomenon. That it is shorthand for the resurrection of the dead (*hē anastasis tōn nekrōn*) is suggested by the appearance of the same phrase in Jesus' response to the Sadducees at 22:31. As indicated above, *anistēmi* is used eschatologically at 12:41 with respect to the (future) resurrected Ninevites. Matthew often compares Jesus' ministry with that of Jonah. Sixty percent of all NT references to Jonah occur in Matthew's Gospel. Luke's Jesus references Jonah at 11:29–32, a passage largely paralleled in Matt 12; but Matthew's Jesus brings Jonah up again (16:4). Soon afterward, Matthew singularly refers to Peter as Simon, son of Jonah (16:17). So important is Jonah to Matthew that the two major figures in his Gospel are both tied to Jonah.[41]

Gathering

In the eschatological program, Jesus designates himself a gatherer: "Whoever is not with me is against me, and whoever does not gather with me scatters" (12:30; cf. 25:24, 26, 32). His gathering involves not only tenderness and protection: "How often have I desired to gather your children together as a hen gathers her brood under her wings, and you were not willing!" (23:37);

---

41. I certainly do not deny that "son of John" was a traditional appellation for Peter (cf. John 1:42), but I think Matthew is combining this tradition with his own penchant for elevating Jonah.

it also brings punishment: "His winnowing fork is in his hand, and he will clear his threshing floor and will gather his wheat into the granary; but the chaff he will burn with unquenchable fire" (3:12) (cf. *episynagō* at 24:31).

"Gathering" is also associated with the religious leaders who oppose Jesus. At the beginning of the Gospel, Herod gathers the chief priests and scribes to advise him regarding the location of Jesus' birth (2:4). At the very end the leaders gather, plotting to pay off the soldiers (28:12). And they gather at numerous points in between (22:34, 41; 26:3, 57; 27:17, 27, 62). Perhaps Matthew describes it most forcefully when he has Jesus make the graphic statement "Wherever the corpse is, there the vultures will gather" (24:28).

What does this mean for the disciples? The only other prominent usage of gathering language (*synagō*) occurs in the extremely important passage about the separation of sheep and goats (25:31–46). In that text we learn that a primary feature of the righteous is their "gathering" of strangers or foreigners, and a primary characteristic of the wicked is their refusal to "gather" foreigners, presumably a reference to Gentiles. The NRSV translates this as "welcome," which might make one think that the Greek word behind it is *lambanō* (receive); but in reality the word is *synagō* (gather). This is a deliberately telling and arresting move on Matthew's part, for he speaks directly to the "church" (*ekklēsia*) as the new synagogue (*synagōgē*), in which Gentiles play a fundamental part. Jesus' instruction to go nowhere among the Gentiles, to go only to the lost sheep of the house of Israel (10:6), has given way to the Great Commission to "all nations" (28:19–20). Matthew thus validates his own mixed church of Jews and Gentiles.

Paradoxically, the goal of eschatological gathering is separation: "So it will be at the end of the age. The angels will come out and separate the evil from the righteous and throw them into the furnace of fire, where there will be weeping and gnashing of teeth" (13:49–50). Who will be subject to this process? "All the nations will be gathered before him, and he will separate people one from another as a shepherd separates the sheep from the goats, and he will put the sheep at his right hand and the goats at the left" (25:32–33). The parable of the Sheep and the Goats concludes with this warning: "These will go away into eternal punishment, but the righteous into eternal life" (25:46). The text is certainly written for the benefit of insiders. This kind of language has two functions in Matthew's community: It consoles them, as they perhaps doubt God's justice, by assuring them that there is a payoff for persevering in ethical behavior. It also warns that evildoers will pay a steep price. Things are not as they appear. In this world, the wicked prosper and the innocent suffer, but in due time, all accounts will be set right.

Basis for Judgment

In many ways Matthew's Gospel, especially the discourse material, reads like an ethics manual. He expects his reader to see that behavior is the basis for judgment: turn the other cheek (5:39), go the second mile (5:41), give secretly (6:4), receive a prophet (10:41), provide a cup of cold water (10:42), do not call people "fool" (5:22), and so on.

Significantly, love and law are inextricably bound together. Only in Matthew does Jesus say: "Because of the increase of lawlessness, the love [*agapē*] of many will grow cold" (24:12). Matthew's particular concern for hypocrisy greatly complicates the issue of judgment. One must live out the details of the ethical mandates provided. If not, one will receive punishment on judgment day. It is not the corollary, however, that those who execute the ethical mandates can automatically be considered worthy of reward because they may, in fact, be performing outward behaviors that are in conflict with their inner motivations. They may appear to be righteous from the outside, when in fact they are nothing but purblind hypocrites. For those who might not quite understand Matthew's point in 7:5 ("You hypocrite, first take the log out of your own eye, and then you will see clearly to take the speck out of your neighbor's eye"), chapter 23 serves as a virtual textbook on hypocrisy, with the Pharisees serving as primary examples.

Remarkably, thirteen of the seventeen NT occurrences of *hypokritēs* occur in Matthew! Matthew's point is made even more powerfully by his choice to refer to specific people, hypocrites, rather than to an abstract notion, hypocrisy. He attacks hypocrites thirteen times, but hypocrisy only once (23:28). When he mentions hypocrisy, the Pharisees are the ones accused, and their hypocrisy correlates with their lawlessness (*anomia*). The extreme danger of hypocrisy lies not only in that it keeps the hypocrite from participating in God's kingdom, but also in that the hypocrite is responsible for barring others as well: "But woe to you, scribes and Pharisees, hypocrites! For you lock people out of the kingdom of heaven. For you do not go in yourselves, and when others are going in, you stop them" (23:13).

Fate of the Good

Economic Language

Matthew uses economic and heaven language when speaking of rewards. In the Sermon on the Mount, he exhorts his listeners to endure persecution with the knowledge that their "wage in the heavens [*misthos en tois ouranois*] will be substantial [*polys*]" (5:12, au. trans.). Matthew's understanding of the motivation for doing right or wrong is reward-based. Good and bad behaviors will receive their reward in kind. Loving someone who loves you back is not "good" behavior; it is ordinary and requires no supererogation, so no reward obtains (5:46). If one practices one's righteousness (*dikaiosynē*) publicly, God will withhold good rewards at the judgment (6:1–6).[42] One must be careful here to avoid oversimplification. Hypocrites may be rewarded with praise, fame, glory, wealth, status (6:2, 5, 16), but these are puny earthly rewards received at the expense of the infinitely greater post-judgment reward. In thinking reminiscent of the OT (see Psalms) and of the rabbis, Matthew defines this reward as a prophet's reward or the reward of the righteous (10:41).[43]

Matthew also uses language of settling accounts (*synairō*) to depict the relationship between God and human beings: "The kingdom of heaven may be compared to a king who wished to settle accounts with his slaves" (18:23). Jesus' death is a "ransom [*lytron*] for many" (20:28), and one assumes that by "many" Matthew means the righteous. When the accounts are settled, "heaven" and, less frequently, "life" are named as specific rewards for those who believe. That "life" (*zōē*) is an eschatological rather than biological term for Matthew is obvious; it is opposed to "eternal fire" in 18:8 and the "hell of fire" in 18:9. Furthermore, when the inquirer asks how to achieve eternal life in 19:16, Jesus omits the *aiōnios* (eternal) in his response. The only life worth talking about is "eternal life." One enters life by keeping "the" commandments (19:17).

The disciples will receive the right to sit on thrones judging the twelve tribes of Israel (19:28). Presumably the author holds out this reward as an encouragement for those presently suffering at the hands of the representatives of Israel's leaders, usually denoted as "Pharisees" in Matthew. When will the good be rewarded? "At the renewal [*en tē palingenesia*] of all things." This word is a hapax legomenon for Matthew (19:28); if occurs in the NT elsewhere only at Titus 3:5; it is customary for apocalyptic literature to speak simultaneously of both an "end" and a "renewal," as in the famous dictum *Endzeit gleicht Urzeit* [the end time will resemble the primordial time]. That Matthew envisions the typical apocalyptic vision of a restored creation is indicated by his attention to Genesis throughout his text, beginning with 1:1: "An account of the genealogy of Jesus the Messiah, the son of David, the son of Abraham [*biblos geneseōs Iēsou Christou huiou David hiou Abraam*]." Genesis 1 uses the language of "heaven and earth": "In the beginning when God created the heavens and the earth [*En archē*

---

42. Carter prefers to translate *dikaiosynē* as "justice" here, commenting that "contemporary readers understand piety in personal religious terms whereas deeds of mercy, radical praying for a new world, and fasting are activities of justice and alternative societal structures" (Personal correspondence, 2/23/2005).

43. See Ephraim Urbach, *The Sages: Their Concepts and Beliefs* (trans. I. Abrahams; 2d, enl. ed.; Jerusalem: Magnes, 1979), ch. 15. See also Chaim Milikowsky, "Which Gehenna? Retribution and Eschatology in the Synoptic Gospels and in Early Jewish Texts," *NTS* 34 (1988): 238–49.

epoiēsen ho theos ton ouranon kai tēn gēn]." Matthew also likes the phrase "heaven and earth" (5:18; 11:25; 24:35; 28:18). It is not accidental, then, that Matthew would use this word "rebirth/renewal" (*palingenesia*), which has Genesis language embedded within it (19:28).

Heaven

Matthew also favors heaven language; one third of all NT occurrences of *ouranos* (heaven) appear in this Gospel.[44] What function does heaven serve? What meaning or meanings does it have for Matthew?

Authority. Heaven is where God the Father resides (5:16; 6:9) and whence God speaks (3:17).[45] It is therefore metonymous with God's authority and with Jesus' ability to act under that authority. Matthew depicts an ironic exchange between Jesus and his opponents at the beginning of chapter 16. They ask for a "sign from heaven [*sēmeion ek tou ouranou*]," thereby contesting his authority. Jesus ridicules them with a play on *ouranos*. The only *ouranos* that they understand is the earthly sky, and even that "heavenly" knowledge is useless because they cannot extrapolate from it that which is of ultimate significance. Heaven is the "throne of God" (5:34), "and whoever swears by heaven, swears by the throne of God and by the one who is seated upon it" (23:22).[46] Matthew's emphasis on power and sovereignty probably is intended to benefit his addressees, who do not have much access to either. This notion of authority arises again in chapter 16, when Peter is given the keys to the kingdom, such that "whatever you bind on earth will be bound in heaven, and whatever you loose on earth will be loosed in heaven" (16:19). This authority is broadened to include the church at 18:18–19.

Relationship of heaven to earth. The connection between heaven and earth is important to Matthew. The ideal situation would be for things on earth to be as they are in heaven, that the kingdom on earth would mirror the kingdom of heaven (6:10). Such is not the case. Matthew's community should find both consolation and conviction in Matthew's three solutions to this problem. First, Christians can pray that God may act to make it so. Second, God has given Peter, and by extension the church, the power to participate in making it happen (16:19; 18:18–19). Finally, in the near but not exactly specified apocalyptic future (see 25:1–13, the parable of the virgins),

---

44. Luke-Acts shows the second greatest interest in heaven, with more than one-fifth of the occurrences. Luke-Acts is also the only place outside of Matthew where *ouranios* language appears. Proportionately speaking, 1 Peter and Hebrews also show great interest in heaven.

45. Matthew uses both the singular and plural of the word: *ouranos* (heaven) and *ouranoi* (heavens).

46. A signature feature of Matthew is his use of *ouranos* in place of "God" in order to avoid mention of the sacred name. Matthew uses "kingdom of heaven" 32 times, Mark and Luke never; Matthew uses "kingdom of God" 5 times; Mark, 14; and Luke, 32.

God will act decisively to make it so. The apocalyptic notion that heaven and earth are on parallel planes is evidenced in the Lord's Prayer, where the goal is to align things on earth with things in heaven. Although they are two distinct planes, with heaven being superior to earth, God nevertheless is the Master of them both (11:25), and God grants that authority to Jesus (28:18). This same use of "heaven" to express authoritative agency is found in 21:25, where Jesus baits his opponents, asking them by what authority or from what source John the Baptist conducted his ministry. When the end is near, heaven will play a prominent role:

> Immediately after the suffering of those days the sun will be darkened, and the moon will not give its light; the stars will fall from heaven, and the powers of heaven will be shaken. Then the sign of the Son of Man will appear in heaven, and then all the tribes of the earth will mourn, and they will see "the Son of Man coming on the clouds of heaven" with power and great glory. And he will send out his angels with a loud trumpet call, and they will gather his elect from the four winds, from one end of heaven to the other. (24:29-31)[47]

Ethical behavior. Because heaven is where God resides, it serves as the compass for the heart as moral agent of human beings. So one should not store up treasures on earth; rather, ethical behavior should be aimed toward heaven (19:21; 6:20).

Heaven also means sky. It is where birds fly (6:26). I would also put Matt 5:18 (which indicates that heaven will "pass away") in this category since Matthew clearly does not signify that God's own realm (as described above) will surcease.

Heaven qualifies kingdom. The phrase "kingdom of heaven" is the focus of John the Baptist's (3:2), Jesus' (4:17), and the disciples' (10:7) proclamations. The genitive *tou ouranou* (of heaven) should be taken both objectively and subjectively here. Objectively, it refers to the proclaimers' revealing the ways of heaven or the will of God. Subjectively, the kingdom originates from heaven. Carter would press it further, to identify the "empire" of heaven as imperial because "it spreads out from and extends the power of heaven."[48] The poor in spirit and the persecuted possess this kingdom (5:3, 10). Some people become eunuchs for its sake (19:12).[49] The kingdom of heaven did

---

47. The statement describing the elect as "in heaven" has proved puzzling to commentators. Davies and Allison (*Matthew*, 3:364) call it "odd" and suggest that it represents an assimilation to Deut 30:3-4. Also, they consider it, along with 1 Thess 4:17, as denoting "a rapture to heaven." Senior (*Matthew*, 271) adds a number of other OT allusions related to God's gathering of the elect, but offers no detailed argument about why the elect would already be in heaven.

48. Carter, personal correspondence, 2/23/2005.

49. Scholars have commented extensively on this striking phrase. See Carter, *Margins*, 382-84ff. Senior (*Matthew*, 215) considers the eunuchs to be men and women who forgo marriage

not arrive on the scene with Jesus of Nazareth; rather, it began at creation, at the genesis: "Then the king will say to those at his right hand, 'Come, you that are blessed by my Father, inherit the kingdom prepared for you *before the foundation of the world*'" (25:34, emphasis added). The OT prophets worked on behalf of the kingdom, and they were violently killed (11:12; 23:34–35; etc.). Jesus worked on behalf of the kingdom, and he was violently killed. His followers can expect the same.

There are both present and future aspects of the kingdom; its present embodiment is the church. To enter the kingdom of heaven means, in part, to enter Matthew's church. The kingdom has drawn near, its perfection is close at hand, and Matthew's readers are closer to its final fulfillment than anyone before them has ever been (cf. 13:17).

Much of the Parables Discourse (ch. 13) is devoted to describing the kingdom. The kingdom of heaven is mysterious. That some are given knowledge of the kingdom and others are not (13:11) evinces Matthew's notion of election. In no way does this exonerate those who behave unrighteously. The elect or "good seed are the children of the kingdom," and those outside are "weeds," "children of the evil one" (13:38). This notion serves to bolster the author's own church community, identifying them as the elect and their enemies as outside the kingdom. Matthew's church and the kingdom of God are not coextensive, since God's kingdom has yet to fully appear, and only at that time will membership in the kingdom be fully sealed (see 22:1–14). Currently the wicked and the righteous commingle, and the wicked appear to impede the coming of the kingdom. God is aware of this and will not allow the situation to persist, as shown by the parable of the Wheat and Weeds (13:24–30, 36–43). The kingdom is small but disproportionately powerful. Matthew issues these words of encouragement to a community that perceives itself as small, persecuted, and besieged by the overwhelming power of Rome and the synagogue.

Entrance to heaven is a reward given to the exceedingly righteous (5:20), provided that they keep their righteousness off display (6:1). Those who perform the will of the Father will enter; calling Jesus Lord is not enough (7:21). Those who do not forgive fellow church members "from [their] heart" will not enter (18:35). Heavenly rewards are for the faithful (5:12), and especially for the poor in spirit (5:3) and the persecuted (5:11).

Ethnicity and social status in heaven. Abraham, Isaac, and Jacob reside in heaven. Matthew's Jewish opponents, "heirs of the kingdom" whom one might expect to dine with the patriarchs, will be cast into outer darkness.

---

for the sake of the kingdom. Davies and Allison (*Matthew*, 3:23) claim that this refers not to those who *cannot* marry, but to those who *will not* marry because of the demands of the kingdom. Davies and Allison draw an analogy with Paul in 1 Cor 7 and 9.

One might not expect to find in the kingdom Gentiles, coming "from east and west," who will dine with the Jewish patriarchs (8:11–12). The wedding garment is likewise a symbol of the inclusion of Gentiles in the kingdom (22:1–14). Matthew here teaches that, as shocking as it might seem to Matthew's community, the inclusion of the Gentiles is part of God's plan.[50]

Heaven is somewhat hierarchical. Matthew betrays belief that one can break a commandment, teach others to do so, and still be in the kingdom of heaven; such a person will simply be "the least," of a lower rank (*elachistos*) than the great (*megas*), who observe and teach the commandments (5:19). Matthew specifies that the least in the kingdom of heaven is greater than John the Baptist (11:11). The hierarchy in the kingdom of heaven is counterintuitive (see the parable of the Laborers in 20:1–16), but I think the hierarchy is more about this world and the categories the righteous should live by than it is about a ladder of people in heaven. If there were such a ladder, it would be modeled just as it should be on earth, where the last are first, the least are greatest (10:16, 25–28). Matthew likely uses this hierarchy both to warn and to console: to warn those who might be tempted to misuse power for personal aggrandizement, as do the Pharisees, and to console the vast majority, who have no power on earth. This situation will be rectified.

Ouranios (heavenly) appears in Matthew adjectivally to refer to the "heavenly Father" (5:48; 6:14, 26, 32; 15:13; 18:35; 23:9).

Angels reside in heaven (24:36) and descend from there (28:2). Matthew appears to believe that at least some human beings, "the little ones," have personal angels (18:10).[51] What is the force of this verse? Matthew intends to warn the readers against mistreating the little ones or, alternatively, to inspire them to treat the little ones well. "Their angels" are in a position to accuse those who mistreat the "little ones" before God, thus causing a demerit that might bar them from entering heaven (cf. 18:14). Again, we see the use of heaven to inspire ethical behavior. Angels do not participate in romantic relationships (22:30); one might call them angelic eunuchs.

---

50. The question may also be posed in terms of social status. Carter takes this up at length, deciding that the parable of the wedding feast, an allegory, "rehearses the elite's rejection and outlines their judgment. The repetition underlines the gravity of the elite's response, accounts for the fall of Jerusalem in 70 as an act of God's judgment carried out (unwittingly) by Rome, confirms the ongoing place of both Israel and disciples within salvation history, and impresses on the audience as the new tenants charged with mission to Israel the need for fruitfulness and faithfulness in carrying out their mission, especially among the poor" (*Margins,* 432). Matthew also indicates the unlikelihood of the wealthy attaining the kingdom (19:24).

51. For an extraordinarily thorough treatment of angels by an NT scholar, see Susan R. Garrett, *No Ordinary Angel: Jesus and the Angels in the Bible and Today* (New York: Doubleday, forthcoming).

Fate of the Bad

Evil people go to hell or some other undesirable place. Matthew says that evil trees, which necessarily produce evil fruits, are "cut down and thrown into the fire" (7:19). Whither they go bears some attention. Only Matthew, Luke-Acts, and Revelation refer to "Hades," a term taken from Greek culture.[52] Whether Matthew inherits it solely from Q or from the LXX is not certain. However, there is no reason to believe that he is interacting with Greek literature or philosophical texts. In 11:23 Matthew prophetically warns Capernaum that, instead of being exalted to heaven, it will descend into Hades. So Hades is located below the earth, in keeping with the Greek notions of Hades and Tartarus and the Hebrew notion of Sheol. Hades is the opposite of heaven. The same warning with exactly the same wording is found in Luke 10:15 but not in Mark, thereby making this a Q saying. In 16:18, Jesus tells Peter that he will build his church upon this rock, and "the gates of Hades will not prevail against it." As indicated in chapter 1 (above), ancient Greek representations of the underworld depict Hades with gates, like an ancient walled city.[53] More important, Hades represents a force that will fail in its attempts to prevail against the church (16:18). Matthew's readers should expect fierce persecution, in keeping with the warnings made elsewhere in his Gospel.

Matthew also consigns the wicked to the "outer darkness, where there will be weeping and gnashing of teeth" (8:12; 13:42, 50; 22:13; 24:51; 25:30).[54] Six of the seven occurrences of this phrase occur in Matthew.[55] Especially graphic is Matthew's depiction of God's execution of the unjust: "He will cut him in pieces and put him with the hypocrites, where there

---

52. It appears in Matt 11:23; 16:18; Luke 10:15; 16:23; Acts 2:27, 31; Rev 1:18; 6:8; 20:13, 14.

53. See Joel Marcus, "The Gates of Hades and the Keys of the Kingdom (Matt 16:18-19)," *CBQ* 50 (1988): 443–55. Though Marcus's interest lies primarily in deciphering the meaning of "binding and loosing" in Matt 16:19b, he does devote attention to what it might mean for gates to actively attack Christians. He contends that "In the time of Jesus and of the NT writers, the predominant conception of Hades (Sheol) among Jews and Christians was of the abode of the dead, not of the place of their punishment, and this is probably the sense in which 'Hades' is used in Matt 16:18" (444). He contrasts the gates of Hades with the gates of the kingdom to which Peter was given keys so that he might open the gates "not in order to *let something in* but in order to *let something out*," to "permit the extension of God's dominion from the heavenly sphere to the earthly one. The phrase *basileia tōn ouranōn* in 16:19, then, should be understood not as a reference to a place but as a term for God's manifestation of his kingly power" (447).

54. The wicked are Jesus' Jewish opponents in 8:12, and presumably 22:13, since right afterward the Pharisees plot against him. Who is the worthless slave who buried his talents in 25:30? Senior (*Matthew*, 279–80) says that this is a warning for the Christian community itself to live active, responsible lives. He suggests that it may also possibly refer to Jews who "chose to remain within a more defined ethnic and religious community," thus burying their gifts.

55. Luke 13:28 contains the seventh.

will be weeping and gnashing of teeth" (24:51). Once again, we see Matthew's special hatred for hypocrites. The phrase *to skotos to exōteron* (outer darkness) is unique to Matthew among NT and LXX authors.

Gehenna is Matthew's favorite place of punishment. (5:22, 29, 30; 10:28; 18:9; 23:15, 33; NRSV: "hell"). As indicated in chapter 1 (above), Gehenna is a Jewish invention, originally referring to the Valley of Hinnom's Son (cf. 2 Chr 33:6), just west and southwest of Jerusalem, Geh ben Hinnom (Gehinnom in rabbinic literature). In it rubbish was burned, so Gehenna is a fiery place. More than half of the twelve NT occurrences of the word appear in this Gospel and always in hortatory settings. In other words, Matthew uses "hell" to scare the sin out of his readers, taking from Mark the notion that those who allow their bodies to lead them to sin belong there. All Markan Gehenna language is used that way (9:43, 45, 47), and the only occurrence in James is similar (3:6).[56] But Matthew enthusiastically expands on Mark's hell. Even those who call a fellow Christian a fool can expect to be judged worthy of consignment to Gehenna. In a verse that evidences tripartite parallelism, Matthew strings three offenses — anger, insult, and slander — with three punishments — judgment, the council, and Gehenna (5:22).

At certain points Matthew speaks of hell as eternal, but oddly he indicates at 10:28 that hell is a place where God destroys both body and soul. However, if a person's body and soul are destroyed, they are completely annihilated and nothing would seem to remain to endure eternal punishment. These inconsistencies remind us that Matthew is far less concerned to systematize the details of hell and the afterlife than he is to use all possible means for urging the living to behave properly.[57] In 23:15 he warns against following the lead of the Pharisees: "Woe to you, scribes and Pharisees, hypocrites! For you cross sea and land to make a single convert, and you make the new convert twice as much a child of hell [Gehenna] as yourselves," upon which he sentences the scribes and Pharisees ("snakes,... brood of vipers") to Gehenna (23:33).

Fire figures prominently in Matthew. Only the author of Revelation includes more fire. Of all NT texts, only Matthew uses the word *empiprēmi* (set on fire). This occurs, in the parable that alludes to the burning of Jerusalem as a punishment by God (22:7). Matthew has apparently fully redacted

---

56. See Richard Bauckham, "The Tongue Set on Fire by Hell (James 3:6)," in *The Fate of the Dead: Studies on the Jewish and Christian Apocalypses* (NovTSup 93; Leiden: Brill, 1998), 119–48.

57. Luke does not have this difficulty because, in the only occurrence of Gehenna language in Luke, hell is envisioned as a postmortem place of punishment, without any indication that a person is annihilated: "But I will warn you whom to fear: fear him who, after he has killed, has authority to cast into hell. Yes, I tell you, fear him!" (12:5).

the parable. Fire becomes a weapon of judgment.[58] At times Matthew speaks of fire in metaphorical language. For instance, trees that do not bear fruit will be gathered and burned (3:10, 12; 7:19). But elsewhere his use of "fire" exceeds metaphor. Matthew suggests in chapter 13 that there is a literal eschatological reality to which the metaphor refers: "Just as the weeds are collected and burned up with fire, so will it be at the end of the age. The Son of Man will send his angels, and they will collect out of his kingdom all causes of sin and all evildoers, and they will throw them into the furnace of fire, where there will be weeping and gnashing of teeth" (13:40–42). He makes a similar statement in 13:50, where the angels again do the throwing. The fire is eternal (18:8), and it has been prepared for Satan and his workers: "Then he will say to those at his left hand, 'You that are accursed, depart from me into the eternal fire prepared for the devil and his angels'" (25:41). One's fate depends upon whether or not one does the good deeds that the law requires; it does not correlate with confessing Jesus (Matthew is a bit suspicious of words; John exults in them). Mark mentions fire related to judgment only in 9:43–48, but Matthew greatly expands Mark's notion. Mark's fire is unquenchable, but Matthew's is also eternal. Curiously, Matthew does not use fire in relation to Sodom and Gomorrah, as do Luke (17:29) and Jude (7).

Hell thus serves as a hortatory tool to extort moral behavior from Matthew's followers, and it serves as a tool against hypocrisy, using the Pharisees as a negative model. Matthew does not write this as a hortatory word to actual Pharisees in order to convert them to Christianity. Rather, it serves his community as a negative example of morality.

Unlike Paul in 1 Cor 15:24–27, where God rules over all of God's enemies, Matthew appears to consider hell to be outside of God's purview (5:34–35): "But I say to you, Do not swear at all, either by heaven, for it is the throne of God, or by the earth, for it is his footstool, or by Jerusalem, for it is the city of the great King." At 28:18 we learn that "Jesus came and said to them, 'All authority in heaven and on earth has been given to me.'" Jesus does not specifically claim authority over hell, nor does he have the ability or, perhaps more important, the *desire* to quench the unquenchable fire of hell. Furthermore, he does not use his authority when he is lifted up to draw "all people to [him]self" (John 12:32). Rather, the focus is upon his Jonah-esque bodily imprisonment: "For just as Jonah was three days and three nights in the belly of the sea monster, so for three days and three nights the Son of Man will be in the heart of the earth" (Matt 12:40). In John, Jesus uses his power and authority to draw all people to himself upon

---

58. Jude envisions eternal fire (7) and states explicitly that the function of the image is hortatory.

his death, but in Matthew Jesus dies and becomes a prisoner in the belly of the earth.

What is hell like? It is fiery.[59] It is associated with Satan and with eternal punishment: "Then he will say to those at his left hand, 'You that are accursed, depart from me into the eternal fire prepared for the devil and his angels' " (25:41).[60] The wicked are escorted to hell by angels, and will remain there forever: "So it will be at the end of the age. The angels will come out and separate the evil from the righteous" (13:49).

Actors in the Eschatological Scenario

It is appropriate to summarize in one place the main actors in the scenario Matthew stages. In 13:37–43, one finds many of the actors whom Matthew envisions participating in the eschatological scenario: the righteous (children of the kingdom, children of Abraham, followers of Jesus), the wicked (= children of the devil), God (= the Father), the Son of Man (= Jesus), angels, and Satan (= the evil one, the devil, the tempter). The only actors not included here are the Ninevites and the queen of the South, along with Jesus, the righteous, God, and the angels, as discussed above.

The devil and the Jerusalem leaders are linked.[61] The devil is described as evil (*poneros*; 6:13) and as tempting (*peirazo*; 4:1, 3); the same language is used of the Jerusalem leaders (16:1; 19:3). The devil controls all the empires of the earth (4:8), and Matthew sees the Jerusalem leaders as the devil's agents.

We have already discussed the righteous and wicked, but let us take a closer look at some of the other agents in Matthew.

The Father and the Son (of Man)

While the Father (Matthew's preferred designation for God: 5:16, 45, 48; 6:1, 4, 6, 8, 9, 14, 15, 18, 26, 32; 7:11, 21; 23:9; etc.) sets the eschaton in motion by sending Jesus, he takes a backseat as it plays out since he has chosen to hand everything over to the Son (11:27). Carter discusses the implication of Matthew's use of Father. In itself the image is patriarchal and is

---

59. See Davies and Allison (*Matthew*, 3:431) for information on metaphorical and literal interpretations of this image. Augustine adopted the literal; Origen and Gregory of Nyssa opted for the metaphorical.

60. Matthew does not indicate that hell is a place or kingdom ruled over by Satan, as one might imagine from C. S. Lewis's *Screwtape Letters*, in which Satan deploys demons to do his bidding. Matthew does not say that Satan has always lived in or voluntarily made his home in the fire; rather, he seems to imply that Satan's realm is earth, and only at the eschaton will Satan and his angels be cast into a fiery place as punishment. Carter (*Margins*, 496) holds that the devil's angels are those who resist God's will. He appears to think of them as human. This would strengthen the notion that the place prepared for the devil is prepared for the devil's own punishment, not as a special playground of pain overseen by Satan.

61. Jack D. Kingsbury, *The Parables of Jesus in Matthew 13: A Study in Redaction-Criticism* (London: SPCK, 1969), 13.

associated with authority; hence, Father *in heaven*. The Jewish tradition associated Father with the formation and obedience of God's people. Matthew invests the image with resistance to "oppressive power structures" and with "manifesting mercy and life."[62] The primary actor in the final judgment, then, is the Son of Man, who will come soon and dole out just deserts to everyone. "For the Son of Man is to come with his angels in the glory of his Father, and then he will repay everyone for what has been done. Truly I tell you, there are some standing here who will not taste death before they see the Son of Man coming in his kingdom" (16:27–28) (cf. Son of Man = king in 25:31, 34, 40). Throughout Matthew, as in Mark, the Son of Man reflects the eschatological figure who will suffer, be vindicated by God, and then judge at the end of the age. Matthew identifies Jesus with this figure.

Angels

The angels are most striking when one compares Matthew's eschatological scenario with Paul's or John's (cf. John 1:51; 12:29; 20:12). Only Luke-Acts and Revelation surpass Matthew's interest in angels. Occasionally the word (*angelos*) simply means a human rather than supernatural messenger as, for example, when it applies to John the Baptist (11:10). Matthew's angels can appear in dreams (1:20; 2:13, 19) and minister to Jesus (4:11). Germane to this study, *all* (25:31) of the angels accompany the Son of Man at the judgment or are sent to act as his agents: "So it will be at the end of the age. The angels will come out and separate the evil from the righteous and throw them into the furnace of fire, where there will be weeping and gnashing of teeth" (13:49–50). Thus, it appears that their role overlaps that of the Son of Man, who is also said to be the one who will separate people (25:32). Only Matthew uses *aphorizō* (separate) in this way.[63] They serve a military role of sorts and can, therefore, be divided into legions (26:53) and called to arms by a trumpet call (24:31). Paul, even in 1 Thess 4:16, never indicates this weighty a role for angels;[64] certainly John does not.

Angels usually reside in heaven, and they do not marry (22:30). The one exception is found in 25:41, where we hear that God has created an eternal fiery place for the devil and his angels. From heaven, an angel descends during an earthquake and personally rolls the stone away from Jesus' grave (28:2), once again ministering to him (cf. 4:11). At 4:5–6 Satan tempts Jesus

---

62. Carter, *Margins*, 139.

63. Davies and Allison (*Matthew*, 3:423) suggest Ezek 34:17, 20, but there is no mention of angels here nor does Ezekiel use *aphorizō*. Elsewhere in Ezekiel *aphorizō* is used regarding the setting aside of a portion of grain, sheep, land, for the Lord, as in 45:1, 4, 13ff.; 48:9, 20.

64. Carter argues that the military language associated with the angels at 24:27–31 indicates a final cosmic battle resulting in Rome's destruction. "The Gospel out-Romes Rome" with its use of military power in effecting judgment, its drawing upon cosmic creation imagery in effecting new creation, and so on (Carter, personal correspondence, 2/23/2005).

by suggesting that ministering angels will keep him from harm if only Jesus will cast himself off the pinnacle of the temple. He rejects the temptation to jump, and soon after he receives the aid of said ministering angels (4:11). The angel's raiment is impressive: "His appearance was like lightning, and his clothing white as snow" (28:3). He proceeds to validate the resurrection and commission its proclamation (28:5–7). From heaven, guardian angels watch over the earth's "little ones" (18:10).[65]

Satan

Matthew uses *Satanas* (the adversary, Satan), *daimonion* (demon), *diabolos* (the devil), *Beelzebul* (Beelzebul; the devil), *ho peirazōn* (the tempter), and *ho ponēros* (the evil one). In the temptation narrative (4:1–11), Satan, also here as "the devil" and "the tempter," acts much as he does in Job 1–2 insofar as he attempts to make the faithful person abandon his obedience to God. Later Peter will likewise tempt Jesus, leading Jesus to declare, "Get behind me, Satan!" (16:23). That the notion of working miracles by Satan's power had parlance is attested by the accusation that Jesus himself did so (12:27). Jesus makes it clear that he stands falsely accused in this regard. The fate of the devil will be the fate of his children and his angels — they will all be consigned to an eternal fire. Matthew uses the expression *ho ponēros* (the evil one) as a synonym for Satan. Apart from 1 John, no one else in the NT expresses great interest in that appellation. The evil one sows weeds, evil people, simultaneously snatching away the good seed that God sows. The power of "Beelzebul, the ruler of demons," is limited to hurting God's work on earth until the end comes (12:24). For this reason, the disciples must pray to be rescued from him (6:13).

CONCLUSION

In Matthew we have seen something old and something new in comparison with Paul and John. The inclusion of angels as a prominent feature of the eschatological scenario, the vigorous notion of a hell characterized as a place of eternal fire and torment for the wicked, the graphic representation of a group of saints resurrected before the eschaton — all are distinctive contributions of Matthew. A Jew concerned with the law, Matthew writes to a group who perceive themselves to be under pressure. He emphasizes the just aspect of God's nature. Yet, like the psalmist he notices that wicked appear to prosper while the righteous suffer. Jesus serves as a prime example, and

---

65. As Garrett states: "We can conclude, then, that some Jews affirmed the existence of guardian angels at about the time of the birth of Christianity, and that the notion was well established in some circles by the second century C.E." Garrett, *No Ordinary Angel*.

his followers should expect no less. But the sovereign God is observing and will settle accounts in the near future, so Matthew's call is to persevere and trust in God's justice. Matthew worries about justice and speaks vehemently and vindictively, in a way customary of powerless, persecuted groups. He abhors hypocrites first and foremost because righteousness is his primary concern.

Matthew's use of apocalyptic aids his twofold goal: catechesis for converts, especially Gentiles but also Jewish Christians, and pastoral encouragement. It is a striking oddity that the Gospel begins with a strong emphasis on repentance when repentance is not really a prominent theme in the Gospel. John the Baptist is quite taken with the notion of repentance, exhorting his listeners and baptismal candidates to repent because the kingdom of God has drawn near. He attacks the Pharisees and Sadducees who come to be baptized and tells them to bear fruit worthy of repentance, which they patently do not do in the narrative.[66] John characterizes his baptismal practices as a baptism for repentance.[67] Jesus mimics John's exhortation exactly, word for word (4:17; cf. 3:2). We do not hear him mention repentance again until he is chastising some cities for not repenting in the way that the Ninevites did (11:20–21; 12:41). Not once does Jesus mention repentance in the Sermon on the Mount or in any dialogue with another character in the narrative. Not once does one find a character in the story world of the Gospel of Matthew repenting (*metanoeō*).[68] Only Judas is said to change his mind (*metamelomai*). This may indicate that Matthew is not trying to bring readers into the kingdom so much as he is trying to explain what one should do and how one might persevere once one is a part of it. It is a document aimed at those who already are Christians.

What questions drive Matthew's view of death and afterlife? How do those questions compare with the questions of moderns who ask about death and afterlife? In speaking to various groups, it has been my experience that moderns differ from Matthew by placing primary concern upon the fate of the individual rather than the group. Many would follow Matthew insofar as he broadly conceives of death and afterlife as an ethical issue. If you do all the right things, you go to heaven. If you fail to do so, hell will be your eternal home. I have noticed another significant difference. For Matthew, ethics include not only issues of personal piety (when you fast, do not let

---

66. Carter (*Margins*, 96–97) argues that *epi* in 3:7 should be taken to mean that the Pharisees and Sadducees came out against John's ministry, in an act of resistance to his ministry considered as a challenge to the social status quo. I disagree and find it part of Matthew's strategy to give the leaders a chance to do the righteous thing, though they fail to do so, just as Herod fails in the infancy narrative.

67. Josephus refers to the baptism of John the Baptist, in *Ant.* 18.5.2 (116–119).

68. The Ninevites serve only as an example from the past, to influence the characters in the narrative.

anyone know about it; etc.) but also a strong emphasis on care for the marginalized. In my audiences, those who have a robust notion of hell tend to be concerned almost solely with issues of personal piety, whereas those most concerned with issues of social justice rarely show much interest in a doctrine of hell or in apocalyptic, future eschatology. They tend to speak of hell, if at all, in terms of the present, evincing a realized eschatology. Most likely Matthew held all of this together because he was immersed in the Hebrew Scriptures in a way that modern Christians are not. From the Torah to the Prophets, God commands God's people to care for the widow, the orphan, and the alien. Matthew understood this and envisioned hell for those who flouted such commands.

Functions of Beliefs

At various points in this chapter, I have indicated how Matthew's material on death and afterlife serves the community and/or the author. Here I will summarize the ethical, social, liturgical, theological, and pastoral functions of that material.

Ethical

Undoubtedly for Matthew, the ethical function looms largest. Righteous behavior will lead to heavenly rewards, and wicked behavior will lead to severe punishment, as the parable of the sheep and the goats, inter alia, indicates. Hell figures prominently in Matthew's ethical program. He provides the hell material for the benefit of the insiders so that they (1) might be reminded why they should behave righteously and (2) can relish the fact that their enemies will pay a severe penalty for not joining their group. It is hard to imagine that Matthew was writing for the benefit of outsiders in a way that the prospect of hell might terrify them into enlisting in Matthew's church.

Social

Matthew is concerned with the formation and maintenance of a sectarian community. He draws upon, creates, and promulgates specific insider language related to death and afterlife. The community's identity rests, in part, on the propitious fate shared by the elect in the eschaton. Though they experience tension with the parent Jewish tradition and with Rome, that tension should in no way be considered of ultimate concern. The church may be small, but it is powerful and substantial.

Liturgical

The Eucharist is eschatological in nature. Christians can expect that in the afterlife they will dine with Jesus at the messianic banquet. Scripture is a locus of divine revelation; Daniel and Ezekiel prove especially helpful with respect to understanding death and afterlife.

Theological

Three key parties work out the truth in God's purposes:

1. Jesus has the ability and the authority to reveal truth about what will happen to human beings when they die.
2. God is a righteous judge.
3. An apocalyptic scenario is likely, and angels will participate heavily in it.

Pastoral

Insofar as a pastor seeks to mold moral agents and gather together an elect community, Matthew's views of death and afterlife could be considered as functioning pastorally. But whoever uses a Pauline model of providing hope and encouragement would have to recognize that Matthew never uses the noun or verb for hope (*elpis/elpizō*; with the one exception in which he quotes an OT passage). Save 5:4, Matthew never uses the language of comfort or encouragement (*parakaleō*) in relation to death and afterlife considerations.

– F I V E –

DEATH AND AFTERLIFE
IN THE PETRINE TEXTS

For them alone did I descend,

For them pray'd, suffer'd, perish'd I.
Ye ne'er shall gain your wicked end;

Who trusts in Me shall never die.

In endless chains here lie ye now,
Nothing can save you from the slough.

— Goethe, "Thoughts on Jesus Christ's
Descent into Hell"

This complex passage [1 Pet 3:18–22] has long challenged scholars and poses a host of questions concerning the syntax and structure of these verses, their sources and conceptual background, their coherence and meaning, their relation to 4:1–6, their rhetorical function, and their relation to the concept of Christ's "descent into hell," despite the fact that neither "descent" nor "hell" is mentioned here. —John H. Elliott[1]

This [1 Pet 3:19] is a strange text and certainly a more obscure passage than any other passage in the New Testament. I still do not know for sure what the apostle meant. —Martin Luther[2]

T HE TANTALIZING LANGUAGE of both of the texts traditionally ascribed to Peter entice one's attention to death and afterlife. First Peter intrigues with its ambiguous description of Jesus preaching to the spirits in prison, and 2 Peter depicts angels cast into Tartarus, who serve as a warning to the contemporary ungodly. The bulk of this chapter will treat 1 Peter, with some attention given to 2 Peter at the end.

---

1. John H. Elliott, *1 Peter: A New Translation with Introduction and Commentary* (AB 37B; New York: Doubleday, 2000), 638.
2. Quoted in Elliott, *1 Peter*, 647.

INTRODUCTION TO 1 PETER

First Peter is generally classified as a pseudonymous letter composed around 73–92 CE to a mixed audience in Asia Minor.[3] The churches likely consisted of both Jews and Gentiles, though this might not be immediately obvious to the novice reader, who instead might assume a Jewish audience because of such features as the Diaspora language, the dependence on Israel's Scripture and tradition, and the derogatory use of the term "Gentile" (2:12; 4:3). But other internal evidence, such as reference to their former lives of ignorance of God, idol worship (1:18: "You know that you were ransomed from the futile ways inherited from your ancestors, not with perishable things like silver or gold"), and the like, signifies a predominantly pagan audience. Most important, the author infuses the term *ethnē* with new meaning: "This collective term, once used by Israel to designate all non-Israelites (as *gôyîm*), is now employed in 1 Peter to identify collectively all non-Christians as the new 'outsiders' and negative reference group. Here we have one of the several sectarian strategies of the messianic movement in its sectarian phase, in which traditional terminology and social distinctions are taken over from the parent body of Israel but invested with new and different meaning."[4]

It appears that the social status of most of the addressees was rather low. Elliott takes the *paroikos* (alien; 2:11) and *xenos* (stranger, foreigner; 4:12) language rather literally: "This designation indicates that their political, legal, and social situation was a precarious one, similar to the multitude of the déclassé and homeless strangers, who lacked, or were deprived of, local citizenship and its privileges."[5] Whatever their ethnic or social status, suffering appears as a leitmotif in the document.[6] No longer do scholars imagine an empirewide persecution of Christians initiated by the decree of Nero or Domitian; rather, the addressees suffer local persecution on the basis of adhering to a lifestyle strange to their neighbors.[7]

For a community apparently suffering so much persecution, there is surprisingly little death-related vocabulary. The noun "death" (*thanatos*) never occurs. The passive verb "put to death" appears once in relation to Christ's

---

3. For the details of introductory issues, see the standard commentaries. Elliott, *1 Peter*, 3–152, provides a useful overview.

4. Ibid., 96. For an analysis of this technique among other sectarians, such as the Qumran community, the community of the Fourth Gospel, and the Branch Davidians, see Jaime Clark-Soles, *Scripture Cannot Be Broken: The Social Function of the Use of Scripture in the Fourth Gospel* (Boston: Brill, 2003).

5. Elliott, *1 Peter*, 94.

6. Proportionately, 1 Peter harbors the heaviest concentration of suffering language in the NT.

7. The author of 1 Peter expresses high regard for the state as he commands his addressees: "Honor the emperor" (2:17). "For the Lord's sake accept the authority of every human institution, whether of the emperor as supreme, or of governors, as sent by him to punish those who do wrong and to praise those who do right" (2:13–14).

crucifixion (1 Pet 3:18). The varied and colorful language for death found
in Paul, John, and Matthew is replaced by language of suffering (*paschō,
pathēma*), trials (*peirasmos*), and endurance (*hypomenō, hypopherō*). Any
vision of afterlife modeled on the death and resurrection of Jesus serves to
encourage perseverance in the face of persecution. Eschatology serves ethics.
Unlike the Thessalonians, this community does not seem overly concerned
with the fate of dead compatriots. Whereas Paul starkly personifies Death,
1 Peter worries more about the specter of Sin.

DEATH AND AFTERLIFE IN 1 PETER

From the Apostles' Creed's insistence that Jesus "descended into hell" to the
paintings of "the harrowing of Hell," 1 Peter has made important contributions to notions of death and afterlife in the NT. Debate focuses largely
on 3:18–19 and 4:6, as well as on the contours of Petrine cosmology and
anthropology. Although it may be impossible to identify fully the roots of
1 Peter's imagery, we can surmise the message the author conveys regarding
the nature of earthly life and the place of God and human beings within it.[8]

Just as our investigation of Paul centered on 1 Cor 15, so we will center
our investigation of 1 Peter on two particular passages, 3:19 and 4:6, which
will serve as an entrée to wider Petrine thought. Because W. J. Dalton has
provided an excellent study that critically reviews the many interpretive pro-
posals offered, it will be enough for our purposes here simply to outline the
major options presented by Dalton before moving to other considerations.[9]

Questions and Responses regarding 1 Pet 3:19

> For Christ also suffered for sins once for all, the righteous for the
> unrighteous, in order to bring you to God. He was put to death in
> the flesh, but made alive in the spirit, in which also he went and
> made a proclamation to the spirits in prison, who in former times
> did not obey, when God waited patiently in the days of Noah, during
> the building of the ark, in which a few, that is, eight persons, were
> saved through water. [*hoti kai Christos hapax peri hamartiōn epa-
> then, dikaios hyper adikōn, hina hymas prosagagē tō theō thanatōtheis*

---

8. Copious and multifaceted has been the conversation regarding traditional background
materials for these verses. Creed, catechetical material, hymn, and other liturgical contexts have
been postulated. Nestle-Aland prints the passage on the spirits in prison (3:18–19) in verse,
implying that the material is already traditional. But as Dalton observes never before 190 CE
do the patristic writers quote 1 Pet 3:18–20 in support of the harrowing of hell (supposed
triumphant descent of Christ into hell between his crucifixion and his resurrection). William J.
Dalton, *Christ's Proclamation to the Spirits: A Study of 1 Peter 3:18–4:6* (2d ed.; AnBib 33;
Rome: Editrice Pontificio Istituto Biblico, 1989), 28n5.

9. Ibid.

*men sarki zōopoiētheis de pneumati; en hō kai tois en phylakē pneu-
masin poreutheis ekēryxen, apeithēsasin pote hote apexedecheto hē
tou theou makrothymia en hēmerais Nōe kataskeuazomenēs kibōtou
eis hēn oligoi, tout' estin oktō psychai, diesōthēsan di' hydatos.*] (1 Pet
3:18–20)

First Peter 3:18–20 raises numerous questions. For instance, do these verses
constitute a digression in the text, or do they fit there seamlessly and logi-
cally? This essay, bolstered by most scholars, assumes a logical fit.[10] Where
and why did Jesus' proclamation to the spirits in prison occur? Did Jesus
conduct this mission to convert the wicked or simply to announce his victory to the supernatural powers? Does "in prison" refer to Hades, Gehenna,
Tartarus, or none of them? Is prison located below (as in the creedal "he
descended into hell") or in one of the layers of heaven through which Jesus
passed during his postresurrection ascension?

To what does "made alive in the spirit" refer? Does it mean (1) Jesus' resurrection or (2) the period between the crucifixion and resurrection, in which
the disembodied soul of Jesus made a proclamation to some characters somewhere? If it means the latter, that raises an anthropological question: Does
1 Peter have a dualistic concept of the dead person in which the body perishes, but the soul continues to exist, conscious but bodiless?[11] Feinberg's
article proffers eight views on the meaning of the phrase "made alive in
the spirit": "In relation to *pneumati,* there are a number of possible ways
to understand it. The possibilities seem to be at least the following: (1) in
(by) the spirit, i.e., attitude; (2) in (by) the spirit world, i.e., the realm of
disembodied spirits, the underworld; (3) in (by) the spirit, i.e., immaterial
substance; (4) in (by) the spirit, i.e., Christ's divine immaterial substance;
(5) in (by) the realm of the spiritual relationship; (6) in (by) the sphere of
the spirit, i.e., the eternal, the heavenly, thus, giving him a spiritual or glorified body as opposed to a natural body; (7) in (by) the spirit world, i.e.,
angelic spirit worlds (especially the realm or world of evil spirits); or (8) in
(by) the Holy Spirit."[12]

What "gospel" did Christ preach? When did Christ effect this preaching?
Who are the "spirits" to whom the proclamation is made? Three positions,
as presented by Dalton, are outlined below:

10. Westfall argues that the author "uses lexical and logical parallelism to join the two
sentences in 1 Pet. 3:19–22 into a pericope." Cynthia Westfall, "The Relationship between the
Resurrection, the Proclamation to the Spirits in Prison and Baptismal Regeneration: 1 Peter
3:19–22," in *Resurrection* (ed. Stanley E. Porter, Michael A. Hayes, and David Tombs;
Sheffield, UK: Sheffield Academic Press, 1999), 107. As argued below, Dalton agrees.
11. J. Ramsey Michaels, *1 Peter* (WBC 49: Waco: Word, 1988), 203–4, argues that "made
alive in the spirit" refers to Jesus' resurrection.
12. John S. Feinberg, "1 Peter 3:18–20, Ancient Mythology, and the Intermediate State,"
WTJ 48 (1986): 314.

Christ Preaches to the Dead Contemporaries of Noah

The first position holds that the spirits are the souls of Noah's contemporaries who were dwelling in the underworld when Christ's spirit preached to them during the *triduum mortis* (three days of death). Within this view, three differing opinions obtain:

1. *Christ preached in order to convert and thereby save them.* First Peter 3:19 is not used as evidence of Christ's descent into the underworld until Clement of Alexandria (ca. 150–ca. 215 CE), who argues that Christ preached to souls in the underworld to save them.[13] Origen, Cyril, and others in the Greek and Syriac churches joined in Clement's optimistic view of the salvific opportunities for the dead. Later fathers, including Augustine, would render the notion of conversion in the next world heretical.[14] Numerous modern Catholic and Protestant scholars have adopted Clement's optimistic trajectory toward universal salvation.[15]

2. *Christ went to bring "good tidings" to Noah's unbelieving contemporaries, who were converted just before death.* There is a difficulty here insofar as there is no evidence of their conversion. Quite the opposite, according to 2 Pet 2:5–9 and 3:5–7. Nonetheless, one finds Justin Martyr arguing that Jesus did actually descend to preach to the just (those who had converted before their death).[16] Also, some early thinkers conflated Matt 27:51–53 with 1 Peter such that the earthquake in Matthew is a result of Jesus' descending to the dead, preaching to the patriarchs, and liberating them. Obviously, there is a distinction between Clement's converts above and the patriarchs.[17]

While Augustine and those following him declared that there is no conversion after death, Robert Bellarmine, writing in the sixteenth century, argued that Christ led those who had repented just before the flood from purgatory into heaven.[18] This view became more popular than Augustine's and dominated the Roman Catholic discussion after it was introduced.

---

13. The tradition of Christ's descent into the underworld, his harrowing of hell, predates Clement; he is simply the first to use 1 Peter in such an argument. See Holzmeister, 317–43. Irenaeus never alludes to 1 Pet 3:19 when he treats Christ's descent, thereby indicating that he must have interpreted the passage differently from Clement.

14. See Kallistos Ware, "Dare We Hope for the Salvation of All? Origen, St. Gregory of Nyssa and St. Isaac the Syrian," in *The Inner Kingdom* (Crestwood, NY: St. Vladimir's Seminary Press, 2001), 193–215.

15. Dalton, *Christ's Proclamation*, 32–33. Dalton includes F. W. Beare in this stance.

16. In his *Dialogue with Trypho*, Justin made use of a particular logion found in his (interpolated) version of Jeremiah, which supported this view. See Dalton, *Christ's Proclamation*, 34, for further bibliography.

17. Dalton, *Christ's Proclamation*, 37.

18. Ibid., 32.

3. *Christ brought castigation to the souls of Noah's wicked contemporaries. Their condemnation is final.*[19] After presenting these three options, Dalton observes that the problem with the discussion about Christ's descent includes inattention to the occasion and tone of the letter as a whole. The letter is written to encourage persecuted Christians suffering unjustly. Why would the author use this occasion to lecture about how Christ will save the unjust after they have died? Such a message would hardly comfort a persecuted congregation hoping for justice. Next, Dalton argues against a dualistic notion in which Christ's soul separates from his body and then peregrinates. Also, rather than referring to human beings, the "spirits" may actually refer to angelic beings, as evidenced by nonbiblical parallel literature.

Preexistent Christ Preaches through Noah

Dalton next entertains the hypothesis considering the spirits in prison (taken to mean "hell") to be Noah's living contemporaries on earth, to whom the preexistent Christ preached during their lifetimes through Noah, as he built the ark. This was Augustine's answer to the contradictory problem raised if one insists both that Christ preached to the dead while they were still living, and that there is no opportunity to convert after death. This interpretation dominated the discussion for the next one thousand years.[20]

Christ Proclaims to Wicked Angels

According to the third position, the spirits refer to the wicked angelic beings that caused human sin by marrying human women, a situation that resulted in the flood.[21] Within this view, there are two options.

1. *Christ descends.* First, Christ descends during the three days that he is dead (*triduum mortis*) and makes his proclamation to the angels. This interpretation owes a great deal to the book of Enoch. The *telos* of such a visit is simply an announcement of victory on Christ's part, not an attempt to convert the wicked angels.

2. *Christ ascends.* Second, and Dalton's favorite, the bodily resurrected Christ makes the proclamation to the angels residing in the lower heavens on his way upward. This takes into account the *zōopoiētheis de pneumati* (made alive in the spirit) language that, elsewhere in the NT, always refers to Jesus'

---

19. See Bo Reicke, *The Disobedient Spirits and Christian Baptism: A Study of 1 Pet. III 19 and Its Context* (Copenhagen: Munksgaard, 1946). Reicke claims that this is the typical Lutheran view.

20. See also Wayne Grudem, *1 Peter* (TNTC; Grand Rapids: Eerdmans, 1988), 157–58.

21. Westfall ("Relationship," 110n20) considers this to be the most common interpretation today. Against her note, however, Dalton, *Christ's Proclamation* (161), does *not* adhere to the notion of *triduum mortis*.

bodily resurrection. It also makes sense of the *poreuomai* (go, leave) language that is frequently used of Jesus' ascent, but nowhere else of a descent into hell.

Questions and Responses regarding 1 Pet 4:6

Whether 4:6 and 3:19 refer to the same event is an issue that has generated debate. Dalton offers four approaches to interpreting 4:6:[22]

Christ Preaches to All Dead Who Lived before Christ

The first suggests that between his death and resurrection, Christ preached to all the dead who lived before Christ thereby giving them the chance to hear the good news and convert. It would be unjust to consign to prison those who never had the opportunity to accept the gospel. In this case, we have a descent motif and a connection with 3:19. As Dalton observes, however, the idea that 4:6 clearly refers to Christ's preaching to convert the dead does not arise until Protestant liberal scholars at the beginning of the twentieth century promulgate such a view.[23]

Christ Preaches to the Righteous Dead Who Lived before Christ

The second position also argues for a reference to the descent of Christ between his death and resurrection. The difference here lies in the identity of those receiving the message. Whereas the first includes anyone who had never heard the gospel, the second envisions only the righteous of the OT. This interpretation relies on the connection between Matt 27:52 and the *koimaomai* (sleep) language in the OT, used to refer to the death of the just. In Dalton's view, this is a forced interpretation necessitated by the "orthodox" conviction that no one can be converted after death. Like the theory of last-minute conversion before the flood, as discussed with reference to 3:19, Robert Bellarmine popularized this position among Roman Catholics. The just determined their fate before they died. Dalton finds little indication early on that 4:6 was taken as a descent reference.

Problems with the first two positions. While Dalton concedes that the notion of Christ's descent in order to offer conversion is quite popular, he complains that such an idea obscures the context of 4:6 by linking it back to 3:19 rather than to its immediate context: 4:1–5. The beginning of chapter 4 exhorts the Christians to live as Christians and to expect to suffer at the hands of pagan adversaries as a result. Given this fact, it makes more sense to assume that the judgment of "the quick and the dead" in 4:5 (KJV) refers to God's judgment on the pagan adversaries; such a scenario might

---

22. Dalton, *Christ's Proclamation,* 51.
23. Ibid., 63.

encourage and inspire confidence among the suffering Christians to whom the letter is written. It would be odd and out of place, then, to suddenly initiate a disquisition about preaching to the righteous people of the OT.

Apostles Preach to the Spiritually Dead on Earth

The third major proposal imagines apostles preaching to the spiritually dead on earth; this notion dates back to Clement of Alexandria, Cyril, and Augustine. In modern times, Gschwind best articulates the position. The idea runs thus: "The gospel was preached to the spiritually dead (those who were once pagans), in order that they might be judged in the flesh in the eyes of human beings (share the suffering of Christ in enduring persecution), and so live in the spirit in the eyes of God (which corresponds to life free from sin of 4:1)."[24]

The main problem here is that the language of the quick and the dead in 4:5 implies that *nekros* means physically rather than spiritually dead. If it refers to the spiritually dead, one would have to entirely change the meaning of *nekros* one verse later; this does not seem likely.

The Dead as Christians

In the fourth view, the dead refers to Christians who were converted to the gospel but died before the letter was penned. In the eyes of their pagan adversaries, their deaths appear to be a condemnation. First Peter assures the readers, however, that these Christians belong to God and are destined to live forever.[25] Dalton compares the concern here with that in 1 Thess 4:13–18.[26]

One difficulty with this fourth interpretation is that it contradicts the surface meaning of *nekros*. Instead of "dead," the fourth interpretation implies "the living (who are now dead)." Second, if *nekros* in 4:5 is general, why limit *nekros* in 4:6 to "Christian dead"? Finally, the apparent purpose clause in 4:6b causes difficulty and leads to implying that the gospel was preached for the purpose of judging people in the flesh, for the purpose of death. This makes no sense. Hence, it must be taken as a concessive, "though judged in

---

24. Ibid., 57.

25. Proponents of this view (loc. cit.) include J. N. D. Kelly (*A Commentary on the Epistles of Peter and Jude* [HNTC; New York: Harper & Row, 1969]), Friedrich Spitta (*Christi Predigt an die Geister (1 Petr. 3, 19ff.): Ein Beitrag zur neutestamentlichen Theologie* [Göttingen: Vandenhoeck & Ruprecht, 1890], Edward G. Selwyn, *The First Epistle of St. Peter: The Greek Text with Introduction, Notes and Essays* (2d ed.; London: Macmillan, 1947), Joseph A. Fitzmyer ("The First Epistle of Peter," in *The Jerome Biblical Commentary* [ed. R. E. Brown, J. A. Fitzmyer, and R. E. Murphy; vol. 2; Englewood Cliffs, NJ: Prentice-Hall, 1968)], 362–68), and R. H. Mounce (*A Living Hope: A Commentary on 1 and 2 Peter* [Grand Rapids: Eerdmans, 1982]).

26. Dalton, *Christ's Proclamation*, 58–59.

the flesh," rather than as a purpose clause: "so that they might be judged in the flesh."

According to Dalton, part of the interpretive problem today may lie in the fact that first-century eschatology imagined an imminent Parousia; only rarely since then has this been the case in the church.

Dalton's Proposal

From the discussion thus far, one can sense the wide debate regarding 3:19 and 4:6. For each element commentators draw contradictory conclusions. Each conclusion is like a card in a deck. One chooses the various cards one likes, each card representing a separate issue, in order to make up one's own hand. It is a mix and match of sorts. For the sake of the clarity that comes with pursuing one line of interpretation, let us employ Dalton's interpretation as an anchor.

Authorship, Genre, Occasion of the Letter

Against most modern commentators, Dalton maintains Petrine authorship for the letter.[27] Dalton adopts the view that the Apostle Peter is responsible for the pastoral letter (though Silvanus perhaps did the actual composing; 5:12). The text is a pastoral letter written to encourage persecuted Christians, formerly pagans, to remain steadfast and hopeful during the abuse suffered at the hands of their neighbors, who are still pagans. It is not primarily a missionary document aimed at converting those neighbors.[28] Rather, the author takes and provides solace in the fact that when they die, these wicked enemies will receive justice and be annihilated at the imminent Parousia: "While he hoped, no doubt, that some of them would believe and be saved, he tended to see in them enemies of the gospel awaiting judgment rather than potential brothers and sisters within the church."[29]

1 Pet 3:18–4:6

Dalton views 3:18–4:6 as a literary unit with two clearly defined parts: 3:18–22 is doctrinal, and 4:1–6 is hortatory. He argues that 3:19 refers to Christ's postresurrection ascension, during which he announces his victory to the wicked, who reside in a lower heaven. In this line of reasoning, the author never had in mind a concept of Jesus' descent into hell. The language of "going" refers to the ascension, as it does elsewhere in the NT.

---

27. Ibid., 77–91. I do not maintain Petrine authorship, but authorship questions are not relevant to this investigation.

28. The same is argued by David Balch, "The Apologetic Function of the Household Code in 1 Peter," in *Let Wives Be Submissive: The Domestic Code in 1 Peter* (Chico, CA: Scholars Press, 1981), 81–116; and John H. Elliott, *A Home for the Homeless: A Sociological Exegesis of I Peter, Its Situation and Strategy* (Philadelphia: Fortress, 1981).

29. Dalton, *Christ's Proclamation*, 122.

Addressing the main features of Dalton's exegesis of 3:19 and 4:6, we begin with the literary structure of 3:18–4:6. He argues that verses 18 and 22 are hymnic or creedal, and 19–21 come from baptismal catechesis. They share parallel notions pointing to the same event. Both 19 and 22 refer to Christ's going (*poreutheis*). In 3:22 it refers to his ascension, which is connected with his exaltation at "the right hand of God," and the vanquishing of angelic powers. This implies that 3:19 might also refer to the ascension. The point is made clearer when other parallels are considered:

> We see, then, the same general topic treated in 3:19–20 and 3:22: in both cases we have a "going" of the risen Lord, an activity directed towards spirits (angels); in each case these spiritual beings are portrayed as "disobedient" (3:20) or hostile (3:22, implied by the idea of "subjected"). What is the activity of the risen Christ with regard to these spiritual beings? In 3:22 it is described as subjection: hostile beings are subdued. In 3:19 it is described as proclamation. The reader,... not told expressly what is proclaimed,... is supposed to get this from the context. If the analysis above is justified, we would seem to be dealing with a proclamation of victory. The point of the proclamation is that the disobedient spirits are no longer capable of harming those who belong to Christ. As in the case of the angels subject to Christ in 3:22, so in the case of the proclamation to the spirits of 3:19, any discussion about their possible conversion forces the thought into areas beyond the writer's intention.[30]

In this way, Dalton eschews arguments that try to parallel Christ converting sinners in the underworld and Christians converting pagan neighbors; he also repudiates any notion of 1 Peter's interest in universal salvation: "In all this section, 3:3–17, the conversion of pagans is not the motive of Christian suffering. It is rather a question of Christian survival in a hostile pagan world."[31] We do not have here an imitation-of-Christ motif whereby Christians emulate Christ by converting sinners. Rather, 3:18–22 focuses on what Christ did uniquely and without possibility of imitation: he died "once for all,... to bring [people] to God" (v. 18).

So, rather than an imitation theme, 3:18–22 presents a typology that aligns Christians with Noah. Just as Noah and his family remained righteous and were saved from the wicked world around them through water, while the wicked around them perished, so too are the Christians saved through baptismal water while the wicked around them perish.[32]

---

30. Ibid., 118–19.
31. Ibid., 126.
32. Ibid., 125.

Petrine Anthropology

The statement "He was put to death in the flesh, but made alive in the spirit [*thanatōtheis men sarki zōopoiētheis de pneumati*]" (v. 18) leads us to ask about Petrine anthropology. For his part, Dalton argues that the NT evinces a monistic anthropology: "Terms such as 'flesh' and 'spirit' are aspects of human existence, not parts of a human compound."[33] Later Greek thinkers, such as Clement, influenced by Plato, held a dualistic notion. As soon as this became widespread, it was easy to imagine Christ's peripatetic soul as separate from his body. Dalton argues here that Peter draws upon traditional creedal expressions: "put to death" refers to Jesus' death, and "brought to life" refers to his bodily resurrection.[34] That *zōopoieō* (make alive) is synonymous with *egeirō* (raise up) is indicated by 2 Cor 1:9 and Rom 4:17 as well as 1 Cor 15 and John 5:21. Nowhere in Peter or elsewhere in the NT is there room for the notion that Jesus' body was separated from his soul and traveled about. "The contrast of flesh-spirit appears often in the New Testament.... It can be said with confidence that in *none* of the cases... is the flesh-spirit distinction to be taken as a distinction between body and soul. In most cases the distinction is quite clear: it refers to two orders of being, the flesh representing human nature in its weakness, its proclivity to evil, its actual evil once it opposes the influence of God; the spirit representing the consequence of God's salvation, the presence and activity among us of the Spirit of God."[35]

Whatever "spirit" might mean with reference to Christ (his divinity, pre-existence, the Holy Spirit), there is no reason to think of it as Christ's wandering "soul." Dalton insists on the primacy of the resurrection of the body for NT Christians, a primacy now lost and replaced by Greek categories that unduly color the exegesis of modern scholars.[36]

What of the dative case in which flesh and spirit are rendered? While some would consider a causal dative to be rendered "brought to life by the Spirit," such would not make sense for the first clause. The two datives are paralleled and, therefore, should be rendered in a way that honors the parallelism. Therefore, it is more likely that we have datives of reference

---

33. Ibid., 64.

34. For an analogy, cf. Rom 8:11.

35. Dalton, *Christ's Proclamation*, 138. See also J. Louis Martyn, "The Galatians' Role in the Spirit's War of Liberation," in *Galatians: A New Translation* (AB 33A; New York: Doubleday, 1997), 524–40, referred to in chapter 2, on Paul (above).

36. Dalton, *Christ's Proclamation*, 141. Michaels (*1 Peter*, 302–4) makes a similar point: "Any attempt to distinguish between ... [*zōopoiētheis pneumati*, "made alive in the spirit"] and Jesus' bodily resurrection must do so by showing that only Jesus' 'soul' or 'spirit' was quickened while his body remained in the tomb, and this ... is not borne out by Peter's ... [*sarki-pneumati*] distinction."

(adverbial datives), which might be rendered "in reference to," or more specifically for Dalton "in the sphere of."[37]

In discussing Petrine anthropology Elliott largely agrees with Dalton.[38] *Sarx* denotes "the tissue, muscle, or fleshly part of one's anatomy, in contrast to bones, blood, and internal organs. When contrasted ... to *spirit* it refers more generally to the physical and mortal dimension of one's life."[39] *Sarx* and *pneuma* "denote the differing but complementary physical and spiritual states of Christ's existence (similar to the contrasts between *sarx* and *pneuma* in Rom 8:10; 1 Cor 5:5; Gal 5:16–25; 1 Tim 3:16; cf. also the similar comparisons of states in 1 Cor 15:42–44).... In 1 Pet 1:24 *sarx* designates all human mortals, and later in 4:1, 2 and 6 the dative of respect, *sarki*, again denotes the physical, mortal dimension in which Christ and the believers experienced suffering."[40] *Psychē* is used six times in 1 Peter and always means person or life; it is never contrasted with the body.[41] The particular meaning of *syneidēsis* (2:19; 3:16, 21) has been cause for debate. Dalton places 1 Peter's use of the word in a baptismal context and states: "While we think primarily of a feeling of innocence or of guilt, the New Testament thinks of an attitude or disposition toward God."[42] *Ennoia* (4:1) appears to mean something like "practical insight," though Johnson prefers "mental attitude."[43] *Sarx* "indicates the sphere of earthly, and often sinful, existence."[44] Flesh and spirit refer not to body parts but to spheres of influence, the first merely human as opposed to the second as incorporation of the divine. This approximates our earlier discussion of Paul, guided by Martyn's apocalyptic categories flesh and spirit (see ch. 2, above).

---

37. Dalton, *Christ's Proclamation*, 141.
38. See especially Elliott, *1 Peter*, 645–47.
39. Ibid., 645.
40. Ibid. Elliott (*1 Peter*, 645–46) eschews any notion of a descent of Christ to Hades in 1 Peter.
41. Elliott (ibid., 344) explains: "Here, and in the Bible generally, ... [*pscyhē*] denotes not an entity within or distinguishable from the human body but human beings in their entirety as *living beings* animated by the breath of God.... For our author, the total persons, personal selves as living beings and not their 'spiritual souls' alone, are the object of divine salvation.... This holistic sense of the term differs notably from Pauline usage, where *psychē, psychikos* can also designate the lower, sensual, and inferior dimension of human personality, a *psychikos anthrōpos* as contrasted to a *pneumatikos* ('spiritual') person (1 Cor 2:14) or an inferior 'physical body' (*sōma psychikon*) in contrast to a superior 'spiritual body' (*sōma pneumatikon*; 1 Cor 15:44). The dissimilarity is among the several elements of word usage, thought, and style that distinguish 1 Peter from the writings of Paul."
42. Dalton, *Christ's Proclamation*, 211. For a full discussion of *syneidēsis* in 1 Peter, see ibid., 210–14. Dalton not only presents his own argument, but also provides an extensive relevant bibliography on the term in both 1 Peter and the rest of the NT canon.
43. Sherman E. Johnson, "The Preaching to the Dead," *JBL* 79 (1960): 50.
44. Dalton, *Christ's Proclamation*, 237.

Detailed Analysis of 1 Pet 3:19

What are we to make of the *en hō* (in which) in verse 19? Does it refer to Christ going "in the spirit," or does it refer to the time at which this occurred? The former depends on an indefensible assumption that spirit means "soul," and that Jesus' soul traveled about while awaiting resurrection of his body. Hence, it most likely refers to the occasion upon which this proclamation took place. Some would argue that the occasion is determined by *epathen* (he suffered) at the time of his suffering or death (v. 18).[45] But this would ignore the second half of the chronological movement from his suffering to his being made alive (resurrected). If Jesus is unified and dead, it must refer to the time after he was resurrected. This is in keeping with the chronology of Christ's death and resurrection seen everywhere else in the NT (cf. Acts 2:31).[46]

Much has been made of how or whether verse 19 connects with what precedes or what follows, and the role of *en hō* (in which) figures prominently in the debates. Westfall names three major positions. First, *en hō* refers back to *pneumati* (either the Holy Spirit or a spiritual state). This would mean that Jesus, made alive in his spirit after death, went to hell as a spirit. It could also refer to "the spiritual sphere of the existence of Christ's pre-existent state."[47] A second argument refers it back to the resurrection in verse 18, leading to the conclusion that 19–20 proves that he was made alive and that his proclamation was made between the crucifixion and resurrection. A third view holds that the phrase is adverbial, either indicating time (at which time), cause (because of this), or "a marker of activity that bears some relationship to something else (in the case of)."[48] It is by no means clear which meaning is intended, though in other instances in 1 Peter it has an adverbial function.

Who are the *pneumasin* (spirits)? Are they "the souls of human beings who perished in the flood"?[49] Or are they the fallen angels from Gen 6:2?[50] Dalton takes spirits to mean supernatural beings, as in Matt 12:45 and Luke 10:20. This usage also appears in *1 Enoch* (as in 15:10; 19:1), a book that

---

45. There are several variants, but the basic division is between reading *epathen* (he suffered) or *apethanen* (he died).

46. Dalton, *Christ's Proclamation*, 147–48.

47. Westfall, "Relationship," 131n80.

48. Ibid.

49. Dalton, *Christ's Proclamation*, 151. Leonhard Goppelt (*A Commentary on I Peter* [ed F. Hahn; trans., augmented by J. E. Alsup; Grand Rapids: Eerdmans, 1993], 249–50) and Heinz-Jürgen Vogels (*Christi Abstieg ins Totenreich und das Läuterungsgericht an den Toten: Eine bibeltheologisch-dogmatische Untersuchung zum Glaubensartikel "descendit ad inferos"* [Freiburg: Herder, 1976], 101–11) argue thus.

50. For a lengthy list of scholars who support this view, see Dalton, *Christ's Proclamation*, 151n27.

probably heavily influences 1 Pet 3. In common with *1 Enoch*, 1 Peter shares the following, thus allowing Dalton to argue for *pneumasin* as the fallen angels: "1. a journey of Christ (*poreutheis*), 2. a proclamation (*ekēruxen*), 3. to the spirits (*tois pneumasin*), 4. in prison (*en phylakē*), 5. who rebelled, or disobeyed (*apeithēsasin*), 6. in the setting of the flood (*en hēmerais Nōe*)."[51]

Westfall argues that the temporal clauses indicate that the spirits in prison and the eight on the ark all belong to the antediluvian period. That is where the association ends, however. The eight are obedient and therefore gain entrance into the ark, while those outside the ark are not obedient and do not enter. There is further temporal contrast between "back then" (the time of the flood) and now (the time after the resurrection and ascension). The readers correlate with the eight souls; the resurrection of Jesus correlates with the ark.[52] Just as the eight were saved (*diesōthēsan*), the readers are now saved (*nun sōzei*).

What is the force of *kēryssō* here? Dalton shows that the verb does not necessarily mean "to preach the gospel with the intention of converting the hearers to a life of Christian faith." Rather, he sees an analogy with Noah, who "does not preach a sermon to his contemporaries: he is the herald of an event."[53] In the same way, Jesus' subjection of the powers equates to his proclamation to the spirits that salvation has come once for all in the person of Jesus. This is, once again, in keeping with the author's interest in encouraging beleaguered Christians rather than converting the wicked. "The author is interested much more in Christians than in angels."[54] It is not clear who does the preaching. It may be Jesus, or Noah, or Enoch.[55] But Westfall argues that to focus on the question of the subject of *kēryssō* is to miss the point; the author leaves the preacher unidentified and wants the focus placed upon the "spirits in prison" instead. There are five different parties in the pericope: the spirits in prison; the eight souls on the ark; those saved by baptism; Jesus Christ, who is at the right hand of God; and the powers subject to Jesus.[56]

What is the nature of the "prison" (*phylakē*) in which the spirits are held? First, it is a temporary, penultimate place of captivity, preceding final judgment. That it is envisioned as a place (rather than a mere "condition")

51. Ibid., 167. Though Westfall ("Relationship," 127–30) explains positively Dalton, the latter is not without critics on adducing *1 Enoch*. See Feinberg, "1 Peter 3:18–20," 321–25; and Grudem, *1 Peter*, 206–23.

52. Westfall, "Relationship," 114.

53. Dalton, *Christ's Proclamation*, 158.

54. Ibid. Dalton does see an occasional missionary nod, but rarely (3:1; perhaps 2:12).

55. The three options for identity of the subject dpends on whether the third-person singular verg is used anaphorically, cataphorically, or exophorically. Westfall, "Relationship," 110n22.

56. Westfall, "Relationship," 111.

is indicated by the author's use of the verb "to go" (*poreuomai*).[57] If 1 Peter is considered analogously with *1 Enoch,* the spirits are wicked (in Petrine terms, "disobedient," as in 3:20 KJV) fallen angels. In the NT, there are two goings. Jesus descends (*katebē*) to the abode of the dead only in Eph 4:9.[58] Then he goes (*poreuomai*) or ascends into heaven (as numerous texts say).[59] Ephesians 4:8 reads: "Therefore it is said, 'When he ascended on high he made captivity itself a captive; he gave gifts to his people' " (cf. Heb 9:11–10:14). This, taken with the evidence from *2 Enoch* that depicts evil spirits (angels/princes) as residing in the second (*2 En.* 7.1; 18.3) and fifth (*2 En.* 7.2; 18.1) heavens, makes a reasonable case for Jesus proclaiming to spirits as he ascends to heaven, rather than a "harrowing of hell" scenario.

Detailed Analysis of 1 Pet 3:20–21

[spirits in prison,] who in former times did not obey, when God waited patiently in the days of Noah, during the building of the ark, in which a few, that is, eight persons, were saved through water. And baptism, which this prefigured, now saves you — not as a removal of dirt from the body, but as an appeal to God for a good conscience, through the resurrection of Jesus Christ. [*apeithēsasin pote hote apexedecheto hē tou theou makrothymia en hēmerais Nōe kataskeuazomenēs kibōtou eis hēn oligoi, tout' estin oktō psychai, diesōthēsan di' hydatos. ho kai hymas antitypon nyn sōzei baptisma, ou sarkos apothesis rhypou alla syneidēseōs agathēs eperōtēma eis theon, di' anastaseōs Iēsou Christou.*] (1 Pet 3:20–21)

Here 1 Peter provides a typological reading of Noah (cf. 2 Pet 2:5, 9; 3:5–9; Matt 24:37–39; Luke 17:26–27). Why eight? Perhaps to make the point to the contemporary Christians that, just as there were few then, there are few now. They should be encouraged, not discouraged by their small numbers.

---

57. Dalton (*Christ's Proclamation,* 160) makes an important point: "Nowhere in biblical literature is the world of the dead, as such, called . . . [*phylakē,* prison]. It is true that in the Syriac Peshitta version of 1 Peter 3:19, . . . [*en phylakē*] is rendered by 'in Sheol.' This is an interpretation rather than a strict translation, which derives from the later church tradition, found in Syriac writings, of Christ's 'harrowing of hell.' In this tradition, Sheol is regarded as a prison in the keeping of Satan, from which Christ at his descent to Sheol, liberated all the souls of the dead. This later, nonbiblical tradition cannot be used to interpret the text of 1 Pet. 3:19." On the other hand, *phylakē* is used in the NT for the prison in which Satan is chained (cf. Rev 20:7), Dalton. 160.

58. With respect to other passages one may want to consider concerning Jesus' whereabouts between his death and resurrection, see Acts 2:24–28, 31 (which deals with the Psalm 16:8–11 quotation) and Matt 12:39–40 (which employs a Jonah metaphor).

59. *Poreuomai* so used: John 14:2–3, 12, 28; 16:7, 28; 20:17. Acts 1:10–11; 1 Pet 3:19, 22. *Anabaino* so used: John 6:62; 20:17; Acts 2:34; Eph 4:8–9.

What does it mean that the eight persons were saved *di' hydatos*? Should the *dia* be translated locally or instrumentally? Given the baptismal setting, probably the latter.[60]

Were they saved by means of baptism? For our discussion of death and afterlife, this question is irrelevant. If in 3:19 we had material from baptismal catechesis, in 3:22 we have hymnic material. As in 3:19, which also uses the language of Christ's "going," 3:22 depicts the risen Christ vanquishing wicked powers, using language similar to that found in Ps 110:1; 1 Cor 15:24–25; Eph 1:20–22; 6:12.[61]

Westfall views the antitype language not as corresponding but as contrastive. So baptism does not correspond to the flood; rather, the salvation comes by being kept *out of* the water, which was a means of destruction. Those who argue for correspondence take *di' hydatos* (through water) in an instrumental sense, so that water is the means of salvation. Those who take it as contrastive take it locally, finding the water a threat from which one needs salvation.[62]

Analysis of 1 Pet 4:1–6

What does the author mean by saying, "For whoever has suffered in the flesh has finished with sin" (4:1)? It cannot be comparing the Christian to Christ since Christ did not suffer in the flesh to finish with (his) sin; he was innocent all along (2:22–23; 3:18). So, unlike Paul (in Rom 6:3–11), Peter does not identify the death of Christ with the Christian's death to sin; Christians do not share in Christ's death that way for Peter. Dalton sees sin here and in 2:24 and 4:8 as sins committed (by others than Christ) rather than Pauline *hamartia* (Sin).[63]

First Peter 4:5–6 is riddled with interpretive difficulties. The passage is an important part of the interpretation of 3:18–22, with its question about

---

60. After going back and forth between the two options, Dalton (*Christ's Proclamation*, 195) concludes that " 'through' is to be taken both instrumentally and locally, though, from the context, the emphasis should fall on the former." On the other hand, while Elliott (*1 Peter*, 667) observes that Michaels (*1 Peter*, loc. cit.) favors the instrumental (paralleling v. 21, which is also instrumental: "through the resurrection"), Elliott finds the similarity "more formal than substantive." The passive form *diesōthēsan* (saved) "clearly implies God as the saving Agent, a use of the passive typical of Petrine style." Tradition holds that Noah was saved *from* water, not by means of water. Elliott (*1 Peter*, 667) holds that *diesōthēsan* is a locative: Noah was saved "in the midst of" the water or "while passing through" the water. Westfall ("Relationship," 112): "Though many scholars see baptism as 'corresponding to' the flood, it is better seen as a contrast. In the flood the eight in the ark were saved by being kept out of the water, which was a means of destruction. In the early Church baptism entailed intentionally placing the believer in the water." Fitzmyer, "First Peter," 336 (58:18): "Just as Noah was saved by passage through the waters of the flood, so the Christian will be saved by passage through the waters of baptism — its antitype."
61. Dalton, *Christ's Proclamation*, 217.
62. This includes Westfall, "Relationship," 112–14.
63. Dalton, *Christ's Proclamation*, 223.

whether to understand that Christ's soul separated from his body and went to a subterranean place to preach to the dead. Dalton lists four major options regarding the proclamation of the gospel (4:6):

1. Christ preaches to all the dead during the *triduum mortis,* thereby giving them a chance to convert.

2. Christ brings the good news of salvation during the *triduum mortis* to the just of the OT.

3. Apostles preach to the *spiritually* dead on earth.

4. Someone preaches to people on earth, but these Christian converts die before the Parousia (cf. 1 Thess 4).

Dalton opts for the fourth. Clearly 1 Peter has an imminent apocalyptic eschatology (4:7), much like that found in 1 Thess 4.[64] The suffering of the Christians is part of the "birth pangs" of that ensuing glory (cf. 1:7, 13; 4:13; and 1:5, 12; 5:1).[65] Whereas the doubt about the dead Christians appears to be raised by other Christians at Thessalonica, in 1 Peter it comes from the pagan camp. The pagan in 1 Peter may point out to the Christian that Christians actually die, like everyone else; they receive no special treatment. But the author reminds them that the dead Christians do have a reward waiting for them. This the believers may not fully understand, but God does.[66]

Let us look at some of the particular difficulties relevant to our topic. First, what of the expression *zōntas kai nekrous* (living and dead)? Who are they? Dalton argues for an eschatological context in which *all people* will

---

64. Dubis argues that 1 Peter should be viewed in light of the Judeo-Christian messianic woes tradition as seen in numerous intertestamental texts as well as Revelation; Dubis considers 1 Peter as heavily apocalyptic. He draws especially upon the work of the SBL Apocalypse Group's definition, supplemented by the work of A. Y. Collins on the hortatory function of apocalyptic. See Mark Dubis, *Messianic Woes in First Peter: Suffering and Eschatology in 1 Peter 4:12–19* (Studies in Biblical Literature 33; New York: Peter Lang, 2002), 37–45. On the other hand, Elliott (*1 Peter,* 112) downplays the apocalyptic elements of 1 Peter and contrasts it with the apocalyptic eschatology of Paul, the Gospels, and 2 Peter: "In contrast to Paul (Gal 1:12) and the author of Revelation (Rev 1:1–2), our author makes no claim to be passing on any privileged revelation. Nor does one find here a dualistic contrast as in Paul, between the present evil age and the coming age (e.g., Rom 8:18–21, 38; Gal 1:4; 2 Cor 5:17) or the duality of corrupt flesh versus Spirit. No cosmic clash is presented between the forces of good and evil, despite the references to God, the Devil (5:9), and the cosmic powers (3:22). Our author presents no pessimistic view of the present age, but manifests a positive outlook marked by confidence in God's power and hope for the future (1:13, 21; 3:15)." To summarize, while Elliott finds ample emphasis on eschatology in 1 Peter, he does not interpret it as strongly apocalyptic. The debate continues over how apocalyptic 1 Peter is.

65. Dalton, *Christ's Proclamation,* 226.

66. Dalton compares 1 Peter to the book of Wisdom in provocative and interesting ways (ibid., throughout).

give an account before God, those still living and those who have died.[67] According to Westfall, Lenski distinguishes the dead in v. 5 (all the people who will face the Judge) from the dead in v. 6 (those who were already dead). Westfall argues that "it is better to equate the terms in interpreting the passage."[68]

So, 3:19 and 4:6 in one respect refer to quite different things: 3:19 refers to Christ proclaiming his victory to the wicked spirits on his way up to the right hand of God. But 4:6 refers to the normal course of Christian preaching on earth in the context of pagans, who ridicule not only the Christians' conversions but also their physical deaths. There is a link, however between Christ and the Christian:

1. Christ, "*put to death in the flesh,* [but] brought to life in the spirit" (3:18);

2. the Christian, "*judged in the flesh in the eyes of people,* but living in the spirit in the eyes of God" (4:6; au. trans.).

The Christian not only is saved by water (baptism) from the world of evil, but also is called to adopt the life of suffering manifested by Jesus. Just as God vindicated Christ and resurrected him, so too will God vindicate the Petrine Christians and resurrect them at the judgment. The author thus provides a word of profound encouragement.

Summary for 1 Peter

Despite scholars' penchant for claiming clarity and certainty with respect to their own interpretations, it is by no means clear exactly what 1 Peter signifies regarding Christ's proclamation to the spirits.[69] Just as Christ probably experienced no intermediate state in 1 Peter's view, neither does a discussion of an intermediate state for human beings arise.

---

67. This differs from 1 Thess 4:13–18 in that 1 Peter is clearer than Paul. Paul may or may not envision all people being raised for judgment.

68. Westfall, "Relationship," 122n60.

69. For example, Johnson ("Preaching to the Dead," 51) concludes his analysis with this proclamation: "The implication of the passage then, is *clear* [emphasis added]. It deals with the comprehensive work of Christ in saving all who will respond to the proclaimed word. This embraces those who have died under the old covenant. The formula which the author quotes referred only to the announcement of judgment to the disobedient spirits, and he does not change this; but he uses it as an example of Christ's redemptive work *ad inferos.* Wherever Christ goes he brings both judgment and salvation." Scharlemann claims: "For this section of First Peter *clearly* [emphasis added] teaches that Christ descended to the region of the damned, to those who deliberately rejected God's grace in the time of Noah, in order to make proclamation to them." See Martin H. Scharlemann, " 'He Descended into Hell': An Interpretation of 1 Peter 3:18–20," *Concordia Journal* 15 (1989): 320. Scharlemann canvasses Lutheran documents and argues his case from a Lutheran stance.

There is no ground for seeing in 1 Pet 3:19 the activity of Christ's soul in the interval between his death and resurrection. Later church tradition may be interested in such activity, but the thought of 1 Peter is far from such categories. If modern exegetes wish to find in 1 Pet 3:19 the descent of Christ to the world of the dead, they should see there the action, not of a soul, but of the whole risen Lord. Such is the influence of the once-prevailing interpretation (that the text deals with the descent of Christ's soul), that scholars are still tempted to see in 1 Pet 3:19 some activity of Christ before his resurrection. It should be evident that such an interpretation does not come from the text, but is imposed upon it.[70]

I have presented Dalton's argument because (1) it provides a sustained, detailed, exhaustive analysis and interpretation and (2) using his argument has allowed me to raise the main lines of argumentation and the daedal exegetical issues entailed.

Eschatological Scenario

What does the above debate imply for the original audience of 1 Peter? In reviewing Dalton, Grassi quotes: "The writer of 1 Peter and his readers belonged to a Church which eagerly awaited the second coming of the Lord, which preferred to understand redemption not so much in the juridical categories of 'satisfaction' or 'merit' as in the more picturesque category of a victorious battle won by Christ over the devil and evil spirits; [a Church] which appreciated and read avidly a whole world of intertestamental literature which has never been formally included in the canon of Scriptures."[71]

Actors in the Eschatological Scenario

All of humanity, "the quick and the dead" (4:5 KJV), will be judged at the Parousia according to their deeds (1:17). Who will judge, God or Christ? God is seen as universal Judge in the NT (1 Pet 1:17; 2:23; cf. Rom 2:6; 3:6; 14:10), but when the stereotyped phrase "judge the living and the dead" appears, it refers to Christ (Matt 25:31–46; Luke 21:34–36; Acts 17:31; 1 Cor 4:4–5, cf. Rom 2:16).[72] The main and important point of 1 Pet 4:6 is to bolster beleaguered Christians, who are being ridiculed and persecuted by their pagan neighbors. Indeed, this is the pastoral purpose of the entire letter. It is not that the author suddenly takes an interest in saving these wicked reprobates, whom he paints as wholly bad rather than simply misguided. Dalton

---

70. Dalton, *Christ's Proclamation*, 140.
71. Joseph A. Grassi, Review of William J. Dalton, *Christ's Proclamation to the Spirits: A Study of 1 Peter 3:18–4:6*, TS 27, no. 1 (1966): 105.
72. Dalton, *Christ's Proclamation*, 231.

argues that *euangelizomai* (4:6) should be taken as "Christ was preached": in the course of Christians preaching the gospel on earth, Christ was the content of the preaching, not the one preaching. Dalton's interpretation is iconoclastic. "The dead" here simply refers to "those who have died," and not to shades inhabiting tenebrous depths. The dead will rise at the judgment, not a moment before. It is the universal NT view that the preaching is done on earth before people die (see the "dead in Christ" of 1 Thess 4:16). In interpreting 1 Peter, it is best to adhere to what is exemplified elsewhere in the NT than to rely on post-NT developments.

Westfall concentrates on three main parties in the section 3:8–4:6, specifically in 3:19–22. The Gentiles play a negative role characterized by obloquy, blasphemy, and captiousness.[73] They believe they are in a powerful position. Ironically, the author argues that the believers, the ostensibly oppressed, actually inhabit the superior position, provided they maintain a good conscience (3:16). God's authority is brought up in at least three ways. First, God hears the righteous and ignores entreaties of the wicked (3:12). Second, since the resurrection and ascension, Jesus is Lord over all angels and authorities (3:22). The believers find themselves in this interim period between the resurrection and the final judgment. Third, because all believers, alive or dead, have already established themselves with God, they need not fear judgment day because it will merely serve to vindicate their good consciences; in contrast, the wicked will be in for a rude awakening (1:17–21; 4:7, 17; 5:10).

Dubis discusses the angels, both the good ones at 1:12 and the bad ones in 3:19, 22. The angels have no advantage over Peter's audience (1:12). The role of the devil with respect to discipline, suffering, and testing appears somewhat confusing since God's testing is a good thing (1:6), but the devil's tempting is not (5:8). However, this same tension exists from Job onward: Satan is both the enemy of humankind and a servant of God's purposes.[74] The Spirit participates in the eschaton (4:6–7, 13–14). The gift of the Spirit indicates that restoration has begun, that the full receipt of glory is near.

---

73. The author's negative connotation for Gentiles requires some explanation given that he was probably writing to a group that consisted largely of Gentiles. He has infused the word with new meaning so that his Christian readers are "former Gentiles": they no longer behave in typically pagan ways, and they now belong to God's covenant people, unlike the Gentiles who have refused to undergo baptism and become part of the group (such as those identified by 2:12). First Peter 2:9–10 puts it eloquently: "But you are a chosen race, a royal priesthood, a holy nation, God's own people, in order that you may proclaim the mighty acts of him who called you out of darkness into his marvelous light. Once you were not a people, but now you are God's people; once you had not received mercy, but now you have received mercy."

74. See especially Neil Forsyth, *The Old Enemy: Satan and the Combat Myth* (Princeton: Princeton University Press, 1987); and Susan R. Garrett, *The Temptations of Jesus in the Gospel of Mark* (Grand Rapids: Eerdmans, 1998). Dubis (*Messianic Woes*, 94–95), who does not include Forsyth or Garrett in his bibliography, has a tidy paragraph on the subject.

Events in the Eschatological Scenario

With respect to chronology, the messianic woes comprise the first act in the drama of the unfolding of the eschatological judgment. Observe the language of 1:20: "He was destined before the foundation of the world, but was revealed at the end of the ages [*phanerōthentos de ep' eschatou tōn chronōn*] for your sake." Here the past tense is used to describe the end of the ages. With Jesus' suffering and resurrection, the end of the ages has arrived. First come the messianic woes, beginning with the passion and cross of Jesus, which are marked by cosmological and ethical indicators: pestilence, hail, war on the one hand, increased lawlessness and persecution of believers on the other. Second comes the judgment of believers. They suffer as part of God's judgment, but with redemptive ends. Then comes judgment of unbelievers.

The eschatological tribulation involves fire (*pyrōsis*; 4:12). For the wicked, the fire destroys (4:17–18); for the righteous, it tests (*peirasmos*) and refines (4:12), a metaphor drawn from refining metals (cf. Mal 3:2–3).[75] The agent of testing is God. The tradition of God testing people appears in the OT as well as in apocryphal and pseudepigraphical Jewish texts, though not necessarily with the eschatological tenor of 1 Peter. First Peter and Revelation both use the idea of testing as part of the eschatological scenario for believers and the wicked alike.

The 1 Peter scenario also involves judgment (*krima*, referring to the last judgment): "The messianic woes were inaugurated in the Messiah's own experience and the readers continue to suffer these woes. Yet the age of glory will soon follow (indeed, it has already dawned since the 'Spirit of glory' (*doxa*) now rests upon the readers; 4:14). These woes are the vehicle of God's judgment upon sinful humanity. Furthermore, these woes found their focus in Jesus' experience upon the cross. God's judgment was centered in Jesus, but it moves from there to impact those united to Christ, and only afterwards will it finally extend to unbelievers."[76] While there is some disagreement, the *krima* of 4:17 is generally taken to mean God's judgment on the church, not simply against apostates, but upon the faithful.

Petrine Cosmology

Where is the abode of these fallen angels? Dalton argues for a development in thought from the OT netherworld of Sheol to a seven-layered heaven.[77]

---

75. For a fuller discussion of the eschatological use of *pyrōsis* (fiery ordeal), see Dubis, *Messianic Woes*, 76–95. For the Stoic eschatological notion of fire, see A. A. Long, *Hellenistic Philosophy: Stoics, Epicureans, Sceptics* (2nd ed.; Berkeley: University of California Press, 1986), 146–56.

76. Dubis, *Messianic Woes*, 144–45.

77. See also Feinberg, "1 Peter 3:18–20," 303–36, who argues that 1 Pet 3:18–20 presents Christ as preaching through Noah (by the Holy Spirit) to the disembodied spirits (imprisoned)

Apocalyptic thinking includes a spatial element in addition to the temporal. First Peter refers to heaven: the inheritance of the believers lies there (1:4), Jesus is there (3:22), the Holy Spirit is sent from there (1:12). Dalton has argued convincingly that the spirits in prison dwell in a heavenly realm (cf. above, on *2 Enoch*). As the Creator (4:19), God will create a new eschatological order. First Peter does not have any hell language (Tartarus, Apollyon, Hades, Gehenna, outer darkness) so one would be hard-pressed to argue that such a place is part of his cosmology.

The Fate of Believers

In 1 Peter, believers are called "the righteous" and "us" (4:17–18). Unbelievers are "those who do not obey the gospel," "ungodly/impious," "Gentiles," and "sinners" (4:3, 17–18). Christians can be finished with sin to some degree: "The Christian, who has made the pledge to follow Christ in suffering and who has seriously started out on this way, is finished with sin. This does not mean that all Christians are sinless, since the participle has the force of an implied condition: to the degree Christians share the sufferings of Christ, to that degree they cut themselves off from sin. This, after all, was the purpose of Christ's own suffering, 'that you might give up sins and live for righteousness' (2:24)."[78] Because Christ suffered or died (textual variants in 3:18) once for all, the just for unjust, Christians are united with God. "The unjust are the Christians viewed as people brought by Christ from a state of sin to a state of righteousness."[79] The author thus has in mind that Christ died for Christians, not that he died for all people.[80] Christians receive eternal life and "glory," which will be revealed on the Day of the Lord (4:13; 5:4). All good things await them (5:10). This view has much in common with what Paul says in 1 Thessalonians.

The readers of 1 Peter (indeed all Christians; 5:9) should expect to suffer as a preliminary part of the eschatological tribulation. This is seen especially

---

who rejected Noah's message. In the article (303–4) he provocatively states: "This...discussion will be limited to a careful exegesis of 1 Pet 3:18–20 in an attempt to discern whether it teaches anything about an underworld, anything about Christ preaching in hell for any reason, or anything about his transferring OT saints to heaven....I shall attempt to demonstrate that the passage in question has nothing to do with any of those ideas, but should be understood as a reference to Christ preaching by the Holy Spirit through Noah to the people of Noah's day....As to the larger question of whether Scripture teaches anything about an underworld, I do not think so, though the demonstration of that claim is a matter for further study. My point is simply that if Scripture does teach the notion, and if it is not a vestige of Greco-Roman or Jewish mythology, one must demonstrate that to be true on grounds other than an appeal to 1 Pet 3:18–20."

78. Dalton, *Christ's Proclamation*, 224.

79. Ibid., 133–34.

80. Again, Dalton (ibid., 134n39) warns: "1 Peter is above all concerned with building up the confidence and self-esteem of threatened Christian communities, not with the extension of salvation (whether to fallen angels or to other human beings) outside the church."

through the use of *dei* (it is necessary) language (1:6; 4:12; 5:9), which indicates a belief that "a certain measure of sufferings must be filled up prior to the eschaton."[81] Christians will suffer the messianic woes together with the wicked. The suffering comes at the hands of their human neighbors, and at the hands of Satan, but ultimately, God is the cause (1:6–7; 3:17; 4:12, 19; 5:6).[82] The believer's suffering is part of the messianic woes, which anticipate God's judgment. In that time of crisis, the true character of the righteous and the wicked is revealed. Additionally, the righteous are tested and purified, while the wicked are put on notice and, perhaps, given the opportunity to convert. Believers will be judged.[83]

Dubis points out that 1 Peter coheres with the temporal element of apocalyptic thinking, which concerns itself with protohistory, history, and eschatology. The protohistory in 1 Peter is visible in the language of predestination and election. Christ's suffering was foreordained (1:20), *believers* were elected/chosen (1:1–2), and *unbelievers* were predestined (2:8). History appears throughout, with references to the Exodus, Sarah and Abraham, exile, Noah, and so on. The eschatological crisis, including the judgment that marks the end of history, is already taking place at the time of the readers (4:12). Believers are currently experiencing God's judgment (4:17), and the rest of humanity will experience it imminently (cf. 1:17; 2:23; 4:6 for further judgment language). Believers will share in Jesus' glory, meaning that Christians will experience resurrection just as Jesus did. Creation will also experience redemption (1:4). Dubis makes this argument by attending to *klēronomia* language, which refers to "the Jewish expectation of a new creation."[84] God is "Creator," *ktistēs*, a hapax legomenon in the NT (4:19). Dubis calls 4:12–19 "the most eschatologically-charged pericope in the entire book."[85]

The Fate of Unbelievers

Given the extensive discussion about the recipients of Christ's proclamation after his death, we must distinguish between two sets of unbelievers: (1) unbelievers who lived and died before Christ, and (2) unbelievers who lived and died after Christ. Our concern here lies with the latter since they are the group most relevant to the audience of 1 Peter: many such unbelievers are perceived as being responsible for the suffering and persecution of Petrine Christians.

---

81. Dubis, *Messianic Woes*, 71.
82. Ibid., 176.
83. The idea is not foreign to the NT. Dubis invokes Heb 10:30, 2 Thess 1:4–5; 1 Cor 11:32. For a discussion of OT and intertestamental parallels in which God first judges God's own people (for redemptive ends), see ibid., 148–57.
84. Ibid., 41.
85. Ibid., 188.

The author asks our very question in 4:17–18: "For the time has come for judgment to begin with the household of God; if it begins with us, what will be the end for those who do not obey the gospel of God? And 'If it is hard for the righteous to be saved, what will become of the ungodly and the sinners?'" The author gives no answer, not wanting to encourage an attitude of vengeance but rather of humility (5:5–6). This, however, does not mean good news for the unbeliever. On the contrary, unbelievers can expect condemnation. Possibly the hardest thing 1 Peter has to say about unbelievers is in 2:7–8: "To you then who believe, he is precious; but for those who do not believe, 'The stone that the builders rejected has become the very head of the corner,' and 'A stone that makes them stumble, and a rock that makes them fall.' They stumble because they disobey the word, as they were destined to do." It is clear from 4:17 that judgment is in order for unbelievers. By the verb *apeitheō* (disobey) they are linked to the wicked spirits of 3:19–20.[86]

Dubis argues that "the wicked will not be among the eschatological survivors of the messianic woes. They will not 'appear' anywhere since they will be wiped from the face of the earth, and will have no place in the apocalypticist's new creation."[87] Elliott consistently insists that 1 Peter is a much kinder, gentler text than is ordinarily assumed. Despite the language implying that God has set some people up to disobey (2:8) while others are "elect," Elliott views 1 Peter as optimistic about the conversion of nonbelievers. He recognizes, however, that these nonbelievers — variously called "those who do not believe," those who have rejected Jesus, those who disobey, Gentiles, the impious, and sinners — are repeatedly contrasted with believers throughout the letter.[88] Unbelievers get no second chance after death; they must believe before they die or they will be put to shame:

> The view that claims a relation between 4:6 and 3:19 and finds here in 4:6 an accent not only on universal judgment but also *universal salvation*, however, runs contrary to the thought of 1 Peter in general and to the point of vv 1–6 in particular. Throughout the letter, salvation is made contingent upon faith in Jesus Christ and fidelity to the will of God here and now, with no hint of a second opportunity of repentance after death. The author's intention here, as throughout the letter, is the exhortation and consolation of the faithful, those who in their lifetime have heard the gospel and are "in Christ." Here attention is given to the deceased among the believers as examples of the prospect facing all the community. The point of 4:6 is not the universal judgment and

---

86. See 1 Pet 4:3–5 for their lifestyle and punishment.
87. Dubis, *Messianic Woes*, 167.
88. Elliott, *1 Peter*, 428.

salvation of all but the vindication of oppressed believers, the deceased as well as the living, as Christ himself was vindicated (2:4; 3:18, 22). The concept of universal salvation is a noble idea but is not advocated in this letter and ought not to be read into this passage.[89]

Function of Beliefs

The beliefs regarding death and afterlife in 1 Peter work in a sixfold manner, with ethical, pastoral, theological, liturgical, apologetic, and social functions:

Ethical: Promoting Ethical Behavior and Faithfulness

First, a hortatory function is served as these beliefs promote ethical behavior. As Dubis argues: "First Peter thus fully expects his worldview to shape the ethical thought and action of his readers. In this way 1 Peter manifests marked commonality with the hortatory function of other apocalyptic literature."[90] The author is especially concerned that his charges not be tempted into lawlessness. Lawlessness increases as the eschaton approaches, so Christians might be tempted, especially Christians who formerly were pagans. The author enjoins the audience to avoid apostatizing in order to save their lives.

Elliott duly recognizes that the material on death and resurrection relates tightly to ethics. In the first part of his commentary, he identifies semantic fields that signify major themes in 1 Peter. One-third of the data he cites relates to eschatology and ethics.[91] In addition, he identifies eight different features illustrating the *"predominantly hortatory tone"* of the letter:

1. the broad semantic field of terms for conduct (mentioned above);

2. fifty-four imperatival constructions;

3. the predominant use of second-person plural pronouns;

4. the paraenetic use of *oun*;

5. numerous antitheses, frequently contrasting believers and non-believers;

6. imperatives followed by supporting indicatives;

7. the persistent stress on conduct consistent with God's will; and

8. exhortations supported by OT citations or allusions that also conclude preceding imperatives.[92]

---

89. Ibid, 742.
90. Dubis, *Messianic Woes*, 43.
91. Elliott, *1 Peter*, 63.
92. Ibid., 67–68.

Pastoral: Encouraging the Powerless Persecuted

A pastoral function is served as the author encourages the powerless during persecution. "The function of this passage [3:18–4:6] in the structure of the letter is to provide the foundation for Christian confidence in persecution."[93] This author sugarcoats nothing; proportionately speaking, he uses the language of suffering more than any other NT writer. He substantiates his view by drawing on the OT: "All flesh is like grass" (1:24). Petrine Christians were anything but Panglossian.

Theological: Declaring God's Sovereignty

Third, a theological function is served as 1 Peter declares God's sovereignty through Jesus' suffering, death, resurrection, and ascension.

Liturgical: Drawing upon the Tradition

Almost everything that 1 Peter has to say about death and afterlife is tied to the liturgical practice of baptism; this highlights the importance of baptism for the Petrine community. There is evidence of both hymnic and creedal material. Thus, talk of death and afterlife in 1 Peter serves, in part, to tie people more closely to the various liturgical traditions of the Petrine church.

Apologetic: Defending Christian Hope

First Peter 3:15b contains this imperative: "Always be ready to make your defense [*apologia*] to anyone who demands from you an accounting [*logos*] for the hope [*elpis*] that is in you." The word *apologia* appears only eight times in the NT, and only once in the Petrine material.[94]

Elliott insists that in 1 Peter the word "apology" means reply or response, not "legal defense."[95] I see no reason to restrict the meaning to one or the other; the term clearly has juridical overtones. Elliott's appeal to Phil 1:7, 16 as an argument against a juridical connotation fails to convince given that there Paul is in chains (by legal authorities) for the gospel. In addition, since Paul regularly employed forensic rhetoric, any appeal to his own speech would argue for a juridical meaning, not against it.

David Balch contends that the *Haustafel* of 1 Peter (2:11–3:12) serves an apologetic function.[96] Like me, Balch allows room for a broader meaning of "apologia" than does Elliott:

---

93. Dalton, *Christ's Proclamation*, 26.

94. Half of the occurrences are Pauline (1 Cor: 9:3; 2 Cor 7:11; Phil 1:7, 16). Two appear in Luke's presentation of Paul: Acts 22:1, in which Paul defends himself, and 25:14–16, in which Festus presents *ta kata ton Paulon* (Paul's case). The other occurs in 2 Tim 4:16, in reference to Paul's earlier life. Thus all of the occurrences outside of 1 Peter refer to Paul.

95. Elliott, *1 Peter*, 626–27.

96. Balch, *Let Wives Be Submissive*, 81–116.

The "defense" is to be given "to anyone who asks" (3:15), so this verse does not specifically contemplate a legal defense before a governor. But this exhortation is supported by the reference to Christ which follows. Christ was "put to death in the flesh" (3:18), an expression which "possibly [puts] some accent on His judicial trial and condemnation" (cf. 4:6). Further, the author probably intended a parallel between the Christian who was to give an "account" (*logon*; 3:15) to the pagans and the "account" (*logon*; 4:5) to be given in the future by the pagans "to the one prepared to judge the living and the dead," a phrase which has an unmistakably judicial flavor. I conclude that the code in 1 Peter exhorted Christians to the kind of "good conduct" which a Roman governor would have approved. However, the writer of 1 Peter seems to view the judicial trial of Christians as a possibility, not as a present reality.[97]

Social: Creating a Strong, Faithful Group; Discouraging Apostasy

A social function is served whereby the author seeks to create a strong, faithful group not subject to apostasy. Westfall treats this under "interpersonal/interactional meaning," summarized in 1 Peter 5:12: "I have written this short letter to encourage you and to testify that this is the true grace of God. Stand fast in it." She writes: "The author catches his readers' attention by including them in the analogy, and using it as a basis both to exhort them and to encourage them." The purpose of the section [3:8–4:6] is to encourage the recipients to verbalize their faith in spite of the risk.[98] In this regard, Westfall identifies all the speech-related semantics.

In attending to what 1 Peter contributes to the question of death and afterlife in the NT, we do well to regard seriously Westfall's contention that 3:18–22 does not aim to "teach information about . . . the intermediate state of Old Testament or New Testament believers, or the antediluvian situation."[99] We are in the realm of analogy, not propositions here. She argues that the author and readers share cultural information not obvious to us; hence, the confusion about the actor of *kēryssō* (proclaim), the referent for *en hō*, and the identity of the spirits.

Throughout his work, Elliott deftly emphasizes the social aspects of the epistle. He claims: "The contrast and conflict on which 1 Peter focuses is not cosmological but social — the contrast between a holy community united with God and a society alienated from God. The author speaks not of "new creation," however, but of personal rebirth and transformed communal life

---

97. Ibid., 94–95.
98. Westfall, "Relationship," 134.
99. Ibid., 124.

in a hostile environment. The perspective thus is eschatological but without any apocalyptic shadowing.... The end, for this author, is a time of redemption through Christ, of a testing of faith through suffering, of impartial judgment, and of a culmination of the salvation promised to the elect and holy people of God — a time calling for vigilance, fidelity, joy, trust, and hope."[100]

DEATH AND AFTERLIFE IN 2 PETER

The author of 2 Peter says that his is the "second letter" (3:1) to the audience, probably indicating knowledge of 1 Peter. Scholars both ancient and modern have expressed profound skepticism regarding Petrine authorship of 2 Peter. They consider the letter pseudonymous and tend to date it around 130 CE. It contains some of the NT's most colorful imagery of judgment and posthumous existence and therefore deserves our attention, however brief.

The general outline of the fate of believers and nonbelievers is not difficult to discern. The author maintains a starkly apocalyptic eschatology and envisions an imminent eschaton. The letter is both apologetic and polemical and as such rebuts the opponents, who deny God's imminent judgment. Second Peter confidently presents the eschatological scenario. Where 1 Peter exhibits some humility with respect to discernment of eschatological details, 2 Peter exhibits certain knowledge. Jesus will return soon. At that time, fire will destroy the present heaven and earth and all the ungodly who reside therein, and a new heaven and earth will be instituted, which will be inhabited solely by the just. "But by the same word (*logos*) the present heavens and earth have been reserved for fire, being kept until the day of judgment (*hēmera kriseōs*) and destruction (*apoleia*) of the godless" (3:7). The just will enjoy imperishability (1:4).[101]

Until the eschaton, the ungodly should expect to be consigned to hell as they await their ultimate destruction (*apōleia*: 2:1, 3; 3:7, 16). Second Peter's vitriolic philippic threatens to overwhelm even readers most inclined to be vindictive. The opponents are variously labeled "ungodly" (2:6), "blots and blemishes" (2:13), unrighteous (2:21), and likened to "irrational animals,... born to be caught and killed" (2:12). The author argues by analogy: Just as water was used by God to enact God's wrath upon the earth in days of old, so now fire will destroy (3:6–7). Just as God cast the wicked angels into Tartarus, which served as a temporary place of punishment ("cast them into hell [Tartarus] and committed them to chains of

---

100. Elliott, *1 Peter*, 112.
101. See Jerome H. Neyrey, *2 Peter, Jude: A New Translation with Introduction and Commentary* (AB 37C; New York: Doubleday, 1993), 157–59.

deepest darkness to be kept until the judgment [*seirais zophou tartarōsas paredōken eis krisin tēroumenous*]"; 2:4), so God will do to the ungodly (*asebēs*; 2:6). They die and reside consciously in a place of punishment until the eschaton, at which point they will be utterly destroyed:

> For if God did not spare the angels when they sinned, but cast them into hell [Tartarus] and committed them to chains of deepest darkness to be kept until the judgment; and if he did not spare the ancient world, even though he saved Noah, a herald of righteousness, with seven others, when he brought a flood on a world of the ungodly; and if by turning the cities of Sodom and Gomorrah to ashes [*tephrōsas*] he condemned [*katekrinen*] them to extinction [*katastrophē*] and made them an example [*hypodeigma*] of what is coming to the ungodly,... then the Lord knows how to rescue the godly from trial, and to keep the unrighteous under punishment until the day of judgment.... These are waterless springs and mists driven by a storm; for them the deepest darkness has been reserved. (2 Pet 2:4–6, 9, 17)

Eschatological Scenario

In striking contrast to the other texts studied in this book, 2 Peter has no room for Satan. The opponents are held morally responsible for their choices: they have no one to blame for their destruction but themselves. God is sovereign and judges justly. The author does allude to the myth of the Watchers, which implies belief in sinful angels; but sinful angels do not influence the opponents (as they do in, e.g., *1 En.* 6–16). Jesus' role in the eschatological scenario is to return, and that will be the occasion for God's judgment.[102]

Functions of Death and Afterlife Teaching in 2 Peter
Ethical: Behave, or Else...

The author has in mind quite specific ethical behaviors that constitute godly living. Second Peter 1:5–7 reads: "You must make every effort to support your faith with goodness, and goodness with knowledge, and knowledge with self-control, and self-control with endurance, and endurance with godliness, and godliness with mutual affection, and mutual affection with love." If one follows these mandates, one will abide in the new heaven and new earth with other well-behaved believers. If not, one will be utterly destroyed and relegated to extinction. If one dies before the eschaton and is ungodly, one can expect to reside in Tartarus, deepest darkness, in chains. The author is less clear as to where dead believers reside.

---

102. For a discussion of whether 2 Peter considers Jesus to be God, see Neyrey, *2 Peter, Jude,* 147–48.

Social: Identifying Insiders and Outsiders

The author uses the death and afterlife material to create strong social boundaries so that insiders and outsiders are clearly demarcated and assigned their appropriate destinies. Neyrey contends: "Typical of NT writers, the author attends to the boundaries of the group.... Boundary making and maintenance thus seems to be the primary ritual here."[103]

Apologetic: Defense against Opponents

The author bolsters the confidence of the readers, who hear the opponents scoffing at their beliefs (3:3–4). He gives believers a sense of superiority over the vilifiers and equips them to defend God against the delay of the Parousia (ch. 3).[104]

---

103. Ibid., 137.
104. For a fuller description of the specific ways in which the author engages popular theodicy, see ibid., 122–28.

– S I X –

CONCLUSIONS
AND DIRECTIONS
FOR FURTHER RESEARCH

I N WHAT FOLLOWS I intend to summarize briefly some of the main findings on functions, variety, similarity, and "the quick and the dead." Then I will preview avenues for further investigation.

BELIEFS FUNCTION

Beliefs concerning death and afterlife do *function*. Long before NT authors entered the fray, ancients of many types — philosophers, OT authors, politicians, religionists, magicians, and poets — knew this. In each chapter we have suggested various functions, including political, pastoral/psychological, liturgical, ethical, apologetic, theological, and social.

Political

Virgil's *Aeneid* served the political aims of Augustus; without it, Lucretius the Epicurean would probably not have enlisted in the emperor's army. Setzer helps us to recognize the way Paul's teaching on resurrection undermines power structures in the church and empire. Presumably, any time an author declares the sovereignty of God, this implicitly puts the emperor in his proper place (far beneath God).

Pastoral

All of our authors are concerned in some way to alleviate the fear associated with death and one's ultimate fate. Paul teaches the Thessalonians about appropriate grief and the power of hope. The Fourth Evangelist (FE) assures believing readers that they are never orphaned but dwell intimately with Christ now and forever. The author of 1 Peter bolsters the confidence of his dejected, powerless, and marginalized parishioners.

222

Liturgical

Some of the texts display liturgical elements associated with the teachings. For instance, 1 Peter 3, which has caused so much consternation regarding Christ's supposed "descent to hell," clearly has baptismal themes.[1] Matthew's eschatological messianic banquet is tied to the church's Eucharist.

Ethical

Some authors, notably Matthew and 2 Peter, use the graphic threats of fiery damnation to inspire virtuous behavior. For Matthew, the ethical may be the *primary* function. Though he has no hell, Paul, too, warns that all will be judged according to their deeds on the Day of the Lord. We saw in the chapter devoted to 1 Peter that this function looms large. The epistle's genre is primarily hortatory.

Apologetic

An apologetic function is served when the FE depicts Jesus, known to have died as a common criminal crucified by the powers of Rome, as being perfectly in control of his own death and resurrection. By accentuating Jesus' aplomb, the FE aggrandizes Jesus' authority among his followers and depicts him as a sage like Socrates. To Socrates' disciples, as to the Samaritan woman and the Jews of the Fourth Gospel (FG), Jesus would insist: "I am greater than Socrates." Paul, too, bolsters his authority by means of death and afterlife teachings in 1 Cor 15. In 2 Peter, teachings on death and afterlife help with the defense against scoffing because of the Parousia's delay. In 1 Peter, all teachings are related to the goal of providing "a defense [*apologia*]...for the hope [*elpis*] that is within [Christians]" (3:15).

Theological

To say something about one's convictions regarding death and afterlife is to say something about the nature and character of the God in question. To be sure, none of our authors wants to paint God as one-dimensional, but they often do choose to emphasize one or two features among a number. Paul's sovereign God (unlike the Roman emperor) is the Creator. God created human bodies and will provide resurrection bodies as well. Scripture, written for our instruction, teaches us about the character of this God. The FE stresses the intimacy between God, Christ, and the created order. He also serves to remind us that theology is an umbrella that can also shelter questions of anthropology, cosmology, eschatology, Christology, pneumatology, and so on. For Matthew, God thunders about as the righteous judge, a point

---

1. Paul also uses death and resurrection language in relation to baptism (Rom 6).

that will be eminently displayed during the apocalyptic scenario which will mark the eschaton.

Social

By this category I have shown that particular beliefs about death and afterlife serve to draw social boundaries around a community. So, like the Epicureans, the FG community's convictions threw into relief the in-group (John's community) versus the out-group (everyone else), thereby helping to establish and maintain sectarian boundaries. Matthew's teachings do the same: the righteous "elect/chosen" are different from the unrighteous. The latter seem to have more power in the contemporary world of Matthew, but the former actually enjoy the ultimate, significant pride of place in God's anthropological hierarchy. We can mention 2 Peter here as well. The social and liturgical overlaps when Neyrey contends that "boundary making seems to be the primary ritual here [in 2 Peter]."[2] First Peter as well seeks to obviate apostasy and establish strict boundaries "between a holy community united with God and a society alienated from God."[3]

VARIETY

There is variety among the authors' views regarding death and afterlife. Sometimes the differences are deep, sometimes they are not.

SIMILARITY

There are similarities among the authors' views. For instance, all authors draw upon OT notions of God, and all authors draw upon traditions of Jesus' powerful, world-altering, ultimate-meaning-making resurrection.

THE QUICK AND THE DEAD

Material about death and afterlife primarily serves to reveal information about the living and how they view anthropology, the body, and the social body. It betrays the fears of the living about their ultimate fate, their relationship to the dead (beloved and despised), and the concern (or lack thereof) displayed by the gods or God.

---

2. Jerome H. Neyrey, *2 Peter, Jude: A New Translation with Introduction and Commentary* (AB 37C; New York: Doubleday, 1993), 137.
3. John H. Elliott, *1 Peter: A New Translation with Introduction and Commentary* (AB 37B; New York: Doubleday, 2000), 112.

HERMENEUTICS

Beliefs related to death and afterlife have hermeneutical implications related to gender, race, class, and empire. We saw this overtly in Virgil and Plato; Byron McCane discusses how such writings served social and cultural functions. In his provocative analysis, apocalyptic generally encouraged the poor, who were in precarious circumstances. Funeral rites allowed the upper classes to move along, remarry, and so on. Setzer has already contributed to this discussion. We need more focused studies on the NT materials.

DOCTRINE

Beliefs related to death and afterlife have doctrinal implications related to, inter alia, Christology (in what ways does Jesus' death and resurrection address the problem of death and afterlife?), soteriology (what constitutes salvation, and how does one obtain it?), eschatology (what is the fate of various human beings?), theodicy, scriptural authority (when some thinkers have heaven and hell and some do not, which are more authoritative for us and why?). However, by far the most important question for me is theology: what kind of God is implied by one's stated beliefs concerning death and afterlife?

ETHICAL AND SPIRITUAL IMPLICATIONS

What are the ethics involved in imagining a space where only those who believe as you do enjoy special benefits from God? What does it do to your soul to cast those outside of one's own communion into outer darkness, hell, or the like? What kind of person does it make you if you hold belief A versus belief B? What difference would it make if you switched to belief B?

HISTORY-OF-IDEAS

The subject matter has historical aspects. How do ideas about death and afterlife develop over time, if they do at all?[4]

WIRKUNGSGESCHICHTE

This subject has social aspects: what evidence exists for the history-of-effects (*Wirkungsgeschichte*) for various notions and texts?

---

4. Alan Segal, *Life after Death: A History of the Afterlife in Western Religion* (New York: Doubleday, 2004), explores the idea in the Jewish, Christian, and Islamic West.

CROSS-DISCIPLINARY POSSIBILITIES

The topic has rich (perhaps limitless) cross-disciplinary potential. At present the lines are somewhat drawn among anthropologists, classicists, musicians, artists, NT scholars, OT scholars, Hebrew Bible scholars, psychologists, literature students, philosophers, and scientists. Collaborative work would yield far greater insights.

CROSS-CULTURAL, INTERRELIGIOUS POTENTIAL

The topic also has immense cross-cultural, interreligious potential. What would it be like if scholars knowledgeable about particular religious traditions engaged in lively exchange about the subject of death and afterlife? Such a dialogue would be fruitful among traditions that share Scriptures, and also among those who do not.[5]

PRACTICAL THEOLOGY AND PASTORAL CARE

While Abraham lived through "summer's parching heat," Jesus died young; but didn't both show us that it is by its content rather than by its duration that a lifetime is measured? (William Sloane Coffin, *Credo,* 166)

Without death, we'd never live. Without discovering the limits of our talents, we'd never discover who we are. And, finally, hard choices have a potential for riches beyond any reckoning, "for eye hath not seen nor ear heard nor the heart of man received the good things that God hath prepared for those who love him." Deserted by his disciples, in agony on the cross, barely thirty years old, Christ said, "It is finished." And thus ended the most complete life ever lived. (William Sloane Coffin, *Credo,* 167)

No church should ever dismiss, demean, or in any way deny the awe-someness of death, nor the fear of it that eats away at the heart of each of us, making us from time to time both insecure and militant — a lethal combination in any individual or nation. Worse yet, because our lives so often cry out for rebuke and forgiveness, we also fear that

---

5. I have recently read two engaging pieces of work on Islam and Buddhism, respectively, and would find it fruitful to work collaboratively with such thinkers: Jane Idleman Smith and Yvonne Yazbeck Haddad, *The Islamic Understanding of Death and Resurrection* (New York: Oxford University Press, 2002); and Ruben Habito, "The Resurrection of the Dead, and Life Everlasting: From a Futuristic to a Realized Christianity," in *The Sound of Liberating Truth: Buddhist-Christian Dialogues* (ed. Sallie B. King and Paul O. Ingram; Richmond, UK: Curzon, 1999), 223–38.

we may deserve to die. So every church worthy of the name, Sunday in and Sunday out, must proclaim the Good News that Christ is the "Lamb of God that taketh away the sins of the world," that "God was in Christ reconciling the world unto itself," and yes, that there is more mercy in God than sin in us. And just as in life, so in death "nothing can separate us from the love of God." We may not know what lies beyond the grave, but we know who is there. Death is inevitable and death is awesome, but it is the fear of death that is its sting. Remove that fear, and there's not a one of us that cannot say with Paul, "O death, where is thy sting?" "O grave, where is they victory?" (William Sloane Coffin, *Credo,* 172)

The topic of death and afterlife relates heavily to practical theology and issues of pastoral care. Death and afterlife are existential matters of the most urgent kind. Those who minister in or participate in the Christian faith will want to school themselves in the ways past Christians have addressed the issue as part of formulating their own ideas. The concept of death and the experience of death are so important that they deserve not to be handled sloppily but with utmost diligence so that, when the time comes, one may offer a witness that is simultaneously humble and life-giving.

BIBLIOGRAPHY

Arnim, Hans Friedrich August von, ed. *Stoicorum veterum fragmenta*. 4 vols. Leipzig: Teubner, 1903–24.

Aune, David E., ed. *The Gospel of Matthew in Current Study: Studies in the Memory of William G. Thompson, S.J.* Grand Rapids: Eerdmans, 2001.

Bailey, R. E. "Life after Death: A New Testament Study in the Relation of Body and Soul." Ph.D. diss., University of Edinburgh, 1962.

Bainbridge, William Sims. *The Sociology of Religious Movements*. New York: Routledge, 1997.

Balch, David L. *Let Wives Be Submissive: The Domestic Code in 1 Peter.* Studies in Biblical Literature: Monograph Series 26. Chico, CA: Scholars Press, 1981.

Barrett, C. K. *A Commentary on the Second Epistle to the Corinthians*. Harper's New Testament Commentaries. New York: Harper & Row, 1973.

Bassler, Jouette M. "*Skeuos*: A Modest Proposal for Illuminating Paul's Use of Metaphor in 1 Thessalonians 4:4." Pages 53–66 in *The Social World of the First Christians: Essays in Honor of Wayne A. Meeks*. Edited by L. Michael White and O. Larry Yarbrough. Minneapolis: Augsburg Fortress, 1995.

Bauckham, Richard. *The Fate of the Dead: Studies on the Jewish and Christian Apocalypses*. Supplements to Novum Testamentum 93. Leiden: Brill, 1998.

Bauer, Walter. *Orthodoxy and Heresy in Earliest Christianity.* Edited by Robert Kraft and Gerhard Krodel. 2d ed. Mifflintown, PA: Sigler, 1996.

Beard, Mary, John North, and Simon Price. *Religions of Rome*. 2 vols. Cambridge, UK: Cambridge University Press, 1998.

Beare, Francis W. *The First Epistle of Peter: The Greek Text with Introduction and Notes*. 3d ed. Oxford: Blackwell, 1970.

Bernstein, Alan E. *The Formation of Hell: Death and Retribution in the Ancient and Early Christian Worlds*. Ithaca, NY: Cornell University Press, 1993.

Blass, Friedrich, and Albert Debrunner. *A Greek Grammar of the New Testament and Other Early Christian Literature.* Translated and revised by Robert W. Funk. Chicago: University of Chicago Press, 1961.

Boring, M. Eugene. *1 Peter*. Abingdon New Testament Commentaries. Nashville: Abingdon, 1999.

Boyarin, Daniel. "Paul and the Genealogy of Gender." Pages 13–41 in *A Feminist Companion to Paul*. Edited by Amy-Jill Levine with Marianne Blickenstaff. London: T&T Clark, 2004.

Bremmer, Jan. *The Rise and Fall of the Afterlife*. London: Routledge, 2002.

Brown, Raymond E. *An Introduction to the New Testament*. New York: Doubleday, 1997.

Bruce, F. F. *1 and 2 Corinthians*. Grand Rapids: Eerdmans, 1980.

Carter, Warren. "Are There Imperial Texts in the Class? Intertextual Eagles and Matthean Eschatology as 'Lights Out' Time for Imperial Rome (Matthew 24:27–31). *Journal of Biblical Literature* 122 (2003): 467–87.

———. *Matthew and the Margins: A Sociopolitical and Religious Reading.* Maryknoll, NY: Orbis, 2000.

Cassem, N. H. "Grammatical and Contextual Inventory of the Use of *Kosmos* in the Johannine Corpus with Some Implications for a Johannine Cosmic Theology." *New Testament Studies* 19 (1972–73): 81–91.

Cavallin, Hans Clemens Caesarius. *Life After Death: Paul's Argument for the Resurrection of the Dead in I Cor 15.* Part 1, *An Enquiry into the Jewish Background.* Lund, Sweden: Gleerup, 1974.

Chilton, Bruce. " 'Not to Taste Death': A Jewish, Christian and Gnostic Usage." *Studia biblica* 2 (1978): 29–36.

———. "Resurrection in the Gospels." Pages 215–39 in *Death, Life-after-Death, Resurrection, and the World-to-Come in the Judaisms of Antiquity.* Edited by Alan J. Avery-Peck and Jacob Neusner. Vol. 4 of *Judaism in Late Antiquity.* New York: Brill, 1995.

Clark-Soles, Jaime. " 'I Will Raise [Whom?] Up on the Last Day': Anthropology as a Feature of Johannine Eschatology." Pages 29–53 in *New Currents through John: A Global Perspective.* Edited by Francisco Lozada Jr. and Thomas W. Thatcher. Atlanta: Society of Biblical Literature, 2006.

———. *Scripture Cannot Be Broken: The Social Function of the Use of Scripture in the Fourth Gospel.* Boston: Brill Academic Publishers, 2003.

Collins, John J. "The Afterlife in Apocalyptic Literature." Pages 119–39 in *Death, Life-After-Death, Resurrection, and the World-to-Come in the Judaisms of Antiquity.* Edited by Alan J. Avery-Peck and Jacob Neusner. Vol. 4 of *Judaism in Late Antiquity.* New York: Brill, 1995.

Collins, Raymond F. *First Corinthians.* Sacra pagina 7. Collegeville, MN: Liturgical Press, 1999.

Coloe, Mary L. *God Dwells with Us: Temple Symbolism in the Fourth Gospel.* Collegeville, MN: Liturgical Press, 2001.

Conzelmann, Hans. *1 Corinthians: A Commentary on the First Epistle to the Corinthians.* Edited by George W. MacRae. Translated by James W. Leitch. Bibliography and references by James W. Dunkly. Hermeneia. Philadelphia: Fortress, 1975.

Cosgrove, Charles H. *Elusive Israel: The Puzzle of Election in Romans.* Louisville: Westminster John Knox, 1997.

Cotter, Wendy. "Greco-Roman Apotheosis: Traditions and the Resurrection Appearances in Matthew." Pages 127–53 in *The Gospel of Matthew in Current Study: Studies in the Memory of William G. Thompson, S.J.* Edited by David Aune. Grand Rapids: Eerdmans, 2001.

Cullmann, Oscar. *Immortality of the Soul or Resurrection of the Dead? The Witness of the New Testament.* London: Epworth; New York: Macmillan, 1958. Online: http://www.geocities.com/pastorkeith/cullmann.html.

Cumont, Franz. *Afterlife in Roman Paganism.* New Haven: Yale University Press, 1922.

Dalton, William Joseph. *Christ's Proclamation to the Spirits: A Study of 1 Peter 3:18–4:6.* 2d ed. Analecta biblica 23. Rome: Editrice Pontificio Istituto Biblico, 1989.

Davies, Jon. *Death, Burial and Rebirth in the Religions of Antiquity.* Religion in the First Christian Centuries. Edited by Deborah Sawyer and John Sawyer. London: Routledge, 1999.

Davies, W. D., and Dale C. Allison. *A Critical and Exegetical Commentary on the Gospel according to Saint Matthew.* 3 vols. Edinburgh: T&T Clark, 1988.

DeMaris, Richard. "Christian Religion and Baptism for the Dead (1 Cor. 15:19): Insights from Archaeology and Anthropology." *Journal of Biblical Literature* 114 (1995): 661–82.

Dillon, John. *The Middle Platonists: 80 B.C. to A.D. 220.* Ithaca, NY: Cornell University Press, 1977.

Douglas, Mary. *Purity and Danger: An Analysis of Concepts of Pollution and Taboo.* London: Ark Paperbacks, 1984.

Dowling, Melissa Barden. "A Time to Regender: The Transformation of Roman Time." *Kronoscope* 3, no. 2 (2003): 169–83.

Dubis, Mark. *Messianic Woes in First Peter: Suffering and Eschatology in 1 Peter 4:12–19.* Studies in Biblical Literature 33. New York: Peter Lang, 2002.

Elliott, John H. *1 Peter: A New Translation with Introduction and Commentary.* Anchor Bible 37B. New York: Doubleday, 2000.

———. *A Home for the Homeless: A Sociological Exegesis of 1 Peter, Its Situation and Strategy.* Philadelphia: Fortress, 1981.

Elliott, Neil. "The Anti-Imperial Message of the Cross." Pages 167–83 in *Paul and Empire: Religion and Power in Roman Imperial Society.* Edited by Richard A. Horsley. Harrisburg, PA: Trinity, 1997.

Ellis, E. Earle. "II Corinthians V:1–10 in Pauline Eschatology." *New Testament Studies* 6 (1960): 211–24.

Fee, Gordon D. *The First Epistle to the Corinthians.* New International Commentary on the New Testament. Edited by F. F. Bruce. Grand Rapids: Eerdmans, 1987.

———. *Paul's Letter to the Philippians.* Grand Rapids: Eerdmans, 1995.

———. *Philippians.* InterVarsity Press New Testament Commentary Series. Downers Grove, IL: InterVarsity, 1999.

Feinberg, John S. "1 Peter 3:18–20, Ancient Mythology, and the Intermediate State." *Westminster Theological Journal* 48 (1986): 303–36.

Felton, Debbie. *Haunted Greece and Rome: Ghost Stories from Classical Antiquity.* Austin: University of Texas Press, 1999.

Fitzmyer, Joseph A. "The First Epistle of Peter." Pages 362–68 in *The Jerome Biblical Commentary.* Edited by Raymond E. Brown, Joseph A. Fitzmyer, and Roland E. Murphy. Vol. 2. Englewood Cliffs, NJ: Prentice-Hall, 1968.

———. "Pauline Anthropology." Page 818 in *The Jerome Biblical Commentary.* Edited by Raymond E. Brown, Joseph A. Fitzmyer, and Roland E. Murphy. Vol. 2. Englewood Cliffs, NJ: Prentice-Hall, 1968.

Ford, J. Massyngberde, *Redeemer, Friend and Mother: Salvation in Antiquity and in the Gospel of John.* Philadelphia: Fortress, 1997.

Forsyth, Neil. *The Old Enemy: Satan and the Combat Myth.* Princeton: Princeton University Press, 1987.

Friedman, Richard Elliot, and Shawna Dolansky Overton. "Death and Afterlife: The Biblical Silence." Pages 35–57 in *Death, Life-after-Death, Resurrection and the World-to-Come in the Judaisms of Antiquity*. Edited by Alan J. Avery-Peck and Jacob Neusner. Vol. 4 of *Judaism in Late Antiquity*. Leiden: Brill, 1995.

Furley, David John. "Epicurus." Pages 532–34 in *The Oxford Classical Dictionary*. Edited by Simon Hornblower and Antony Spawforth. 3d ed., rev. New York: Oxford University Press, 2003.

Furnish, Victor Paul. *2 Corinthians*. Anchor Bible Commentary Series 32A. Garden City, NY: Doubleday, 1984.

Gager, John G. *Reinventing Paul*. New York: Oxford University Press, 2000.

Garrett, Susan R. *No Ordinary Angel: Jesus and the Angels in the Bible and Today*. New York: Doubleday, forthcoming.

———. *The Temptations of Jesus in Mark's Gospel*. Grand Rapids: Eerdmans, 1998.

Goldingay, John. "Death and Afterlife in the Psalms." Pages 61–85 in *Death, Life-after-Death, Resurrection and the World-to-Come in the Judaisms of Antiquity*. Edited by Alan J. Avery-Peck and Jacob Neusner. Vol. 4 of *Judaism in Late Antiquity*. New York: Brill, 1995.

Goppelt, Leonhard. *A Commentary on I Peter*. Edited by F. Hahn. Translated and augmented by J. E. Alsup. Grand Rapids: Eerdmans, 1993.

Grabbe, Lester L. "Eschatology in Philo and Josephus." Pages 163–85 in *Death, Life-after-Death, Resurrection and the World-to-Come in the Judaisms of Antiquity*. Edited by Alan J. Avery-Peck and Jacob Neusner. Vol. 4 of *Judaism in Late Antiquity*. New York: Brill, 1995.

Grassi, Joseph A. Review of William Joseph Dalton, *Christ's Proclamation to the Spirits: A Study of 1 Peter 3:18–4:6*. *Theological Studies* 27, no. 1 (1966): 103–5.

Grieb, A. Katherine. *The Story of Romans: A Narrative Defense of God's Righteousness*. Louisville: Westminster John Knox, 2002.

Grudem, Wayne. *1 Peter*. Tyndale New Testament Commentaries. Grand Rapids: Eerdmans, 1988.

Gundry, Robert H. *Sōma in Biblical Theology: With Emphasis on Pauline Anthropology*. Grand Rapids: Academie Books, 1987.

Habito, Ruben. "The Resurrection of the Dead, and Life Everlasting: From a Futuristic to a Realized Christianity." Pages 223–38 in *The Sound of Liberating Truth: Buddhist-Christian Dialogues*. Edited by Sallie B. King and Paul O. Ingram. Richmond, UK: Curzon, 1999.

Hallote, Rachel S. *Death, Burial, and Afterlife in the Biblical World: How the Israelites and Their Neighbors Treated the Dead*. Chicago: Ivan R. Dee, 2001.

Hanhart, Karel. *The Intermediate State in the New Testament*. Groningen: printed by V. R. B. Kleine, 1966.

Harris, Murray J. "Paul's View of Death." Pages 317–28 in *New Dimensions in New Testament Study*. Edited by Richard N. Longenecker and Merrill C. Tenney. Grand Rapids: Zondervan, 1974.

———. *Raised Immortal: Resurrection and Immortality in the New Testament*. Grand Rapids: Eerdmans, 1985.

Hays, Richard. *Echoes of Scripture in the Letters of Paul.* New Haven: Yale University Press, 1989.

———. *The Faith of Jesus Christ: An Investigation of the Narrative Substructure of Galatians 3:1–4:11.* Chico, CA: Scholars Press, 1983.

———. "Paul: The *Koinōnia* of His Sufferings." Pages 16–59 in *The Moral Vision of the New Testament: Community, Cross, New Creation; A Contemporary Introduction to New Testament Ethics.* San Francisco: HarperSanFrancisco, 1996.

Heller, Mark. *The Ontology of Physical Objects: Four-Dimensional Hunks of Matter.* Cambridge, UK: Cambridge University Press, 1990.

———. "Temporal Parts of Four-Dimensional Objects." *Philosophical Studies* 46 (1984): 323–34.

Himmelfarb, Martha. *Ascent to Heaven in Jewish and Christian Apocalypses.* New York: Oxford University Press, 1993.

Holloway, Paul A. *Consolation in Philippians: Philosophical Sources and Rhetorical Strategy.* Cambridge, UK: Cambridge University Press, 2001.

———. "Notes and Observations *Bona Cogitare*: An Epicurean Consolation in Phil 4:8–9." *Harvard Theological Review* 91 (1998): 89–96.

Holst-Warhaft, Gail. *Dangerous Voices: Women's Laments and Greek Literature.* London: Routledge, 1992.

Hopkins, Keith. *Death and Renewal.* Cambridge, UK: Cambridge University Press, 1983.

Horsley, Richard A. "1 Corinthians: A Case Study of Paul's Assembly as an Alternative Society." Pages 242–52 in *Paul and Empire: Religion and Power in Roman Imperial Society.* Edited by Richard A. Horsley. Harrisburg, PA: Trinity, 1997.

Jackson, Paul N. *An Investigation of* Koimaomai *in the New Testament: The Concept of Eschatological Sleep.* Mellen Biblical Press Series 45. Lewiston, NY: Mellen Biblical Press, 1996.

Jaffee, Martin S. *Early Judaism.* Upper Saddle River, NJ: Prentice Hall, 1997.

Jewett, Robert. *A Chronology of Paul's Life.* Philadelphia: Fortress, 1979.

———. *Paul's Anthropological Terms: A Study of Their Use in Conflict Settings.* Leiden: Brill, 1971.

Johnson, Sherman E. "The Preaching to the Dead." *Journal of Biblical Literature* 79 (1960): 48–51.

Keck, Leander. "Death and Afterlife in the New Testament." Pages 83–96 in *Death and Afterlife: Perspectives of World Religions.* Edited by Hiroshi Obayashi. New York: Greenwood, 1992.

Kelly, J. N. D. *A Commentary on the Epistles of Peter and Jude.* Harper's New Testament Commentaries. New York: Harper & Row, 1969.

Kingsbury, Jack D. *The Parables of Jesus in Matthew 13: A Study in Redaction-Criticism.* London: SPCK, 1969.

Kittel, G., and G. Friedrich, eds. *Theological Dictionary of the New Testament.* Translated by G. W. Bromiley. 10 vols. Grand Rapids: Eerdmans, 1964–76.

Koester, Craig. "The Death of Jesus and the Human Condition: Exploring the Theology of John's Gospel." Pages 141–57 in *Life in Abundance: Studies in Tribute to Raymond E. Brown, S.S.* Edited by John R. Donahue. Collegeville, MN: Liturgical Press, 2005.

Koester, Helmut. "Imperial Ideology and Paul's Eschatology in 1 Thessalonians." Pages 158–66 in *Paul and Empire: Religion and Power in Roman Imperial Society*. Edited by Richard A. Horsley. Harrisburg, PA: Trinity, 1997.

Kuck, David W. *Judgment and Community Conflict: Paul's Use of Apocalyptic Judgment Language in 1 Corinthians 3:5–4:5*. Supplements to Novum Testamentum 66. Leiden: Brill, 1992.

Kysar, Robert. *John, the Maverick Gospel*. Rev. ed. Louisville: Westminster John Knox, 1993.

Lambrecht, Jan. *Second Corinthians*. Sacra pagina 8. Collegeville, MN: Liturgical Press, 1999.

Layton, Bentley. *The Gnostic Scriptures: A New Translation with Annotations and Introductions*. Anchor Bible Reference Library. New York: Doubleday, 1995.

Levine, Amy-Jill, ed., with Marianne Blickenstaff. *A Feminist Companion to Matthew*. Sheffield, UK: Sheffield Academic Press, 2001.

———. *A Feminist Companion to Paul*. London: T&T Clark, 2004.

Long, A. A. *Hellenistic Philosophy: Stoics, Epicureans, Sceptics*. Berkeley: University of California Press, 1974. 2nd ed. 1986.

Longenecker, Richard, ed. *Life in the Face of Death: The Resurrection Message of the New Testament*. Grand Rapids: Eerdmans, 1998.

MacMullen, Ramsey. *Paganism in the Roman Empire*. New Haven: Yale University Press, 1981.

Malherbe, Abraham J. "Determinism and Free Will in Paul: The Argument of 1 Corinthians 8–9." Pages 231–55 in *Paul in His Hellenistic Context*. Edited by Troels Engberg-Pedersen. Minneapolis: Fortress, 1995.

Marcus, Joel. "The Gates of Hades and the Keys of the Kingdom (Matt 16:18–19)." *Catholic Biblical Quarterly* 50 (1988): 443–55.

Martin, Dale. *The Corinthian Body*. New Haven: Yale University Press, 1995.

———. "Cutting Too Close for Comfort: Paul's Letter to the Galatians in Its Anatolian Cultic Context." *Catholic Biblical Quarterly* 66 (2004): 647–49.

———. "The Queer History of Galatians 3:28: No Male and Female." Pages 77–90 in *Sex and the Single Savior: Gender and Sexuality in Biblical Interpretation*. Louisville: Westminster John Knox, 2006.

Martyn, J. Louis. "The Galatians' Role in the Spirit's War of Liberation." Pages 524–40 in *Galatians: A New Translation*. Anchor Bible 33A. New York: Doubleday, 1997.

McCane, Byron R. "Rest in Peace or Roast in Hell: Funerary versus Apocalyptic Portraits of Paradise." Pages 488–500 in *Zeichen aus Text und Stein: Studien auf dem Weg zu einer Archäologie des Neuen Testaments*. Edited by Stefan Alkier and Jürgen Zangenberg. Texte und Arbeiten zum neutestamentlichen Zeitalter 42. Tübingen: Francke, 2003. Repr., in Byron R. McCane, *Roll Back the Stone: Death and Burial in the World of Jesus*. Harrisburg, PA: Trinity, 2003.

McDannell, Colleen, and Bernhard Lang. *Heaven: A History*. New Haven: Yale University Press, 2001.

Meeks, Wayne A. "The Ethics of the Fourth Evangelist." Pages 317–26 in *Exploring the Gospel of John*. Edited by Alan Culpepper and Clifton Black. Louisville: Westminster John Knox, 1996.

————. *The First Urban Christians: The Social World of the Apostle Paul.* New Haven: Yale University Press, 1983.

————. "The Image of the Androgyne: Some Uses of a Symbol in Earliest Christianity." *History of Religions* 13 (1974): 165–208.

Metzger, Bruce M. *A Textual Commentary on the Greek New Testament.* 2d ed. New York: United Bible Societies, 1994.

Meyer, M. W., ed. *The Ancient Mysteries: A Sourcebook.* San Francisco: Harper & Row, 1987.

Michaels, J. Ramsey. *1 Peter.* Word Biblical Commentary 49. Waco: Word, 1988.

Milikowsky, Chaim. "Which Gehenna? Retribution and Eschatology in the Synoptic Gospels and in Early Jewish Texts." *New Testament Studies* 34 (1988): 238–49.

Mounce, R. H. *A Living Hope: A Commentary on 1 and 2 Peter.* Grand Rapids: Eerdmans, 1982.

Neyrey, Jerome H. *2 Peter, Jude: A New Translation with Introduction and Commentary.* Anchor Bible 37C. New York: Doubleday, 1993.

Oepke, A. "*Apōleia.*" Pages 396–97 in vol. 1 of *Theological Dictionary of the New Testament.* Edited by G. Kittel and G. Friedrich. Translated by G. W. Bromiley. 10 vols. Grand Rapids: Eerdmans, 1964–76.

Osei-Bonsu, J. "The Intermediate State in the New Testament." *Scottish Journal of Theology* 44 (1991): 169–94.

Pagels, Elaine. *The Gnostic Gospels.* New York: Random House, 1979.

Park, Joseph S. *Conceptions of Afterlife in Jewish Inscriptions: With Special Reference to Pauline Literature.* Tübingen: Mohr Siebeck, 2000.

Pelikan, Jaroslav. *The Emergence of the Catholic Tradition (100–600).* Chicago: University of Chicago Press, 1971.

Perkins, Pheme. *Resurrection: New Testament Witness and Contemporary Reflection.* Garden City, NY: Doubleday, 1984.

Pomeroy, Sarah, ed. *Plutarch's "Advice to the Bride and Groom," and "A Consolation to His Wife": English Translations, Commentary, Interpretive Essays, and Bibliography.* New York: Oxford University Pres, 1999.

Przybylski, Benno. *Righteousness in Matthew and His World of Thought.* Cambridge, UK: Cambridge University Press, 1980.

Reicke, Bo. *The Disobedient Spirits and Christian Baptism: A Study of I Peter III:19 and Its Context.* Copenhagen: Munksgaard, 1946. Repr., New York: AMS, 1984.

Rissi, Matthias. *Studien zum zweiten Korintherbrief: Der alte Bund — Der Predigt — Der Tod.* Abhandlungen zur Theologie des Alten und Neuen Testaments. Zurich: Zwingli, 1969.

Robinson, John A. T. *The Body: A Study in Pauline Theology.* London: SCM, 1952.

————. "The New Look at the Fourth Gospel." Pages 338–50 in *Papers Presented to the International Congress on "The Four Gospels in 1957" Held at Christ Church, Oxford, 1957.* Edited by K. Aland et al. Studia evangelica 1; Texte und Untersuchungen zur Geschichte der altchristlichen Literatur 73. Berlin: Akademie Verlag, 1959. Repr. as "The New Look on the Fourth Gospel." Pages 94–106 in *Twelve New Testament Studies.* Studies in Biblical Theology 34. London: SCM, 1962.

Roetzel, Calvin. *Paul: The Man and the Myth*. Columbia: University of South Carolina Press, 1998.

Roetzel, Calvin J. " 'As Dying, and Behold We Live': Death and Resurrection in Paul's Theology." *Interpretation* 46 (1992): 5–18.

Russell, Jeffrey Burton. *A History of Heaven: The Singing Silence*. Princeton: Princeton University Press, 1997.

Saldarini, Anthony. *Pharisees, Scribes, and Sadducees in Palestinian Society: A Sociological Approach*. Grand Rapids: Eerdmans, 2001.

Sampley, J. Paul. *Walking between the Times: Paul's Moral Reasoning*. Minneapolis: Fortress, 1991.

Scharlemann, Martin H. " 'He Descended into Hell': An Interpretation of 1 Peter 3:18–20." *Concordia Journal* 15 (1989): 311–22.

———. Review of William Joseph Dalton, *Christ's Proclamation to the Spirits: A Study of 1 Peter 3:18–4:6. Journal of Biblical Literature* 84 (1965): 470–72.

Schnackenburg, Rudolph. *The Gospel of Matthew*. Translated by Robert R. Barr. Grand Rapids: Eerdmans, 2002.

Schneiders, Sandra. *Written That You May Believe: Encountering Jesus in the Fourth Gospel*. New York: Crossroad, 2003.

Schneiders, Sandra M. "The Resurrection (of the Body) in the FG: A Key to Johannine Spirituality." Pages 168–98 in *Life in Abundance: Studies in Tribute to Raymond E. Brown, S.S.* Edited by John R. Donahue. Collegeville, MN: Liturgical Press, 2005.

Schweizer, Eduard. *The Good News according to Matthew*. Translated by David E. Green. Atlanta: John Knox, 1975.

Segal, Alan. *Life after Death: A History of the Afterlife in Western Religion*. New York: Doubleday, 2004.

———. *Paul the Convert: The Apostolate and Apostasy of Saul the Pharisee*. New Haven: Yale University Press, 1990.

Segal, Charles. *Lucretius on Death and Anxiety: Poetry and Philosophy in "De rerum natura*. Princeton: Princeton University Press, 1990.

Selwyn, Edward G. *The First Epistle of St. Peter: The Greek Text with Introduction, Notes and Essays*. 2d ed. London: Macmillan, 1947.

Senior, Donald. *Matthew*. Abingdon New Testament Commentaries. Nashville: Abingdon, 1998.

———. *What Are They Saying about Matthew?* Rev. and enl. ed. New York: Paulist Press, 1996.

Setzer, Claudia. *Resurrection of the Body in Early Judaism and Early Christianity: Doctrine, Community, and Self-Definition*. Leiden: Brill, 2004.

Smith, Abraham. *Comfort One Another: Reconstructing the Rhetoric and Audience of 1 Thessalonians*. Louisville: Westminster John Knox, 1995.

Smith, Jane Idleman, and Yvonne Yazbeck Haddad. *The Islamic Understanding of Death and Resurrection*. New York: Oxford University Press, 2002.

Sourvinou-Inwood, Christiane. *'Reading' Greek Death: To the End of the Classical Period*. Oxford: Clarendon, 1995

Stanton, Graham. *A Gospel for a New People: Studies in Matthew*. Edinburgh: T&T Clark, 1992.

Syreeni, Kari. "Between Heaven and Earth: On the Structure of Matthew's Symbolic Universe." *Journal for the Study of the New Testament* 40 (1990): 3–13.

Tartt, Donna. *The Secret History*. New York: Knopf, 1992.

Thiselton, Anthony. *The First Epistle to the Corinthians: A Commentary on the Greek Text*. Grand Rapids: Eerdmans, 2000.

Thurston, Bonnie, and Judith M. Ryan. *Philippians and Philemon*. Edited by Daniel J. Harrington. Collegeville, MN: Liturgical Press, 2005.

Tissot, James. *The Life of Our Saviour Jesus Christ: Three Hundred and Sixty-Five Compositions from the Four Gospels*. Translated by Mrs. Arthur Bell (N. d'Anvers). New York: McClure-Tissot, 1899.

Trumbower, Jeffrey. *Born from Above: The Anthropology of the Gospel of John*. Tübingen: Mohr, 1992.

Trumbower, Jeffrey A. *Rescue for the Dead: The Posthumous Salvation of Non-Christians in Early Christianity*. Oxford: Oxford University Press, 2001.

Urbach, Ephraim E. *The Sages, Their Concepts and Beliefs*. Translated by Israel Abrahams. 2d, enl. ed. Jerusalem: Magnes, 1979.

Wardy, Robert B. B., "Atomism." Pages 208–10 in *The Oxford Classical Dictionary*. Edited by Simon Hornblower and Antony Spawforth. 3d ed., rev. New York: Oxford University Press, 2003.

Ware, Kallistos, "Dare We Hope for the Salvation of All? Origen, St. Gregory of Nyssa, and St. Isaac the Syrian." Pages 193–215 in *The Inner Kingdom*. Vol. 1 of *The Collected Works*. Crestwood, NY: St. Vladimir's Seminary Press, 2001.

Westfall, Cynthia, "The Relationship between the Resurrection, the Proclamation to the Spirits in Prison and Baptismal Regeneration: 1 Peter 3:19–22." Pages 106–35 in *Resurrection*. Edited by Stanley E. Porter, Michael A. Hayes, and David Tombs. Journal for the Study of the New Testament, Supplement Series 186. Sheffield: Sheffield Academic Press, 1999.

White, L. Michael, and O. Larry Yarbrough, eds. *The Social World of the First Christians*. Minneapolis: Fortress, 1995.

Wire, Antoinette. "Christ and Gender: A Study of Difference and Equality in Galatians 3:28." Pages 430–77 in *Jesus Christus als die Mitte der Schrift*. Edited by Judith Gundry-Volf. Berlin: de Gruyter, 1997.

Wolff, Hans W. *Anthropology of the Old Testament*. Translated by Margaret Kohl. Philadelphia: Fortress, 1974.

Wright, J. Edward. *The Early History of Heaven*. New York: Oxford University Press, 2000.

Wright, N. T. *The Resurrection of the Son of God*. Minneapolis: Fortress, 2003.

INDEX OF
BIBLICAL REFERENCES

GENERAL INDEX

Abaddon. *See* hell, language of

abyss. *See* hell, language of

afterlife, 9–14, 18–38, 51–52, 55–59, 222–27. *See also* eschatology, heaven, hell, reward and punishment

anaireō (to kill), 165

androgyne, myth of, 78–79

angels, 172, 187–88
  eschatological role of, 187
  judged by believers, 82
  in OT, 21
  reside in heaven, 21, 182, 187
  wicked, fallen, disobedient, 204, 206
    fate of, 192, 220
    in hell, 187
    Jesus and, 187–88, 196–97, 201
    in layered heaven, 206, 213
    See also demons, Satan

anthropology, 28, 112, 113–23, 159–64
  FE on, 112–23, 148, 151
  Greek, 39–48
  Matthean, 151, 159–64
  OT, 9–10, 14–18, 118, 151, 161
  Pauline, 62–70, 151
  Petrine, 195, 202–3
  Philo and Josephus on, 28
  See also blood, body, flesh, human, mind, *psychē*, soul, spirit

anthrōpos. See human

apocalypse, apocalyptic
  faux pas, 111, 131, 134
  functions of
    catechesis, 189
    hortatory, 189, 216, 217
    social and cultural inequities, 24–25, 189, 225
  Dead Sea Scrolls community and, 134
  FE and, 111–12, 127, 141
  intertestamental, 80
  Matthean, 80, 153, 164, 178–80
  Pauline, 61, 77, 80
  Petrine, 208, 213, 219
  See also eschatology, fire, Judgment Day, Parousia, Son of Man

apokteinō (to kill), 165–67

apologetic (defense), 149, 217–18, 221, 223

apostles, false (super apostles), 89, 92–97

apothnēskō (to die; to cease biological life), 165. *See also* death

Appolyon, *see* hell, language of

apollymi (to destroy, to perish, to lose), 73, 165–67

Aristophanes, 40

Aristotle, 27, 41–42, 50, 51, 52, 53

ascension. *See* Jesus/Christ, ascension

atomistic theory. *See* Epicurus

authority. *See* power and authority

Babylonian/Assyrian beliefs, 20, 29–30

baptism
  for the dead, 75–76
  death and afterlife and, 217
  the Flood and, 201–2, 207, 209
  as genderless experience, 78–79
  as putting on the Spirit, 94–95
  for repentance, 189
  as salvific, 209

bāśār, 16. *See also* flesh

Beelzebul, 26, 153. *See also* Satan

behavior. *See* ethics

belief
  functions of, 190–91, 216–21, 222–27
    assuages anxiety, fear of punishment, 139, 147
    knowledge as, 140
    vs. works, 151
  See also believers, knowledge

believers (the just, the righteous)
  as doers, 151, 160
  encouragement of, 101, 205, 210, 211
  fate of as present reality, 113, 128–30
    bestowed realized immortality, 113, 132–33
    enlivened by God, Jesus, Holy Spirit, 128
  fate of as future, 97, 105, 213–14
  fate of as imminent, 219–20
    death, 86, 97, 98–102, 131, l32, 137, 208
    eternal life, 127
    judged, 85, 86, 127, 151, 152, 176, 211, 214, 215
    as judges, 84
    predestined, 214
    resurrected, 60, 97, 113, 127, 152, 214

250

Epictetus, 93
Epicureanism/Epicurus, 41–42, 44, 50–53,
    56, 58, 135–49
  beliefs of
    anthropology, 42, 52–53
    atomistic theory, 50, 136, 137, 140–41
    death, 52, 140–41, 143
    eschatology, realized, 147
    God/gods, 44, 51
    im/mortality, 51
    judgment and punishment, 51, 52
    soul and body, 42
    theodicy, 51
  community characterized by
    friendship, 138, 145, 147
    freedom from disturbance/trouble in,
      53, 138–39, 147
    freedom from judgment/punishment in,
      139, 141
    happiness, 50
  and community of FE, 135–49
  See also church, Hellenism, Lucretius,
    Stoicism
eschatology, NT, 152–54, 170–88, 210–16,
  220
  components/characteristics of
    actors, 153, 186–88, 210–12
    events, 212
    imminence of eschaton, 74, 170
    judgment of believers and unbelievers,
      82, 166, 212, 214, 219–20
    parousia. *See* parousia
    present/earthly and future/heavenly
      blurred, 122, 170
    physical death, 127
    realized vs. future, 70, 81–86, 87n89,
      95–96, 111–13, 127, 147, 190
    righteousness of God, 63
    signs of eschaton, 170, 208, 212
    suffering, 208, 214
  diachronic vs. synchronic methodology in,
    111–13, 131–35
  functional influences on
    anthropology, 123, 132
    apologetic, 149, 217
    ethics, 154, 149, 194, 216–17
    liturgy, 191, 217
    pastoral, 148, 191, 217
    social, 149, 190
    theological, doctrinal, 148, 225
  influenced by
    anthropology, 123
    apocalyptic, 153, 168, 208, 214, 219
    Deuteronomistic theology, 152, 153
    Greco-Roman beliefs, 56–59
    Josephus, 28

eschatology, influenced by (*continued*)
    Philo, 27, 28
    Scripture, 156
  See also anthropology, apocalypse, fire,
      Judgment Day, parousia, resurrection,
      Son of Man, end
eternal life, 127–28, 129, 146, 148, 178
  described as
    different kind of life, 128
    Father/Jesus abide with believer, 125,
      128, 146
    gift, inheritance, reward, 128, 178
    Holy-Spiritual life, 131, 132
    only for the psyche, 122
    present reality, 123, 125, 139–40, 146
    a sharing in the life to come, 73
  in non-Christian thought
    Egyptian, 30
    Roman and Mystery religions, 37–38
  See also heaven, immortality, resurrection
ethics, 30, 61, 177, 190, 223, 225
  related to
    belief/knowledge, 68, 76–77, 81, 89,
      190, 216–17, 221, 225
    body/flesh, 68, 70, 87n89, 89, 96–97,
      163
    death and afterlife, 18, 61, 69, 76–77,
      80, 135, 156, 190, 194, 216–17
    eschatology, 81, 154, 190, 194
    gospel, 80
    heaven, 28, 180
    hell, 80, 96, 184, 185, 190, 223
    judgment, 81–83, 86, 89, 127, 177, 223
    resurrection, 69, 76–77, 109, 216–17
    scripture, 154
  function of, 223
    elicit good behavior, 89, 127, 156, 176,
      180, 185, 216–17, 220–21, 223
    personal piety, 190
    social justice, 190
  types of
    Epicurean, 53, 143, 144, 146, 149
    FE, 145, 146, 149
    Matthew, 163, 177
    Paul, 60–109
    Plato, Virgil, and Plutarch, 33
    Stoic, 48–50
  See also evil works, good works, justice, re-
      ward and punishment, righteousness,
      sin, wickedness
evil works (*porneia*), 86
  determinism and, 47
  heart as source of, 160–61
  knowledge of as judgment, 142
  punishment for, 127, 151, 152, 189–90
  vice lists, 86
  See also ethics, judgment, sin, wickedness

CPSIA information can be obtained
at www.ICGtesting.com
Printed in the USA
LVHW011034090721
692214LV00013BA/603